Guide Library

Hillwood Museum
Washington, D.C.

THE MEMOIRS OF
ALEXANDER HERZEN

VOLUME ONE

Most of the memoirs of Alexander Herzen (1812-1870) were published in Russian in his lifetime: in his periodicals *The Pole Star* (*Polyárnaya zvezdá*) and *The Bell* (*Kólokol*), and in the book *Prison and Exile* (London, 1854, 1858); and in *My Past and Thoughts* (*Byloye i dumy*) (3 vols., London and Geneva, 1861-6). The first separate and fairly complete edition of the memoirs, *Byloye i dumy*, was published in 1921 in Berlin, by Slovo, in five volumes. The translation of this edition, by Constance Garnett, was first published in 1924-7 by Chatto & Windus, London, in six volumes. For the present four-volume edition, Mrs Garnett's translation has been revised by Humphrey Higgens, with additions translated from the *Collected Works* of Herzen issued by the Academy of Sciences of the U.S.S.R. (30 vols., Moscow, 1954-64).

My Past and Thoughts

THE MEMOIRS OF
ALEXANDER HERZEN

VOLUME ONE

Translated by Constance Garnett
Revised by Humphrey Higgens

With an Introduction by
ISAIAH BERLIN

1968
ALFRED · A · KNOPF
NEW YORK

Library of Congress Catalog Card Number 66-12398

Introduction © Isaiah Berlin 1968
Revised translation © Chatto & Windus Ltd 1968
Printed in Great Britain by
Richard Clay (The Chaucer Press) Ltd
Bungay, Suffolk

CONTENTS

PART I

Nursery and University 1812-1834

PART II

Prison and Exile 1834-1838

PART III

Vladimir on the Klyazma 1838-1839

Preface to the Revised Edition of 1968

By HUMPHREY HIGGENS

Texts: The memoirs of Alexander Ivanovich Herzen, *Byloye i dumy*, were first published (A) in the original Russian in a separate (separate, that is, from Herzen's voluminous other works) and fairly complete edition in 5 volumes by Slovo (Berlin, 1921), and it was from this edition that Constance Garnett made her translation (B), *My Past and Thoughts*, in 6 volumes (which contained a long Introduction prefaced to the 6th volume), published by the present publishers in 1924-7.

In revising Mrs Garnett's translation I have made use, besides A and B above, of (C) A. I. Herzen : *The Collected Works*, edited and published by the Academy of Sciences of the U.S.S.R. in 30 volumes, of which 29 had been published in September 1964 (Moscow, 1954-65), particularly of volumes VIII-XI which contain the text of the memoirs with an *apparatus criticus,* variant readings, notes and an index of persons and publications referred to; and (D) of the 3-volume edition of *Byloye i dumy*, published by the Gosudarstvennoye Izdatel'stvo Khudozhestvennoy Literatury (Moscow, 1958). The notes in this edition are much shorter than in C, above, but are very serviceable. I am indebted to this edition for some of my footnotes. Its index includes few references to publications (my own index is an index only of persons) and is otherwise not absolutely reliable. I have made little use of (E) the edition of Herzen's *Complete Works and Letters* edited by M. K. Lemke in 22 volumes (Petrograd, 1919-25).

The present revised edition of Constance Garnett's translation (B) is referred to as F.

Most of Herzen's memoirs were published from time to time in *The Pole Star* (*Polyárnaya zvezdá*) and *The Bell* (*Kólokol*), both of which were printed and published at Herzen's Free Russian Press in London.

Everything that appeared in B is in the present edition, including passages in the second part of volume VI of that publication which are not strictly speaking memoirs but have been retained because they are of interest and because there is no other version of them in English.

Certain passages which were not in B appear in this edition, most of them in the fourth volume. The longest of these are: accounts of two love-affairs of Herzen's, the first while he was engaged, but not yet married. It is omitted from A (two lines of asterisks indicate the omission) and therefore does not appear in B. The second 'affair', which took place during the early years of his married life, is briefly referred to in a footnote in A, and this note is given in B. With the help of D the accounts of these incidents are restored to their places in the text. There is a whole chapter, called 'The German Emigrants', which appears in D but not in A: it is given in the present version. The beginning of 'Apogee and Perigee' is restored to its place with the help of D. There is a small part of a conversation between Herzen and Baron James Rothschild that is omitted from A, and it is hard to see why: this also has been restored. For a complete list of such passages as these see the paragraph of this preface headed *'Translation'*.

Certain changes have been made in the order in which passages appear in B; but it is impossible to produce an ideal order because passages, or parts of them, leap forwards or backwards in time, anticipate or drop behind; and the work never had a final touch from the author's hand.

The text in the more recent editions differs—except for the omissions and inclusions referred to above—very little from that of A. There are a few verbal variations, to some of which I have drawn attention by way of example.

I have usually left untranslated phrases and short remarks in French, German and Italian, with which Herzen is so free. I have considered it my business to deal with the text in Russian; hence where passages are given in A and B in the original French, for instance, but in D have been translated into Russian (as, for example, the letters from Cœurderoy and Pechërin who also appears in the French transliteration of his name, Pétchérine) I have translated the French into English.

Proper names which in any text are indicated by the initial letter, or by this and the rest of the name in brackets, I have printed, if the full name is known, in full without brackets.

Notes: i: At the end of the volumes. At the end of each volume of C there are copious notes, attention to which is drawn by asterisks

in the text. I have plundered these notes with a free hand; my pick-
ing and stealings, where they are of considerable length, appear at
the end of each volume and attention is drawn to them in the same
way. I have seldom interpolated remarks of my own, and where I
have done so this is indicated.

ii: footnotes. There are four kinds: footnotes by Constance Garnett, indicated by (*Tr.*); those borrowed from C, indicated by (*A.S.*);
notes by myself, indicated by (*R.*), and Herzen's own footnotes from
A, which are given without any ascription.

Transliteration: I have been chiefly guided by the system used by
the Royal Geographical Society. Russian surnames, however, that are
familiar to the English reader I have left in the familiar form: *e.g.*
Dostoyevsky, not Dostoyevskiy and Herzen, not Gertsen; and those
surnames of women which should be in the feminine form I have
printed in the masculine: *e.g.* Anna Borisovna Meshchersky, not
Meshcherskaya. (This does not apply to the names of places, streets
or rivers: *e.g.* Neglinnaya). The Russian Christian name Nikolay is
so transliterated; the Tsar and the Saint are called Nicholas. The
hard sign and the soft sign are not indicated in the text.

Translation: Translating Herzen is not easy. His language, says
Dr E. Lampert (*Studies in Rebellion* [Routledge & Kegan Paul,
1957], page 156), 'is spiced with extravagant vocabulary, with
violations of Russian syntax, and a maze of Gallicisms, Anglicisms
and Germanisms, which became more pronounced the longer he
lived abroad'. I have tried to keep the English version as close as possible to the Russian original, notably in metaphors and similes, provided that the English is lucid, even if not elegant.

The passages which I have myself translated (not revised) are:

i: from the Russian:
Herzen's dedication to Ogarëv (Vol. I, pp. xliii-xlvi).
Herzen's affair with Madame Medvedev (Vol. I, pp. 325-7).
A dozen lines at the end of Chapter 23 (Vol. I, p. 365).
Letters to Natalya A. Herzen (Vol. I, pp. 374-9).
Herzen's affair with Katerina (Vol. II, pp. 474-7).
Part of a conversation with Baron James Rothschild (Vol. II,
pp. 763-4).
From Herzen's Diary (Vol. II, pp. 929-32).
From the Diary of Natalya A. Herzen (Vol. II, pp. 1004-9).

A*

Certain words present difficulty. (i) Various words like banish, expel, deport, exile, emigrant, refugee: Herzen sometimes uses the Russian equivalent, and sometimes transliterates the French, or whatever it may be, and he is not quite consistent in his usage. (Nor, for that matter, is English: banish, deport and exile are often used indifferently, when perhaps the word used should be 'relegate'. For instance Herzen was banished from Petersburg and Moscow and relegated, at different times, to Perm, Vyatka, Vladimir and Novgorod.) To be exiled means, I take it, to be expelled from one's native country. It is wrong, then, to talk of Russians being exiled to Siberia (which is part of their own country and to which, by the way, Herzen was never sent): 'relegated' is usually the correct word. Herzen, moreover, was never exiled—he went to live abroad of his own free will—until he had been summoned to return to Russia and had refused. 'Exile' is used also ambiguously to mean both one who has been expelled from his country and a voluntary emigrant. I have avoided the word 'expatriate' which, however, would be no anachronism, for it was used by Shelley and by the *Quarterly Review* in 1812. I deplore the promiscuous use of the termination -*ee* to signify someone to whom something is done, and still more when it is used to signify someone who has done something ('escapee'); but it is a pity that 'banishee' does not exist: after all, we have 'garnishee'.

The word *meshchanin* (with its abstract *meshchanstvo*) is very difficult to translate. In Tsarist times it was translated 'citizen', 'bourgeois', 'commoner'; in a modern Russian-English dictionary one finds: 'lower middle class citizen; fig. bourgeois, Philistine, narrow-minded (humdrum) person; gigman' (shade of Carlyle!). The best account I know of the *meshchanin* and *meshchanstvo*[1] is in *Melkiy Bes*, by Fëdor Sologub, translated into English as *The Little Demon* by Ronald Wilks (The New English Library, 1962). It is hard to find an English equivalent for the word—impossible, I should say, to translate it consistently. Pushkin, for instance, insists time after time in his verse that he is a *meshchanin*: what is one to make of that? And Constance Garnett, translating a passage of Herzen, speaks of 'Napoleon III . . . carousing with commoners in the City' (of London). Most often, however, she uses *bourgeois* or *petit bourgeois,* and certainly this usually suits the context. (The passage where the expression is thickest on the ground is in 'Ends and Beginnings', Herzen's first letter to Turgenev (Vol. IV, pp. 1682ff.). One must not forget that when he preferred it Herzen would use *bourgeois*, etc., transliterated into Russian, as also he did (see above) 'emigrant' and 'refugee'.

Genealogy: I have included a genealogical table of the family of Yakovlev, beginning with Herzen's grandfather and including, so far as I have been able, all his relations, however distant, who are mentioned in the memoirs or are relevant to them.

Acknowledgements: First, of course, to the late Constance Garnett herself. There were translations into English of Russian works that had been translated into French (hence, for instance, the use of *tch* for *ch*); but it was the energy and speed of work of Mrs Garnett which made a vast amount of Russian literature available to the English reader. A list of her translations from Russian occupies a page and three quarters in Carolyn G. Heilbrun: *The Garnett Family* (Macmillan, New York; George Allen & Unwin, 1961), and includes most of the works of Turgenev, Dostoyevsky and Chekhov; *Anna Karenina* and *War and Peace* and other works of Tolstoy: with these the list is by no means finished.

I have derived assistance from several books, and they are referred to in the footnotes. The one which I have found most helpful, and enjoyable, is E. H. Carr: *The Romantic Exiles* (Gollancz, 1963):

[1] On 5 April, 1962, *Literaturnaya Gazeta* published an issue devoted to the 150th anniversary of Herzen's birth. It contains much information and comment; Herzen's attitude to *meshchanstvo* is mentioned on p. 1, col. 5.

one might almost call it requisite and necessary reading for the windows it opens on the political and domestic life of Herzen himself and his associates, from the engaging but almost impossible Bakunin, of whom it was said that on the first day of a revolution he was an absolute treasure but on the second he should be shot; to the quite impossible (though Herzen did not find him so) and not in the least engaging Dolgorukov.

I also acknowledge with much gratitude the invaluable help that has been given me in my work of revision by Sir Isaiah Berlin; the many hours and much kindness afforded me by Madame S. P. Botcharsky, and the invaluable research done by Miss Helen Roy.

Introduction

By ISAIAH BERLIN

ALEXANDER HERZEN, like Diderot, was an amateur of genius whose opinions and activities changed the direction of social thought in his country. Like Diderot too, he was a brilliant and irrepressible talker: he talked equally well in Russian and in French to his intimate friends and in the Moscow salons—always in an overwhelming flow of ideas and images; the waste, from the point of view of posterity (just as with Diderot) is probably immense: he had no Boswell and no Eckermann to record his conversation, nor was he a man who would have suffered such a relationship. His prose is essentially a form of talk, with the vices and virtues of talk: eloquent, spontaneous, liable to the heightened tones and exaggerations of the born story-teller, unable to resist long digressions which themselves carry him into a network of intersecting tributaries of memory or speculation, but always returning to the main stream of the story or the argument; but above all, his prose has the vitality of spoken words—it appears to owe nothing to the carefully composed formal sentences of the French *'philosophes'* whom he admired or to the terrible philosophical style of the Germans from whom he learnt; we hear his voice—almost too much—in the essays, the pamphlets, the autobiography, as much as in the letters and scraps of notes to his friends.

Civilised, imaginative, self-critical, Herzen was a marvellously gifted social observer; the record of what he saw is unique even in the articulate nineteenth century. He had an acute, easily stirred and ironical mind, a fiery and poetical temperament, and a capacity for vivid, often lyrical, writing—qualities that combined and reinforced each other in the succession of sharp vignettes of men, events, ideas, personal relationships, political situations and descriptions of entire forms of life in which his writings abound. He was a man of extreme refinement and sensibility, great intellectual energy and biting wit, easily irritated *amour propre* and a taste for polemical writing; he was addicted to analysis, investigation, exposure; he saw himself as an expert 'unmasker' of appearances and conventions, and drama-

xiii

tised himself as a devastating discoverer of their social and moral core. Tolstoy, who had little sympathy with Herzen's opinions, and was not given to excessive praise of his contemporaries among men of letters, especially when they belonged to his own class and country, said towards the end of his life that he had never met anyone with 'so rare a combination of scintillating brilliance and depth'. These gifts make a good many of Herzen's essays, political articles, day-to-day journalism, casual notes and reviews, and especially letters written to intimates or to political correspondents, irresistibly readable even to-day, when the issues with which they were concerned are for the most part dead and of interest mainly to historians.

Although much has been written about Herzen—and not only in Russian—the task of his biographers has not been made easier by the fact that he left an incomparable memorial to himself in his own greatest work—translated by Constance Garnett as *My Past and Thoughts*—a literary masterpiece worthy to be placed by the side of the novels of his contemporaries and countrymen, Tolstoy, Turgenev, Dostoyevsky. Nor were they altogether unaware of this. Turgenev, an intimate and life-long friend (the fluctuations of their personal relationship were important in the life of both; this complex and interesting story has never been adequately told) admired him as a writer as well as a revolutionary journalist. The celebrated critic Vissarion Belinsky discovered, described and acclaimed his extraordinary literary gift when they were both young and relatively unknown. Even the angry and suspicious Dostoyevsky excepted him from the virulent hatred with which he regarded the pro-Western Russian revolutionaries, recognised the poetry of his writing, and remained well-disposed towards him until the end of his life. As for Tolstoy, he delighted both in his society and his writings: half a century after their first meeting in London he still remembered the scene vividly.[1]

---

[1] P. Sergeyenko, in his book on Tolstoy, says that Tolstoy told him in 1908 that he had a very clear recollection of his visit to Herzen in his London house in March 1861. 'Lev Nikolayevich remembered him as a not very large, plump little man, who generated electric energy. "Lively, responsive, intelligent, interesting", Lev Nikolaevich explained (as usual illustrating every shade of meaning by appropriate movements of his hands), "Herzen at once began talking to me as if we had known each other for a long time. I found his personality enchanting. I have never met a more attractive man. He stood head and shoulders above all the politicians of his own and of our time".' (P. Sergeyenko, *Tolstoi i ego sovremenniki*, Moscow, 1911, pp. 13-14.)

It is strange that this remarkable writer, in his lifetime a celebrated European figure, the admired friend of Michelet, Mazzini, Garibaldi and Victor Hugo, long canonised in his own country not only as a revolutionary but as one of its greatest men of letters, is, even to-day, not much more than a name in the West. The enjoyment to be obtained from reading his prose—for the most part still untranslated —makes this a strange and gratuitous loss.

Alexander Herzen was born in Moscow on the 6th April, 1812, some months before the great fire that destroyed the city during Napoleon's occupation after the battle of Borodino. His father, Ivan Alexandrovich Yakovlev, came of an ancient family distantly related to the Romanov dynasty. Like other rich and well-born members of the Russian gentry, he had spent some years abroad, and, during one of his journeys, met, and took back to Moscow with him, the daughter of a minor Württemberg official, Luiza Haag, a gentle, submissive, somewhat colourless girl, a good deal younger than himself. For some reason, perhaps owing to the disparity in their social positions, he never married her according to the rites of the Church. Yakovlev was a member of the Orthodox Church; she remained a Lutheran.[2] He was a proud, independent, disdainful man, and had grown increasingly morose and misanthropic. He retired before the war of 1812, and at the time of the French invasion was living in bitter and resentful idleness in his house in Moscow. During the occupation he was recognised by Marshal Mortier, whom he had known in Paris, and agreed—in return for a safe conduct enabling him to take his family out of the devastated city—to carry a message from Napoleon to the Emperor Alexander. For this indiscretion he was sent back to his estates and only allowed to return to Moscow somewhat later. In his large and gloomy house on the Arbat he brought up his son, Alexander, to whom he had given the surname Herzen, as if to stress the fact that he was the child of an irregular liaison, an affair of the heart. Luiza Haag was never accorded the full status of a wife, but the boy had every attention lavished upon him. He received the normal education of a young Russian nobleman of his time, that is to say, he was looked after by a host of nurses and serfs, and taught by private tutors, German and French, carefully chosen by his neurotic, irritable, devoted, suspicious father. Every care was taken to develop his gifts. He was a lively and imag-

[2] There is evidence, although it is not conclusive, that she was married to him according to the Lutheran rite, not recognised by the Orthodox Church.

inative child and absorbed knowledge easily and eagerly. His father loved him after his fashion: more, certainly, than his other son, also illegitimate, born ten years earlier, whom he had christened Yegor (George). But he was, by the eighteen-twenties, a defeated and gloomy man, unable to communicate with his family or indeed anyone else. Shrewd, honourable, and neither unfeeling nor unjust, a 'difficult' character like old Prince Bolkonsky in Tolstoy's *War and Peace*, Ivan Yakovlev emerges from his son's recollections a self-lacerating, grim, shut-in, half-frozen human being, who terrorised his household with his whims and his sarcasm. He kept all doors and windows locked, the blinds permanently drawn, and, apart from a few old friends and his own brothers, saw virtually nobody. In later years his son described him as the product of 'the encounter of two such incompatible things as the eighteenth century and Russian life'—a collision of cultures that had destroyed a good many among the more sensitive members of the Russian gentry in the reigns of Catherine II and her successors. The boy escaped with relief from his father's oppressive and frightening company to the rooms occupied by his mother and the servants; she was kind and unassuming, crushed by her husband, frightened by her foreign surroundings, and seemed to accept her almost Oriental status in the household with uncomplaining resignation. As for the servants, they were serfs from the Yakovlev estates, trained to behave obsequiously to the son and probable heir of their master. Herzen himself, in later years, attributed the deepest of all his social feelings (which his friend, the critic Belinsky, diagnosed so accurately), concern for the freedom and dignity of human individuals, to the barbarous conditions that surrounded him in childhood. He was a favourite child, and much spoiled; but the facts of his irregular birth and of his mother's status were brought home to him by listening to the servants' gossip and, on at least one occasion, by overhearing a conversation about himself between his father and one of his old army comrades. The shock was, according to his own testimony, profound: it was probably one of the determining factors of his life.

He was taught Russian literature and history by a young university student, an enthusiastic follower of the new Romantic movement, which, particularly in its German form, had then begun to dominate Russian intellectual life. He learned French (which his father wrote more easily than Russian) and German (which he spoke with his mother) and European, rather than Russian, history—his tutor was a French refugee who had emigrated to Russia after the French Revolution. The Frenchman did not reveal his political opinions, so Herzen tells us, until one day, when his pupil asked him why Louis XVI had been executed; to this he replied in an altered voice, 'Because he was a traitor to his country', and finding the boy responsive, threw off his reserve and spoke to him openly about the liberty and equality of men. Herzen was a lonely child, at once pampered and cramped, lively and bored; he read voraciously in his father's large library, especially French books of the Enlightenment. He was fourteen when the leaders of the Decembrist conspiracy were hanged by the Emperor Nicholas I. He later declared that this event was the critical turning point of his life; whether this was so or not, the memory of these aristocratic martyrs in the cause of Russian constitutional liberty later became a sacred symbol to him, as to many others of his class and generation, and affected him for the rest of his days. He tells us that a few years after this, he and his intimate friend Nick Ogarëv, standing on the Sparrow Hills above Moscow, took a solemn 'Hannibalic' oath to avenge these fighters for the rights of man, and to dedicate their own lives to the cause for which they had died.

In due course he became a student in the University of Moscow, read Schiller and Goethe, and somewhat later the French utopian socialists, Saint-Simon, Fourier and other social prophets smuggled into Russia in defiance of the censorship, and became a convinced and passionate radical. He and Ogarëv belonged to a group of students who read forbidden books and discussed dangerous ideas; for this he was, together with most other 'unreliable' students, duly arrested and, probably because he declined to repudiate the views imputed to him, condemned to imprisonment. His father used all his influence to get the sentence mitigated, but could not save his son from being exiled to the provincial city of Vyatka, near the borders of Asia, where he was not indeed kept in prison, but put to work in the local administration. To his astonishment, he enjoyed this new test of his powers; he displayed administrative gifts and became a far more competent and perhaps even enthusiastic official than he was later prepared to admit, and helped to expose the corrupt and brutal governor, whom he detested and despised. In Vyatka he became involved in a passionate love affair with a married woman, behaved badly, and suffered agonies of contrition. He read Dante, went through a religious phase, and began a long and passionate correspondence with his first cousin Natalie, who, like himself, was illegitimate, and lived as a companion in the house of a rich and despotic aunt. As a result of his father's ceaseless efforts, he was transferred to the city of Vladimir, and with the help of his young Moscow friends, arranged the elopement of Natalie. They were married in Vladimir against their relations' wishes. He was in due course allowed to return to Moscow and was appointed to a government post in Petersburg. Whatever his ambitions at the time, he remained indomitably independent and committed to the radical cause. As a result of an indiscreet letter, opened by the censors, in which he had criticised the behaviour of the police, he was again sentenced to a period of exile, this time in Novgorod. Two years later, in 1842, he was once more permitted to return to Moscow. He was by then regarded as an established member of the new radical intelligentsia, and, indeed, as an honoured martyr in its cause, and began to write in the progressive periodicals of the time. He always dealt with the same central theme: the oppression of the individual; the humiliation and degradation of men by political and personal tyranny; the yoke of social custom, the dark ignorance, and savage, arbitrary misgovernment which maimed and destroyed human beings in the brutal and odious Russian Empire.

Like the other members of his circle, the young poet and novelist Turgenev, the critic Belinsky, the future political agitators Bakunin and Katkov (the first in the cause of revolution, the second of reaction), the literary essayist Annenkov, his own intimate friend Ogarëv, Herzen plunged into the study of German metaphysics and French sociological theory and history—the works of Kant, Schelling, and, above all, Hegel: Saint-Simon, Augustin Thierry, Leroux, Mignet and Guizot. He composed arresting historical and philosophical essays, and stories dealing with social issues; they were published, widely read and discussed, and created a considerable reputation for their author. He adopted an uncompromising position. A leading representative of the dissident Russian gentry, his socialist beliefs were caused less by a reaction against the cruelty and chaos of the *laissez faire* economy of the bourgeois West—for Russia, then in its early industrial beginnings, was still a semi-feudal, socially and economically primitive society—than as a direct response to the agonising social problems in his native land: the poverty of the masses, serfdom and lack of individual freedom at all levels, and a

lawless and brutal autocracy.[3] In addition, there was the wounded
national pride of a powerful and semi-barbarous society, whose
leaders were aware of its backwardness, and suffered from mingled
admiration, envy and resentment of the civilised West. The radicals
believed in reform along democratic, secular, Western lines; the
Slavophils retreated into mystical nationalism, and preached the
need for return to native 'organic' forms of life and faith that,
according to them, had been all but ruined by Peter I's reforms, which
had merely encouraged a sedulous and humiliating aping of the
soulless, and, in any case, hopelessly decadent West. Herzen was an
extreme 'Westerner', but he preserved his links with the Slavophil
adversaries—he regarded the best among them as romantic reactionaries, misguided nationalists, but honourable allies against the Tsarist
bureaucracy—and later tended systematically to minimise his differences with them, perhaps from a desire to see all Russians who
were not dead to human feeling ranged in a single vast protest
against the evil régime.

In 1847 Ivan Yakovlev died. He left the greater part of his fortune
to Luiza Haag and her son, Alexander Herzen. With immense faith
in his own powers, and burning with a desire (in Fichte's words
that expressed the attitude of a generation) 'to be and do something
in the world', Herzen decided to emigrate. Whether he wished or
expected to remain abroad during the rest of his life is uncertain,
but so it turned out to be. He left in the same year, and travelled in
considerable state, accompanied by his wife, his mother, two friends,
as well as servants, and, crossing Germany, towards the end of
1847 reached the coveted city of Paris, the capital of the civilised
world. He plunged at once into the life of the exiled radicals and
socialists of many nationalities who played a central role in the
fermenting intellectual and artistic activity of that city. By 1848,
when a series of revolutions broke out in country after country in
Europe, he found himself with Bakunin and Proudhon on the
extreme left wing of revolutionary socialism. When rumours of his
activities reached the Russian government, he was ordered to return
immediately. He refused. His fortune in Russia and that of his

---

[3] The historical and sociological explanation of the origins of Russian socialism and of Herzen's part in it cannot be attempted here. It has been treated in
a number of (untranslated) Russian monographs, both pre- and post-revolutionary.
The most detailed and original study of this topic to date is *Alexander Herzen and
the Birth of Russian Socialism, 1812-1855* (1961) by Professor Martin Malia.

mother were declared confiscated. Aided by the efforts of the banker James Rothschild who had conceived a liking for the young Russian 'baron' and was in a position to bring pressure on the Russian government, Herzen recovered the major portion of his resources, and thereafter experienced no financial want. This gave him a degree of independence not then enjoyed by many exiles, as well as the financial means for supporting other refugees and radical causes.

Shortly after his arrival in Paris, before the revolution, he con- tributed a series of impassioned articles to a Moscow periodical controlled by his friends, in which he gave an eloquent and violently critical account of the conditions of life and culture in Paris, and, in particular, a devastating analysis of the degradation of the French bourgeoisie, an indictment not surpassed even in the works of his contemporaries Marx and Heine. His Moscow friends for the most part received this with disfavour: they regarded his analyses as characteristic flights of a highly rhetorical fancy, irresponsible ex- tremism, ill suited to the needs of a misgoverned and backward country compared to which the progress of the middle classes in the West, whatever its shortcomings, was a notable step forward towards universal enlightenment. These early works—*The Letters from Avenue Marigny* and the Italian sketches that followed—possess qualities which became characteristic of all his writings: a rapid torrent of descriptive sentences, fresh, lucid, direct, interspersed with vivid and never irrelevant digressions, variations on the same theme in many keys, puns, neologisms, quotations real and imagin- ary, verbal inventions, gallicisms which irritated his nationalistic Russian friends, mordant personal observations and cascades of vivid images and incomparable epigrams, which, so far from either tiring or distracting the reader by their virtuosity, add to the force and swiftness of the narrative. The effect is one of spontaneous improvi- sation: exhilarating conversation by an intellectually gay and exceptionally clever and honest man endowed with singular powers of observation and expression. The mood is one of ardent political radicalism imbued with a typically aristocratic (and even more typi- cally Muscovite) contempt for everything narrow, calculating, self- satisfied, commercial, anything cautious, petty or tending towards compromise and the *juste milieu*, of which Louis Philippe and Guizot are held up to view as particularly repulsive incarnations. Herzen's outlook in these essays is a combination of optimistic idealism—a vision of a socially, intellectually and morally free society, the beginnings of which, like Proudhon, Marx, and Louis Blanc, he saw in the French working class; faith in the radical revolution which alone could create the conditions for their liberation; but with this, a deep distrust (something that most of his allies did not share) of all general formulae as such, of the programmes and battle cries of all the political parties, of the great, official historical goals—progress, liberty, equality, national unity, historic rights, human solidarity—principles and slogans in the name of which men had been, and doubtless would soon again be, violated and slaughtered, and their forms of life condemned and destroyed. Like the more extreme of the left wing disciples of Hegel, in particular like the anarchist Max Stirner, Herzen saw danger in the great magnificent abstractions the mere sound of which precipitated men into violent and meaningless slaughter—new idols, it seemed to him, on whose altars human blood was to be shed tomorrow as irrationally and uselessly as the blood of the victims of yesterday or the day before, sacrificed in honour of older divinities—church or monarchy or the feudal order or the sacred customs of the tribe, that were now discredited as obstacles to the progress of mankind. Together with this scepticism about the meaning and value of abstract ideals as such, in contrast with the concrete, short-term, immediate goals of identifiable living individuals—specific freedoms, reward for the day's work—Herzen spoke of something even more disquieting—a haunting sense of the ever widening and unbridgeable gulf between the humane values of the relatively free and civilised élites (to which he knew himself to belong) and the actual needs, desires and tastes of the vast voiceless masses of mankind, barbarous enough in the West, wilder still in Russia or the plains of Asia beyond. The old world was crumbling visibly, and it deserved to fall. It would be destroyed by its victims—the slaves who cared nothing for the art and the science of their masters; and indeed, Herzen asks, why should they care? Was it not erected on their suffering and degradation? Young and vigorous, filled with a just hatred of the old world built on their fathers' bones, the new barbarians will raze to the ground the edifices of their oppressors, and with them all that is most sublime and beautiful in Western civilisation; such a cataclysm might be not only inevitable but justified, since this civilisation, noble and valuable in the eyes of its beneficiaries, has offered nothing but suffering, a life without meaning, to the vast majority of mankind. Yet he does not pretend that this makes the prospect, to those who, like him, have tasted the riper fruits of civilisation, any less dreadful.

It has often been asserted by both Russian and Western critics that Herzen arrived in Paris a passionate, even utopian idealist, and that it was the failure of the Revolution of 1848 which brought about his disillusionment and a new, more pessimistic realism. This is not sufficiently borne out by the evidence.[4] Even in 1847, the sceptical note, in particular pessimism about the degree to which human beings can be transformed, and the still deeper scepticism about whether such changes, even if they were achieved by fearless and intelligent revolutionaries or reformers, ideal images of whom floated before the eyes of his Westernising friends in Russia, would in fact lead to a juster and freer order, or on the contrary to the rule of new masters over new slaves—that ominous note is sounded before the great debâcle. Yet, despite this, he remained a convinced, ultimately optimistic revolutionary. The spectacle of the workers' revolt and its brutal suppression in Italy and in France, haunted Herzen all his life. His first-hand description of the events of 1848-9, in particular of the drowning in blood of the July revolt in Paris, is a masterpiece of 'committed' historical and sociological writing. So, too, are his sketches of the personalities involved in these upheavals, and his reflections upon them. Most of these essays and letters remain untranslated.

Herzen could not and would not return to Russia. He became a Swiss citizen, and to the disasters of the Revolution was added a personal tragedy—the seduction of his adored wife by the most intimate of his new friends, the radical German poet Georg Herwegh, a friend of Marx and Wagner, the 'iron lark' of the German Revolution, as Heine half ironically called him. Herzen's progressive, somewhat Shelleyan, views on love, friendship, equality of the sexes, and the irrationality of bourgeois morality, were tested by this crisis and broken by it. He went almost mad with grief and jealousy: his love, his vanity, his deeper assumptions about the basis of all human relationships, suffered a traumatic shock from which he was never fully to recover. He did what few others have ever done: described every detail of his own agony, every step of his altering relationship with his wife, with Herwegh and

---

[4] The clearest formulation of this well-worn and almost universal thesis is to be found in Mr E. H. Carr's lively and well documented treatment of Herzen in his *The Romantic Exiles* and elsewhere. Mr Malia's book avoids this error.

Herwegh's wife, as they seemed to him in retrospect; he noted every communication that occurred between them, every moment of anger, despair, affection, love, hope, hatred, contempt and agonised, suicidal self-contempt. Every tone and *nuance* in his own moral and psychological condition are raised to high relief against the background of his public life in the world of exiles and conspirators, French, Italian, German, Russian, Austrian, Hungarian, Polish, who move on and off the stage on which he himself is always the central, self-absorbed, tragic hero. The account is not unbalanced—there is no obvious distortion—but it is wholly egocentric. All his life Herzen perceived the external world clearly, and in proportion, but through the medium of his own self-romanticising personality, with his own impressionable, ill-organised self at the centre of his universe. No matter how violent his torment, he retains full artistic control of the tragedy which he is living through, but also writing. It is, perhaps, this artistic egotism, which all his work exhibits, that was in part responsible both for Natalie's suffocation and for the lack of reticence in his description of what took place: Herzen takes wholly for granted the reader's understanding, and still more, his undivided interest in every detail of his own, the writer's, mental and emotional life. Natalie's letters and desperate flight to Herwegh show the measure of the increasingly destructive effect of Herzen's self-absorbed blindness upon her frail and *exalté* temperament. We know comparatively little of Natalie's relationship with Herwegh: she may well have been physically in love with him, and he with her: the inflated literary language of the letters conceals more than it reveals; what is clear is that she felt unhappy, trapped and irresistibly attracted to her lover. If Herzen sensed this, he perceived it very dimly. He appropriated the feelings of those nearest him as he did the ideas of Hegel or George Sand: that is, he took what he needed, and poured it into the vehement torrent of his own experience. He gave generously, if fitfully, to others; he put his own life into them, but for all his deep and lifelong belief in individual liberty and the absolute value of personal life and personal relationships, scarcely understood or tolerated wholly independent lives by the side of his own; his description of his agony is scrupulously and bitterly detailed and accurate, never self-sparing, eloquent but not sentimental, and remorselessly self-absorbed. It is a harrowing document. He did not publish the story in full during his lifetime, but now it forms part of his memoirs.

Self-expression—the need to say his own word—and perhaps the craving for recognition by others, by Russia, by Europe, were primary needs of Herzen's nature. Consequently, even during this, the darkest period of his life, he continued to pour out a stream of letters and articles in various languages on political and social topics; he helped to keep Proudhon going, kept up a correspondence with Swiss radicals and Russian émigrés, read widely, made notes, conceived ideas, argued, worked unremittingly both as a publicist and as an active supporter of left wing and revolutionary causes. After a short while Natalie returned to him in Nice, only to die in his arms. Shortly before her death, a ship on which his mother and one of his children, a deaf-mute, were travelling from Marseilles, sank in a storm. Their bodies were not found. Herzen's life had reached its lowest ebb. He left Nice and the circle of Italian, French and Polish revolutionaries to many of whom he was bound by ties of warm friendship, and with his three surviving children went to England. America was too far away and, besides, seemed to him too dull. England was no less remote from the scene of his defeats, political and personal, and yet still a part of Europe. It was then the country most hospitable to political refugees, civilised, tolerant of eccentricities or indifferent to them, proud of its civil liberties and its sympathy with the victims of foreign oppression. He arrived in London in 1851.

He and his children wandered from home to home in London and its suburbs, and there, after the death of Nicholas I had made it possible for him to leave Russia, his most intimate friend, Nicholas Ogarëv, joined them. Together they set up a printing press, and began to publish a periodical in Russian called *The Pole Star*—the first organ wholly dedicated to uncompromising agitation against the Imperial Russian régime. The earliest chapters of *My Past and Thoughts* appeared in its pages. The memory of the terrible years 1848-51 obsessed Herzen's thoughts and poisoned his blood stream: it became an inescapable psychological necessity for him to seek relief by setting down this bitter history. This was the first section of his Memoirs to be written. It was an opiate against the appalling loneliness of a life lived among uninterested strangers[5] while political

---

[5] Herzen had no close English friends, although he had associates, allies and admirers. One of these, the radical journalist W. J. Linton, to whose *English Republic* Herzen had contributed articles, described him as 'short of stature, stoutly built, in his last days inclined to corpulence, with a grand head, long chestnut

reaction seemed to envelop the entire world, leaving no room for
hope. Insensibly he was drawn into the past. He moved further and
further into it and found it a source of liberty and strength. This is
how the book which he conceived on the analogy of *David Copperfield* came to be composed.[6] He began to write it in the last months
of 1852. He wrote by fits and starts. The first two parts were
probably finished by the end of 1853. In 1854 a selection which he
called *Prison and Exile*—a title perhaps inspired by Silvio Pellico's
celebrated *I Miei Prigioni,* was published in English. It was an
immediate success; encouraged by this, he continued. By the spring
of 1855, the first five parts of the work were completed; they were
all published by 1857. He revised part IV, added new chapters to it
and composed part V; he completed the bulk of part VI by 1858.
The sections dealing with his intimate life—his love and the early
years of his marriage, were composed in 1857: he could not bring
himself to touch upon them until then. This was followed by an
interval of seven years. Independent essays such as those on Robert
Owen, the actor Shchepkin, the painter Ivanov, Garibaldi (*Camicia
Rossa*), were published in London between 1860 and 1864; but these,
although usually included in the Memoirs, were not intended for
them. The first complete edition of the first four parts appeared in
1861. The final section—part VIII and almost the whole of part VII
—were written, in that order, in 1865-7. Herzen deliberately left
some sections unpublished: the most intimate details of his personal
tragedy appeared posthumously—only a part of the chapter entitled
Oceano Nox was printed in his lifetime. He omitted also the story
of his affairs with Medvedeva in Vyatka and with the serf girl

---

hair and beard, small, luminous eyes, and rather ruddy complexion. Suave in his
manner, courteous, but with an intense power of irony, witty, . . . clear, concise
and impressive, he was a subtle and profound thinker, with all the passionate
nature of the "barbarian", yet generous and humane.' (*Memories*, London, 1895,
pp. 146-7.) And in his *European Republicans,* published two years earlier, he spoke
of him as 'hospitable and taking pleasure in society, . . . a good conversationalist,
with a frank and pleasing manner', and said that the Spanish radical Castelar
declared that Herzen, with his fair hair and fair beard, looked like a Goth, but possessed the warmth, vivacity, 'verve and inimitable grace' and 'marvellous variety' of a
Southerner. Turgenev and Herzen were the first Russians to move freely in
European society. The impression that they made did a good deal, though perhaps
not enough, to dispel the myth of the dark 'Slav soul', which took a long time to die;
perhaps it is not altogether dead yet.

  [6] 'Copperfield is Dickens's *Past and Thoughts*', he said in one of his letters in the
early sixties; humility was not among his virtues.

Katerina in Moscow—his confession of them to Natalie cast the first
shadow over their relationship, a shadow that never lifted; he could
not bear to see it in print while he lived. He suppressed, too, a
chapter on 'The German Emigrants' which contains his un-
flattering comments on Marx and his followers, and some characteris-
tically entertaining and ironical sketches of some of his old friends
among the Russian radicals. He genuinely detested the practice of
washing the revolutionaries' dirty linen in public, and made it clear
that he did not intend to make fun of allies for the entertainment
of the common enemy. The first authoritative edition of the Memoirs
was compiled by Mikhail Lemke in the first complete edition of
Herzen's works, which was begun before, and completed some years
after, the Russian Revolution of 1917. It has since been revised in
successive Soviet editions. The fullest version is that published in the
new exhaustive edition of Herzen's works, a handsome monument of
Soviet scholarship—which at the time of writing is still incomplete.

The Memoirs formed a vivid and broken background accompani-
ment to Herzen's central activity: revolutionary journalism, to
which he dedicated his life. The bulk of it is contained in the most
celebrated of all Russian periodicals published abroad—*Kólokol*—
The Bell—edited by Herzen and Ogarëv in London and then in
Geneva from 1857 until 1867, with the motto (taken from Schiller)
Vivos voco. The Bell had an immense success. It was the first systematic instrument of revolutionary propaganda directed against the
Russian autocracy, written with knowledge, sincerity and mordant
eloquence; it gathered round itself all that was uncowed not only in
Russia and the Russian colonies abroad, but also among Poles and
other oppressed nationalities. It began to penetrate into Russia by
secret routes and was regularly read by high officials of State, including, it was rumoured, the Emperor himself. Herzen used the copious
information that reached him in clandestine letters and personal mes-
sages, describing various misdeeds of the Russian bureaucracy to
expose specific scandals—cases of bribery, miscarriage of justice,
tyranny and dishonesty by officials and influential persons. *The Bell*
named names, offered documentary evidence, asked awkward questions and exposed hideous aspects of Russian life. Russian travellers
visited London in order to meet the mysterious leader of the mounting opposition to the Tsar. Generals, high officials and other loyal
subjects of the Empire were among the many visitors who thronged
to see him, some out of curiosity, others to shake his hand, to

express sympathy or admiration. He reached the peak of his fame, both political and literary, after the defeat of Russia in the Crimean War and the death of Nicholas I. The open appeal by Herzen to the new Emperor to free the serfs and initiate bold and radical reforms 'from above', and, after the first concrete steps towards this had been taken in 1859, his paean of praise to Alexander II under the title of 'Thou hast Conquered, O Galilean', created the illusion on both sides of the Russian frontier that a new liberal era was at last dawning, in which a degree of understanding—perhaps of actual co-operation—could be achieved between Tsardom and its opponents. This state of mind did not last long. But Herzen's credit stood very high—higher than that of any other Russian in the West: in the late fifties and early sixties, he was the acknowledged leader of all that was generous, enlightened, civilised, humane in Russia. More than Bakunin and even Turgenev, whose novels formed a central source of knowledge about Russia in the West, Herzen counteracted the legend, ingrained in the minds of progressive Europeans (of whom Michelet was perhaps the most representative), that Russia consisted of nothing save only the government jack-boot on the one hand, and the dark, silent, sullen mass of brutalised peasants on the other—an image that was the by-product of the widespread sympathy for the principal victim of Russian despotism, the martyred nation, Poland. Some among the Polish exiles spontaneously conceded this service to the truth on Herzen's part, if only because he was one of the rare Russians who genuinely liked and admired individual Poles, worked in close sympathy with them, and identified the cause of Russian liberation with that of all her oppressed subject nationalities. It was, indeed, this unswerving avoidance of chauvinism that was among the principal causes of the ultimate collapse of *The Bell* and of Herzen's own political undoing.

After Russia, Herzen's deepest love was for Italy and the Italians. The closest ties bound him to the Italian exiles, Mazzini, Garibaldi, Saffi and Orsini. Although he supported every liberal beginning in France, his attitude towards her was more ambiguous. For this there were many reasons. Like Tocqueville (whom he personally disliked), he had a distaste for all that was centralised, bureaucratic, hierarchical, subject to rigid forms or rules; France was to him the incarnation of order, discipline, the worship of the state, of unity, and of despotic, abstract formulae that flattened all things to the same rule and pattern—something that had a family resemblance to the great

slave states—Prussia, Austria, Russia; with this he constantly con-
trasts the decentralised, uncrushed, untidy, 'truly democratic'
Italians, whom he believes to possess a deep affinity with the free
Russian spirit embodied in the peasant commune with its sense of
natural justice and human worth. To this ideal even England seemed
to him to be far less hostile than legalistic, calculating France: in
such moods he comes close to his romantic Slavophil opponents.
Moreover, he could not forget the betrayal of the Revolution in Paris
by the bourgeois parties in 1848, the execution of the workers, the
suppression of the Roman Revolution by the troops of the French
Republic, the vanity, weakness and rhetoric of the French radical
politicians—Lamartine, Marrast, Ledru-Rollin, Félix Pyat. His
sketches of the lives and behaviour of leading French exiles in
England are masterpieces of amused, half-sympathetic, half contemp-
tuous description of the grotesque and futile aspects of every political
emigration condemned to sterility, intrigue and a constant flow of
self-justifying eloquence before a foreign audience too remote or
bored to listen. Yet he thought well of individual members of it:
he had for a time been a close ally of Proudhon, and despite their
differences, he continued to respect him; he regarded Louis Blanc as
an honest and fearless democrat, he was on good terms with Victor
Hugo, he liked and admired Michelet. In later years he visited
at least one Paris political salon—admittedly, it was that of a Pole—
with evident enjoyment: the Goncourts met him there and left a
vivid description in their journal of his appearance and his conversation.[7] Although he was half German himself, or perhaps because

[7] See entry in the *Journal* under *8th February 1865*—'Dinner at Charles Edmond's
(Chojecki) . . . A Socratic mask with the warm and transparent flesh of a Rubens
portrait, a red mark between the eyebrows as from a branding iron, greying beard
and hair. As he talks there is a constant ironical chuckle which rises and falls in
his throat. His voice is soft and slow, without any of the coarseness one might have
expected from the huge neck; the ideas are fine, delicate, pungent, at times subtle,
always definite, illuminated by words that take time to arrive, but which always
possess the felicitous quality of French as it is spoken by a civilised and witty
foreigner.

'He speaks of Bakunin, of his eleven months in prison, chained to a wall, of his
escape from Siberia by the Amur River, of his return by way of California, of his
arrival in London, where, after a stormy, moist embrace, his first words to Herzen
were "Can one get oysters here?".'

Herzen delighted the Goncourts with stories about the Emperor Nicholas walking
in the night in his empty palace, after the fall of Eupatoria during the Crimean
War, with the heavy, unearthly steps of the stone statue of the Commander in
'Don Juan'. This was followed by anecdotes about English habits and manners—'a
country which he loves as the land of liberty'—to illustrate its absurd, class conscious,

of it, he felt, like his friend Bakunin, a strong aversion from what
he regarded as the incurable philistinism of the Germans, and what
seemed to him peculiarly unattractive combination of craving for
blind authority, with a tendency to squalid internecine recriminations
in public, more pronounced than among other *émigrés*. Perhaps his
hatred of Herwegh, whom he knew to be a friend both of Marx
and of Wagner, as well as Marx's onslaughts on Karl Vogt, the
Swiss naturalist to whom Herzen was devoted, played some part in
this. At least three of his most intimate friends were pure Germans.
Goethe and Schiller meant more to him than any Russian
writers. Yet there is something genuinely venomous in his account
of the German exiles, quite different from the high spirited sense of
comedy with which he describes the idiosyncracies of the other
foreign colonies gathered in London in the fifties and sixties—a city,
if we are to believe Herzen, equally unconcerned with their absurdities and their martyrdoms. As for his hosts, the English, they seldom
appear in his pages. Herzen had met Mill, Carlyle and Owen. His
first night in England was spent with English hosts. He was on
reasonably good terms with one or two editors of radical papers
(some of whom, like Linton and Cowen, helped him to propagate
his views, and to preserve contact with revolutionaries on the continent as well with clandestine traffic of propaganda to Russia),
and several radically inclined Members of Parliament, including
minor ministers. In general, however, he seems to have had even less
contact with Englishmen than his contemporary and fellow exile,
Karl Marx. He admired England. He admired her constitution; the
wild and tangled wood of her unwritten laws and customs brought
the full resources of his romantic imagination into play. The entertaining passages of *My Past and Thoughts* in which he compared the
French and the English, or the English and the Germans, display
acute and amused insight into the national characteristics of the
English. But he could not altogether like them: they remained for
him too insular, too indifferent, too unimaginative, too remote from
the moral, social and aesthetic issues which lay closest to his own heart,
too materialistic and self satisfied. His judgments about them,
always intelligent and sometimes penetrating, are distant and tend

---

unyielding traditionalism, particularly noticeable in the relations of masters and
servants. The Goncourts quote a characteristic epigram made by Herzen to illustrate
the difference between the French and the English characters. They faithfully report
the story of how James Rothschild managed to save Herzen's property in Russia.

to be conventional. A description of the trial in London of a French radical who had killed a political opponent in a duel in Windsor Great Park is wonderfully executed, but remains a piece of *genre* painting, a gay and brilliant caricature. The French, the Swiss, the Italians, even the Germans, certainly the Poles, are closer to him. He cannot establish any genuine personal relationship with the English. When he thinks of mankind he does not think of them.

Apart from his central preoccupations, he devoted himself to the education of his children, which he entrusted in part to an idealistic German lady, Malwida von Meysenbug, afterwards a friend of Nietzsche and Romain Rolland. His personal life was intertwined with that of his intimate friend Ogarëv, and of Ogarëv's wife who became his mistress; in spite of this the mutual devotion of the two friends remained unaltered—the Memoirs reveal little of the curious emotional consequences of this relationship.

For the rest, he lived the life of an affluent, well born man of letters, a member of the Russian, and more specifically, Moscow gentry, uprooted from his native soil, unable to achieve a settled existence or even the semblance of inward or outward peace, a life filled with occasional moments of hope and even exultation, followed by long periods of misery, corrosive self-criticism, and most of all overwhelming, omnivorous, bitter nostalgia. It may be this, as much as objective reasons, that caused him to idealise the Russian peasant, and to dream that the answer to the central 'social' question of his time—that of growing inequality, exploitation, dehumanisation of both the oppressor and the oppressed—lay in the preservation of the Russian peasant commune. He perceived in it the seeds of the development of a non-industrial, semi-anarchist socialism. Only such a solution, plainly influenced by the views of Fourier, Proudhon and George Sand, seemed to him free from the crushing, barrack-room discipline demanded by Western communists from Cabet to Marx; and from the equally suffocating, and, it seemed to him, far more vulgar and philistine ideals contained in moderate, half-socialist doctrines, with their faith in the progressive role of developing industrialism preached by the forerunners of social democracy in Germany and France and of the Fabians in England. At times he modified his view: towards the end of his life he began to recognise the historical significance of the organised urban workers. But all in all, he remained faithful to his belief in the Russian peasant commune as an embryonic form of a life in which the quest for individual freedom was reconciled with the need for collective activity and responsibility. He retained to the end a romantic vision of the inevitable coming of a new, just, all-transforming social order.

Herzen is neither consistent nor systematic. His style during his middle years has lost the confident touch of his youth, and conveys the consuming nostalgia that never leaves him. He is obsessed by a sense of blind accident, although his faith in the values of life remains unshaken. Almost all traces of Hegelian influence are gone. 'The absurdity of facts offends us . . . it is as though someone had promised that everything in the world will be exquisitely beautiful, just and harmonious. We have marvelled enough at the deep abstract wisdom of nature and history; it is time to realise that nature and history are full of the accidental and senseless, of muddle and bungling.' This is highly characteristic of his mood in the sixties; and it is no accident that his exposition is not ordered, but is a succession of fragments, episodes, isolated vignettes, a mingling of *Dichtung* and *Wahrheit*, facts and poetic licence. His moods alternate sharply. Sometimes he believes in the need for a great, cleansing, revolutionary storm, even were it to take the form of a barbarian invasion likely to destroy all the values that he himself holds dear. At other times he reproaches his old friend Bakunin, who joined him in London after escaping from his Russian prisons, for wanting to make the revolution too soon; for not understanding that dwellings for free men cannot be constructed out of the stones of a prison; that the average European of the nineteenth century is too deeply marked by the slavery of the old order to be capable of conceiving true freedom, that it is not the liberated slaves who will build the new order, but new men brought up in liberty. History has her own tempo. Patience and gradualism—not the haste and violence of a Peter the Great—can alone bring about a permanent transformation. At such moments he wonders whether the future belongs to the free, anarchic peasant, or to the bold and ruthless planner; perhaps it is the industrial worker who is to be the heir to the new, unavoidable, collectivist economic order.[8] Then again he returns to his early moods of disillusionment and wonders whether men in general really desire freedom: perhaps only a few do so in each generation, while most human beings only want good government, no matter at whose hands; and he echoes de Maistre's bitter epigram about Rousseau:

---

[8] This is the thesis in which orthodox Soviet scholars claim to discern a belated approach to those of Marx.

'Monsieur Rousseau has asked why it is that men who are born free are nevertheless everywhere in chains; it is as if one were to ask why sheep, who are born carnivorous, nevertheless everywhere nibble grass.' Herzen develops this theme. Men desire freedom no more than fish desire to fly. The fact that a few flying fish exist does not demonstrate that fish in general were created to fly, or are not fundamentally quite content to stay below the surface of the water, forever away from the sun and the light. Then he returns to his earlier optimism and the thought that somewhere—in Russia—there lives the unbroken human being, the peasant with his faculties intact, untainted by the corruption and sophistication of the West. But this Rousseau-inspired faith, as he grows older, grows less secure. His sense of reality is too strong. For all his efforts, and the efforts of his socialist friends, he cannot deceive himself entirely. He oscillates between pessimism and optimism, scepticism and suspicion of his own scepticism, and is kept morally alive only by his hatred of all injustice, all arbitrariness, all mediocrity as such—in particular by his inability to compromise in any degree with either the brutality of reactionaries or the hypocrisy of bourgeois liberals. He is preserved by this, buoyed up by his belief that such evils will destroy themselves, and by his love for his children and his devoted friends, and by his unquenchable delight in the variety of life and the comedy of human character.

On the whole, he grew more pessimistic. He began with an ideal vision of human life, largely ignored the chasm which divided it from the present—whether the Russia of Nicholas, or the corrupt constitutionalism in the West. In his youth he glorified Jacobin radicalism and condemned its opponents in Russia—blind conservatism, Slavophil nostalgia, the cautious gradualism of his friends Granovsky and Turgenev, as well as Hegelian appeals to patience and rational conformity to the inescapable rhythms of history, which seemed to him designed to ensure the triumph of the new bourgeois class. His attitude, before he went abroad, was boldly optimistic. There followed, not indeed a change of view, but a cooling-off, a tendency to a more sober and critical outlook. All genuine change, he began to think in 1847, is necessarily slow; the power of tradition (which he at once mocks at and admires in England) is very great; men are less malleable than was believed in the eighteenth century, nor do they truly seek liberty, only security and contentment; communism is but Tsarism stood on its head, the replacement of one yoke by another; the ideals and watchwords of politics turn out, on examination, to be empty formulae to which devout fanatics happily slaughter hecatombs of their fellows. He no longer feels certain that the gap between the enlightened élite and the masses can ever, in principle, be bridged (this becomes an obsessive refrain in later Russian thought), since the awakened people may, for unalterable psychological or sociological reasons, despise and reject the gifts of a civilisation which will never mean enough to them. But if all this is even in small part true, is radical transformation either practicable or desirable? From this follows Herzen's growing sense of obstacles that may be insurmountable, limits that may be impassable, his empiricism, scepticism, the latent pessimism and despair of the middle sixties. This is the attitude which some Soviet scholars interpret as the beginning of an approach on his part towards a quasi-Marxist recognition of the inexorable laws of social development—in particular the inevitability of industrialism, above all of the central role to be played by the proletariat. This is not how Herzen's Russian left wing critics interpreted his views in his lifetime, or for the half century that followed. To them, rightly or wrongly, these doctrines seemed symptomatic of conservatism and betrayal. For in the fifties and sixties, a new generation of radicals grew up in Russia, then a backward country in the painful process of the earliest, most rudimentary beginnings of slow, sporadic, inefficient industrialisation. These were men of mixed social origins, filled with contempt for the feeble liberal compromises of 1848, with no illusions about the prospects of freedom in the West, determined on more ruthless methods; accepting as true only what the sciences can prove, prepared to be hard, and if need be, unscrupulous and cruel, in order to break the power of their equally ruthless oppressors; bitterly hostile to the aestheticism, the devotion to civilised values, of the 'soft' generation of the forties. Herzen realised that the criticism and abuse showered upon him as an obsolete aristocratic dilettante by these 'nihilists' (as they came to be called after Turgenev's novel *Fathers and Sons,* in which this conflict is vividly presented for the first time) was not altogether different from the disdain that he had himself felt in his own youth for the elegant and ineffective reformers of Alexander I's reign; but this did not make his position easier to bear. What was ill-received by the tough-minded revolutionaries pleased Tolstoy, who said more than once that the censorship of Herzen's works in Russia was a characteristic blunder on the

B

part of the government; the government, in its anxiety to stop young men from marching towards the revolutionary morass, seized them and swept them off to Siberia or prison long before they were even in sight of it, while they were still on the broad highway; Herzen had trodden this very path, he had seen the chasm, and warned against it, particularly in his 'Letters to an Old Comrade'. Nothing, Tolstoy argued, would have proved a better antidote to the 'revolutionary nihilism' which Tolstoy condemned, than Herzen's brilliant analyses. 'Our young generation would not have been the same if Herzen had been read by them during the last twenty years'. Suppression of his books, Tolstoy went on, was both a criminal, and from the point of view of those who did not desire a violent revolution, an idiotic policy. At other times, Tolstoy was less generous. In 1860, six months before they met, he had been reading Herzen's writings with mingled admiration and irritation: 'Herzen is a man of scattered intellect, and morbid *amour-propre*', he wrote in a letter, 'but his breadth, ability, goodness, elegance of mind are Russian'. From time to time various correspondents record the fact that Tolstoy read Herzen, at times aloud to his family, with the greatest admiration. In 1896, during one of his angriest, most anti-rationalist moods, he said 'What has Herzen said that is of the slightest use?'—as for the argument that the generation of the forties could not say what it wanted to say because of the rigid Russian censorship, Herzen wrote in perfect freedom in Paris and yet managed to say 'nothing useful'. What irritated Tolstoy most was Herzen's socialism. In 1908 he complained that Herzen was 'a narrow socialist', even if he was 'head and shoulders above the other politicians of his age and ours'. The fact that he believed in politics as a weapon was sufficient to condemn him in Tolstoy's eyes. From 1862 onwards, Tolstoy had declared his hostility to faith in liberal reform and improvement of human life by legal or institutional change. Herzen fell under this general ban. Moreover, Tolstoy seems to have felt a certain lack of personal sympathy for Herzen and his public position—even a kind of jealousy. When, in moments of acute discouragement and irritation, Tolstoy spoke (perhaps not very seriously) of leaving Russia forever, he would say that whatever he did, he would not join Herzen or march under his banner: 'he goes his way, I shall go mine'. He seriously underrated Herzen's revolutionary temperament and instincts. However sceptical Herzen may have been of specific revolutionary doctrines or plans in Russia—and no-one was more so—he believed to the end of his life in the moral and social need and the inevitability, sooner or later, of a revolution in Russia—a violent transformation followed by a just, that is a socialist, order. He did not, it is true, close his eyes to the possibility, even the probability, that the great rebellion would extinguish values to which he was himself dedicated—in particular, the freedoms without which he and others like him could not breathe. Nevertheless, he recognised not only the inevitability but the historic justice of the coming cataclysm. His moral tastes, his respect for human values, his entire style of life, divided him from the tough-minded younger radicals of the sixties, but he did not, despite all his distrust of political fanaticism, whether on the right or on the left, turn into a cautious, reformist liberal constitutionalist. Even in his gradualist phase he remained an agitator, an egalitarian and a socialist to the end. It is this in him that both the Russian populists and the Russian Marxists—Mikhaylovsky and Lenin—recognised and saluted.

It was not prudence or moderation that led him to his unwavering support of Poland in her insurrection against Russia in 1863. The wave of passionate Russian nationalism which accompanied its suppression, robbed him of sympathy even among Russian liberals. *The Bell* declined in circulation. The new, 'hard' revolutionaries needed his money, but made it plain that they looked upon him as a liberal dinosaur, the preacher of antiquated humanistic views, useless in the violent social struggle to come. He left London in the late sixties and attempted to produce a French edition of *The Bell* in Geneva. When that too failed, he visited his friends in Florence, returning to Paris early in 1870, before the outbreak of the Franco-Prussian War. There he died of pleurisy, broken both morally and physically, but not disillusioned; still writing with concentrated intelligence and force. His body was taken to Nice, where he is buried beside his wife. A life-size statue still marks his grave.

Herzen's ideas have long since entered into the general texture of Russian political thought—liberals and radicals, populists and anarchists, socialists and communists, have all claimed him as an ancestor. But what survives to-day of all that unceasing and feverish activity, even in his native country, is not a system or a doctrine but a handful of essays, some remarkable letters, and the extraordinary amalgam of memory, observation, moral passion, psychological analysis and political description, wedded to a major literary talent, which has immortalised his name. What remains is, above all, a passionate and inextinguishable temperament and a sense of the movement of nature and of its unpredictable possibilities, which he felt with an intensity which not even his uniquely rich and flexible prose could fully express. He believed that the ultimate goal of life was life itself; that the day and the hour were ends in themselves, not a means to another day or another experience. He believed that remote ends were a dream, that faith in them was a fatal illusion; that to sacrifice the present, or the immediate and foreseeable future to these distant ends must always lead to cruel and futile forms of human sacrifice. He believed that values were not found in an impersonal, objective realm, but were created by human beings, changed with the generations of men, but were nonetheless binding upon those who lived in their light; that suffering was inescapable, and infallible knowledge neither attainable nor needed. He believed in reason, scientific methods, individual action, empirically discovered truths; but he tended to suspect that faith in general formulae, laws, prescription in human affairs was an attempt, sometimes catastrophic, always irrational, to escape from the uncertainty and unpredictable variety of life to the false security of our own symmetrical fantasies. He was fully conscious of what he believed. He had obtained this knowledge at the cost of painful, and, at times, unintended, self-analysis, and he described what he saw in language of exceptional vitality, precision and poetry. His purely personal credo remained unaltered from his earliest days: 'Art, and the summer lightning of individual happiness: these are the only real goods we have', he declared in a self-revealing passage of the kind that so deeply shocked the stern young Russian revolutionaries in the sixties. Yet even they and their descendants did not and do not reject his artistic and intellectual achievement.

Herzen was not, and had no desire to be, an impartial observer. No less than the poets and the novelists of his nation, he created a style, an outlook, and, in the words of Gorky's tribute to him, 'an entire province, a country astonishingly rich in ideas',[9] where everything is immediately recognisable as being his and his alone, a country into which he transplants all that he touches, in which things, sensations, feelings, persons, ideas, private and public events, institutions, entire cultures, are given shape and life by his powerful and coherent historical imagination, and have stood up against the forces of decay in the solid world which his memory, his intelligence

[9] *Istoriya Russkoy Literatury*, p. 206, Moscow, 1939.

and his artistic genius recovered and reconstructed. *My Past and Thoughts* is the Noah's ark in which he saved himself, and not himself alone, from the destructive flood in which many idealistic radicals of the forties were drowned. Genuine art survives and transcends its immediate purpose. The structure that Herzen built in the first place, perhaps, for his own personal salvation, built out of material provided by his own predicament—out of exile, solitude, despair—survives intact. Written abroad, concerned largely with European issues and figures, these reminiscences are a great permanent monument to the civilised, sensitive, morally preoccupied and gifted Russian society to which Herzen belonged; their vitality and fascination have not declined in the hundred years that have passed since the first chapters saw the light.

GENEALOGICAL TABLE

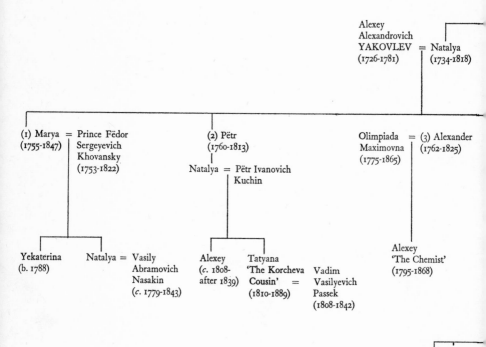

Alexey
Alexandrovich
YAKOVLEV = Natalya
(1726-1781)   (1734-1818)

(1) Marya = Prince Fëdor   (2) Pëtr   Olimpiada = (3) Alexander
(1755-1847) Sergeyevich   (1760-1813)   Maximovna   (1762-1825)
             Khovansky   (1775-1865)
             (1753-1822)   Natalya = Pëtr Ivanovich
                                      Kuchin

                                                                    Alexey
                                                                    'The Chemist'
                                                                    (1795-1868)

Yekaterina   Natalya = Vasily   Alexey   Tatyana
(b. 1788)   Abramovich   (c. 1808-   'The Korcheva   Vadim
                        Nasakin   after 1839) Cousin'   =   Vasilyevich
                        (c. 1779-1843)   (1810-1889)   Passek
                                                                  (1808-1842)

                                                               Alexander
                                                               'Sasha'
                                                               (1839-1906)

Prince
Boris
Meshchersky

Anna Borisovna
(1738-1827)

+ Kseniya　　　Luiza　　　+ (6) Ivan　　　+ ?　　　　　(4) Yelizaveta = Pavel Ivanovich　　　(5) Lev
Ivanovna　　　Haag　　　(1767-1846)　　　　　　　　(1763-1822)　　Golokhvastov　　　'The Senator'
Zakharin　　　(1795-1851)　　　　　　　　　　　　　　　　　　　(d. 1812)　　　(1764-1839)

Natalya　　　　(2) Alexander　　(1) Yegor　　　　　　Dmitry　　　　　Nikolay
Alexandrovna = Ivanovich　　　Ivanovich　　　　　(1796-1849)　　　(1800-184?)
Zakharin　　　HERZEN　　　　Herzen
(1817-1852)　　(1812-1870)　　(1803-1882)

Nikolay　　　　Natalya　　　　Olga
'Kolya'　　　　'Tata'　　　　(b. 1850)
(1843-1851)　　(1844-1936)

TRANSLATOR'S NOTE

A few words about Herzen's parentage will make his narrative more intelligible to the English reader. Herzen's father, Ivan Yakovlev, was a very wealthy nobleman belonging to one of the most aristocratic families of Russia. In 1811, at the age of forty-two, he married (so Brückner tells us in his *History of Russian Literature*)[1] at Stuttgart a girl of sixteen, whose name was Henrietta Haag, though she was always in Russia called Luiza Ivanovna, as easier to pronounce. As he neglected to repeat the marriage ceremony in Russia, their son was there illegitimate. Yakovlev is said to have given him the surname Herzen,[2] because he was the 'child of his heart'.

C. G.

---

[1] But see p. xv, fn. (*R.*)

[2] There was also, though, another illegitimate son, ten years older than Alexander Ivanovich Herzen, namely Yegor Ivanovich, who had also been given the surname of Herzen. See, p. 13, footnote[17]. (*R.*)

MY PAST AND THOUGHTS

To N. P. OGARËV[1]

This book speaks chiefly of two persons. One of them is no more:[2] *you are still left, and therefore it is to you, my friend, that it rightly belongs.*

Iskander

1st July, 1860
Eagle's Nest, Bournemouth

Many of my friends have advised me to begin a complete edition of *My Past and Thoughts*, and there is no difficulty about this, at least so far as Parts I and II are concerned. But they say that the fragments which appeared in *The Pole Star* are rhapsodical and lacking in unity, are broken off at haphazard, sometimes anticipate, sometimes lag behind. I feel that this is true, but I cannot put it right. To make additions, to arrange the chapters in chronological order, would not be a difficult matter; but to recast entirely, *d'un jet*—that I will not undertake.

My Past and Thoughts was not written consecutively: between some chapters there lie whole years. Therefore the whole of it retains the colour of its own time and of varying moods—I should not care to rub this off.

These are not so much notes as a confession, round which, *à propos* of which, have been assembled memories snatched from here and there in the *Past*, and ideas from my *Thoughts*, which here and there have remained behind. Moreover, in these annexes, superstructures, extensions, there *is* a unity: at least I think so.

These notes are not a first experiment. I was twenty-five when I first began to write something in the way of reminiscences. This is how it happened: I had been transferred from Vyatka to Vladimir, and I was horribly bored. I found the stop before Moscow tantalizing, outrageous. I was in the situation of a man who is kept at the last coach-stage for want of horses.

In reality this was very nearly the most 'pure, most earnest period of a youth which had begun to come to an end'.[3] And my boredom

---

[1] For Nikolay Platonovich Ogarëv see E. H. Carr: *The Romantic Exiles* (Gollancz, 1933), chapters VII, XVI. (*R.*)

[2] Natalya Alexandrovna, Herzen's first cousin and wife. (*R.*)

[3] See *Prison and Exile.*

xliii

was lucid and contented, as with children on the day before a holiday or a birthday. Every day letters arrived, written in a fine hand;* I was proud of them and happy, and they helped me to grow. None the less separation was a torment, and I did not know how to set about pushing aside that eternity—some four months!* I listened to the advice that was given me and began at leisure to make notes of my memories of Krutitsky and Vyatka. Three note-books were filled . . . and then the past was flooded by the light of the present.

Belinsky read them in 1840 and liked them, and he printed two of the note-books in *Otechestvenniye Zapiski* (*Notes of the Fatherland*), the first and third; the other must be still lying about somewhere in our house in Moscow, if it has not been used to light the fire.

Fifteen years went by;[4] 'I was living a lonely life in London, near Primrose Hill, cut off from the whole world by distance, by the fog and by my own desire.

'I had not a single close friend in London. There were people for whom I had a regard, and who had the same for me, but no one who was my intimate. All of them, as they came and went and met each other, were interested only in general matters, in the business of the whole of humanity, or at least of a whole people; their acquaintance, one might say, was impersonal. Months would pass and there would not be a single word of what I wanted to talk about.

'. . . Meanwhile I was hardly beginning at that time to come to myself, to recover from a series of fearful events, misfortunes, mistakes.* The history of the recent years of my life presented itself to me with greater and greater clarity, and I perceived with dismay that no one but myself was aware of it, and that the truth would die with me.

'I determined to write: but one memory summoned up hundreds of others; all the old, the half-forgotten, rose again: boyhood's dreams, the hopes of youth, a young man's intrepidity, prison and exile—those early misfortunes that had left no bitterness in my heart, but had passed like thunderstorms in Spring, refreshing and strengthening my young life with their impact.'

Now I was not writing to gain time: there was nowhere I was in a hurry to go to.

When I began this new work I absolutely forgot the existence of *Notes of a Young Man*,[5] and came upon them by chance in the British Museum when I was going through some Russian magazines.

---

[4] Introduction to *Prison and Exile*, written in May, 1854.
[5] See Vol. IV, pp. 1799-1857. (R.)

I had copies made and read them through. The feeling they aroused was a strange one: I perceived so palpably how much older I had grown in those fifteen years, that at first I was amazed. At that time I had still been playing with life, and with my very happiness, as though there was to be no end to it. The tints of *Notes of a Young Man* were so rosy that I could take nothing from it: it belonged to the time of my youth, and it must be left as it was. Its morning's light was not suited to my evening's labour. There was much truth in it, but also much that was mischievous; more than that, there remained upon it the mark, quite evident to me, of Heine, whom I had read with admiration at Vyatka. In *My Past and Thoughts* the marks of life are visible, and no others are to be seen.

My work progressed slowly. . . . Much time is needed for any event to settle into a perspicuous thought—not a comforting one: melancholy, perhaps, but one that can be reconciled with one's intelligence. Without this there may be sincerity, but truth there cannot be!

Several attempts were unsuccessful and I threw them away. Finally, when this year I was reading my latest note-books to a friend of my youth,[6] I myself recognized the familiar features, and I stopped. My labour was over.

It is very possible that I have greatly overestimated it, that in these rough sketches there is much that is hidden away, but only for me; perhaps I read into it much more than was written; what I have said inspires me with dreams, and works like hieroglyphs to which I hold the key. Perhaps I alone hear spirits knocking beneath these lines . . . perhaps: but the book is no less dear to me for that. For a long time it had taken the place for me both of people and of what I had lost. The time had come to part with the book, too.

All that is personal soon crumbles away, and to this destitution one has to submit. This is not despair, not senility, not coldness and not indifference: it is grey-haired youth, one of the forms of convalescence or, better, that process itself. Only by this means is it humanly possible to survive certain wounds.

In a monk, of whatever age he may be, one is continually meeting both an old man and a young man. By burying everything personal he has returned to his youth. He has begun to live easily, on a grand scale—sometimes too grand. . . . In reality a man now and again

[6] N. M. Satin. (*A.S.*)

has a feeling of futility and loneliness among impersonal generalities, the elements of history, and the shapes of the future which pass across their surface like the shadows of clouds. But what follows from this? People would like to preserve everything, both the roses and the snow; they would like the clusters of ripe grapes to be lapped round with May flowers. The monks used to escape from the temptation to murmur by means of prayer. We have no prayers: we have work. Work is our prayer. It is possible that the fruit of both will be the same, but for the moment that is not what I am talking about.

Yes, in life there is a predilection for a recurring rhythm, for the repetition of a *motif*. Who does not know how close old age is to childhood? Look closely, and you will see that on both sides of the full climax of life, with its crowns of flowers and thorns, with its cradles and its graves, epochs often repeat themselves which are similar in their chief features. What youth has not had is already lost; what youth has dreamt of, without an actual sight of it, comes out brighter and more composed, likewise without being actually seen, from behind the clouds and the red glow in the sky.

. . . When I think how we two, now when we are nearly fifty, are standing at the first machine for the manufacture of free speech in Russia,[7] it seems that our childish Grütli* on the Sparrow Hills were not thirty-three years ago, and even three seems a lot!

Life . . . lives, peoples, revolutions, beloved faces have appeared, changed and vanished between the Sparrow Hills and Primrose Hill; already their traces have almost been swept away by the pitiless whirl-wind of events. Everything round me is changed: the Thames flows instead of the Moscow River, and I am surrounded by a strange people . . . and there is no more a way for us back to our country . . . only the dream of two boys, one of thirteen, the other of eleven, has remained intact!

May *My Past and Thoughts* settle my account with my personal life and be its summary. My remaining thoughts belong to my work: my remaining powers, to the struggle!

> *Thus have we kept, we two, our [lofty] league:*
> *We two again will tread the cheerless track,*
> *Tell of the truth, unconscious of fatigue,*
> *On fancies and on persons turn our back.*[8]

[7] H.'s printing-press in London, with a fount of Russian type. (*R.*)

[8] The final lines of Ogarëv's poem, *To Iskander*: the word 'lofty' is omitted from the first line. (*A.S.*)

PART I

NURSERY
AND UNIVERSITY
(1812—1834)

'When memories of the past return
And the old road again we tread,
Slowly the feelings of old days
Come back to life within the soul;
Old griefs and joys are here unchanged,
Again the once familiar thrill
Stirs echoes in the troubled heart;
And for remembered woes we sigh.'

N. P. OGARËV: Humorous Verse

Chapter I

Childhood

'Vera Artamonovna, come tell me once more how the French came to Moscow,' I used to say, rolling myself up in the quilt and stretching in my crib, which was sewn round with canvas that I might not fall out.

'Oh! what's the use of telling you? You've heard it so many times; besides it's time to go to sleep. You had better get up a little earlier to-morrow,' the old woman would usually answer, although she was as eager to repeat her favourite story as I was to hear it.

'But do tell me a little bit. How did you find out? How did it begin?'

'This was how it began. You know what your papa[1] is—he is always putting things off; he was getting ready and getting ready, and all of a sudden he was ready! Everyone was saying "It's time to set off; what is there to wait for? There's almost no one left in the town." But no: Pavel Ivanovich[2] and he kept talking of how they would go together, and first one wasn't ready and then the other. At last we were packed and the carriage was ready; the family sat down to lunch, when all at once our head cook ran into the dining-room as pale as a sheet, and announced: "The enemy has marched in at the Dragomilovsky Gate." How all hearts did sink! "The power of the Cross be with us!" we cried. What a panic there was! While we were bustling about, sighing and groaning, we looked and down the street came galloping dragoons in those helmets with horses' tails streaming behind. The gates had all been shut, and here was your papa left behind, and a fine party there was going to be, and you with him; your wet nurse Darya still had you at the breast, you were so weak and delicate.'

And I smiled with pride, pleased that I had taken part in the war.

[1] Yakovlev, Ivan Alexeyevich (1767-1846). (*R.*)
[2] Golokhvastov, the husband of my father's younger sister, Yelizaveta.

3

'At the beginning we got along somehow, for the first few days, that is; it was only that two or three soldiers would come in and ask by signs whether there wasn't anything to drink; we would take them a glass each, of course, and they would go away, and touch their caps to us, too. But then, you see, when fires began and kept getting worse and worse, there was such disorder, plundering and all sorts of horrors. At that time we were living in the lodge at the princess's[3] and the house caught fire; then Pavel Ivanovich said, "Let's go to my house: it is built of stone; it stands far back in the courtyard and the outer walls are properly built."

'So we went, masters and servants all together—there was no difference made; we went out into the Tverskoy Boulevard and the trees were beginning to burn—we made our way at last to the Golokhvastovs' house and it was simply blazing, flames from every window. Pavel Ivanovich was dumbfounded, he couldn't believe his eyes. Behind the house there is a big garden, you know; we went into it thinking we should be safe there. We sat there on the seats grieving, when, all at once, a mob of drunken soldiers were upon us; one set about trying to pull off Pavel Ivanovich's sheepskin travelling coat; the old man would not give it up, and the soldier pulled out his sword and struck him smack in the face with it so that he kept the scar to the end of his days; the others set upon us: one soldier tore you from your nurse, opened your baby-clothes to see if there were any money-notes or diamonds hidden among them, saw there was nothing there, and so in a rage he deliberately tore your clothes to pieces and flung them down. As soon as they had gone away, we were in trouble again. Do you remember our Platon who was sent for a soldier? He was dreadfully fond of drink and that day he was very full of courage; he tied on a sabre and walked about like that. The day before the enemy entered, Count Rostopchin[4] had distributed all sorts of weapons at the arsenal; so that was how he had got hold of a sabre. Towards the evening he saw a dragoon ride into the yard; there was a horse standing near the stable, the dragoon wanted to take it, but Platon rushed headlong at him and, catching hold of the bridle, said: "The horse is ours, I won't give it you." The dragoon threatened him with a pistol, but seemingly it was not loaded;

---

[3] Anna Borisovna Meshchersky. (*A.S.*) See p. 298. (*R.*)
[4] Rostopchin, Fëdor Vasilevich, Count (1763-1826), Governor of Moscow in 1812. Believed to have set fire to the city when the French entered. (*Tr.*)

the master himself saw what was happening and shouted to Platon:
"Let the horse alone, it's not your business." But not a bit of it!
Platon pulled out his sabre and struck him again and again. "Well,"
thought we, "now the hour of our death is come; when his comrades
see him, it will be the end of us." But when the dragoon fell off
Platon seized him by the feet and dragged him to a pit full of lime
and threw him in, poor fellow, and he was still alive; his horse stood
there and did not stir from the place, but stamped its foot on the
ground as though it understood; our servants shut it in the stable; it
must have been burnt there. We all hurried out of the courtyard, the
fire was more and more dreadful; worn out and with nothing to eat,
we got into a house that was still untouched, and set about getting
some rest; in less than an hour, our people were shouting from the
street: "Come out, come out! Fire! Fire!" Then I took a piece of
green baize from the billiard table and wrapped you in it to keep you
from the night air; and so we made our way as far as the Tverskoy
Square. There the French were trying to put the fire out, because
some great man of theirs was living in the governor's house; we
simply sat in the street; sentries were walking everywhere, others
were riding by on horseback. And you were screaming, straining
yourself with crying, your nurse had no more milk, no one had a bit
of bread. Natalya Konstantinovna was with us then, a bold wench,
you know; she saw that some soldiers were eating something in a
corner, took you and went straight to them, showed you and said
"*manger* for the little one"; at first they looked at her so sternly and
said "*allez, allez*," but she fell to scolding them. "Ah, you cursed
brutes," she said, "You this and that"; the soldiers did not understand a word, but they burst out laughing and gave her some bread
soaked in water for you and a crust for herself. Early in the morning
an officer came up and gathered together all the men and your papa
with them, leaving only the women and Pavel Ivanovich who was
wounded, and took them to put out the fire in the houses nearby, so
we remained alone till evening; we sat and cried and that was all.
When it was dusk, the master came back and with him some sort of
officer. . . .'

Allow me to take the old woman's place and continue her narrative. When my father had finished his duties as a fire-brigade man,
he met by the Strastny monastery a squadron of Italian cavalry; he
went up to their officer and told him in Italian the situation his
family was in. When the Italian heard *la sua dolce favella* he prom-

ised to speak to the Duke of Treviso,[5] and as a preliminary measure to put a sentry to guard us and prevent barbarous scenes such as had taken place in the Golokhvastovs' garden. He sent an officer to accompany my father with these instructions. Hearing that the whole party had eaten nothing for two days, the officer led us all to a shop that had been broken into; the choicest tea, with the buds in it, and Levant coffee had been thrown about on the floor, together with a great number of dates, figs, and almonds; our servants stuffed their pockets full: there was no lack of dessert. The sentry turned out to be of the greatest use to us: a dozen times gangs of soldiers began molesting the luckless group of women and servants encamped in the corner of Tverskoy Square, but they moved off immediately at his command.

Mortier remembered that he had known my father in Paris and informed Napoleon; Napoleon ordered him to be presented next morning. In a shabby, dark blue, short coat with bronze buttons, intended for sporting wear, without his wig, in high boots that had not been cleaned for several days, with dirty linen and unshaven chin, my father—who worshipped decorum and strict etiquette—made his appearance in the throne room of the Kremlin Palace at the summons of the Emperor of the French.

Their conversation which I have heard many times is fairly correctly given in Baron Fain's[6] History and in that of Mikhaylovsky-Danilevsky.

After the usual phrases, abrupt words and laconic remarks, to which a deep meaning was ascribed for thirty-five years, till men realised that their meaning was often quite trivial, Napoleon blamed Rostopchin for the fire, said that it was vandalism, declared as usual his invincible love of peace, maintained that his war was against England and not against Russia, boasted that he had set a guard on the Foundling Hospital and the Uspensky Cathedral, complained of Alexander, and said that he was surrounded by bad advisers and that his (Napoleon's) peaceful inclinations were not known to the Emperor.

My father observed that it was rather for the victor to make offers of peace.

[5] Mortier, Edouard Adolphe (1768-1835), Duke of Treviso, general under the Revolution and Napoleon, Marshal of France. Killed, 1835, by the infernal machine of Fieschi. (Tr.)

[6] Fain, François, Baron (1778-1837), French historian and secretary of Napoleon. (Tr.)

'I have done what I could; I have sent to Kutuzov:[7] he will not enter into negotiations and does not bring my proposals to the cognisance of the Tsar. If they want war, it is not my fault—they shall have war.'

After all this comedy my father asked him for a pass to leave Moscow.

'I have ordered no passes to be given to any one; why are you going? What are you afraid of? I have ordered the markets to be opened.'

The Emperor of the French apparently forgot at that moment that, in addition to open markets, it is as well to have a house with a roof, and that life in the Tverskoy Square in the midst of enemy soldiers was anything but agreeable.

My father pointed this out to him; Napoleon thought a moment and suddenly asked:

'Will you undertake to convey a letter from me to the Emperor? On that condition I will command them to give you a permit to leave the town with all your household.'

'I would accept your Majesty's offer,' my father observed, 'but it is difficult for me to guarantee that it will reach him.'

'Will you give me your word of honour that you will make every effort to deliver the letter in person?'

'*Je m'engage sur mon honneur, Sire.*'

'That is enough. I will send for you. Are you in need of anything?'

'Of a roof for my family while I am here. Nothing else.'

'The duc de Trévise will do what he can.'

Mortier did, in fact, give us a room in the Governor-General's house, and gave orders that we should be furnished with provisions; his *maître d'hôtel* even sent us wine. A few days passed in this way, after which Mortier sent an adjutant, at four o'clock one morning, to summon my father to the Kremlin.

The fire had attained terrific dimensions during those days; the scorched air, opaque with smoke, was becoming insufferably hot. Napoleon was dressed and was walking about the room, looking careworn and out of temper; he was beginning to feel that his singed laurels would before long be frozen, and there would be no getting out of it here with a jest, as in Egypt. The plan of the campaign was absurd; except Napoleon, everybody knew it: Ney, Narbonne, Ber-

[7] Kutuzov, Mikhail Illarionovich (1745-1813), Commander-in-chief of the Russian army in 1812. (*Tr.*)

thier, and officers of lower rank; to all objections he had replied with
the cabbalistic word 'Moscow'; in Moscow even he guessed the truth.

When my father went in, Napoleon took a sealed letter that was
lying on the table, handed it to him and said, bowing him out: 'I
rely on your word of honour.' On the envelope was written: '*A mon
frère l'Empereur Alexandre.*'

The permit given to my father has survived; it is signed by the
Duke of Treviso and countersigned by the *oberpolitsmeyster* of Moscow, Lesseps. A few outsiders, hearing of our permit, joined us, begging my father to take them in the guise of servants or relations. An
open wagonette was given us for the wounded old man, my mother
and my nurse; the others walked. A few Uhlans escorted us on horseback as far as the Russian rearguard, at the sight of which they
wished us a good journey and galloped back. A minute later the
Cossacks surrounded the strange refugees and led them to the head-
quarters of the rearguard. There Wintsengerode and Ilovaysky the
Fourth were in command.

Wintsengerode, hearing of the letter, told my father that he would
send him on immediately, with two dragoons, to the Tsar in Petersburg.

'What's to be done with your people?' asked the Cossack general,
Ilovaysky. 'It is impossible for them to stay here. They are not out of
musket-shot, and a real action may be expected any day.'

My father begged that we should, if possible, be taken to his Yaroslavl estate, but incidentally observed that he had not a kopeck with
him.

'We will settle up afterwards,' said Ilovaysky, 'and do not worry
yourself: I give you my word to send them.'

My father was taken by the military courier system along a road
made of fascines in the style of those days. For us Ilovaysky procured
some sort of an old conveyance and sent us to the nearest town with
a party of French prisoners and an escort of Cossacks; he provided us
with money for our expenses until we reached Yaroslavl, and altogether did everything he possibly could in the bustle and apprehension of wartime.

Such was my first journey in Russia; my second was unaccom-
panied by French Uhlans, Cossacks from the Urals and prisoners of
war—I was alone but for a drunken gendarme sitting by my side.[8]

[8] See chapter 13. (*A.S.*)

My father was taken straight to Count Arakcheyev[9] and detained in his house. The Count asked for the letter, but my father told him he had given his word of honour to deliver it in person; Arakcheyev promised to ask the Tsar, and, next day, informed him by letter that the Tsar had charged him to take the letter and to deliver it immediately. He gave a receipt for the letter: that, too, has survived. For a month my father remained under arrest in Arakcheyev's house; no one was allowed to see him except S. S. Shishkov,[10] who came at the Tsar's command to question him concerning the details of the fire, of the enemy's entry into Moscow, and his interview with Napoleon; he was the first eye-witness to arrive in Petersburg. At last Arakcheyev informed my father that the Tsar had ordered his release, and did not hold him to blame for accepting a permit from the enemy in consideration of the extremity in which he was placed. On setting him free Arakcheyev commanded him to leave Petersburg immediately without seeing anybody except his elder brother, to whom he was allowed to say good-bye.

On reaching at nightfall the little Yaroslavl village, my father found us in a peasant's hut (he had no house on that estate). I was asleep on a bench under the window; the window did not close properly, and the snow, drifting through the crack, covered part of the bench and lay, not thawing, on the window-sill.

Everyone was in a state of great perturbation, especially mother.[11] A few days before my father's arrival, the village elder and some of the house-serfs had run hastily in the morning into the hut where she was living, trying to explain something by gestures and insisting on her following them. At that time my mother did not speak a word of Russian; all she could make out was that the matter concerned Pavel Ivanovich; she did not know what to think; the idea occurred to her that they had killed him, or that they meant to kill him and afterwards her. She took me in her arms, and trembling all over, more dead than alive, followed the elder. Golokhvastov was in another hut and they went into it; the old man really was lying dead beside the table at which he had been about to shave; a sudden stroke of paralysis had cut short his life instantaneously.

[9] Arakcheyev, Aleksey Andreyevich, Count (1769-1834), Minister of War and the most powerful and influential man of the reign of Alexander I, whose intimate friend he was, hated and dreaded for his cruelty. (*Tr.*)

[10] Probably A. S. Shishkov, Secretary of State under Alexander I. (*A.S.*) See p. 153 fn. (*R.*)

[11] Luiza Ivanovna, née Haag. For the reason why she did not speak Russian see page 21. (*R.*)

My mother's position may well be imagined (she was then seven-teen), in the midst of these *half-savage* bearded men, dressed in bare sheepskins, talking in a completely unknown language, in a little smoke-blackened hut; and all this in November of the terrible winter of 1812. Her one support had been Golokhvastov; she wept day and night after his death. But these *savages* pitied her from the bottom of their hearts, in all their kindness and simplicity; and the village elder sent his son several times to the town to get raisins, cakes, apples, and bread-rings for her.

Fifteen years later the elder was still living and used sometimes, grey with age and somewhat bald, to come to Moscow. My mother used customarily to regale him with tea and to talk to him about the winter of 1812, saying how she had been so afraid of him and how, without understanding each other, they had made the arrangements for the funeral of Pavel Ivanovich. The old man used still to call my mother—as he had then—Yuliza Ivanovna, instead of Luiza, and used to tell how I was not at all afraid of his beard and would readily let him take me into his arms.

From the province of Yaroslavl we moved to that of Tver, and at last, a year later, made our way back to Moscow. By that time my father's brother,[12] who had been ambassador to Westphalia and had afterwards gone on some commission to Bernadotte, had returned from Sweden; he settled in the same house with us.

I still remember, as in a dream, the traces of the fire, which re-mained until early in the 'twenties: great burnt-out houses without window frames or roofs, tumble-down walls, empty spaces fenced in, with remains of stoves with chimneys on them.

Tales of the fire of Moscow, of the battle of Borodino, of the Bere-zina, of the taking of Paris were my cradle-songs, my nursery stories, my Iliad and my Odyssey. My mother and our servants, my father and Vera Artamonovna were continually going back to the terrible time which had impressed them so recently, so intimately, and so acutely. Then the returning generals and officers began crowding into Moscow. My father's old comrades of the Izmaylovsky regi-ment, now the heroes of a bloody war scarcely ended, were often at our house. They found relief from their fatigues and battles in des-cribing them. This was in reality the most brilliant moment of the Petersburg period; the consciousness of strength gave new life, and all practical affairs and troubles seemed to be put off till the morrow

---

[12] Yakovlev, Lev Alexeyevich (1764-1839), 'The Senator.' (*A.S.*)

when work would begin again : now all that was wanted was to revel in the joys of victory.

From these gentlemen my eager ears heard even more about the war than from Vera Artamonovna. I was particularly fond of the stories told by Count Miloradovich;[13] he spoke with the greatest vivacity, with lively mimicry, with roars of laughter, and more than once I fell asleep, on the sofa behind him, to the sound of them.

Of course, in such surroundings I was a desperate patriot and intended to go into the army; but an exclusive sentiment of nationality never leads to any good; it led me to the following incident. Among others who used to visit us was the Comte de Quinsonas, a French *émigré* and a lieutenant-general in the Russian service. A desperate royalist, he took part in the celebrated fête of Versailles, at which the King's life-guards trampled underfoot the popular cockade and at which Marie Antoinette drank to the destruction of the revolution. This French count, a tall, thin, graceful old man with grey hair, was the very model of politeness and elegant manners. There was a peerage awaiting him in Paris, where he had already been to congratulate Louis XVIII on getting his situation. He had returned to Russia to dispose of his estate. Unluckily for me this most courteous of the generals of all the Russian armies had to begin speaking of the war in my presence.

'But surely you must have been fighting against us?' I remarked with extreme naïveté.

'*Non, mon petit, non; j'étais dans l'armée russe.*'

'What?' said I, 'you, a Frenchman, and fighting in our army? That's impossible!'

My father glanced sternly at me and changed the subject. The Count heroically set things right by saying to my father that 'he liked such *patriotic* sentiments'. My father had not liked them, and when the Count had gone away he gave me a terrible scolding. 'This is what comes of rushing headlong into conversation about all sorts of things you don't understand and can't understand; it was out of fidelity to *his* king that the Count served under *our* emperor.'

I certainly did not understand that.

My father had spent twelve years abroad and his brother still longer; they tried to arrange their life in the foreign style while

---

[13] One of the generals of the campaign of 1812. Military Governor-General of Petersburg at the accession of Nicholas in 1825, and killed in the rising of December 14th. (*Tr.*)

avoiding great expense and retaining all Russian comforts. Their life never was so arranged, either because they did not know how to manage or because the nature of a Russian landowner was stronger in them than their foreign habits. The management of their land and house was in common, the estate was undivided, an immense crowd of house-serfs peopled the ground floor, and consequently all conditions for disorder were present.

Two nurses looked after me, one Russian and one German. Vera Artamonovna and Madame Proveau were very kind women, but it bored me to watch them all day long knitting stockings and bickering together, and so at every favourable opportunity I ran away to the half of the house occupied by my uncle, the Senator (the one who had been an ambassador), to see my one friend, his valet Calot.

I have rarely met a kinder, gentler, milder man; utterly alone in Russia, parted from all his own people, with difficulty speaking broken Russian, his devotion to me was like a woman's. I spent whole hours in his room, worried him, got in his way, played pranks —he bore it all with a good-natured smile; cut all sorts of marvels out of cardboard for me and carved various trifles out of wood (and how I loved him for it!). In the evenings he used to bring me up picture-books from the library—the Travels of Gmelin[14] and of Pallas,[15] and a fat book of *The World in Pictures*,[16] which I liked so much that I looked at it until the binding, although of leather, gave way; for a couple of hours at a time Calot would show me the same pictures, repeating the same explanation for the thousandth time.

Before my birthday and my name-day Calot would lock himself up in his room, from which came the sounds of a hammer and other tools; often he would pass along the corridor with rapid steps, locking his door after him every time, sometimes carrying a little saucepan of glue, sometimes a parcel with things wrapped up. It may well be imagined how much I longed to know what he was making; I used to send the house-serf boys to try and find out, but Calot kept a sharp look-out. We somehow discovered, on the staircase, a little crack which looked straight into his room, but it was of no help to us; all we could see was the upper part of the window and the port-

---

[14] Gmelin, Johann Georg (1709-1755), a learned German who travelled in the East. (*Tr.*)

[15] Pallas, Peter Simon (1741-1811), German traveller and naturalist who explored the Urals, Kirghiz Steppes, Altai mountains, and parts of Siberia. (*Tr.*)

[16] *Orbis sensualium pictus* by Yan Amos Komensky (1592-1670), a Czech pedagogue and humanist. (*R.*)

rait of Frederick II with a huge nose and huge star, and the expression of an emaciated hawk. Two days before the event the noise would cease and the room would be opened—everything in it was as usual, except for scraps of coloured and gold paper here and there; I would flush crimson, devoured with curiosity, but Calot, with an air of strained gravity, refused to approach the delicate subject.

I lived in agonies until the momentous day. At five o'clock in the morning I was awake and thinking of Calot's preparations; at eight o'clock he would himself appear in a white cravat, a white waistcoat, and a dark-blue tail-coat—with empty hands. When would it end? Had he spoiled it? And time passed and the ordinary presents came, and Yelizaveta Alexeyevna Golokhvastov's footman had already appeared with a costly toy, wrapped up in a napkin, and the Senator had already brought me some marvel, but the uneasy expectation of the surprise troubled my joy.

All at once, as it were casually, after dinner or after tea, Nurse would say to me:

'Go downstairs just a minute; there is somebody asking for you.'

At last, I thought, and went down, sliding on my arms down the banisters of the staircase. The doors into the ball-room were thrown open noisily, music was playing. A transparency with my monogram was lit up, serf-boys dressed up as Turks offered me sweetmeats, then followed a puppet show or indoor fireworks. Calot, perspiring with his efforts, was with his own hands setting everything in motion, and was no less enraptured than I was.

What presents could be compared with such an entertainment! I have never been fond of *things*, the bump of ownership and acquisitiveness has never been developed in me at any age, and now, after the prolonged suspense, the numbers of candles, the tinsel and the smell of gunpowder! Only one thing was lacking—a comrade of my own age, but I spent all my childhood in solitude,[17] and certainly was not over-indulged in that respect.

---

[17] My father had, besides me, another son ten years older.† I was always fond of him, but he could not be a companion to me. From his twelfth to his thirtieth year he was always in the hands of the surgeons. After a series of tortures, endured with extreme fortitude and rendering his whole existence one intermittent operation, the doctors declared his disease incurable. His health was shattered; circumstances and character contributed to the complete ruin of his life. The pages in which I speak of his lonely and melancholy existence have been omitted. I do not wish to print them without his consent.

† Yegor Ivanovich Herzen (1803-82). (*A.S.*)

My father and the Senator had an elder brother,[18] between whom and the two younger brothers there was an open feud, in spite of which they managed their estate in common or rather ruined it in common. The triple control and the quarrel together led to glaring disorganisation. My father and the Senator did everything to thwart the elder brother, who did the same by them. The village elders and peasants lost their heads: one brother was demanding wagons; another, hay; a third, firewood; each gave orders, each sent his authorised agents. The elder brother would appoint a village elder, the younger ones would remove him in a month, upon some nonsensical pretext, and appoint another whom their senior would not recognise. With all this, of course, backbiting, slander, spies and favourites were naturally plentiful, and under it all the poor peasants, who found neither justice nor defence, were harassed on all sides and oppressed with the double burden of work and the disorganisation caused by the capricious demands of their owners.

The first consequence of the feud between the brothers that made some impression upon them, was the loss of their great lawsuit with the Counts Devier, though justice was on their side. Though their interests were the same, they could never agree on a course of action; their opponents naturally profited by this. In addition to the loss of a large and fine estate, the Senate sentenced each of the brothers to pay costs and damages to the amount of thirty thousand paper roubles. This lesson opened their eyes and they made up their minds to divide their property. The preliminary negotiations lasted for about a year, the estate was carved into three fairly equal parts and they were to decide by casting lots which was to come to which. The Senator and my father visited their elder brother, whom they had not seen for several years, to negotiate and be reconciled; then there was a rumour that he would visit us to complete the arrangements. The rumour of the visit of this elder brother[19] excited horror and anxiety in our household.

---

[18] There were originally four brothers: Pëtr, the grandfather of 'the cousin from Korcheva' mentioned in Chapter 3; Alexander, the elder brother here described, who is believed to have been the model from whom Dostoevsky drew the character of Fëdor Pavlovich in *The Brothers Karamazov*; Lev, always referred to as 'the Senator', and Ivan, Herzen's father. Of the sisters one was Yelizaveta Alexeyevna Golokhvastov and one was Marya Alexeyevna Khovansky. The family of the Yakovlevs was one of the oldest and most aristocratic in Russia. (*Tr.*)

[19] This brother, Alexander, had an illegitimate daughter, Natalya, who became the wife of her first cousin, the author of this book. (*R.*)

He was one of those grotesquely odd creatures who are only possible in Russia, where life is so odd as to be grotesque. He was a man gifted by nature, yet he spent his whole life in absurd actions, often almost crimes. He had received a sound education in the French style, was very well read—and spent his time in debauchery and empty idleness up to the day of his death. He, too, had served at first in the Izmaylovsky regiment, had been something like an aide-de-camp in attendance on Potëmkin, then served in some mission, and returning to Petersburg was made Procurator of the Synod. Neither diplomatic nor monastic surroundings could restrain his unbridled character. For his quarrels with the heads of the Church he was removed from his post; for a slap in the face, which he either tried to give, or gave, to a gentleman at an official dinner at the Governor-General's, he was banished from Petersburg. He went to his Tambov estate; there the peasants nearly murdered him for his brutality and amorous propensities; he was indebted to his coachman and his horses for his life.

After that he settled in Moscow. Deserted by all his relations and also by his acquaintances, he lived in solitude in his big house in the Tverskoy Boulevard, oppressing his house-serfs and ruining his peasants. He amassed a great library of books and collected a regular harem of serf-girls, both of which he kept under lock and key. Deprived of every occupation and concealing a passionate vanity, often extremely naïve, he amused himself by buying unnecessary things, and bringing unnecessary lawsuits, which he pursued with great bitterness. His lawsuit concerning an Amati violin lasted *thirty* years, and ended in his winning it. After another lawsuit he succeeded by extraordinary efforts in winning a wall which was common to two houses, the possession of which was of no use to him whatever. Being himself on the retired list, he used, on reading in the newspapers of the promotions of his fellow-soldiers, to buy such orders as had been given to them, and lay them on his table as a mournful reminder of the decorations he might have received!

His brothers and sisters were afraid of him and had nothing to do with him; our servants would go a long way round to avoid his house for fear of meeting him, and would turn pale at the sight of him; women went in terror of his impudent persecution; the house-serfs had special services said that they might not come into his possession.

So this was the terrible man who was to visit us. Extraordinary excitement prevailed throughout the house from early morning; I had never seen this legendary 'enemy-brother', though I was born in his house, where my father stayed when he came back from foreign parts; I longed to see him and at the same time I was frightened—I do not know why, but I was terribly frightened.

Two hours before his arrival, my father's eldest nephew,[20] two intimate acquaintances and a good-natured stout and flabby official who was in charge of the legal business arrived. They were all sitting in silent expectation, when suddenly the butler came in, and, in a voice unlike his own, announced that the brother 'had graciously pleased to arrive'.

'Show him up,' said the Senator, with perceptible agitation, while my father began taking snuff, the nephew straightened his cravat, and the official hawked and coughed. I had been ordered to go upstairs but, trembling all over, I stayed in the next room.

Slowly and majestically the 'brother' advanced, and the Senator and my father went to meet him. He was holding an ikon with both hands before his chest, as people do at weddings and funerals, and in a drawling voice, a little through his nose, he addressed his brothers in the following words:

'With this ikon our father blessed me before his end, charging me and our late brother Pëtr to watch over you and to be a father to you in his place . . . if our father knew of your conduct to your elder brother! . . .'

'Come, *mon cher frère*,' observed my father in his studiously indifferent voice, 'you have carried out our father's last wish well indeed. It would be better to forget these memories, painful to you as well as to us.'

'How? What?' shouted the devout brother. 'Is this what you have summoned me for? . . .' and he flung down the ikon, so that the silver setting gave a metallic clink. At this point the Senator shouted in a voice still more terrifying. I rushed headlong upstairs and only had time to see the official and the nephew, no less scared, retreating to the balcony.

What was done and how it was done, I cannot say; the frightened servants huddled into corners out of sight, no one knew anything of what happened, and neither the Senator nor my father ever

[20] D. P. Golokhvastov. (*A.S.*)

spoke of this scene before me. Little by little the noise subsided and the partition of the estate was carried out, whether then or an another day I do not remember.

My father received Vasilevskoye, a big estate in the Ruzsky district, near Moscow. We spent the whole summer there the following year; meanwhile the Senator bought himself a house on the Arbat, and we went to live alone in our great house, deserted and deathlike. Soon afterwards my father too bought a house in Old Konyushennaya Street.

With the Senator there departed first Calot, and secondly the source of all animation in our house. The Senator alone had prevented the hypochondriacal disposition of my father from prevailing; now it had full sway. The new house was gloomy; it suggested a prison or a hospital; the ground floor was vaulted and the thick walls made the windows look like the embrasures of a fortress. The house was surrounded on all sides by a courtyard unnecessarily large.

To tell the truth, it is more of a wonder that the Senator managed to live so long under the same roof as my father than that they parted. I have rarely seen two men so complete a contrast as they were.

The Senator was of a kindly disposition, and fond of amusements; he had spent his whole life in the world of artificial light and of official diplomacy, the world that surrounded the court, without a notion that there was another more serious world, although he had been not merely in contact with but intimately connected with all the great events from 1789 to 1815. Count Vorontsov had sent him to Lord Grenville[21] to find out what General Bonaparte was going to undertake after abandoning the Egyptian army. He had been in Paris at the coronation of Napoleon. In 1811 Napoleon had ordered him to be detained in Cassel, where he was ambassador 'at the court of King Jerome',[22] as my father used to say in moments of vexation. In fact, he took part in all the great events of his time, but in a queer way, irregularly.

When a captain in the Life Guards of the Izmaylovsky regiment, he was sent on a mission to London; Paul, seeing this in the muster-

---

[21] British Foreign Secretary in 1791, and Prime Minister, 1806 and 1807, when the Act for the abolition of the slave trade was passed. (*Tr.*)

[22] I.e., of Jérôme Bonaparte, king of Westphalia from 1807 to 1813. (*Tr.*)

roll, ordered him to return at once to Petersburg. The soldier-diplomat set off by the first ship and appeared on parade.

'Do you want to remain in London?' Paul asked in his hoarse voice.

'If it should please your Majesty to permit me,' answered the captain-diplomat.

'Go back and lose no time,' said Paul in his hoarse voice, and he did go back, without even seeing his relations, who lived in Moscow.

While diplomatic questions were being settled by bayonets and grape-shot, he was an ambassador and concluded his diplomatic career at the time of the Congress of Vienna, that bright festival of all the diplomats. Returning to Russia he was appointed court chamberlain in Moscow, where there is no court. Though he knew nothing of Russian Law and legal procedure, he got into the Senate, became a member of the Council of Guardians, a director of the Mariinsky Hospital, and of the Alexandriinsky Institute, and he performed all his duties with a zeal that was hardly necessary, with a censoriousness that only did harm and with an honesty that no one noticed.

He was never at home, he tired out two teams of four strong horses in the course of the day, one set in the morning, the other after dinner. Besides the Senate, the sittings of which he never neglected, and the Council of Guardians, which he attended twice a week, besides the Hospital and the Institute, he hardly missed a single French play, and visited the English Club three times a week. He had no time to be bored: he was always busy and interested. He was always going somewhere, and his life rolled lightly on good springs through a world of official papers and red tape.

Moreover, up to the age of seventy-five he was as strong as a young man, was present at all the great balls and dinners, took part in every ceremonial assembly and annual function, whether it was of an agricultural or medical or fire insurance society or of the Society of Natural Philosophy . . . and, on the top of it all, perhaps because of it, preserved to old age some degree of human feeling and a certain warmth of heart.

No greater contrast to the sanguine Senator, who was always in motion and only occasionally visited his home, can possibly be imagined than my father, who hardly ever went out of his courtyard, hated the whole official world and was everlastingly freakish and discontented. We also had eight horses (very poor ones), but our stable was something like an almshouse for broken-down nags; my father kept them partly for the sake of appearances and partly so that the two coachmen and the two postillions should have something to do, besides fetching the *Moscow News* and getting up cock-fights, which they did very successfully between the coachhouse and the neighbour's yard.

My father had scarcely been in the service at all; educated by a French tutor, in the house of a devoutly religious aunt, he entered the Izmaylovsky regiment as a sergeant at sixteen, served until the accession of Paul, and retired with the rank of captain in the Guards. In 1801 he went abroad and remained until the end of 1811, wandering from one country to another. He returned with my mother three months before my birth, and after the fire of Moscow he spent a year on his estate in the province of Tver, and then returned to live in Moscow, trying to order his life so as to be as solitary and dreary as possible. His brother's liveliness hindered him in this.

After the Senator left us, everything in the house began to assume a more and more gloomy aspect. The walls, the furniture, the servants, everything bore a look of discontent and suspicion, and I need hardly say that my father himself was of all the most discontented. The unnatural stillness, the whispers and cautious footsteps of the servants, did not suggest attentive solicitude, but oppression and terror. In the rooms everything was stationary; for five or six years the same books would lie in the very same places with the same markers in them. In my father's bedroom and study the furniture was not moved nor the windows opened for years together. When he went away into the country he took the key of his room in his pocket, that they might not venture to scrub the floor or wash the walls in his absence.

Chapter 2

Youth

UNTIL I was ten years old I noticed nothing strange or special in my position; it seemed to me simple and natural that I should be living in my father's house; that in his part of it I should be on my best behaviour, while my mother lived in another part of the house, in which I could be as noisy and mischievous as I liked. The Senator spoiled me and gave me presents, Calot carried me about in his arms, Vera Artamonovna dressed me, put me to bed, and gave me my bath, Madame Proveau took me out for walks and talked to me in German; everything went on in its regular way, yet I began pondering on things.

Stray remarks, carelessly uttered words, began to attract my attention. Old Madame Proveau and all the servants were devoted to my mother, while they feared and disliked my father. The scenes which sometimes took place between them were often the subject of conversation between Madame Proveau and Vera Artamonovna, both of whom always took my mother's side.

My mother certainly had a good deal to put up with. Being an extremely kind-hearted woman, with no strength of will, she was completely crushed by my father, and, as always happens with weak characters, put up a desperate opposition in trifling matters and things of no consequence. Unhappily, in these trifling matters my father was nearly always in the right, and the dispute always ended for him in triumph.

'If I were in the mistress's place,' Madame Proveau would say, for instance, 'I would simply go straight back to Stuttgart; much comfort she gets—nothing but fads and unpleasantness, and deadly dullness.'

'To be sure,' Vera Artamonovna would assent, 'but that's what ties her, hand and foot,' and she would point with her knitting-needle towards me. 'How can she take him with her—what to? And as for

20

leaving him here alone, with the way we live—why, even if one was no relation, one would have pity on him!'

Children in general have far more insight than is supposed; they are quickly distracted and forget for a time what has struck them, but they go back to it persistently, especially if it is anything mysterious or frightening and with wonderful perseverance and ingenuity they go on probing until they reach the truth.

Once I became curious, within a few weeks I had found out all the details of my father's meeting with my mother, had heard how she had brought herself to leave her parents' home, how she had been hidden at the Senator's in the Russian Embassy at Cassel, and had crossed the frontier dressed as a boy; all this I found out without putting a single question to anyone.

The first result of these discoveries was to estrange me from my father because of the scenes of which I have spoken. I had seen them before, but I used to think all that quite normal—part of the regular order of things; for I was so accustomed to the fact that everyone in the house, not excepting the Senator, was afraid of my father, and that he was given to scolding everyone, that I saw nothing strange in it. Now I began to think so no longer, and the thought that some of it was endured on my account sometimes threw a dark, oppressive cloud over my bright, childish imagination.

A second idea that took root in me from that time was that I was far less dependent on my father than children are as a rule. I liked this feeling of independence which I imagined for myself.

Two or three years later two of my father's old comrades in the regiment, P. K. Essen, the Governor-General of Orenburg, and A. N. Bakhmetev, formerly Governor in Bessarabia, a general who had lost his leg at Borodino, were sitting with my father. My room was next to the ballroom in which they were. Among other things my father told them that he had been speaking to Prince Yusupov about putting me into the civil service.

'There's no time to be lost,' he added; 'you know that it will take him years to reach any kind of decent rank in the service.'

'What a strange idea, dear friend, to make him a clerk,' Essen said, good-naturedly. 'Leave it to me, and I will get him into the Ural Cossacks. We'll get him a commission, that's all that matters: after that he will make his way, like the rest of us.'

My father did not agree and said that he had grown to dislike everything military, and that he hoped in time to get me a post on some mission to a warm country, where he would go to end his days.

Bakhmetev, who had taken little part in the conversation, got up on his crutches and said:

'It seems to me that you ought to think very seriously over Pëtr Kirillovich's advice. If you don't want to put his name down at Orenburg, you might put him down here. We are old friends, and it's my habit to say openly what I think; if you put him into the civil service and the university you will do no good to *your young man*, nor to society either. He is quite obviously *in a false position*; only the military service can open a career for him and put him right. Before he gets command of a company, all dangerous ideas will have subsided. Military discipline is a grand schooling, and after that it all depends on him. You say that he has abilities, but you don't mean to say that none but fools go into the army, do you? What about us and all our set? There's only one objection you can make—that he will have to serve longer before he gets a commission, but it's just over that that we can help you.'

This conversation had as much effect as the remarks of Madame Proveau and Vera Artamonovna. By that time I was thirteen* and such lessons, turned over and over, and analysed from every point of view during weeks and months of complete solitude, bore their fruit. The result of this conversation was that, although I had till then, like all boys, dreamed of the army and a uniform, and had been ready to cry at my father's wanting me to go into the civil service, my enthusiasm for soldiering suddenly cooled, and my craving and weakness for epaulettes, aiguillettes and striped trousers, were by degrees completely eradicated. My dying passion for a uniform had, however, one last flicker. A cousin of ours, who had been at a boarding-school in Moscow and used sometimes to spend a holiday with us, had entered the Yamburgsky regiment of Uhlans. In 1825 he came to Moscow as an ensign and stayed a few days with us. My heart throbbed when I saw him with all his little cords and laces, with a sword, and a four-cornered shako worn a little on one side and fastened with a chin-strap. He was a boy of seventeen and short for his age. Next morning I dressed up in his uniform, put on his sword and shako and looked at myself in the glass. Goodness! how handsome I thought myself in the short dark-blue jacket with red braid! And the tassels and the pompom, and the pouch . . . what were the yellow nankeen breeches and the short camlet jacket which I used to wear at home, in comparison with these?

The cousin's visit might have destroyed the effect of the general's talk, but soon circumstances turned me against the army again, and this time for good.

The spiritual result of my meditations on my 'false position' was much the same as that which I had deduced from the talk of my two nurses. I felt myself more independent of society, of which I knew absolutely nothing, felt that in reality I was thrown on my own resources, and with somewhat childish conceit thought I would show the old generals what I was made of.

With all this it may well be imagined how drearily and monotonously the time passed in the strange convent-like seclusion of my father's house. I had neither encouragement nor distraction; my father had spoilt me until I was ten, and now he was almost always dissatisfied with me; I had no companions, my teachers called to give lessons and went away, and, seeing them out of the yard, I used to run off on the sly, to play with the house-serf boys, which was strictly forbidden. The rest of my time I spent wandering aimlessly about the big, dark rooms, which had their windows shut all day and were only dimly lit in the evening, doing nothing or reading anything that turned up.

The servants' hall and the maids' room provided the only keen enjoyment left me. There I had complete liberty; I took the side of one party against another, discussed their business with my friends, and gave my opinion upon them, knew all their intimate affairs, and never dropped a word in the drawing-room about the secrets of the servants' hall.

I must pause upon this subject. Indeed, I do not intend to avoid digressions and episodes; that is part of every conversation; indeed of life itself.

Children as a rule are fond of servants; their parents forbid them, especially in Russia, to associate with servants; the children do not obey them because in the drawing-room it is dull, while in the maids' room it is lively. In this case, as in thousands of others, parents do not know what they are about. I do not imagine that our hall was a less wholesome place for children than our 'tea-room' or 'sitting-room'. In the servants' hall children pick up coarse expressions and bad manners, that is true; but in the drawing-room they pick up coarse ideas and bad feelings.

The very orders to children to keep away from those with whom they are continually in contact is immoral.

A great deal is said among us about the complete depravity of servants, especially when they are serfs. They certainly are not distinguished by exemplary strictness of conduct, and their moral degradation can be seen from the fact that they put up with too much and are too rarely moved to indignation and resistance. But that is not the point. I should like to know what class in Russia is less depraved? The nobility[1] or the officials? The clergy, perhaps?

Why do you laugh?

The peasants, perhaps, are the only ones who could put up some kind of claim to be different. . . .

The difference between the nobleman and the serving man is very small. I hate the demagogues' flattery of the mob, particularly since the troubles of 1848, but the aristocrats' slander of the people I hate even more. By picturing servants and slaves as degraded animals, the slave-owners throw dust in people's eyes and stifle the voice of conscience in themselves. We are not often better than the lower classes, but we express ourselves more gently and conceal our egoism and our passions more adroitly; our desires are not so coarse, and the ease with which they are satisfied and our habit of not controlling them make them less conspicuous; we are simply wealthier and better fed and consequently more fastidious. When Count Almaviva recited to the Barber of Seville the catalogue of the qualities he expected from a servant, Figaro observed with a sigh: 'If a servant must have all these virtues, are there many gentlemen fit to be lackeys?'

Dissoluteness in Russia as a rule does not go deep; it is more savage and dirty, noisy and coarse, dishevelled and shameless than profound. The clergy, shut up at home, drink and overeat themselves with the merchants. The nobility get drunk in public, play cards until they are ruined, thrash their servants, seduce their housemaids, manage their business affairs badly and their family life still worse. The officials do the same, but in a dirtier way, and in addition are guilty of grovelling before their superiors and pilfering. As far as stealing in the literal sense goes, the nobility are less guilty: they take openly

---

[1] The word *dvoryanstvo* includes both nobility and gentry. '*Aux termes de la loi du 12 janvier 1682, tous les gentilshommes russes sont égaux en droits, sans acception de titre ou d'origine.*' (P. Dolgorouky: *Notice sur les Principales Familles de la Russie* (Berlin, 1858), page 3). (*R.*)

what belongs to others; besides, when it suits them they are just as grasping as other people.

All these amiable weaknesses are to be met with in a still coarser form in officials who stand below the fourteenth grade,[2] and in gentlefolk who are dependent not on the Tsar but on the landowners. But in what way they are worse than others as a class, I do not know.

Going over my recollections, not only of the serfs in our house and in the Senator's, but also of two or three households with which we were intimate for twenty-five years, I do not remember anything particularly vicious in their behaviour. Petty thefts, perhaps, . . . but on that matter all ideas are so dulled by the serfs' position, that it is difficult to judge; *human property* does not stand on much ceremony with its kith and kin, and is pretty cavalier with the master's goods. It would be only fair to exclude from this generalisation the confidential servants, the favourites of both sexes, masters' mistresses and tale-bearers; but in the first place they are an exception—these Kleinmikhels of the stable[3] and Benckendorfs[4] from the cellar, Perekusikhins[5] in striped linen gowns, and barefoot Pompadours; moreover, they do behave better than any of the rest: they only get drunk at night and do not pawn their clothes at the gin-shop.

The simple-minded immorality of the rest revolves round a glass of vodka and a bottle of beer, a merry talk and a pipe, absences from home without leave, quarrels which sometimes end in fights, and cunning tricks played on masters who expect of them something inhuman and impossible. Of course, the lack of all education on the one hand, and on the other the simplicity of the peasant serfs have introduced into their manners much that is ugly and distorted, but for all that, like the negroes in America, they have remained half infantile; trifles amuse them, trifles distress them; their desires are limited, and are rather naïve and human than vicious.

Alcohol and tea, the tavern and the eating-house, are the two

---

[2] Peter I's Table of Ranks, 24th January, 1722, was drawn up in three parallel columns, civil, military and court, each divided into fourteen ranks or classes, most of which were given Latin or German names. It established a bureaucratic hierarchy based on ability rather than birth. (*R.*)

[3] Kleinmikhel, Pëtr Andreyevich, Minister of Means of Communication under Nicholas I. (*Tr.*)

[4] Benckendorf, Alexander Khristoforovich, Chief of Gendarmes, and favourite of Nicholas I. (*Tr.*)

[5] Perekusikhin, Marya Savvishna, favourite of Catherine II. (*Tr.*)

permanent passions of the Russian servant; for their sake he steals, for their sake he is poor, on their account he endures persecution and punishment and leaves his family in poverty. Nothing is easier than for a Father Mathew,[6] from the height of his teetotal intoxication, to condemn drunkenness and, while sitting at the tea-table, to wonder why it is that servants go for their tea to the eating-house, instead of drinking it at home, although at home it is cheaper.

Alcohol stupefies a man, it enables him to forget himself, stimulates him and induces an artificial gaiety; this stupefaction and stimulation are the more agreeable the less the man is developed and the more he is bound to a narrow, empty life. How can a servant not drink when he is condemned to the everlasting waiting in the hall, to perpetual poverty, to being a slave, to being sold? He drinks to excess—when he can—because he cannot drink every day; that was observed fifteen years ago by Senkovsky in the *Library of Good Reading*.[7] In Italy and the South of France there are no drunkards, because there is plenty of wine. The savage drunkenness of the English working man is to be explained in exactly the same way. These men are broken in the helpless and unequal conflict with hunger and poverty; however hard they have struggled they have met everywhere a leaden legal code and harsh resistance that has flung them back into the dark depths of common life, and condemned them to the never-ending, aimless toil that eats away mind and body alike. It is not surprising that a man who spends six days as a lever, a cog, a spring, a screw, on Saturday afternoon breaks savagely out of the penal servitude of factory work, and drinks himself silly in half an hour, the more so since his exhaustion cannot stand much. The moralists would do better to drink Irish or Scotch whisky themselves and hold their tongues, or their inhuman philanthropy may call down terrible retribution on them.

Drinking tea at the eating-house means something quite different to servants. Tea at home is not the same thing for the house-serf; at home everything reminds him that he is a servant; at home he is in the dirty servants' room, he must get the samovar himself; at

<hr />

[6] Father Mathew (1790-1856), an Irish priest, who had remarkable success in a great temperance campaign based on the religious appeal. (*Tr.*)

[7] Senkovsky, Joseph Ivanovich (1800-1878), of Polish origin, was a whimsical critic on the reactionary side who placed a miserable poetaster, Timofeyev, above Pushkin and preferred Le Sage to Fielding. Under the pseudonym Baron Brambeus, he wrote sensational and bombastic novels. He edited a serial publication, the *Library of Good Reading,* employing poor young men of talent to write for it. (*Tr.*)

home he has a cup with a broken handle, and any minute his master may ring for him. At the eating-house he is a free man, he is a gentleman; for him the table is laid and the lamps are lit; for him the waiter runs with the tray; the cup shines, the tea-pot glitters, he gives orders and is obeyed, he enjoys himself and gaily calls for pressed caviare or a turnover with his tea.

In all this there is more childish simplicity than dissoluteness. Impressions quickly take possession of them but do not send down roots; their minds are continually occupied, or rather distracted, by casual subjects, small desires, trivial aims. A childish belief in everything marvellous turns a grown-up man into a coward, and the same childish belief comforts him at the most difficult moments. I was filled with wonder when I was present at the death of two or three of my father's servants; it was then that one could judge of the simple-hearted carelessness with which their lives had passed, of the absence of great sins upon their conscience; if there was anything, it had all been settled at confession with the priest.

This resemblance between servants and children accounts for their mutual attraction. Children hate the aristocratic ideas of the grown-ups and their benevolently condescending manners, because they are clever and understand that in the eyes of grown-up people they are children, while in the eyes of servants they are people. Consequently they are much fonder of playing cards or lotto with the maids than with visitors. Visitors play for the children's benefit with condescension, give way to them, tease them and stop playing whenever they feel like it; the maids, as a rule, play as much for their own sakes as for the children's; and that gives the game interest.

Servants are extremely devoted to children, and this is not the devotion of a slave, but the mutual affection of the *weak* and the *simple*.

In old days there used to be a patriarchal dynastic affection between landowners and their house-servants, such as exists now in Turkey. To-day there are in Russia no more of those devoted servants, attached to the line and the family of their masters. And that is easy to understand. The landowner no longer believes in his power, he does not believe that he will have to answer for his serfs at the terrible Day of Judgment, but simply makes use of his power for his own advantage. The servant does not believe in his subjection and endures violence not as a chastisement and trial from God, but simply because he is defenceless; the big fish swallows the little ones.

B*

I used to know in my youth two or three examples of those zealots of slavery, of whom eighty-year-old landowners speak with a sigh, telling stories of their unflagging service and their great diligence, and forgetting to add in what way their fathers and themselves repaid such self-sacrifice.

On one of the Senator's estates a feeble old man called Andrey Stepanov was living in peace, that is, on free rations.

He had been valet to the Senator and my father when they were serving in the Guards, and was a good, honest, and sober man, who looked into his young masters' eyes, and, to use their own words, 'guessed from them what they wanted', which, I imagine, was not an easy task. Afterwards he looked after the estate near Moscow. Cut off from the beginning of the war of 1812 from all communication, and afterwards left alone, without money, on the ashes of a village which had been burnt to the ground, he sold some beams to escape starvation. The Senator, on his return to Russia, proceeded to set his estate in order, and at last came to the beams. He punished his former valet by sending him away in disgrace, depriving him of his duties. The old man, burdened with a family, trudged off to pick up what food he could. We sometimes had to drive through the village where Andrey Stepanov lived, and stay there for a day or two. The feeble old man, crippled by paralysis, used to come every time leaning on his crutch, to pay his respects to my father and to have a talk with him.

The devotion and the gentleness with which he talked, his sorrowful appearance, the locks of yellowish grey hair on each side of his bald pate, touched me deeply.

'I have heard, sir,' he said on one occasion, 'that your brother has thought proper to receive another decoration. I am getting old, your honour, I shall soon give up my soul to God, and yet the Lord has not vouchsafed to me to see your brother in his decorations: if only I might once before my end behold his honour in his ribbons and all his insignia!'

I looked at the old man: his face was so childishly candid, his bent figure, his painfully twisted face, lustreless eyes, and weak voice —all inspired confidence; he was not lying, he was not flattering, he really longed before his death to see, in 'his decorations and insignia', the man who for fifteen years could not forgive him the loss of a few beams. Was this a saint, or a madman? But perhaps it is only madmen who attain saintliness?

The new generation has not this idolatrous worship, and if there are cases of serfs not caring for freedom, that is simply due to indolence and material considerations. It is more depraved, there is no doubt, but it is a sign that it is nearer to its ending; if they want to see anything on their master's neck, it is certainly not the Vladimir ribbon.

Here I will say something of the situation of our servants in general.

Neither the Senator nor my father oppressed the house-serfs particularly: that is, they did not ill-treat them physically. The Senator was hasty and impatient, and consequently often rough and unjust, but he had so little contact with the house-serfs and took so little notice of them that they scarcely knew each other. My father wearied them with his caprices, never let pass a look, a word or a movement, and was everlastingly lecturing them; to a Russian this is often worse than blows and abuse.

Corporal punishment was almost unknown in our house, and the two or three cases in which the Senator and my father resorted to the revolting method of the police station were so exceptional that all the servants talked about it for months afterwards; and it was only provoked by glaring offences.

More frequently house-serfs were sent for soldiers, and this punishment was a terror to all the young men; without kith or kin, they still preferred to remain house-serfs, rather than to be in harness for twenty years. I was greatly affected by those terrible scenes. . . . Two soldiers of the police would appear at the summons of the landowner: they would stealthily, in a casual, sudden way, seize the appointed victim. The village elder commonly announced at this point that the master had the evening before ordered that he was to be produced at the recruiting-office, and the man would try through his tears to put a brave face on it, while the women wept: everyone made him presents and I gave him everything I could, that is, perhaps a neckerchief worth twenty kopecks.

I remember, too, by father's ordering some village elder's beard to be shaved off, because he had spent the *obrok*[8] which he had collected. I did not understand this punishment, but was struck by the appearance of this old man of sixty; he was in floods of tears, and kept bowing to the ground and begging for a fine of a hundred silver

[8] Payment in money or kind by a serf in lieu of labour for his master. (*Tr.*)

roubles in addition to the *obrok* if only he might be spared this disgrace.

When the Senator was living with us, the common household consisted of thirty men and almost as many women; the married women, however, performed no service: they looked after their own families; there were five or six maids and laundresses, who never came upstairs. To these must be added the *boys and girls* who were being trained in their duties, that is, in sloth and idleness, in lying and the use of corn-spirit.

To give an idea of the life in Russia of those days, I think it will not be out of place to say a few words on the maintenance of the house-serfs. At first they used to be given five paper roubles a month for victuals, and afterwards six. The women had a rouble a month less, and children under ten had half the full allowance. The servants made up 'artels'[9] and did not complain of the allowance being too small, which shows how extraordinarily cheap provisions were. The highest wage was a hundred roubles a year, while others received half that amount and some only thirty roubles. Boys under eighteen got no wages at all. In addition to their wages, servants were given clothes, greatcoats, shirts, sheets, blankets, towels and mattresses made of canvas; boys, who did not get wages, were allowed money for their physical and moral purification, that is, for the bath-house and for preparing for communion. Taking everything into account, a servant cost about three hundred paper roubles a year; if to this we add a share of medicine, of a doctor and of the surplus stores brought from the country, even then it is not over 350 roubles. This is only a *quarter* of the cost of a servant in Paris or London.

Slave-owners usually take into account the *insurance* premium of slavery, that is, the maintenance of wife and children by the owner, and a meagre crust of bread somewhere in the village for the slave in old age. Of course this must be taken into account; but the cost is greatly lessened by the *fear* of corporal punishment, the impossibility of changing their condition, and a much lower scale of maintenance.

I have seen enough of the way in which the terrible consciousness of serfdom destroys and poisons the existence of house-serfs, the way in which it oppresses and stupefies their souls. Peasants, especially those who pay a fixed sum in lieu of labour, have less feeling of their

[9] i.e., clubs or guilds for messing or working together. (*Tr.*)

personal bondage; they somehow succeed in not believing in their complete slavery. But for the house-serf, sitting on a dirty locker in the hall from morning till night, or standing with a plate at table, there is no room for doubt.

Of course there are people who live in the hall like fish in water, people whose souls have never awakened, who have acquired a taste for their manner of life and who perform their duties with a sort of artistic relish.

Of that class we had one extremely interesting specimen, our footman Bakay, a man of tall figure and athletic build, with solid, dignified features and an air of the greatest profundity; he lived to an advanced age, imagining that the position of a footman was one of the greatest consequence.

This worthy old man was perpetually angry or a little drunk, or angry and a little drunk at once. He took an exalted view of his duties and ascribed a solemn importance to them: with a peculiar bang and crash he would throw up the steps of the carriage and slam the carriage door with a report like a musket-shot. With a gloomy air he stood up stiff and rigid behind the carriage, and every time there was a jolt over a rut he would shout in a thick and displeased voice to the coachman: 'Steady!' regardless of the fact that the rut was already five paces behind.

Apart from going out with the carriage, his chief occupation, a duty he had voluntarily undertaken, consisted of training the serf-boys in the aristocratic manners to be employed in the hall. When he was sober, things went fairly well, but when his head was a little dizzy, he became incredibly pedantic and tyrannical. I sometimes stood up for my friends, but my authority had little influence on Bakay, whose temper was of a Roman severity; he would open the door into the *salon* for me and say:

'This is not the place for you; be pleased to leave the room or I shall carry you out.'

He lost no opportunity of abusing the boys, and often added a cuff to his words, or 'beat butter', that is, with his thumb and little finger dexterously gave them a sly flip on the head with the sharpness and force of a spring.

When at last he had chased the boys out and was left alone, he transferred his persecution to his one friend, Macbeth, a big Newfoundland dog, whom he used to feed, comb and fondle. After sitting in solitude for two or three minutes he would go out into the yard, call Macbeth to join him on the locker, and begin a conversation.

'What are you sitting out there in the yard in the frost for, stupid, when there is a warm room for you? What a beast! What are you staring for, eh? Have you nothing to say?'

Usually a slap would follow these words. Macbeth would sometimes growl at his benefactor; and then Bakay would upbraid him in earnest:

'You may go on feeding a dog, but he will still remain a dog; he will show his teeth at anyone, without caring who it is . . . the fleas would have eaten him up if it had not been for me!'

And offended by his friend's ingratitude he would wrathfully take a pinch of snuff and fling what was left between his fingers on Macbeth's nose. Then the dog would sneeze, clumsily wipe out of his eyes with his paw the snuff that had fallen on his nose, and, leaving the locker indignantly, would scratch at the door; Bakay would open it with the word 'Rascal' and give him a kick as he went. . . . Then the boys would come back, and he would set to flipping them on the head again.

Before Macbeth we had a setter called Berta; she fell very ill and Bakay took her on to his mattress and looked after her for two or three weeks. Early one morning I went out into the hall. Bakay tried to say something to me, but his voice broke and a big tear rolled down his cheek—the dog was dead. There is a fact for the student of human nature! I do not for a moment suppose that he disliked the boys; it was simply a case of a severe character, accentuated by drink and unconsciously grown accustomed to the spirit that prevailed in the hall.

But besides these amateurs of slavery, what gloomy images of martyrs, of hopeless victims, pass mournfully before my memory!

The Senator had a cook, Alexey, a sober, industrious man of exceptional talent who made his way in the world. The Senator himself got him taken into the Tsar's kitchen, where there was at that time a celebrated French cook. After being trained there he got a post in the English Club, grew rich, married and lived like a gentleman; but the strings which tied him to serfdom would not let him sleep soundly at night, nor take pleasure in his situation.

After having a service celebrated to the Iversky Madonna, Alexey plucked up his courage and presented himself before the Senator to ask for his freedom for five thousand paper roubles. The Senator was proud of *his* cook, just as he was proud of *his* painter, and so he would not take the money, but told the cook that he should be set free for nothing at his master's death.

The cook was thunderstruck; he grieved, grew thin and worn, turned grey and . . . being a Russian, took to drink. He neglected his work; the English Club dismissed him. He was engaged by the Princess Trubetskoy, who worried him by her petty niggardliness. Being on one occasion extremely offended by her, Alexey, who was fond of expressing himself eloquently, said, speaking through his nose with his air of dignity:

'What an opaque soul dwells in your luminous body!'

The princess was furious; she turned the cook away, and, as might be expected from a Russian lady, wrote a complaint to the Senator. The Senator would have done nothing to him, but, as a courteous gentleman, he felt bound to send for the cook, gave him a good cursing and told him to go and beg the princess's pardon.

The cook did not go to the princess but went to the pot-house. Within a year he had lost everything, from the capital he had saved up for his ransom to the last of his aprons. His wife struggled and struggled on with him, but at last went off and took a place as a nurse. Nothing was heard of him for a long time. Then the police brought Alexey, wild-looking and in tatters; he had been picked up in the street, he had no lodging, he migrated from tavern to tavern. The police insisted that his master should take him. The Senator was distressed and perhaps conscience-stricken, too; he received him rather mildly and gave him a room. Alexey went on drinking, was noisy when he was drunk and imagined that he was composing verses; he certainly had some imagination of an incoherent sort. We were at that time at Vasilevskoye. The Senator, not knowing what to do with the cook, sent him there, thinking that my father would bring him to reason. But the man was too completely shattered. I saw in his case the concentrated anger and hatred against the masters which lies in the heart of the serf: he would talk with a grinding of the teeth and with gesticulations which, especially in a cook, might have been dangerous. He was not afraid to give full rein to his tongue in my presence; he was fond of me and would often, patting me familiarly on the shoulders, say that I was:

'A good branch of a rotten tree.'

After the Senator's death my father gave him his freedom at once.

It was too late and simply meant getting rid of him; he just disappeared.

Besides Alexey I cannot help recalling another victim of serfdom. The Senator had a serf aged about five-and-thirty who acted as his secretary. My father's eldest brother, who died in 1813, had sent him as a boy to a well-known doctor to be trained as a *feldsher* (or doctor's assistant) that he might be of use in a village hospital which his master was intending to found. The doctor procured permission for him to attend the lectures at the Academy of Medicine and Surgery; the young man had abilities, he learned Latin, German, and something of doctoring. At five-and-twenty he fell in love with the daughter of an officer, concealed his condition from her and married her. The deception could not last long. After his master's death, the wife learned with horror that they were serfs. The Senator, his new owner, did not oppress them in any way, indeed he was fond of young Tolochanov, but the quarrel with the wife persisted; she could not forgive her husband for the deception and ran away from him with another man. Tolochanov must have been devoted to her, for from that time he sank into a melancholy that bordered upon madness, spent his nights in debauchery, and, having no means of his own, squandered his master's money. When he saw that he could not set things right, on the 31st of December, 1821, he poisoned himself.

The Senator was not at home; Tolochanov went in to my father in my presence and told him that he had come to say good-bye to him and to ask him to tell the Senator that he had spent the money that was missing.

'You are drunk,' my father told him. 'Go and sleep it off.'

'I shall soon go for a long sleep,' said the doctor, 'and I only beg you not to bear resentment against me.'

Tolochanov's tranquil air alarmed my father and, looking more intently at him, he asked:

'What's the matter with you, are you raving?'

'Not at all, sir, I have only taken a wineglassful of arsenic.'

They sent for a doctor and the police, gave him an emetic, and made him drink milk. When he was on the point of vomiting, he restrained himself and said:

'Stay there, stay there, I did not swallow you for that.'

Afterwards, when the poison began to act more violently, I heard his moans and his voice repeating in agony,

'It burns! it burns! it's fire!'

Someone advised him to send for a priest; he refused, and told Calot that there could not be a life beyond the grave, that he knew too much anatomy to believe that. At midnight he asked the doctor, in German, what time it was, then saying, 'Well, it's the New Year: I wish you a happy one,' he died.

In the morning I rushed to the little lodge that served as a bath-house; Tolochanov had been taken there; the body was lying on the table, looking just as it had when he died, in a swallow-tail coat without a cravat, with his chest bare, and his features were terribly distorted and had even turned black. This was the first dead body I saw; I went away almost fainting. And the playthings and pictures I had had given me for the New Year did not comfort me. Tolochanov's blackened face hovered before my eyes and I kept hearing his 'It burns! it's fire!'

I will say only one thing more, to conclude this gloomy subject: the hall had no really bad influence upon me at all. On the contrary, it awakened in me from my earliest years an invincible hatred for every form of slavery and every form of tyranny. At times, when I was a child, Vera Artamonovna would say by way of the greatest rebuke for some naughtiness: 'Wait a bit, you will grow up and turn into just such another master as the rest.' I felt this a horrible insult. The old woman need not have worried herself—just such another as the rest, anyway, I have not become.

Besides the hall and the maids' room I had one other distraction, and in that I was not hindered in any way. I loved reading as much as I hated lessons. My passion for unsystematic reading was, indeed, one of the chief obstacles to serious study. I never could, for instance, then or later, endure the theoretical study of languages, but I very soon learnt to understand and gabble them incorrectly, and at that stage I remained, because it was sufficient for my reading.

My father and the Senator had between them a fairly large library, consisting of French books of the eighteenth century. The books lay about in heaps in a damp, unused room on the ground floor of the Senator's house. Calot had the key. I was allowed to rummage in these literary granaries as I liked, and I read and read to my heart's content. My father saw two advantages in it, that I should learn French more quickly and that I was occupied—that is, I was sitting quiet and in my own room. Besides, I did not show him all the books I read, nor lay them on the table; some of them were hidden in a bureau.

What did I read? Novels and plays, of course. I read fifty volumes of the French *Répertoire* and the Russian *Theatre*; in every volume there were three or four plays. Besides French novels my mother had the Tales of Lafontaine and the comedies of Kotzebue, and I read them two or three times. I cannot say that the novels had much influence on me; and though like all boys I pounced eagerly on all equivocal or somewhat improper scenes, they did not interest me particularly. A play which I liked beyond all measure and read over twenty times, (and moreover in the Russian translation in *Theatre*,) the *Marriage of Figaro*,[10] had much greater influence on me. I was in love with Cherubino and the Countess, and what is more, I was myself Cherubino; my heart throbbed as I read it and without clearly recognising it I was conscious of a new sensation. How enchanting I thought the scene in which the page is dressed up as a girl, how intensely I longed to hide somebody's ribbon in my bosom and kiss it in secret. In reality I had in those years no feminine society.

I only remember that occasionally on Sundays Bakhmetev's two daughters used to come from their boarding-school to visit us. The younger, a girl of sixteen, was strikingly beautiful. I was overwhelmed when she entered the room and never ventured to address a word to her, but kept stealing looks at her lovely dark eyes and dark curls. I never dropped a hint to anyone on the subject and the first breath of love passed unknown to anyone, even to her.

Years afterwards, when I met her, my heart throbbed violently and I remembered how at twelve years old I had worshipped her beauty.

I forgot to say that *Werther* interested me almost as much as the *Marriage of Figaro*; half the novel was beyond me and I skipped it, and hurried on to the terrible *dénouement*, over which I wept like a madman. In 1839 *Werther* happened to come into my hands again; this was when I was at Vladimir and I told my wife how as a boy I had cried over it and began reading her the last letters . . . and

---

[10] *Le Mariage de Figaro*, a satirical comedy by Beaumarchais (*né* Caron, 1732-99), a watchmaker's son, who rose to wealth and influence, and by his writings helped to bring about the Revolution. This play and an earlier one, *Le Barbier de Séville*, became popular all over Europe, but are now chiefly remembered through their adaptation to operas by Mozart and Rossini. (*Tr.*)

when I came to the same passage, my tears began flowing again and
I had to stop.

Up to the age of fourteen I cannot say that my father greatly
restricted my liberty, but the whole atmosphere of our house was
oppressive for a lively boy. The persistent and unnecessary fussiness
concerning my physical health, together with complete indifference
to my moral well-being, was horribly wearisome. There were everlasting precautions against my taking a chill, or eating anything
indigestible, and anxious solicitude over the slightest cough or cold
in the head. In the winter I was kept indoors for weeks at a time and,
when I was allowed to go out, it was only wearing warm high boots,
thick scarves and such things. At home it was always insufferably
hot from the stoves. All this would inevitably have made me a frail
and delicate child but for the iron health I inherited from my
mother. She by no means shared my father's prejudices, and in
her half of the house allowed me everything which was forbidden
in his.

My education made slow progress without competition, encouragement, or approval; I did my lessons lazily, without method or supervision, and thought to make a good memory and lively imagination
take the place of hard work. I need hardly say that there was no
supervision over my teachers either; once the terms upon which they
were engaged were settled, they might, so long as they turned up at
the proper time and sat through their hour, go on for years without
rendering any account to any one.

One of the queerest episodes of my education at that time was the
engagement of the French actor Dalès to give me lessons in elocution.

'No attention is paid to it nowadays,' my father said to me, 'but my
brother Alexander was reciting *"Le récit de Théramène"*[11] every
evening for six months with his teacher without reaching the perfec-
tion that he insisted upon.'

So I set to work at recitation.

'Well, Monsieur Dalès, I expect you can give dancing lessons?' my
father asked him on one occasion.

Dalès, a fat old man over sixty, who was fully aware of his own
qualities, but no less fully aware of the propriety of being modest
about them, replied: 'that he could not judge of his own talents, but
that he had often given advice in the ballet dances *au grand Opéra*.'

---

[11] The famous passage in Racine's *Phèdre*. (*Tr.*)

'So I supposed,' my father observed, offering him his open snuff-box, a civility he would never have shown to a Russian or a German teacher. 'I should be very glad if you could *le dégourdir un peu*; after his recitation he might have a little dancing.'

'*Monsieur le comte peut disposer de moi.*'

And my father, who was excessively fond of Paris, began recalling the foyer of the opera in 1810, the youth of George,[12] the declining years of Mars,[13] and inquiring about cafés and theatres.

Now imagine my little room, a gloomy winter evening, the windows frozen over and water dripping down a cord from them, two tallow candles on the table and our *tête-à-tête*. On the stage Dalès still spoke fairly naturally, but at a lesson thought it his duty to depart further from nature in his delivery. He read Racine in a sort of chant and at the cæsura made a parting such as an Englishman makes in his hair, so that each line seemed like a broken stick.

At the same time he waved his arm like a man who has fallen into the water and does not know how to swim. He made me repeat every line several times and always shook his head, saying,

'Not right, not right at all, *attention: "Je crains Dieu, cher Abner,"*' then the parting, at which he would close his eyes and with a slight shake of his head, tenderly pushing away the waves with his hand, add: '*et n'ai point d'autre crainte*'.[14]

Then the old gentleman who 'feared nothing but God' looked at his watch, shut the book and took up a chair; *this was my partner.*

Under the circumstances it was not surprising that I never learned to dance.

The lessons did not last long; they were cut short very tragically a fortnight later.

I was at the French theatre with the Senator; the overture was played once, then a second time and still the curtain did not rise. The front rows, wishing to show they knew *their* Paris, began to be noisy in the way the *back rows* are there. The manager came before the curtain, bowed to the right, bowed to the left, bowed straight before him, and said:

'We ask the kind indulgence of the audience; a terrible calamity

---

[12] Mlle George (1787-1867), French actress famous for her performances in classical tragedy. (*Tr.*)

[13] Mlle Mars (1779-1847), French actress famous for her acting in comedies of Molière. (*Tr.*)

[14] From Racine's *Athalie*, Act I, Scene 1. (*A.S.*)

has befallen us, our comrade Dalès'—and the man's voice was actually broken by tears—'has been found in his room stifled by charcoal fumes.'

It was in this violent way the fumes of a Russian stove delivered me from recitations, monologues and solo dances with my partner with her four well-turned mahogany legs.

At twelve years old I was transferred from feminine to masculine hands. About that time my father made two unsuccessful attempts to engage a German to look after me.

A German who looks after children is neither a tutor nor a *dyadka*;[15] it is quite a special profession. He does not teach the children and he does not dress them, but sees that they are taught and dressed, takes care of their health, goes out for walks with them and talks any nonsense to them so long as it is in German. If there is a tutor in the house, the German is under his orders; if there is a *dyadka*, he takes his orders from the German. The visiting teachers who come late owing to unforeseen causes and leave early owing to circumstances over which they have no control, do their best to win the German's favour, and in spite of his complete illiteracy he begins to regard himself as a man of learning. Governesses employ the German in shopping for them and on all sorts of errands, but only allow him to pay his court to them if they suffer from striking physical defects or a complete lack of other admirers. Boys of fourteen will go, without their parents' knowledge, to the German's room to smoke, and he puts up with it because he must have powerful auxiliary resources in order to remain in the house. In fact what mostly happens is that at this time the German is thanked, presented with a watch and discharged. If he is tired of sauntering about the streets with children and receiving reprimands for their having colds, or stains on their clothes, the 'children's German' becomes simply a German, sets up a little shop, sells amber cigarette-holders, eau-de-Cologne and cigars to his former nurslings and carries out for them *secret* commissions of another kind.[16]

The first German who was engaged to look after me was a native of Silesia and was called Jokisch; to my mind the surname was more than sufficient reason not to have engaged him. He was a tall, bald

[15] A man, usually a serf, whose duties resembled those of the *pædagogus* in a household in ancient Rome. (R.)

[16] The organist and music-teacher, I. I. Eck, spoken of in the *Notes of a Young Man*, did nothing but give music lessons and had no influence.

man, distinguished by an extreme lack of cleanliness; he used to boast of his knowledge of agricultural science, and I imagine it must have been on that account that my father engaged him. I looked on the Silesian giant with aversion, and the only thing that reconciled me to him was that he used, as we walked about the Devichy grounds and to the Presnensky ponds, to tell me smutty stories which I passed on to the hall. He stayed no more than a year; he did something disgraceful at our country place and the gardener tried to kill him with a scythe, so my father told him to take himself off.

He was succeeded by a Brunswick-Wolfenbüttel soldier (probably a deserter) called Fëdor Karlovich, who was distinguished by his fine handwriting and extreme stupidity. He had been in the same position in two families before and had acquired some experience, so adopted the tone of a tutor; moreover, when he spoke French he would say 'sh' for 'zh', and invariably put the accent on the wrong syllable.[17]

I had not a particle of respect for him and poisoned every moment of his existence, especially after I had convinced myself that he was incapable of understanding decimal fractions and the rule of three. As a rule there is a great deal of ruthlessness and even cruelty in boys' hearts; with positive ferocity I persecuted the poor Wolfenbüttel *Jäger* with proportion sums; this so interested me that I triumphantly informed my father of Fëdor Karlovich's stupidity, though I was not given to discussing such subjects with him.

Moreover, Fëdor Karlovich boasted to me that he had a new swallow-tail coat, dark blue with gold buttons, and I actually did see him on one occasion setting off to attend a wedding in a swallow-tail coat which was too big for him but had gold buttons. The boy whose duty it was to wait upon him informed me that he had borrowed the coat from a friend who served at the counter of a perfumery shop. Without the slightest sympathy I pestered the poor fellow to tell me where his blue dress-coat was.

'There are so many moths in your house,' he said, 'that I have left it with a tailor I know, to be taken care of.'

'Where does that tailor live?'

'What is that to you?'

'Why not tell me?'

'You needn't poke your nose into other people's business.'

---

[17] The English speak French worse than the Germans, but they only distort the language, while the Germans *degrade* it.

'Well, perhaps not, but it is my name-day in a week, so please do get the blue coat from the tailor for that day.'

'No, I won't. You don't deserve it because you are so impertinent.' And I would threaten him with my finger.

For his final discomfiture Fëdor Karlovich must needs one day brag before Bouchot, my French teacher, of having been a recruit at Waterloo, and of the Germans having given the French a terrible thrashing. Bouchot merely stared at him and took a pinch of snuff with such a terrible air that the conqueror of Napoleon was a good deal disconcerted. Bouchot walked off leaning angrily on his gnarled stick and never referred to him afterwards except as '*le soldat de Vilain-ton*'. I did not know at the time that this pun was perpetrated by Béranger and could not boast of having sprung from Bouchot's fertile fancy.

At last Blücher's companion in arms had some quarrel with my father and left our house; after that my father did not worry me with any more Germans.

While our Brunswick-Wolfenbüttel friend held the field I sometimes used to visit some boys with whom a friend of his lived, also in the capacity of a 'German'; and with these boys we used to take long walks; after his departure I was left again in complete solitude. I was bored, struggled to get out of it, and found no means of escape. As I had no chance of overriding my father's will I might perhaps have been broken in to this existence, if a new intellectual interest and two meetings, of which I will speak in the following chapter, had not soon afterwards saved me. I am quite certain that my father had not the faintest notion what sort of life he was forcing upon me, or he would not have thwarted me in the most innocent desires, nor have refused my most natural requests.

Sometimes he allowed me to go with the Senator to the French theatre, and this was the greatest enjoyment for me; I was passionately fond of seeing acting, but this pleasure brought me as much pain as joy. The Senator used to arrive with me when the play was half over and, as he invariably had an invitation for the evening, would take me away before the end. The theatre was in Apraxin's house, at the Arbatsky Gate, and we lived in Old Konyushennaya Street, that is very close by, but my father sternly forbade my returning without the Senator.

I was about fifteen when my father engaged a priest to give me Divinity lessons, so far as was necessary for entering the University.

The Catechism came into my hands after I had read Voltaire. Nowhere does religion play so modest a part in education as in Russia,
and that, of course, is a great piece of good fortune. A priest is always
paid half-price for lessons in religion, and, indeed, if the same priest
gives Latin lessons also, he is paid more for them than for teaching
the Catechism.

My father regarded religion as among the essential belongings of a
well-bred man; he used to say that one must believe in the Holy
Scriptures without criticism, because one could do nothing in that
domain with reason, and all intellectual considerations merely ob-
scured the subject; that one must observe the rites of the religion in
which one was born, without, however, giving way to excessive devoutness, which was all right for old women, but not proper in men.
Did he himself believe? I imagine that he did believe a little, from
habit, from regard for propriety, and from a desire to be on the safe
side. He did not himself, however, take part in any church observances, sheltering himself behind the delicate state of his health. He
scarcely ever received a priest; at most he would ask him to perform
a service in the empty *salon* and would send him out there a
five-rouble note. In the winter he excused himself on the plea that the
priest and the deacon always brought such chilliness with them that
he invariably caught cold. In the country he used to go to church
and have the priest to his house, but with an eye more to the considerations of society and authority than to God-fearing ones.

My mother was a Lutheran and therefore one degree more religious; on one or two Sundays in every month she would drive to her
church, or as Bakay persisted in calling it, to 'her *Kirche*', and, having nothing better to do, I went with her. There I learned to mimic
the German pastors, their declamation and verbosity, with artistic
finish, and I retained the talent in riper years.

Every year my father commanded me to take the sacrament. I was
afraid of confession, and the church *mise en scène* altogether impressed and alarmed me. With genuine awe I went up to take the
sacrament, but I cannot call it a religious feeling; it was the awe
which is inspired by everything incomprehensible and mysterious,
especially when a grave and solemn significance is attributed to
it; casting spells and telling fortunes affect one in the same way. I
took the sacrament after the early service in Holy Week, and, after
devouring eggs coloured red, *paskha* and Easter cakes, I thought no
more of religion for the rest of the year.

But I used to read the Gospel a great deal and with love, both in the Slavonic and in the Lutheran translation. I read it without any guidance, and, though I did not understand everything, I felt a deep and genuine respect for what I read. In my early youth I was often influenced by Voltairianism, and was fond of irony and mockery, but I do not remember that I ever took the Gospel in my hand with a cold feeling; and it has been the same with me all my life; at all ages and under various circumstances I have gone back to reading the Gospel, and every time its words have brought peace and meekness to my soul.

When the priest began giving me lessons he was surprised to find not only that I had a general knowledge of the Gospel but that I could quote texts, word for word. 'But the Lord God,' he said, 'though He has opened his mind, had not yet opened his heart.' And my theologian, shrugging his shoulders, marvelled at my 'double nature', but was pleased with me, thinking that I should be able to pass my examination.

Soon a religion of a different sort took possession of my soul.

Chapter 3

Political Awakening

ONE winter morning the Senator arrived not at the time he usually visited us; looking anxious, he went with hurried footsteps into my father's study and closed the door, motioning me to remain in the *salon*.

Luckily I had not long to rack my brains guessing what was the matter. The door from the hall opened a little way and a red face, half-hidden in the wolf-fur of a livery overcoat, called me in a whisper; it was the Senator's footman. I rushed to the door.

'Haven't you heard?' he asked.

'What?'

'The Tsar has just died at Taganrog.'

The news impressed me; I had never thought of the possibility of the Tsar's death; I had grown up with a great respect for Alexander, and recalled mournfully how I had seen him not long before in Moscow. When we were out walking, we had met him beyond the Tverskoy Gate; he was slowly riding along with two or three generals, returning from Khodynki, where there had been a review. His face was gracious, his features soft and rounded, his expression tired and melancholy. When he was on a level with us I raised my hat, and he bowed to me, smiling. What a contrast to Nicholas, who always looked like a slightly bald Medusa with cropped hair and moustaches. In the street, at the court, with his children and ministers, with his courtiers and maids of honour, he was incessantly trying whether his eyes had the power of a rattlesnake, of freezing blood in the veins.[1] If Alexander's external gentleness was assumed, surely

[1] The story is told that on one occasion in his own household, in the presence, that is, of two or three heads of the secret police, two or three maids of honour and generals in waiting, he tried his Medusa glance on his daughter Marya Nikolayevna. She is like her father, and her eyes really do recall the terrible look in his. The daughter boldly endured her father's stare. The Tsar turned pale, his cheeks twitched, and his eyes grew still more ferocious; his daughter met him with the same look in hers.

44

such hypocrisy is better than the naked candour of autocracy.

While vague ideas floated through my mind, while portraits of the new Emperor Constantine were sold in the shops, while appeals to take the oath of allegiance were being delivered, and good people were hastening to do so, rumours were suddenly afloat that the Tsesarevich had refused the crown. Then that same footman of the Senator's, who was greatly interested in political news and had a fine field for gathering it—in all the public offices and vestibules of senators, to one or other of which he was always driving from morning to night, for he did not share the privilege of the horses, who were changed after dinner—informed me that there had been rioting in Petersburg and that cannon were being fired in Galernaya Street.

On the following evening Count Komarovsky, a general of the gendarmes, was with us: he told us of the square formed in St Isaac's Square, of the Horse Guards' attack, of the death of Count Miloradovich.

Then followed arrests; 'so-and-so has been taken', 'so-and-so has been seized', 'so-and-so has been brought up from the country', terrified parents trembled for their children. The sky was overcast with gloomy storm-clouds.

In the reign of Alexander political oppression was rare; the Tsar did, it is true, banish Pushkin for his verses and Labzin for having, when he was secretary, proposed to elect the coachman, Ilya Baykov, a member of the Academy of Arts;[2] but there was no systematic persecution. The secret police had not yet grown into an independent body of gendarmes, but consisted of a department under the control of de Sanglain, an old Voltairian, a wit, a great talker, and a humorist in the style of Jouy.[3] Under Nicholas this gentleman himself was

---

Everyone turned pale and trembled; the maids of honour and the generals in waiting dared not breathe, so panic-stricken were they at this cannibalistic imperial duel with the eyes, in the style of that described by Byron in *Don Juan*.* Nicholas got up: he felt that he had met his match.

[2] The President of the Academy proposed Arakcheyev as honorary member. Alexander Fëdorovich Labzin (1766-1825), asked in what the Count's services to the arts consisted. The President was at a loss and answered that Arakcheyev was the man who was closest to the Tsar. 'If that is sufficient reason, then I propose his coachman, Ilya Baykov,' observed the secretary; 'he not only is close to the Tsar, but sits in front of him.' Labzin was a mystic and the editor of the *Messenger of Zion*; Alexander himself was a mystic of the same sort, but with the fall of Golitsyn's ministry he handed over his former 'brethren of Christ and of the inner man' to Arakcheyev to do with as he pleased. Labzin was banished to Simbirsk.

[3] Victor Joseph Étienne de Jouy, a popular French writer (1764-1846). (*Tr.*)

under the supervision of the police and he was considered a liberal, though he was exactly what he had always been; from this fact alone, it is easy to judge of the difference between the two reigns.

Nicholas was completely unknown until he came to the throne; in the reign of Alexander he was of no consequence, and no one was interested in him. Now everyone rushed to inquire about him; no one could answer questions but the officers of the Guards; they hated him for his cold cruelty, his petty fussiness and his vindictiveness. One of the first anecdotes that went the round of the town confirmed the officers' opinion of him. The story was that at some drill or other the Grand Duke had so far forgotten himself as to try and take an officer by the collar. The officer responded with the words: 'Your Highness, my sword is in my hand.' Nicholas drew back, said nothing, but never forgot the answer. After the Fourteenth of December he made inquiries on two occasions as to whether this officer was implicated. Fortunately he was not.[4]

The tone of society changed before one's eyes; the rapid deterioration in morals was a melancholy proof of how little the sense of personal dignity was developed among Russian aristocrats. Nobody (except women) dared utter a warm word about relations or friends, whose hands they had shaken only the day before they had been carried off at night by the police. On the contrary, there were savage fanatics for slavery, some from abjectness, others, worse still, from disinterested motives.

Women alone did not take part in this shameful abandonment of those who were near and dear . . . and women alone stood at the Cross too, and at the blood-stained guillotine there stood, first, Lucile Desmoulins,[5] that Ophelia of the Revolution, always beside the axe,

---

[4] The officer, if I am not mistaken, Count Samoylov, had left the army and was living quietly in Moscow. Nicholas recognised him at the theatre, fancied that he was dressed with rather elaborate originality, and expressed the royal desire that such costumes should be ridiculed on the stage. The theatre director and *patriot*, Zagoskin, commissioned one of his actors to represent Samoylov in some vaudeville. The rumour of this was soon all over the town. When the performance was over, the real Samoylov went into the director's box and asked permission to say a few words to his double. The director was frightened but, afraid of a scene, summoned the actor. 'You have acted me very well,' the Count said to him, 'and the only thing wanting to complete the likeness is this diamond which I always wear; allow me to hand it to you; you will wear it next time you are ordered to represent me.' After this Samoylov calmly returned to his seat. The stupid jest at his expense fell as flat as the proclamation that Chaadayev was mad and other august pranks.

[5] Wife of Camille Desmoulins, who at his execution appealed to the crowd, was arrested and also executed in 1794. (*Tr.*)

waiting for her turn, and later, George Sand, who gave the hand of sympathy and friendship on the scaffold to the youthful fanatic Alibaud.[6]

The wives of men exiled to hard labour lost their civil rights, abandoned wealth and social position, and went to a lifetime of bondage in the terrible climate of Eastern Siberia, under the still more terrible oppression of the police there.[7] Sisters, who had not the right to go with their brothers, withdrew from court, and many left Russia; almost all of them kept a feeling of love for the victims alive in their hearts; but there was no such love in the men: terror consumed it in their hearts, and not one of them dared mention the *unfortunates*.

While I am touching on the subject, I cannot forbear saying a few words about one of those heroic stories of which very little has been heard.

A young French governess was living in the old-fashioned family of the Ivashevs. Ivashev's only son wanted to marry her. This drove all his relations frantic; there was an uproar, tears, petitions. The French girl had not the support of a brother like Chërnov, who on his sister's behalf killed Novosiltsev in a duel and was killed by him. She was persuaded to leave Petersburg, and he to put off for a time his design of marrying her. Ivashev was one of the more active conspirators and he was sentenced to penal servitude for life. His relations did not succeed in saving him from the *mésalliance*. As soon as the dreadful news reached the young girl in Paris, she set off for Petersburg and asked permission to go to the province of Irkutsk to join her betrothed. Benckendorf tried to dissuade her from this criminal intention; he did not succeed and reported the matter to Nicholas. The Tsar directed that the position of women who did not desert their exiled husbands should be explained to her, adding that he would not prevent her going, but that she must know that, if wives who went to Siberia from fidelity to their husbands deserved some indulgence, she had not the slightest right to any since she was wilfully entering into marriage with a criminal.

Nicholas and she both kept their word: she went to Siberia, and he did nothing to alleviate her fate.

'The monarch though severe was just.'[8]

In the prison nothing was known of the permission given her, and

---

[6] Alibaud, Louis (1810-36), attempted to assassinate Louis-Philippe in 1836. (*Tr.*)

[7] See *Russian Women* (1871-72) by Nikolay Alexeyevich Nekrasov (1821-78). (*R.*)

[8] Line from Pushkin's poem, 'The Tsar Nikita'. (*Tr.*)

when the poor girl arrived she had, while a correspondence was carried on with the authorities in Petersburg, to wait in a little settlement inhabited by all sorts of former criminals, with no means of finding out anything about Ivashev or communicating with him.

By degrees she became acquainted with her new companions. Among them was an exiled robber who worked in the prison; she told him her story. Next day the robber brought her a note from Ivashev. A day later he offered to bring her notes from Ivashev and to take her letters to him. He had to work in the prison from morning till evening; at nightfall he would take Ivashev's letter and would set off with it regardless of snowstorms and fatigue, and return to his work by dawn.[9]

At last the permission came and they were married. A few years later penal servitude was exchanged for a settlement. Their situation was somewhat better, but their strength was exhausted; the wife was the first to sink under the weight of all she had gone through. She faded away as a flower of southern lands must fade in the Siberian snows. Ivashev did not survive her: he actually died a year later, but before then he had left this sphere; his letters (which made some impression on the Third Division[10]) bear the traces of an infinitely mournful, holy madness and gloomy poetry; he was not really living after her death, but slowly and solemnly dying.

This chronicle does not end with his death. After Ivashev's exile his father made over his estate to his illegitimate son, begging him to help his poor brother and not to forget him. The exiles left two little boys, helpless, fatherless and motherless, who had neither name nor rights and seemed likely to become *cantonists*[11] and settlers in Siberia. Ivashev's brother entreated Nicholas for permission to take the children. Nicholas granted permission. A few years later he risked another petition: he moved heaven and earth for their father's name to be restored to them; and in this too he was successful.

The accounts of the rising and of the trial of the leaders, and the horror in Moscow, made a deep impression on me; a new

---

[9] The story of V. P. Ivashev and his family is not accurately given by Herzen. The details of it are to be found in O. K. Bylanov: *The Romance of the Decembrists* (Moscow, 1925)—in Russian—in which use has been made of the Ivashev family archives. (*A.S.*)

[10] I.e., the gendarmes, the secret police. (*Tr.*)

[11] '*Cantonists*' were soldiers' sons educated at the government expense and afterwards sent into the army. (*Tr.*)

world was revealed to me which became more and more the centre of my moral existence. I do not know how it came to pass, but, though I had no understanding, or only a very dim one, of what it all meant, I felt that I was not on the same side as the grapeshot and victory, prisons and chains. The execution of Pestel[12] and his associates finally dissipated the childish dream of my soul.

Everyone expected some mitigation of the sentence on the condemned men, since the coronation was about to take place. Even my father, in spite of his caution and his scepticism, said that the death penalty would not be carried out, and that all this was done merely to impress people. But, like everyone else, he knew little of the youthful monarch. Nicholas left Petersburg, and, without visiting Moscow, stopped at the Petrovsky Palace. . . . The inhabitants of Moscow could scarcely believe their eyes when they read in the *Moscow News* the terrible news of the fourteenth of July.*

The Russian people had become unaccustomed to the death penalty; since the days of Mirovich,[13] who was executed instead of Catherine II, and of Pugachëv[14] and his companions, there had been no executions; men had died under the knout, soldiers had run the gauntlet (contrary to the law) until they fell dead, but the death penalty *de jure* did not exist.* The story is told that in the reign of Paul there was some partial rising of the Cossacks on the Don in which two officers were implicated. Paul ordered them to be tried by court martial, and gave the hetman or general full authority. The court condemned them to death, but no one dared to confirm the sentence; the hetman submitted the matter to the Tsar. 'They are a pack of women,' said Paul; 'they want to throw the execution on me: very much obliged to them,' and he commuted the sentence to penal servitude.

Nicholas reintroduced the death penalty into our criminal proceedings, at first illegally, but afterwards he legitimised it into his Code.*

The day after receiving the terrible news there was a religious

---

[12] Pestel, Pavel Ivanovich (1793-1826), leader of the officers in the Southern Army who supported the attempt to overthrow the autocracy and establish constitutional government. The other four who were hanged were Ryleyev, Kakhovsky, Bestuzhev-Ryumin, and Muravëv-Apostol. (*Tr.*)

[13] Mirovich, Vasily Yakovlevich (1740-64), in 1762 tried to rescue from the Schlüsselburg the legitimate heir to the Russian throne, known as Ivan VI, who perished in the attempt. It is said that Catherine had given orders that he was to be murdered if any attempt were made to release him. Mirovich was beheaded. (*Tr.*)

[14] Pugachëv, Emelyan Ivanovich (*c.* 1742-75), the Cossack leader of the great rising of the serfs in 1775. (*Tr.*)

service in the Kremlin.[15] After celebrating the execution Nicholas made his triumphal entry into Moscow. I saw him then for the first time; he was on horseback, riding beside a carriage in which the two empresses, his wife and Alexander's widow, were sitting. He was handsome, but there was a coldness about his looks; no face could have more mercilessly betrayed the character of the man than his. The sharply retreating forehead and the lower jaw developed at the expense of the skull were expressive of iron will and feeble intelligence, rather of cruelty than of sensuality; but the chief point in the face was the eyes, which were entirely without warmth, without a trace of mercy, wintry eyes. I do not believe that he ever passionately loved any woman, as Paul loved Anna Lopukhin,[16] and as Alexander loved all women except his wife; 'he was favourably disposed to them', nothing more.

In the Vatican there is a new gallery in which Pius VII, I believe, placed an immense number of statues, busts, and statuettes, dug up in Rome and its environs. The whole history of the decline of Rome is there expressed in eyebrows, lips, foreheads; from the daughter of Augustus down to Poppaea the matrons have succeeded in transforming themselves into cocottes, and the type of cocotte is predominant and persists; the masculine type, surpassing itself, so to speak, in Antinous and Hermaphroditus, divides into two. On one hand there is sensual and moral degradation, low brows and features defiled by vice and gluttony, bloodshed and every wickedness in the world, petty as in the *hetaira* Heliogabalus, or with pendulous cheeks like Galba; the last type is wonderfully reproduced in the King of Naples. . . . But there is another—the type of military commander in whom everything that makes a good citizen, everything

[15] Nicholas's victory over the Five was celebrated by a religious service in Moscow. In the midst of the Kremlin the Metropolitan Filaret thanked God for the murders. The whole of the Royal Family* took part in the service, near them the Senate and the ministers and in the immense space around, packed masses of the Guards knelt bareheaded, and also took part in the prayers; cannon thundered from the heights of the Kremlin. Never have the gallows been celebrated with such pomp; Nicholas knew the importance of the victory!

I was present at that service, a boy of fourteen lost in the crowd, and on the spot, before that altar defiled by bloody rites, I swore to avenge the murdered men, and dedicated myself to the struggle with that throne, with that altar, with those cannon. I have not avenged them: the Guards and the throne, the altar and the cannon all remain, but for thirty years I have stood under that flag and have never once deserted it. (*The Pole Star, 1855*.)

[16] Paul's mistress, the daughter of Lopukhin, the chief of the Moscow Police, better known under her married name as Princess Gagarin. (*Tr.*)

human, has died out, and there is left nothing but the passion for domination; the mind is narrow and there is no heart at all; they are the monks of the love of power; strength and harshness of will are manifest in their features. Such were the Emperors of the Prae-torian Guard and of the army, whom mutinous legionaries raised to power for an hour. Among their number I found many heads that recalled Nicholas before he wore a moustache. I understand the necessity for these grim and inflexible guards beside one who is dying in frenzy, but what use are they to one who is young, whose career is just starting?

In spite of the fact that political dreams absorbed me day and night, my ideas were not distinguished by any peculiar insight; they were so confused that I actually imagined that the object of the Petersburg rising was, among other things, to put the Tsesarevitch Constantine on the throne, while limiting his power. This led to my being devoted for a whole year to that eccentric creature. He was at that time more popular than Nicholas; for what reason I do not know, but the masses, for whom he had never done anything good, and the soldiers, to whom he had done nothing but harm, loved him. I well remember how during the coronation he walked beside the pale-faced Nicholas with puckered, light-yellow, bristling eye-brows, a bent figure with the shoulders hunched up to the ears, wearing the uniform of the Lettish Guards with a yellow collar. After giving away the bride at the wedding of Nicholas with Russia, he went away to complete the disaffection of Warsaw. Nothing more was heard of him until the 29th of November, 1830.[17]

My hero was not handsome and you could not find such a type in the Vatican. I should have called it the *Gatchina*[18] type, if I had not seen the King of Sardinia.

I need hardly say that now loneliness weighed upon me more than ever, for I longed to communicate my ideas and my dreams to someone, to test them and to hear them confirmed; I was too proudly conscious of being 'ill-intentioned' to say nothing about it, or to speak of it indiscriminately.

My first choice of a confidant was my Russian tutor.

[17] The date when the Polish rebellion broke out. (*Tr.*)
[18] Gatchina was an estate which had belonged to Grigory Orlov. Catherine II bought it from his executors and presented it to Paul. He ran it like a barracks and drilled his battalions there, which were largely composed of criminals and runaways. (*R.*)

C

I. E. Protopopov was full of that vague and generous liberalism which often passes away with the first grey hair, with marriage and a post, but yet does ennoble a man. My teacher was touched, and as he was taking leave embraced me with the words: 'God grant that these feelings may ripen and grow stronger in you.' His sympathy was a great comfort to me. After this he began bringing me much-soiled manuscript copies in small handwriting of poems: 'An Ode to Freedom' and 'The Dagger' by Pushkin, and Ryleyev's 'Thoughts'. I used to copy them in secret . . . (*and now* I print them openly!).

Of course my reading, too, took a different turn. Politics was now in the foreground, and above all the history of the Revolution, of which I knew nothing except from Madame Proveau's tales. In the library in the basement I discovered a history of the 'nineties written by a Royalist. It was so partial that even at fourteen I did not believe it. I happened to hear from old Bouchot that he had been in Paris during the Revolution, and I longed to question him; but Bouchot was a stern and forbidding man with an immense nose and spectacles; he never indulged in superfluous conversation with me; he conjugated verbs, dictated copies, scolded me and went away, leaning on his thick gnarled stick.

'Why did they execute Louis XVI?' I asked him in the middle of a lesson.

The old man looked at me, frowning with one grey eyebrow and lifting the other, pushed his spectacles up on his forehead like a visor, pulled out a large blue handkerchief and, wiping his nose with dignity, said:

'*Parce qu'il a été traître à la patrie.*'

'If you had been one of the judges, would you have signed the death sentence?'

'With both hands.'

This lesson was of more value to me than all the subjunctives; it was enough for me; it was clear that the king had deserved to be executed.

Old Bouchot did not like me and thought me empty-headed and mischievous, because I did not prepare my lessons properly, and he often used to say, 'You'll come to no good', but when he noticed my sympathy with his regicide ideas, he began to be gracious instead of being cross, forgave my mistakes and used to tell me episodes of the year '93, and how he had left France, when 'the dissolute and the dishonest' got the upper hand. He would finish the lesson with the same dignity, without a smile, but now he would say indulgently:

'I really did think that you were coming to no good, but your generous feelings will be your salvation.'

To this encouragement and sympathy from my teacher was soon added a warmer sympathy which had more influence on me.

The granddaughter[19] of my father's eldest brother was living in a little town in the province of Tver. I had known her from my earliest childhood, but we rarely met; she used to come once a year for Christmas or for carnival to stay at Moscow with her aunt. Nevertheless, we became friends. She was five years older than I, but so small and young-looking that she might have been taken for the same age. What I particularly liked her for was that she was the first person who treated me as a human being, that is, did not continually express surprise at my having grown, ask me what lessons I was doing, and whether I was good at them, and whether I wanted to go into the army and into what regiment, but talked to me as people in general talk to each other; though she retained that tone of authority which girls like to assume with boys who are a little younger than themselves.

We had been writing to each other since 1824, and frequently, but letters again mean pens and paper, again the schoolroom table with its blots and pictures carved with a penknife; I longed to see her, to talk to her about my new ideas, and so it may be imagined with what joy I heard that my cousin was coming in February (1826), and would stay with us for some months. I scratched on my table the days of the month until her arrival and blotted them out as they passed, sometimes intentionally forgetting three days so as to have the pleasure of blotting out rather more at once, and yet the time dragged on very slowly; then the time fixed had passed and another was fixed, and that passed, as always happens.

I was sitting one evening with my tutor Protopopov in my schoolroom, and he, as usual, taking a sip of fizzing *kvas* after every sentence, was talking of the hexameter, horribly chopping up, with voice and hand, every line of Gnedich's *Iliad* into feet, when all of a sudden the snow in the yard crunched with a different sound from that made by town sledges, the tied-up bell gave the relic of a tinkle, there were voices in the courtyard . . . I flushed crimson, I had no

---

[19] Tatyana Kuchin, known in Russian literature under her married name, Passek. She wrote *Memoirs*, which throw interesting sidelights on Herzen's narrative. (*Tr.*)

more thought for the wrath of 'Achilles, son of Peleus'; I rushed headlong to the hall and my cousin from Tver, wrapped in fur coats, shawls, and scarves, wearing a hood and high, white fur boots, flushed with the frost and, perhaps, with joy, rushed to kiss me.

People usually recall their early childhood, its griefs and joys, with a smile of condescension, as though like Sofya Pavlovna in *Woe from Wit*,[20] they would say, looking prim: 'Childishness!' As though they had grown better in later years, as though their feelings were keener or deeper. Within three years children are ashamed of their playthings—let them: they long to be grown-up, they grow and change so rapidly, they see that from their jackets and the pages of their schoolbooks; but one would have thought grown-up people might understand that childhood together with two or three years of youth is the fullest, most exquisite part of life, the part that is most our own, and, indeed, almost the most important, for it imperceptibly shapes our future.

So long as a man is advancing with swift footsteps, without stopping or taking thought, so long as he does not come to a precipice or break his neck, he imagines that his life lies before him, looks down on the past and does not know how to appreciate the present. But when experience has crushed the flowers of spring and has chilled the glow on the cheeks of summer, when he begins to suspect that life, properly speaking, is over, and what remains is its continuation, then he returns with different feelings to the bright, warm, lovely memories of early youth.

Nature with her everlasting snares and economic devices *gives* man youth, but *takes* the formed man for herself; she draws him on, entangles him in a web of social and family relations, three-fourths of which are independent of his will; he, of course, gives his personal character to his actions, but he belongs to himself far less than in youth; the lyrical element in the personality is feebler and therefore also his senses and his power of enjoyment—everything —is weaker, except the mind and the will.

My cousin's life was not a bed of roses. Her mother she lost when she was a child. Her father was a desperate gambler, and, like all who have gambling in their blood, he was a dozen times reduced to poverty and a dozen times rich again, and ended all the same by completely ruining himself. *Les beaux restes* of his property he

---

[20] By A. S. Griboyedov. (Act I, scene 7.) (*A.S.*)

devoted to a stud-farm on which he concentrated all his thoughts and feelings. His son, an ensign in the Uhlans, my cousin's only brother and a very good-natured youth, was going the straight road to ruin; at nineteen he was already a more passionate gambler than his father.

At fifty the father, for no reason at all, married an old maid who had been a pupil in the Smolny Convent.[21] Such a complete, perfect type of the Petersburg boarding-school mistress it has never been my lot to meet. She had been one of the best pupils, and afterwards had become *dame de classe* in the school; thin, fair, and short-sighted, there was something didactic and edifying in her very appearance. Not at all stupid, she was full of an icy exaltation in her speech, talked in hackneyed phrases of virtue and devotion, knew chronology and geography by heart, spoke French with a revolting correctness and concealed within her an egotism that bordered on the factitious modesty of a Jesuit. In addition to these traits of the 'seminarists in yellow shawls'[22] she had others which were purely Nevsky or Smolny characteristics. She used to raise to heaven eyes full of tears as she spoke of the visits of their common mother (the Empress Marya Fëdorovna), was in love with the Emperor Alexander and, I remember, used to wear a locket, or a signet ring, with an extract in it of a letter from the Empress Elizabeth, *'Il a repris son sourire de bienveillance!'*

The reader can picture the harmonious trio: the father a gambler, passionately devoted to horses, gypsies, noise, carousals, races and trotting matches; the daughter brought up in complete independence, accustomed to do what she liked in the house; and the learned lady who, from an elderly schoolmistress, had been turned into a young wife. Of course, she did not like her stepdaughter, and of course her stepdaughter did not like her; as a rule great affection can only exist between women of five-and-thirty and girls of seventeen when the former, with resolute self-sacrifice, determine to have no sex.

I am not at all surprised at the usual hostility between stepdaughters and stepmothers: it is natural and it is morally right. The new person put into the mother's place excites aversion in the children; the second marriage is for them like a second funeral. The children's love is vividly expressed in this feeling and it whispers to the

---

[21] Originally a convent, this was a famous girls' school founded by Catherine II. (*Tr.*)

[22] A. S. Pushkin: *Yevgeny Onegin*, III, 28. (*A.S.*)

orphans: 'Your father's wife is not your mother at all.' At first
Christianity understood that with the conception of marriage which
it developed, with the immortality of the soul which it preached, a
second marriage was altogether incongruous; but, making continual
concessions to the world, the Church was too artful by half and
was confronted with the implacable logic of life, with the simple
childish heart that in practice revolts against the pious absurdity of
regarding its father's companion as its mother.

On her side, too, the woman, who comes to her new home from
her wedding and finds a ready-made family awaiting her, is in an
awkward position; she has nothing to do with them, she must affect
feelings which she cannot have, she must persuade herself and
others that another woman's children are as dear to her as if they
were her own.

And therefore I do not in the least blame the lady from the convent
nor my cousin for their mutual dislike, but I understand how the
young girl, unaccustomed to discipline, was fretting to escape to
freedom, wherever that might be, out of the parental home. Her
father was beginning to get old and was more and more under the
thumb of his learned wife. Her brother, the Uhlan, was going from
bad to worse and, in fact, life was not pleasant at home; at last she
persuaded her stepmother to let her come for some months, possibly
even for a year, to us.

The day after her arrival my cousin turned the whole order of
my life, except my lessons, upside down, arbitrarily fixed hours for
our reading together, advised me not to read novels, but recommended Ségur's *Universal History* and the *Travels of Anacharsis*. Her
stoical ideals led her to oppose my marked inclination for smoking
in secret, which I did by rolling the tobacco in paper (cigarettes did
not exist in those days); in general, she liked preaching morality to
me, and if I did not obey her teaching at least I listened meekly.
Luckily she could not keep up to her own standards and, forgetting
her rules, she read Zschokke's[23] tales with me instead of an archæo-
logical novel, and secretly sent a boy out to buy, in winter, buckwheat
cakes and pease-pudding with vegetable oil, and in summer goose-
berries and currants.

[23] Heinrich Zschokke (1771-1848), wrote in German *Tales of Swiss Life*, in five
vols., and also dramas—as well as a religious work *Stunden der Andacht*, in eight
vols., which was widely read up to the middle of the nineteenth century and was
attacked for ascribing more importance to religious feeling than to orthodox belief.
(*Tr.*)

I think my cousin's influence over me was very good; a warm element came with her into the cell-like seclusion of my youth; it fostered and perhaps, indeed, preserved the scarcely developed feelings which might very well have been completely crushed by my father's irony. I learnt to be observant, to be wounded by a word, to care about my friends, to love; I learnt to talk about my feelings. She supported my political aspirations, predicted for me an unusual future and fame, and I, with childish vanity, believed her that I was a future 'Brutus or Fabricius'.

To me alone she confided the secret of her love for an officer in the Alexandriinsky Regiment of Hussars, in a black pelisse and black dolman; it was a genuine secret, for the hussar himself, as he commanded his squadron, never suspected what a pure flame was glowing for him in the bosom of a girl of eighteen. I do not know whether I envied his lot—probably I did a little—but I was proud of having been chosen as her confidant, and imagined (after Werther) that this was one of those tragic passions, which would have a great *dénouement* accompanied by suicide, poison, and a dagger, and the idea even occurred to me that I might go to him and tell him all about it.

My cousin had brought shuttlecocks from Korcheva, and in one of the shuttlecocks there was a pin; she would never play with any other, and whenever it fell to me or anyone else she would take it, saying she was used to playing with it. The demon of mischief, which was always my evil tempter, prompted me to change the pin, that is, to stick it in another shuttlecock. The trick succeeded perfectly: my cousin always took the one with the pin in it. A fortnight later I told her; her face changed, she dissolved into tears and went off to her own room. I was frightened and unhappy and, after waiting for half an hour, went to see her; her door was locked. I begged her to open it; she refused to let me in and said that she was ill, that I was no friend of hers, but a heartless boy. I wrote her a note and besought her to forgive me; after tea we made it up, I kissed her hand, she embraced me and at once explained the full importance of the matter. A year before the hussar had dined with them and after dinner played battledore and shuttlecock with her—it was his shuttlecock that had been marked with a pin. I had pangs of conscience: I thought that I had committed a real sacrilege.

My cousin stayed until October. Her father sent for her to come home, promising to let her come to us at Vasilevskoye the following year. We were horrified at the idea of parting, but so it was: one autumn day a *brichka* came for her; her maid carried off boxes and baskets to pack in it, and our servants put in all sorts of provisions for a full week's journey, and crowded at the entrance to say good-bye. We hugged each other hard, she wept and I wept—the *brichka* drove out into the street, turned into a side-street near the very place where the buckwheat cakes and pease-pudding were sold, and vanished. I walked about in the courtyard: and there it was rather cold and nasty; I went up into my room—and there it seemed cold and empty. I set to work on my lesson for Protopopov, while I wondered where the *brichka* was now, and whether it had passed the town-gate or not.

My only comfort was the thought of our being together again at Vasilevskoye the following June!

For me the country was always a time of renewal; I was passionately fond of country life. The forest, the fields, and the freedom— it was all so new for me who had been brought up in cotton-wool, within brick walls, not daring on any pretext to go out beyond the gate without asking leave and being accompanied by a footman. . . .

'Are we going to Vasilevskoye or not?' From early spring I was quite engrossed by this question. My father invariably said that this year he was going away early, that he longed to see the leaves come out; but he could never be ready before July. Some years he was so much behind that we never went at all. He wrote to the country every winter that the house was to be ready and thoroughly warmed, but this was done from deep considerations of policy rather than quite seriously, in order that the village head-man and the clerk to the *Zemstvo* might be afraid he would soon be coming and look after their work more carefully.

It seemed that we were going. My father told the Senator that he was longing to rest in the country and that the estate needed his inspection, but again weeks went by.

Little by little there seemed more ground for hope: provisions began to be sent off, sugar, tea, all sorts of cereals, and wine—and again there was a pause; then at last an order was despatched to the village elder to send so many peasants' horses by such a day—and so we were going, we were going!

I did not think then how onerous the loss of four or five days, when work in the fields was at its height, must have been to the peasants, but rejoiced with all my heart and hastened to pack my lesson-books and exercise books. The horses were brought, and with inward satisfaction I heard their munching and snorting in the courtyard, and took great interest in the bustle of the coachmen, and the wrangling of the servants as to who should sit in which cart and where each should put his belongings. In the servants' quarters lights were burning until daybreak, and all were packing, dragging sacks and bags from place to place, and dressing for the journey (which was fifty miles at most!). My father's valet was the most exasperated of all, for he realised how important it was to stow things properly; with intense irritation he fiercely ejected everything which had been put in by others, tore his hair with vexation and was quite unapproachable.

My father did not get up a bit earlier next day; in fact I think he got up later than usual, and drank his coffee just as slowly, but at last, at eleven o'clock, he ordered the horses to be put to. Behind the carriage, which had four seats and was drawn by six of my father's own horses, there came three and sometimes four conveyances—a barouche, a *brichka*, a wagon or, instead of it, two carts; all these were filled with the house-serfs and their belongings and, although wagon-loads had been sent on beforehand, everything was so tightly packed that no one could sit with comfort.

We stopped half-way to have dinner and to feed the horses in the big village of Perkhushkovo, the name of which occurs in Napoleon's bulletins. This village belonged to the son of that elder brother of my father's of whom I have spoken in connection with the division of the property. The neglected house of the owner stood on the high-road, surrounded by flat, cheerless-looking fields; but even this dusty vista delighted me after the cramped life of town. In the house the warped floors and stairs shook, noises and footsteps resounded loudly, and the walls echoed them as it were with astonishment. The old-fashioned furniture from the former owner's cabinet of curiosities was living out its day here in exile; I wandered with curiosity from room to room, went upstairs and downstairs and finally into the kitchen. There our man-cook, with a cross and ironical expression, was preparing a hasty dinner. The steward, a grey-haired old man with a swelling on his head, was usually sitting in the kitchen; the cook addressed his remarks to him and criticised the stove and the hearth, while the steward listened to him and from time to time answered laconically: 'May-be; perhaps it's so,' and looked disconsolately at all the upset, wondering when the devil would carry us off again.

The dinner was served on a special English service, made of tin or

c*

some composition, bought *ad hoc*. Meanwhile the horses had been put in; in the hall and vestibule people who were fond of watching meetings and leave-takings of the gentry were gathering together: footmen who were finishing their lives on bread and pure country air, old women who had been prepossessing maids thirty years before, all the locusts of a landowner's household who through no fault of their own eat up the peasants' labour like real locusts. With them came children with flaxen hair; barefooted and dirty, they kept poking forward while the old women pulled them back. The children screamed and the old women screamed at them; and they caught me at every opportunity, and marvelled every year that I had grown so much. My father said a few words to them; some went up to kiss his hand, which he never gave them, others bowed, and we set off.

A few miles from Prince Golitsyn's estate of Vyazma the head-man of Vasilevskoye was waiting for us on horseback at the edge of the forest, and he escorted us on a by-road. In the village by the big house, approached by a long avenue of limes, we were met by the priest, his wife, the church servitors, the house-serfs, several peasants, and Pronka, the fool, the only one with any feeling of human dignity, for he did not take off his greasy hat, but stood smiling at a little distance and took to his heels as soon as anyone from the town servants tried to come near him.

I have seen few places more pleasant to look at than Vasilevskoye. For anyone who knows Kuntsevo and Yusupov's Arkhangelskoye, or Lopukhin's estate facing the Savva monastery, it is enough to say that Vasilevskoye lies on a continuation of the same bank of the Moskva, twenty miles from the monastery. On the sloping side of the river lie the village, the church, and the old manor house. On the other side there is a hill and a small village, and there my father had built a new house. The view from it embraced the country within a radius of ten miles; far and wide rolled seas of quivering corn; homesteads and villages with white churches could be seen here and there; forests of various hues made a semi-circular setting, and the Moskva like a pale blue ribbon ran through it all. Early in the morning I opened the window in my room upstairs and looked and listened and breathed.

And yet I regretted the old stone house, perhaps because it was in it that I first made acquaintance with the country; I so loved the long, shady avenue leading up to it and the garden that had run wild; the house was falling into ruins and a slender, graceful birch tree was growing out of a crack in the wall of the vestibule. On the left an avenue of willows ran along the riverside, beyond it there were reeds and the white sand down to the river; on that sand and among those reeds I used at eleven and twelve years old to play for a whole morning. A bent old man, the gardener, used nearly always to be sitting before the house; he used to triple-distil peppermint liquor, cook berries, and secretly regale me with all sorts of vegetables. There were great numbers of crows in the garden : the tops of the trees were covered with their nests, and they used to circle round them, cawing; sometimes, especially towards the evening, they used to take wing, hundreds at a time, racing after one another with a great clamour; sometimes one would fly hurriedly from tree to tree and then all would be still. . . . And towards night an owl would wail somewhere in the distance like a child, or go off into a peal of laughter. . . . I was afraid of these wild wailing sounds and yet I went to listen to them.

Every year, or, at least, every other year, we used to go to Vasilevskoye. As I went away I used to measure my height on the wall by the balcony, and I went at once on arriving to find how much I had grown. But in the country I could measure not only my physical growth: these periodical returns to the same objects showed me plainly the difference in my inner development. Other books were brought, other objects interested me. In 1823 I was still quite a child; I had children's books with me, and even those I did not read, but was much more interested in a hare and a squirrel which lived in the loft near my room. One of my principal enjoyments consisted in my father's permission to fire a small cannon every evening, an operation which of course entertained all the servants, and grey-haired old men of fifty were as much diverted as I was. In 1827 I brought with me Plutarch and Schiller; early in the morning I used to go out into the forest, as far as I could into the thickest part of it and, imagining that I was in the Bohemian forests,[24] read aloud to myself. Nevertheless, I was greatly interested also in a dam which I was making in a small stream with the help of a serf-boy, and would run a dozen times a day to look at it and repair it. In 1829 and 1830 I was writing a philosophical article on Schiller's *Wallenstein*, and of my old toys none but the cannon retained its charm.

Besides firing the cannon there was, however, another enjoyment

[24] The scene of Schiller's *Die Räuber*. (*A.S.*)

for which I retained an unalterable passion—watching the evenings in the country; now as then such evenings are for me still times of devoutness, peace, and poetry. One of the last serenely bright moments in my life reminds me also of those village evenings. The sun was sinking majestically, brilliantly, into an ocean of fire, was dissolving into it. . . . All at once the rich purple was followed by deep blue dusk, and everything was covered with a smoky mist: in Italy the darkness falls quickly. We mounted our mules; on the way from Frascati to Rome we had to ride through a little village; here and there lights were already twinkling; everything was still, the hoofs of the mules rang on the stone, a fresh and rather damp wind was blowing from the Apennines. As we came out of the village, there was a little Madonna standing in a niche with a lamp burning before her; some peasant girls as they came from work with white kerchiefs on their heads sank on their knees and chanted a prayer; they were joined by some needy *pifferari* who were passing by. I was deeply affected, deeply touched. We looked at each other . . . and rode on at a slow pace to the inn where a carriage was waiting for us. As we drove homewards I talked of the evenings at Vasilevskoye. But what was there to tell?

> '*In silence stood the garden trees,*
> *Among the hills the village lay,*
> *And thither at the fall of night*
> *The lingering cattle wend their way.*'

N. P. Ogarëv: *Humorous Verse.*

. . . The shepherd cracks his long whip and plays on his birch-bark pipe; there is the lowing and bleating and stamping of the herds returning over the bridge, the dog with a bark chases a straying sheep while she runs with a sort of wooden gallop; and then the songs of the peasant girls, on their way home from the fields, come closer and closer; but the path turns off to the right and the sounds recede again. From the houses children, little girls, run out at the creaking gates to meet their cows and sheep; work is over. The children are playing in the street and on the river-bank, their voices ring out with shrill clarity over the river in the evening glow; the scorched smell of barns mingles with the air, the dew begins little by little to spread like smoke over the fields, the wind moves over the forest with a sound as though the leaves were boiling, the summer lightning, quivering, lights up the landscape with a dying, tremulous azure, and Vera Artamonovna, grumbling rather than cross, says, coming upon me under a lime tree:

'How is it there's no finding you anywhere? And tea has been served long ago and everyone is at table. Here I have been looking and looking for you until my legs are tired. I can't go running about at my age; and why are you lying on the damp grass like that? . . . you'll have a cold to-morrow, I'll be bound.'

'Oh, that'll do, that'll do,' I say to the old woman with a laugh; 'I shan't have a cold and I don't want any tea, but you steal me the best of the cream from the very top.'

'Well, you really are a boy, there's no being angry with you . . . what a sweet tooth you've got! I have got the cream ready for you without your asking. Look at the lightning . . . well, that's right! It brings the corn on.'

And I go home skipping and whistling.

We did not go to Vasilevskoye after 1832. My father sold it while I was in exile. In 1843 we stayed at another estate in the Moscow province, in the district of Zvenigorod, about fourteen miles from Vasilevskoye. I could not help going over to visit my old home. And here we were again riding along the same by-road; the familiar fir-wood and the hill covered with nut trees came into view, and then the ford over the river, the ford that had so delighted me twenty years before, the gurgling of the water, the crunching of the pebbles, the shouting coachman and the struggling horses . . . and here was the village and the priest's house where he used to sit on a bench in a dark-brown cassock, simple-hearted, good-natured, red-haired, always in a sweat, always nibbling something and always afflicted with a hiccup; and here was the counting-house where the clerk Vasily Yepifanov, who was never sober, used to write his accounts, huddled up over the paper, holding the pen by the very end with his third finger bent tightly under it. The priest is dead and Vasily Yepifanov is keeping accounts and getting drunk in another village. We stopped at the village head-man's hut, but found only the wife at home, for her husband was in the fields.

A strange element had crept in during those ten years; instead of our house on the hill there was a new one, and a new garden was laid out beside it. As we turned by the church and the graveyard we met a deformed-looking creature, dragging itself along almost on all fours; it was trying to show me something, and I went up: it was a hunchbacked, paralytic old woman, half-crazy, who used to live on charity and work in the former priest's garden. She had been about seventy then and death had just passed by her. She recognised me, shed tears, shook her head and kept saying:

'Ough! why even you are getting old. I only knew you from your walk, while I—there, there, ough! ough! don't talk of it!'

As we were driving back, I saw in the fields in the distance the village head-man, the same as in our time. At first he did not know me, but when we had driven by, as though suddenly coming to himself with a start, he took off his hat and bowed low. When we had driven a little farther I turned round; the head-man, Grigory Gorsky, was still standing in the same place, looking after us; his tall, bearded figure, bowing in the midst of the cornfield, gave us a friendly send-off from the home which had passed into the hands of strangers.

Chapter 4

Nick and the Sparrow Hills

'Write then how in this place (the Sparrow Hills) the story of our lives, yours and mine, developed.'

A Letter, 1833.

THREE years before the time I am speaking of we were walking on the banks of the Moskva at Luzhniki, that is, on the other side of the Sparrow Hills. At the river's edge we met a French tutor of our acquaintance in nothing but his shirt; he was panic-stricken and was shouting, 'He is drowning, he is drowning!' But before our friend had time to take off his shirt or put on his trousers a Ural Cossack ran down from the Sparrow Hills, dashed into the water, vanished, and a minute later reappeared with a frail man, whose head and arms were flopping about like clothes hung out in the wind. He laid him on the bank, saying, 'He'll still recover if we roll him about.'

The people standing round collected fifty roubles and offered it to the Cossack. The latter, without making faces over it, said very simply: 'It's a sin to take money for such a thing, and it was no trouble; come to think of it, he weighs no more than a cat. We are poor people, though,' he added. 'Ask, we don't; but there, if people give, why not take? we are humbly thankful.' Then tying up the money in a handkerchief he went to graze his horses on the hill. My father asked his name and wrote about the incident next day to Essen. Essen promoted him to be a non-commissioned officer. A few months later the Cossack came to see us and with him a pock-marked, bald German, smelling of scent and wearing a curled, fair wig; he came to thank us on behalf of the Cossack—it was the drowned man. From that time he took to coming to see us.

Karl Ivanovich Sonnenberg, that was his name, was at that time completing the German part of the education of two young rascals; from them he went to a landowner of Simbirsk, and from him to a

65

distant relative of my father's. The boy, the care of whose health and German accent had been entrusted to him, and whom Sonnenberg called Nick, attracted me. There was something kind, gentle and pensive about him; he was not at all like the other boys it had been my luck to meet, but nevertheless, we became close friends. He was silent and pensive: I was high-spirited but afraid to rag him.

About the time when my cousin went back to Korcheva, Nick's grandmother died; his mother he had lost in early childhood. There was a great upset in the house and Sonnenberg, who really had nothing to do, fussed about too, and imagined that he was run off his legs; he brought Nick in the morning and asked that he might remain with us for the rest of the day. Nick was sad and frightened; I suppose he had been fond of his grandmother. He poetically recalled her thus in after years:

'When even's golden beams are blent
With rosy vistas, radiant hued,
I call to mind how in our home
The ancient customs we pursued.
On every Sunday's eve there came
Our grey and stately priest arrayed,
And, bowing to the holy shrine,
With his assistants knelt and prayed.
Our grandmamma, the honoured dame,
Would lean upon her spacious chair
And, fingering her rosary,
Would bend her head in whispered prayer.
And through the doorway we could see
The house-servants' familiar faces,
As praying for a ripe old age
They knelt in their accustomed places.
Meantime, upon the window-panes
The evening glow would shine, reflected,
While incense floated through the hall
By censers, swinging wide, projected.
Amid the silence so profound
No sound was heard except the praying
Of mingled voices. On my heart
Some feeling undefined was weighing,
A wistful sadness, dim and vague,

Of fleeting, childish dreams begot.
Unknown to me my heart was full
Of yearning for I knew not what.'
N. P. Ogarëv: *Humorous Verse.*[1]

. . . After we had been sitting still a little I suggested reading
Schiller. I was surprised at the similarity of our tastes; he knew far
more by heart than I did and knew precisely the passages I liked
best; we closed the book and, so to speak, began sounding each
other's sympathies.

From Möros who went with a dagger in his sleeve 'to free the city
from the tyrant', from Wilhelm Tell who waited for Vogt on the
narrow path at Küsznacht, the transition to Nicholas and the Fourteenth of December was easy. These thoughts and these comparisons
were not new to Nick; he, too, knew Pushkin's and Ryleyev's[2] unpublished poems. The contrast between him and the empty-headed
boys I had occasionally met was striking.

Not long before, walking near the Presnensky Ponds, full of my
Bouchot terrorism, I had explained to a companion of my age the
justice of the execution of Louis XVI.

'Quite so,' observed the youthful Prince O., 'but you know he was
God's anointed!'

I looked at him with compassion, ceased to care for him and never
asked to go and see him again.

There were no such barriers with Nick: his heart beat as mine did.
He, too, had cast off from the grim conservative shore, and we had
but to shove off together, and almost from the first day we resolved to
work in the interests of the Tsesarevich Constantine!

Before that day we had few long conversations. Karl Ivanovich
pestered us like an autumn fly and spoilt every conversation with his
presence; he interfered in everything without understanding, made
remarks, straightened Nick's shirt collar, was in a hurry to get home:
in fact, was detestable. After a month we could not pass two days
without seeing each other or writing a letter; with all the impulsiveness of my nature I attached myself more and more to Nick, while
he had a quiet, deep love for me.

From the very beginning our friendship was to take a serious tone.

---

[1] Translated by Juliet Soskice. (*Tr.*)

[2] Ryleyev, Kondrati Fëdorovich (1795-1826), one of the leaders of the Decembrists:
he was hanged for his part in the conspiracy. (*R.*)

I do not remember that mischievous pranks were our foremost interest, particularly when we were alone. Of course we did not sit still: our age came into its own, and we laughed and played the fool, teased Sonnenberg and played with bows and arrows in our courtyard; but at the bottom of it all there was something very different from idle companionship. Besides our being of the same age, besides our 'chemical affinity', we were united by the faith that bound us. Nothing in the world so purifies and ennobles early youth, nothing keeps it so safe as a passionate interest in the whole of humanity. We respected our future in ourselves, we looked at each other as 'chosen vessels', predestined.

Nick and I often walked out into the country. We had our favourite places, the Sparrow Hills, the fields beyond the Dragomilovsky Gate. He would come with Sonnenberg to fetch me at six or seven in the morning, and if I were asleep would throw sand and little pebbles at my window. I would wake up smiling and hasten out to him.

These walks had been instituted by the indefatigable Karl Ivanovich.

In the old-fashioned patriarchal education of Ogarëv, Sonnenberg plays the part of Biron.[3] When he made his appearance the influence of the old male nurse who had looked after the boy was put aside; the discontented oligarchy of the hall were forced against the grain to silence, knowing that there was no overcoming the damned German who fed at the master's table. Sonnenberg made violent changes in the old order of things. The old man who had been nurse positively grew tearful when he learned that the wretched German had taken the young master *himself* to buy ready-made boots at a shop! Sonnenberg's revolution, like Peter I's, was distinguished by a military character even in the most peaceful matters. It does not follow from that that Karl Ivanovich's thin little shoulders had ever been adorned with epaulettes; but nature has so made the German, that if he does not reach the slovenliness and *sans-gêne* of a philologist or a theologian, he is inevitably of a military mind, even though he be a civilian. By virtue of this peculiarity Karl Ivanovich liked tight-fitting clothes, buttoned up and cut with a waist; by virtue of it he was a strict observer of his own rules, and, if he proposed to get up at six o'clock in the morning, he would get Nick up at one minute to six, and in no case later than one minute past, and would go out into the open air with him.

---

[3] Biron, favourite of the Empress Anna Ivanovna, was practically ruler of Russia during her reign and designated as successor by her. (*Tr.*)

The Sparrow Hills, at the foot of which Karl Ivanovich had been so nearly drowned, soon became our 'sacred hills'.

One day after dinner my father proposed to drive out into the country. Ogarëv was with us and my father invited him and Sonnenberg to go too. These expeditions were not a joking matter. Before reaching the town gate we had to drive for an hour or more in a four-seated carriage 'built by Joachim', which had not prevented it from becoming disgracefully shabby in its fifteen years of service, peaceful as they had been, and from being, as it always had been, heavier than a siege gun. The four horses of different sizes and colours which had grown fat and lazy in idleness were covered with sweat and foam within a quarter of an hour; the coachman Avdey was forbidden to let this happen, and so had no choice but to drive at a walk. The windows were usually up, however hot it might be; and with all this we had the indifferently oppressive supervision of my father and the restlessly fussy and irritating supervision of Karl Ivanovich. But we gladly put up with everything for the sake of being together.

At Luzhniki we crossed the river Moskva in a boat at the very spot where the Cossack had pulled Karl Ivanovich out of the water. My father walked, bent and morose as always; beside him Karl Ivanovich tripped along, entertaining him with gossip and scandal. We went on in front of them, and getting far ahead ran up to the Sparrow Hills at the spot where the first stone of Vitberg's temple was laid.

Flushed and breathless, we stood there mopping our faces. The sun was setting, the cupolas glittered, beneath the hill the city extended farther than the eye could reach; a fresh breeze blew on our faces, we stood leaning against each other and, suddenly embracing, vowed in sight of all Moscow to sacrifice our lives to the struggle we had chosen.

This scene may strike others as very affected and theatrical, and yet twenty-six years afterwards I am moved to tears as I recall it; there was a sacred sincerity in it, and our whole life has proved this. But apparently a like destiny defeats all vows made on that spot; Alexander was sincere, too, when he laid the first stone of that temple,[4] which, as Joseph II[5] said (though then mistakenly) at the

---

[4] See Part II, chapter 16. (R.) Alexander I laid the foundation stone on 12th October, 1817. (A.S.)

[5] Joseph II of Austria paid a famous visit to Catherine II of Russia in 1780. (Tr.)

laying of the first stone in some town in Novorossiya, was destined to
be the last.

We did not know all the strength of the foe with whom we were
entering into battle, but we took up the fight. That strength broke
much in us, but it was not that strength that shattered us, and we did
not surrender to it in spite of all its blows. The wounds received from
it were honourable. Jacob's strained thigh was the sign that he had
wrestled in the night with God.

From that day the Sparrow Hills became a place of worship for us
and once or twice a year we went there, and always by ourselves.
There, five years later, Ogarëv asked me timidly and shyly whether I
believed in his poetic talent, and wrote to me afterwards (1833) from
his country house: 'I have come away and feel sad, as sad as I have
never been before. And it's all the Sparrow Hills. For a long time I
hid my enthusiasm in myself; shyness or something else, I don't myself know what, prevented me from uttering it; but on the Sparrow
Hills that enthusiasm was not burdened with solitude: you shared it
with me and those moments have been unforgettable; like memories
of past happiness they have followed me on my way, while round me
I saw nothing but forest; it was all so blue, dark blue, and in my soul
was darkness, darkness.

'Write then,' he concluded, 'how in this place' (that is, on the
Sparrow Hills) 'the story of our lives, yours and mine, began to
unfold.'

Five more years passed. I was far from the Sparrow Hills, but near
me their Prometheus, A. L. Vitberg, stood, austere and gloomy. In
1842, returning finally to Moscow, I again visited the Sparrow Hills,
and once more we stood on the site of the foundation stone and gazed
at the same view, two together, but the other was not Nick.

Since 1827 we had not been parted. In every memory of that time,
general and particular, he with his boyish features and his love for
me was everywhere in the foreground. Early could be seen in him
that sign of grace which is vouchsafed to few, whether for woe or for
bliss I know not, but certainly in order not to be one of the crowd. A
large portrait of Ogarëv as he was at that time (1827-8), painted in
oils, remained for long afterwards in his father's house. In later days
I often stood before it and gazed at him. He is shown with an open
shirt collar; the painter has wonderfully caught the luxuriant chestnut hair, the undefined, youthful beauty of his irregular features and
his rather swarthy colouring; there was a pensiveness in the portrait

that gave promise of powerful thought; an unaccountable melancholy and extreme gentleness shone out from his big grey eyes that suggested the future stature of a mighty spirit; such indeed he grew to be. This portrait, presented to me, was taken by a woman who was a stranger; perhaps these lines will meet her eyes and she will send it to me.

I do not know why the memories of first love are given such precedence over the memories of youthful friendship. The fragrance of first love lies in the fact that it forgets the difference of the sexes, that it is passionate friendship. On the other hand, friendship between the young has all the ardour of love and all its character, the same delicate fear of touching on its feelings with a word, the same mistrust of self and absolute devotion, the same agony at separation, and the same jealous desire for exclusive affection.

I had long loved Nick and loved him passionately, but had not been able to resolve to call him my friend, and when he was spending the summer at Kuntsevo I wrote to him at the end of a letter: 'Whether your friend or not, I do not yet know.' He first used the second person singular in writing to me and used to call me his Agathon after Karamzin,[6] while I called him my Raphael after Schiller.[7]

You will smile, perhaps, but let it be a mild, good-natured smile, such as one smiles when one thinks of the time when one was fifteen. Or would it not be better to muse over the question, 'Was I like that when I was blossoming out?'[8] and to bless your fate if you have had youth (merely being young is not enough for this), and to bless it doubly if you had a friend then.

The language of that period seems affected and bookish to us now; we have become unaccustomed to its vague enthusiasm, its confused fervour that passes suddenly into languid tenderness or childish laughter. It would be as absurd in a man of thirty as the celebrated *Bettina will schlafen*,[9] but in its proper time this language of youth, this *jargon de la puberté*, this change of the psychological voice is very sincere; even the shade of bookishness is natural to the age of theoretical knowledge and practical ignorance.

---

[6] Karamzin, Nikolay Mikhaylovich (1766-1826), author of a great *History of the Russian State*, and also of novels in the sentimental romantic style of his period. (*Tr.*)

[7] In the *Philosophische Briefe*. (*Tr.*)

[8] From A. S. Pushkin: *Onegin's Travels* (*A.S.*)

[9] See the *Tagebuch* of Bettina von Arnim for the account of her famous first interview with Goethe. (*Tr.*)

Schiller remained our favourite.[10] The characters of his dramas were living persons for us; we analysed them, loved and hated them, not as poetic creations but as living men. Moreover we saw ourselves in them. I wrote to Nick, somewhat troubled by his being too fond of Fiesco, that behind every Fiesco stands his Verrina.[11] My ideal was Karl Moor,[12] but soon I was false to him and went over to the Marquis of Posa.[13] I imagined in a hundred variations how I would speak to Nicholas, and how afterwards he would send me to the mines or the scaffold. It is a strange thing that almost all our day-dreams ended in Siberia or the scaffold and hardly ever in triumph; can this be the way the Russian imagination turns, or is it the effect of Petersburg with its five gallows and its penal servitude reflected on the young generation?

And so, Ogarëv, hand in hand we moved forward into life! Fearlessly and proudly we advanced, generously we responded to every challenge and single-heartedly we surrendered to every inclination. The path we chose was no easy one; we have never left it for one moment: wounded and broken we have gone forward and no one has outdistanced us. I have reached . . . not the goal but the spot where the road goes downhill, and involuntarily I seek thy hand that we may go down together, that I may press it and say, smiling mournfully, 'So this is all!'

Meanwhile in the dull leisure to which events have condemned me, finding in myself neither strength nor freshness for new labours, I am writing down *our* memories. Much of that which united us so closely has settled in these pages. I present them to thee. For thee they have a double meaning, the meaning of tombstones on which we meet familiar names.[14]

. . . And is it not strange to think that had Sonnenberg known how to swim, or had he been drowned then in the Moskva, had he been pulled out not by a Cossack of the Urals but by a soldier of the Apsheronsky infantry, I should not have met Nick or should have met him later, differently, not in that room in our old house, where,

---

[10] Schiller's poetry has not lost its influence on me. A few months ago I read *Wallenstein*, that titanic work, aloud to my son. The man who has lost his taste for Schiller has grown old or pedantic, has grown hard or forgotten himself. What is one to say of these precocious *altkluge Burschen* who know his defects so well at seventeen?

[11] Characters in *Die Verschwörung des Fiesco zu Genua*. (R.)

[12] and [13] In *Die Räuber* and *Don Carlos*. (R.)

[14] Written in 1853.

smoking cigars on the sly, we entered so deeply into each other's lives and drew strength from each other.

He did not forget our "old house".

> 'Old Home! My old friend! I have found thee,
> Thy cold desolation I see;
> The past is arising before me,
> And sadly I gaze upon thee.
> Unswept and untended the courtyard,
> Neglected and fallen the well,
> Green leaves that once whispered and murmured
> Lie yellow and dead where they fell.
> The house is dismantled and empty,
> The plaster is spread on the grass,
> The heavy grey clouds wander sadly
> And weep for thy plight as they pass.
> I entered. The rooms were familiar:
> 'Twas here—when we children were young—
> The peevish old man sat and grumbled:
> We feared his malevolent tongue.
> And this room, my friend, oh! my comrade!
> We shared, one in heart and in mind,
> What bright golden thoughts were conceived here
> In days that lie dimly behind!
> A star shimmered faint through the window:
> The words that are left on the wall
> Were written when youth was triumphant,
> Inspirer, dictator of all!
> In this little room love and friendship
> Were fostered. What joys did they bring!
> But now, in its drear empty corners
> The spiders' webs broaden and cling.
> And suddenly, smitten with terror,
> Methought in the graveyard near by
> I stood and I called on my loved ones,
> The dead did not answer my cry . . .'

> N. P. Ogarëv: *The Old House*.[15]

[15] Translated by Juliet Soskice (*Tr.*)

Chapter 5

My Father

THE insufferable dreariness of our house grew greater every year. If my time at the University had not been approaching, if it had not been for my new friendship, my political inclinations and the liveliness of my disposition, I should have run away or perished.

My father was hardly ever in a good humour; he was perpetually dissatisfied with everything. A man of great intelligence and great powers of observation, he had seen, heard, and remembered an immense amount; an accomplished man of the world, he could be extremely amiable and interesting, but he did not care to be so and sank more and more into wayward unsociability.

It is hard to say exactly what it was that put so much bitterness and spleen into his blood. Periods of passion, of great unhappiness, of mistakes and losses were completely absent from his life. I could never fully understand what was the origin of the spiteful mockery and irritability that filled his soul, the mistrustful unsociability and the vexation that consumed him. Did he bear with him to the grave some memory which he confided to no one, or was this simply the result of the combination of two elements so absolutely opposed to each other as the eighteenth century and Russian life, with the intervention of a third, terribly conducive to the development of capricious humour, the idleness of the serf-owning landed gentleman?

Last century produced in the West, particularly in France, a wonderful lode of men endowed with all the weak points of the Regency and all the strong points of Rome and Sparta. These men, Faublas[1] and Regulus together, opened wide the doors of the Revolution and were the first to rush in, crowding each other in their haste to reach the 'window' of the guillotine. Our age no longer produces these single-minded, violent natures; the eighteenth century, on the con-

[1] The hero of *La Vie du Chevalier de Faublas* (1787), by Louvet de Couvray, is the type of the effeminate rake and fashionable exquisite of the period. (*Tr.*)

trary, called them forth everywhere, even where they were not needed, even where they could not develop except into something grotesque. In Russia men exposed to the influence of this mighty Western wind became eccentric, but not historical figures. Foreigners at home, foreigners abroad, idle spectators, spoilt for Russia by Western prejudices and for the West by Russian habits, they were a sort of intellectual superfluity and were lost in artificial life, in sensual pleasure and in unbearable egoism.

To this circle belonged the Tatar Prince, N. B. Yusupov, a Russian grandee and a European *grand seigneur*, a foremost figure in Moscow, conspicuous for his intelligence and his wealth. About him gathered a perfect galaxy of grey-headed gallants and *esprits forts*, all the Masalskys[2] and Santis[3] and *tutti quanti*. They were all quite cultured, well-educated people; having no work in life they flung themselves upon pleasure, pampered themselves, loved themselves, good-naturedly forgave themselves all transgressions, exalted their gastronomy to the level of a Platonic passion and reduced love for women to a sort of voracious gourmandise.

The old sceptic and epicurean Yusupov, a friend of Voltaire and Beaumarchais,[4] of Diderot and Casti,[5] really was gifted with artistic taste. To convince oneself of this, it is enough to make one visit to Arkhangelskoye and look at his galleries, that is, if they have not yet been sold bit by bit by his heir. He was magnificently fading out of life at eighty, surrounded by marble, painted and *living* beauty. In his house near Moscow Pushkin conversed with him, and dedicated to him a wonderful epistle, and Gonzaga[6] painted, to whom Yusupov dedicated his theatre.

By his education, by his service in the Guards, by position and connections, my father belonged to this circle, but neither his character nor his health permitted him to lead a frivolous life to the age of

---

[2] Masalsky, Pëtr Grigorevich (d. 1839) an intimate friend of M. M. Speransky. (*A.S.*)

[3] Santis, Alexander Lvovich, Count, (1769-1838), lieutenant-general; governor of Kiev, 1811. (*A.S.*)

[4] Pierre-Augustin Caron de, see p. 36, fn. (*R.*)

[5] Casti (1721-1803), an Italian poet, 'attached by habit and taste to the polished and frivolous society of the *ancien régime*, his sympathies were nevertheless liberal', satirised Catherine II, and when exiled on that account from Vienna, had the spirit to resign his Austrian pension. The *Talking Animals*, a satire on the predominance of the foreigner in political life, is his best work. The influence of his poems on Byron is apparent in *Don Juan*. (*Tr.*)

[6] Gonzaga was a Venetian painter who came to Petersburg in 1792 to paint scenery for the Court Theatre. He planned the celebrated park at Pavlovsk. (*Tr.*)

seventy: and he went to the opposite extreme. He tried to organise for himself a life of solitude, and there he found waiting for him a deadly dullness, the more because he tried to arrange it entirely *for himself*. His strength of will changed into obstinate caprice, and his unemployed energies spoilt his character, and made it disagreeable.

When he was being educated, European civilisation was still so new in Russia that to be educated meant being so much the less Russian. To the end of his days he wrote more fluently and correctly in French than in Russian. He had literally not read one single book in Russian, not even the Bible, though, indeed, he had not read the Bible in other languages either; he knew the subject-matter of the Holy Scriptures generally from hearsay and from extracts, and had no curiosity to look further into it. He had, it is true, a respect for Derzhavin[7] and Krylov:[8] Derzhavin because he had written an ode on the death of his uncle, Prince Meshchersky, and Krylov because he had been a second with him at N. N. Bakhmetev's duel. My father did once pick up Karamzin's *History of the Russian Empire*, having heard that the Emperor Alexander had read it, but he laid it aside, saying contemptuously: 'It is nothing but Izyaslaviches and Olgoviches: to whom can it be of interest?'

For people he had an open, undisguised contempt—for everyone. Never under any circumstances did he count upon anybody, and I do not remember that he ever applied to any one with any considerable request. He himself did nothing for any one. In his relations with outsiders he demanded one thing only, the observance of the proprieties; *les apparances, les convenances* made up the whole of his moral religion. He was ready to forgive much, or rather to overlook it, but breaches of good form and good manners put him beside himself, and in such cases he was without any tolerance, without the slightest indulgence or compassion. I was rebellious so long against this injustice that at last I understood it. He was convinced beforehand that every man is capable of any evil act; and that, if he does not commit it, it is either that he has no need to, or that the opportunity does not present itself; in the disregard of formalities he saw a personal affront, a disrespect to himself; or a 'plebeian education', which in his opinion excluded a man from all human society.

[7] Derzhavin, Gavril Romanovich (1743-1816), was poet-laureate to Catherine II, and wrote numerous patriotic and a few other odes. (*Tr.*)

[8] Krylov, Ivan Andreyevich (1768-1844), was a very popular writer of fables in verse. (*Tr.*)

'The soul of man,' he used to say, 'is darkness, and who knows what is in any man's soul? I have too much business of my own to be interested in other people's, much less to judge and criticise their intentions; but I cannot be in the same room with an ill-bred man: he offends me, *il me froisse*; of course he may be the best-hearted man in the world and for that he will have a place in para-dise, but I don't want him. What is most important in life is *esprit de conduite*, it is more important than the most superior intellect or any kind of learning. To know how to be at ease everywhere, to put yourself forward nowhere; the utmost courtesy with all and no familiarity with any one.'

My father disliked every sort of *abandon*, every sort of frankness; all this he called familiarity, just as he called every feeling sentiment-ality. He persistently posed as a man superior to all such petty trifles; for the sake of what, with what object? What was the higher interest to which the heart was sacrificed?—I do not know. And for whom did this haughty old man, who despised men so genuinely and knew them so well, play his part of impartial judge?—for a woman whose will he had broken although she sometimes contradicted him; for an invalid who lay always at the mercy of the surgeon's knife; for a boy whose high spirits he had developed into disobe-dience; for a dozen lackeys whom he did not reckon as human beings!

And how much energy, how much patience were spent on it, how much perseverance; and with what marvellous sureness the part was played through to the end in spite of age and illness. Truly the soul of man is darkness.

Later on when I was arrested, and afterwards when I was sent into exile, I saw that the old man's heart was more open to love and even to tenderness than I had thought. I never thanked him for it, not knowing how he would take my gratitude.

Of course he was not happy: always on his guard, always dissatis-fied, he saw with a pang the hostile feelings he roused in all his household; he saw the smile vanish from the face and the words checked at his entrance; he spoke of it with mockery, with vexation, but made not a single concession and went his way with extreme per-sistence. Mockery, irony, cold, caustic, utter contempt, were the tools which he wielded like an artist; he employed them equally against us and against the servants. In early youth one can bear many things better than jeers, and until I went to prison I was actually estranged from my father, and joined with the maids and men-servants in waging a little war against him.

Add to everything else the fact that he had persuaded himself that he was dangerously ill, and was continually undergoing treatment; besides our own household doctor he was visited by two or three others and had three or four consultations a year at least. Visitors, seeing his continually unfriendly face and hearing nothing but complaints of his health, which was far from being so bad as he thought, became fewer. He was angry at this but never reproached a single person nor invited one. A terrible dullness reigned in the house, particularly on the endless winter evenings—two lamps lit a whole suite of rooms; wearing high cloth or lamb's-wool boots (like *valenki*[9]), a velvet cap and a long, white lambskin coat, bowed, with his hands clasped behind his back, the old man walked up and down, followed by two or three brown dogs, and never uttering a word.

A cautiousness, directed towards objects of no value, grew with his melancholy. He managed the estate badly for himself and badly for his peasants. The head-men and his *missi dominici* robbed their master and the peasants; yet everything that could be seen was subjected to double supervision: candles were saved and the thin *vin de Graves* was replaced by sour Crimean wine at the very time when a whole forest was cut down in one village, and in another he was sold his own oats. He had his privileged thieves; the peasant whom he made collector of *obrok*[10] in Moscow and whom he sent every summer to inspect the head-man, the kitchen-garden, the forest, and the field work, in ten years bought a house in Moscow. From a child I hated this 'minister without portfolio'; on one occasion he beat an old peasant in the courtyard in my presence. I was so furious that I clutched him by the beard and almost fainted. From that time until he died in 1845 I could not look at him calmly. I several times asked my father where did Shkun get the money to buy a house.

'That's what sobriety does,' the old man answered; 'he never takes a drop of liquor.'

Every year near the time of carnival the peasants from the Penza province used to bring from near Kerensk *obrok* in kind. For a fortnight a trail of poor-looking wagons was crawling along the road, laden with pigs' carcasses, sucking pigs, goslings, fowls, groats, rye, eggs, butter, and sacking. The arrival of the Kerensk peasants was a

[9] Felt knee-boots. (R.)
[10] See p. 29, fn.

holiday for all the house-serfs; they robbed the peasants and cheated them at every step, and without the slightest right to do so. The coachmen charged them for the water in the well, and would not let them water horses without payment. The women made them pay for warmth in their huts; they had to pay homage to one aristocrat of the hall with a sucking pig and a towel, to another with a goose and some butter. All the time they stayed in the master's courtyard the servants kept up a sumptuous banquet, *solyanki*[11] were made, sucking pigs were roasted, and the hall was continually full of the fumes of onion, burnt fat, and the corn-spirit which had just been consumed. For the last two days of these junketings Bakay did not go into the hall and did not finish dressing, but sat in the outer kitchen with an old livery greatcoat thrown over his shoulders, without his waistcoat and jacket. He was growing visibly thinner and becoming swarthier and older. My father put up with all this fairly calmly, knowing that it was inevitable and could not be hindered.

After the frozen victuals had been received, my father—and the most remarkable point about it is that the farce was repeated every year—used to summon the cook, Spiridon, and send him to Okhotny Ryad and the Smolensky market to find out the prices; the cook returned with fabulously low prices, less than half the real ones. My father would tell him he was a fool and send for Shkun or Slepushkin. The latter had a fruit stall at the Ilyinsky Gate. They both considered the cook's prices terribly low, made inquiries and brought back prices rather higher. At last Slepushkin offered to buy it all wholesale, eggs and sucking pigs and butter and rye 'to save any disturbance to your health, sir'. Of course he offered a price somewhat higher than the cook's. My father agreed. Slepushkin would bring him some oranges and little cakes to bind the bargain, and bring the cook a two-hundred-rouble note.

This Slepushkin was in high favour with my father and often borrowed money from him; he was unusual in having made a profound study of the old man's character.

He would ask for five hundred roubles for two months, and a day before the two months were up would appear in the hall with a cake of some sort on a dish and five hundred roubles on the cake. My father would take the money, Slepushkin would make a bow and ask for his hand to kiss, which his master never gave. But about three days later Slepushkin would come again to borrow money and ask for fifteen hundred roubles. My father would give it and Slepushkin would again bring it by the time fixed. My father used to hold him up as an example, but a week later he would raise the stake, and in that way enjoyed the use of some five thousand roubles a year in ready money to speculate with, for the trifling interest of two or three cakes, a few pounds of figs and walnuts, and a hundred or so oranges and apples from the Crimea.

In conclusion I will mention how some hundreds of acres of building timber disappeared in Novoselye. In the 'forties M. F. Orlov who, I remember, had been given the capital by Countess Anna Alexeyevna[12] to purchase an estate for his children, began treating for the Tver estate which had come to my father from the Senator. They agreed on the price and the business seemed to be settled. Orlov went to inspect the land and, when he had, he wrote to my father that on the map he had shown him a forest, but that there was no such forest.

'That's a clever man,' said my father, 'he took part in the conspiracy and wrote a book *des finances*, but as soon as it comes to business you can see what a silly fellow he is. These Neckers! Well, I'll ask Grigory Ivanovich to ride over; he's not a conspirator, but he's an honest man and knows his work.'

Grigory Ivanovich, too, went over to Novoselye and brought the news that *there was no forest*, but only a stage setting of a forest, so that neither from the big house nor from the high-road did the theft of the trees catch the eye. After the partition of the estate the Senator had been at the very least five times to Novoselye, and yet the secret had never leaked out.

To give a full idea of our manner of life I will describe a whole day from the morning; it was just the monotony that was one of the most deadly things: our life went like an English clock regulated to go slowly—quietly, evenly, loudly recording each second.

At nine o'clock in the morning the valet who sat in the room next the bedroom informed Vera Artamonovna, my ex-nurse, that the master was getting up. She went to prepare the coffee which he always drank alone in his study. Everything in the house assumed a different look: the servants began sweeping the rooms, or at any rate

[12] Countess A. A. Orlov-Chesmensky. (*A.S.*)

made a show of doing something. The hall, empty until then, filled up, and even the big Newfoundland dog Macbeth sat before the stove and watched the fire without blinking.

Over his coffee the old man read the *Moscow News* and the *Journal de St Pétersbourg*. I may mention that orders had been given for the *Moscow News* to be warmed, that his hands might not be chilled by the dampness of the paper, and that he read the political news in the French text, finding the Russian obscure. At one time he used to take in a Hamburg newspaper, but could not reconcile himself to the fact that Germans printed in the German letters, and each time pointed out to me the difference between the French print and the German, saying that these freakish Gothic letters with their little tails weakened the eyesight. Later on he subscribed to the *Journal de Francfort*, but in the end he confined himself to the newspapers of his own country.

When he had finished reading he would observe that Karl Ivanovich Sonnenberg was already in the room. When Nick was fifteen Karl Ivanovich had tried setting up a shop but, having neither goods nor customers, after wasting on this profitable undertaking the money he had somehow scraped up, he retired from it with the honourable title of 'merchant of Reval'. He was by then well over forty, and at that agreeable age he led the life of a bird of the air or a boy of fourteen, that is, did not know where he would sleep next day nor on what he would dine. He took advantage of my father's being somewhat well-disposed towards him; we shall now see what this meant.

In 1830 my father bought near our house another, bigger, better, and with a garden. The house had belonged to Countess Rostopchin, wife of the celebrated Governor of Moscow. We moved into it; after that he bought a third house which was quite unnecessary, but was next it. Both these houses stood empty; they were not let for fear of fire (the houses were insured) and disturbance from tenants. Moreover they were not kept in repair, so they were on the sure road to ruin. In one of them the homeless Karl Ivanovich was permitted to live on condition that he did not open the gates after ten o'clock (not a difficult condition, since the gates were never closed), and that he bought his own firewood and did not get it from our store supplies (he did indeed buy it—from our coachman), and that he served my father in the capacity of an agent for private errands, that is, he came in the morning to inquire whether there were any orders, appeared for dinner and came in the evening, if there was no one else there, to entertain him with stories and the news.

Simple as Karl Ivanovich's duties might appear to be, my father knew how to inject so much bitterness into them that my poor merchant of Reval, accustomed to all the calamities which can fall upon the head of a man with no money, with no brains, who is small in stature, pock-marked and a German, could not endure it perpetually. At intervals of two years or eighteen months, Karl Ivanovich, deeply offended, would declare that 'this is absolutely intolerable', would pack up, buy or exchange various articles of questionable soundness and dubious quality, and set off for the Caucasus. Ill-luck usually pursued him with ferocity. On one occasion his wretched nag—he was driving his own horse to Tiflis and the Kale Redoubt—fell down not far from the land of the Don Cossacks; on another, half his load was stolen from him; on another his two-wheeled gig upset and his French perfumes were spilt over the broken wheel, unappreciated by any one, at the foot of Elbrus; then he would lose something, and when he had nothing left to lose he lost his passport. Ten months later, as a rule, Karl Ivanovich, a little older, a little more battered, a little poorer, with still fewer teeth and less hair, would quite meekly present himself before my father with a store of Persian flea and bed-bug powder, of faded silks and rusty Circassian daggers, and would settle once more in the empty house on the conditions of running errands and using his own firewood to heat his stove.

Observing Karl Ivanovich, my father would at once commence some slight military operations against him. Karl Ivanovich would inquire after his health, the old man would thank him with a bow and then after a moment's thought would inquire, for instance;

'Where do you buy your pomade?'

I must mention here that Karl Ivanovich, the ugliest of mortals, was a fearful dangler after women, considered himself a Lovelace, dressed with pretensions to smartness and wore a curled golden wig. All this, of course, had long ago been weighed and assessed by my father.

'At Bouïs's on the Kuznetsky Most,' Karl Ivanovich would answer abruptly, somewhat piqued, and he would cross one leg over the other like a man ready to stand up for himself.

'What's the scent called?'

'*Nachtviolen,*' answered Karl Ivanovich.

'He cheats you: *la violette* is a delicate scent, *c'est un parfum*; but

that's something strong, repellent—they embalm bodies with something of that sort! My nerves have grown so weak it's made me feel
positively sick; tell them to give me the eau-de-Cologne.'

Karl Ivanovich would himself dash for the flask.

'Oh no, you must call someone, or you will come still closer. I
shall be ill; I shall faint.'

Karl Ivanovich, who was reckoning on the effect of his pomade in
the maids' room, would be deeply chagrined.

After sprinkling the room with eau-de-Cologne my father would
invent some errands: to buy some French snuff and English mag-
nesia, and to look at a carriage advertised for sale in the papers
(he never bought anything). Karl Ivanovich, pleasantly bowing
himself out and sincerely glad to get away, would be gone till
dinner.

After Karl Ivanovich the cook appeared; whatever he had bought
or whatever he had written down, my father thought extremely
expensive.

'Ough, ough, how expensive! Why, is it because no supplies have
come in?'

'Just so, sir,' answered the cook, 'the roads are very bad.'

'Oh very well, till they are mended you and I will buy less.'

After this he would sit down to his writing-table and write reports
and orders to the villages, cast up his accounts, between whiles scolding me, receiving the doctor and chiefly—quarrelling with his valet.
The latter was the greatest sufferer in the whole house. A little,
sanguine man, hasty and hot-tempered, he seemed to have been expressly created to irritate my father and provoke his sermons. The
scenes that were repeated between them every day might have filled a
farce, but it was all perfectly serious. My father knew very well that
the man was indispensable to him and often put up with his rude
answers, but never ceased trying to train him, in spite of his unsuccessful efforts for thirty-five years. The valet on his side would not have
put up with such a life if he had not had his own distractions: more
often than not he was somewhat tipsy by dinner-time. My father
noticed this, but confined himself to roundabout allusions, advising
him, for instance, to munch a little black bread and salt that he
might not smell of vodka. Nikita Andreyevich had a habit, when he
had had too much to drink, of bowing and scraping in a peculiar way
as he handed the dishes. As soon as my father noticed this, he would
invent some errand for him—would send him, for instance, to ask

E

the barber Anton if he had changed his address, adding to me in French,

'I know he has not moved, but the fellow is not sober, he will drop the soup-tureen and smash it, drench the cloth and give me a turn. Let him go out for an airing. *Le grand air* will help.'

To such stratagems the valet usually made some reply, but if he could find nothing to say he would go out, muttering between his teeth. Then his master would call him and in the same calm voice ask him what he had said.

'I didn't address a single word to you.'

'To whom were you speaking, then? Except you and me there is no one in this room or the next.'

'To myself.'

'That's very dangerous; that's the way madness begins.'

The valet would depart in a rage and go to his room next to my father's bedroom; there he used to read the *Moscow News* and plait hair for wigs for sale. Probably to relieve his anger he would take snuff furiously; whether his snuff was particularly strong or the nerves of his nose were weak I cannot say, but this was almost always followed by his sneezing violently five or six times.

The master would ring. The valet would fling down his handful of hair and go in.

'Was that you sneezing?'

'Yes, sir.'

'Bless you.' And he would give a sign with his hand for the valet to withdraw.

On the last day of carnival, all the servants, according to ancient custom, would come in the evening to ask their master's forgiveness: on these solemn occasions my father used to go into the great hall, accompanied by his valet. Then he would pretend not to recognise some of them.

'Who is that venerable old man standing there in the corner?' he would ask the valet.

'Danilo, the coachman,' the valet would answer abruptly, knowing that all this was only a dramatic performance.

'Good gracious! how he has changed. I really believe that it is entirely from drink that men get old so quickly; what does he do?'

'He hauls the firewood in for the stoves.'

The old man assumed an expression of insufferable pain.

'How is it that in thirty years you have not learned how to speak?

. . . Hauls: what's that—hauling firewood?—firewood is carried, not hauled. Well, Danilo, thank God, the Lord has thought me worthy to see you once more. I forgive you all your sins for this year, the oats which you waste so immoderately, and for not cleaning the horses, and do you forgive me. Go on hauling firewood while you have the strength, but now Lent is coming, so take less drink; it is bad for us at our age, and besides it is a sin.'

In this style he conducted the whole inspection.

We used to dine between three and four o'clock. The dinner lasted a long time and was very boring. Spiridon was an excellent cook, but my father's economy on the one hand, and his own on the other, rendered the dinner somewhat meagre, in spite of the fact that there were a great many dishes. Beside my father stood a red clay bowl into which he himself put various bits of food for the dogs; moreover, he used to feed them from his own fork, which gave fearful offence to the servants and consequently to me. Why? It is hard to say. . . .

Visitors on the whole seldom called upon us and dined more rarely still. I remember out of all those who visited us one man whose arrival to dinner would sometimes smooth the wrinkles out of my father's face, N. N. Bakhmetev. He was the brother of the lame general of that name and was himself a general also, though long on the retired list. My father and he had been friends as long before as the time when both had been officers in the Izmaylovsky regiment. They had indulged themselves together in the days of Catherine, and in the reign of Paul had both been court-martialled, Bakhmetev for having fought a duel with someone and my father for having been his second; then one of them had gone away to foreign lands as a tourist, and the other to Ufa as Governor. There was no likeness between them. Bakhmetev, a stout, healthy and handsome old man, liked a meal and getting a little drunk after it; was fond of lively conversation and many other things. He used to boast that he had eaten as many as a hundred sour-dough pies at a time; and when he was about sixty he could, with complete impunity, make away with up to a dozen buckwheat pancakes drowned in a pool of butter. These experiments I have witnessed more than once.

Bakhmetev had some shade of influence over my father, or at any rate did keep him in check. When Bakhmetev noticed that my father's ill-humour was beyond bounds, he would put on his hat and say with a military scrape :

'Good-bye—you are ill and stupid to-day; I meant to stay to dinner, but I cannot endure sour faces at table! *Gehorsamer Diener!*'

And my father by way of explanation would say to me: 'The impresario! What a lively fellow N. N. still is! Thank God, he's a healthy man and cannot understand a suffering Job like me; there are twenty degrees of frost, but he dashes here all the way from Pokrovka in his sledge as though it were nothing . . . while I thank the Creator every morning that I have woken up alive, that I am still breathing. Oh . . . oh . . . ough . . . ! it's a true proverb; the well-fed don't understand the hungry!'

This was the utmost indulgence that could be expected from him.

From time to time there were family dinners at which the Senator, the Golokhvastovs and others were present, and these dinners were not given casually, nor for the sake of any pleasure to be derived from them, but were due to profound considerations of economy and policy. Thus on the 20th February, the Senator's name-day, there was a dinner at our house, and on the 24th June, my father's name-day, the dinner was at the Senator's, an arrangement which, besides setting a moral example of brotherly love, saved each of them from giving a much bigger dinner at home.

Then there were various *habitués*; Sonnenberg would appear *ex officio*, and having just before dinner swallowed a glass of vodka and had a bite of Reval anchovy at home he would refuse a minute glass of some specially infused vodka; sometimes my last French tutor would come, a miserly old fellow with saucy phiz, fond of talking scandal. Monsieur Thirié so often made mistakes, pouring wine into his tumbler instead of beer and drinking it off apologetically, that at last my father would say to him,

'The *vin de Graves* stands on your right side, so you won't make a mistake again,' and Thirié, stuffing a huge pinch of snuff into his broad nose that turned up on one side, would spill snuff on his plate.

Among these visitors one was an extremely comic person. A little bald old man, invariably dressed in a short, narrow swallow-tail coat, and in a waistcoat that ended where now the waistcoat properly begins, and carrying a thin little cane, he was in his whole figure the embodiment of a period twenty years earlier, in 1830 of 1810 and in 1840 of 1820. Dmitri Ivanovich Pimenov, a counsellor of state by rank, was one of the governors of the Sheremetevsky Almshouse, and was, moreover, interested in literature. Scantily endowed by nature and brought up on the sentimental phrases of Karamzin, on Marmontel[13] and Marivaux,[14] Pimenov might have been the middle brother between Shalikov and Panayev.[15] The Voltaire of this honourable phalanx was the head of the secret police under Alexander, Yakov Ivanovich de Sanglain, and its promising young man, Pimen Arapov.[16] They were all in a close relationship with the universal patriarch Ivan Ivanovich Dmitriyev;[17] he had no rivals, but there was Vasily Lvovich Pushkin.[18] Pimenov went every Tuesday to Dmitriyev, 'the Ancient of Days', to discuss, in his house in Sadovaya Street, beauties of style and the corruption of the language of to-day. Pimenov himself had been tempted by the slippery career of Russian literature; first he had published the *Thoughts of the Duc de La Rochefoucauld*, then a treatise 'On Feminine Beauty and Charm'. Of this treatise, which I have not taken in my hand since I was sixteen, I remember only long comparisons in the style in which Plutarch compares his heroes; of the fair with the dark: 'Though a fair woman is this and that and the other, yet a dark woman is this and that and the other. . . .' Pimenov's chief peculiarity lay not in his having once published books that no one ever read, but in the fact that if he began laughing he could not stop, and his laughter would grow into fits of whooping-cough, with explosions and dull rolls of thunder. He knew this and therefore, when he had a presentiment that something laughable was coming, began little by little to take measures; he brought out a pocket-handkerchief, looked at his watch, buttoned up his coat, hid his face in his hands and, when the crisis came, stood up, turned to the wall, leaned against it and writhed in agony for half an hour or more, then, crimson and exhausted by the paroxysm, he would sit down mopping the perspiration from his bald head, though the fit would keep seizing him again for long afterwards.

Of course my father did not think him worth a farthing—he was

---

[13] Marmontel (1723-99), author of the *Contes Moraux* and other stories. (*Tr.*)

[14] Marivaux (1688-1763), author of numerous plays and a novel called *Marianne*—all distinguished by an excessive refinement of sentiment and language. (*Tr.*)

[15] Pëtr Ivanovich Shalikov and Vladimir Ivanovich Panayev were insignificant writers of the early part of the nineteenth century. (*Tr.*)

[16] Arapov, Pimen Nikolayevich (1796-1861), wrote some twenty plays, but is chiefly remembered for the *Chronicle of the Russian Theatre* (published after his death), a chronological record of everything performed on the Russian stage up to 1825. (*Tr.*)

[17] I. I. Dmitriyev (1760-1837) wrote a number of fables and songs, of which 'The Little Dove' is the best known. He was a great patron of young literary men, and in 1810 was made Minister of Justice. (*Tr.*)

[18] V. L. Pushkin, a minor poet, uncle of the famous A. S. Pushkin. (*Tr.*)

gentle, kind, awkward, a literary man and poor, and therefore not worth considering on any ground—but he had taken good note of his convulsive risibility. On the strength of it he would make him laugh until everyone else in the room too, under his influence, started laughing in the same unnatural way. The cause of our derision would look at us with a slight smile, as a man looks at a crowd of noisy puppies.

Sometimes my father played dreadful tricks on the unfortunate amateur of feminine charm and beauty.

'Engineer-Colonel So-and-so,' the servant would announce.

'Ask him in,' my father would say, and turning to Pimenov he would add: 'Please be on your guard when he is here, Dmitri Ivanovich; he has an unfortunate tic and when he talks now and then he makes a strange sound as though he had a chronic eructation.' Thereupon he would give a perfect imitation of the colonel. 'I know you are given to laughing, but please restrain yourself.'

This was enough. At the second word the colonel uttered, Pimenov would take out his handkerchief, make a parasol of his hands, and at last jump up.

The colonel would look at him in amazement, while my father would say to me with great composure:

'What is the matter with Dmitri Ivanovich? *Il est malade*, it's spasms; tell them to make haste and give him a glass of cold water, and you fetch some eau-de-Cologne.'

On such occasions Pimenov would snatch up his hat and laugh all the way to the Arbatsky Gate, stopping at cross-roads and leaning against lamp-posts.

For several years he came regularly every other Sunday to dine with us, and his punctuality in coming and his unpunctuality if he missed a Sunday angered my father equally, and he would persecute him. Yet the good-natured man went on coming, and coming on foot from the Red Gate to old Konyushennaya Street till he died, and not at all funnily. After ailing for a long time the solitary old bachelor, as he lay dying, saw with his own eyes his housekeeper carry off his things, his clothes, even the linen from his bed, leaving him entirely uncared for.

But the real *souffre-douleurs* at dinner were various old women, the needy, nomadic hangers-on of Princess M. A. Khovansky, my father's sister. For the sake of a change, and also partly to find out how everything was going on in our house, whether there had been any quarrels in the family, whether the cook had not had a fight with his wife, and whether the master had not found out that Palashka or Ulyasha was with child, they would sometimes come on holidays to spend a whole day. It must be noted that these widows had forty or fifty years before, when they were still unmarried, been dependants in the household of my father's aunt, old Princess Mesh-chersky, and afterwards in that of her daughter,[19] and had known my father since those days; that in this interval between their unsettled youth and the nomadic life of their old age they had spent some twenty years quarrelling with their husbands, restraining them from drunkenness, looking after them when they were paralysed, and taking them to the churchyard. Some had been trailing from one place to another in Bessarabia with a garrison officer and an armful of children; others had spent years with a criminal charge hanging over their husbands; and all these experiences of life had left upon them the marks of government offices and provincial towns, a dread of the powers of this world, a spirit of abasement and a sort of dull-witted bigotry.

Amazing scenes took place with them.

'Why is this, Anna Yakimovna; are you ill that you don't eat anything?' my father would ask.

Shrinking together the widow of some inspector in Kremenchug, a wretched old woman with a worn, faded face, who always smelt strongly of sticking plaster, would answer with cringing eyes and deprecating fingers:

'Forgive me, Ivan Alexeyevich, sir, I am really ashamed, but there, it is my old-fashioned ways, sir. Ha, ha, ha, it's the fast before the Assumption now.'

'Oh, how tiresome! You are always so pious! It's not what goes into the mouth, dear lady, that defiles, but what comes out of it; whether you eat one thing or another, it all goes the same way; now what comes out of the mouth, you must watch over . . . your judgments of your neighbours. Come, you had better dine at home on such days, or we shall have a Turk coming next asking for pilau; I don't keep a restaurant à la carte.'

The frightened old woman, who had intended as well to ask for some dish made of flour or cereals, would fall upon the *kvas* and salad, making a show of eating a terrific meal.

[19] See p. 4 fn. (R.)

But it is noteworthy that she, or any of the others, had only to begin eating meat during a fast for my father, though he never touched Lenten food himself, to say, shaking his head sadly:

'I should not have thought it was worth-while for you, Anna Yakimovna, to forsake the customs of your forefathers for the last few years of your life. I sin and eat meat, as comports with my many infirmities; but you, as you're allowed, thank God, have kept the fasts all your life and suddenly . . . what an example for *them*.'

He motioned towards the servants. And the poor old woman had to betake herself to *kvas* and salad again.

These scenes made me very indignant; sometimes I was so bold as to intervene and remind him of the contrary opinion he had expressed. Then my father would rise from his seat, take off his velvet cap by the tassel and, holding it in the air, thank me for the lesson and beg pardon for his forgetfulness; then he would say to the old lady:

'It's a terrible age! It's no wonder you eat meat during a fast, when children teach their parents! What are we coming to? It's dreadful to think of it! Luckily you and I won't see it.'

After dinner my father lay down to rest for an hour and a half. The servants at once dispersed to beer-shops and eating-houses. At seven o'clock tea was served; then sometimes someone would arrive, the Senator more often than anyone; it was a time of leisure for all of us. The Senator usually brought various items of news and told them eagerly. My father affected complete inattention as he listened to him: he assumed a serious face, when his brother had expected him to be dying of laughter, and would cross-question him, as though he had not heard the point, when the Senator had been telling some astonishing story.

The Senator came in for it in a very different way when he contradicted or differed from his younger brother (which rarely happened, however), and sometimes, indeed, when he did not contradict at all, if my father was particularly ill-humoured. In these tragi-comic scenes, what was funniest was the Senator's natural vehemence and my father's factitious *sang froid*.

'Well, you are ill to-day,' the Senator would say impatiently, and he would seize his hat and rush off.

Once in his vexation he could not open the door and pushed at it with all his might, saying, 'What a confounded door!' My father

went up, coolly opened the door inwards, and in a perfectly composed voice observed:

'This door does its duty: it opens this way, and you try to open
it that way, and lose your temper.'

It may not be out of place to mention that the Senator was two
years older than my father and addressed him in the second person
singular, while the latter as the younger brother used the plural form,
'you'.

When the Senator had gone, my father would retire to his bedroom, would each time inquire whether the gates were closed, would
receive an answer in the affirmative, would express doubts on the
subject but do nothing to make sure. Then began a lengthy routine
of washings, fomentations, and medicines; his valet made ready on a
little table by the bed a perfect arsenal of different objects—phials,
nightlights, pill-boxes. The old man as a rule read for an hour
Bourrienne's *Mémorial de Sainte Hélène*[20] and other memoirs; then
came the night.

Such was our household when I left it in 1834: so I found it in
1840, and so it continued until his death in 1846.

At thirty, when I returned from exile, I realised that my father
had been right in many things, that he had unhappily an offensively
good understanding of men. But was it my fault that he preached
the truth itself in a way so provoking to a youthful heart? His mind,
chilled by a long life in a circle of depraved men, put him on his
guard against everyone, and his callous heart did not crave for
reconciliation; so he remained on hostile terms with everyone on
earth.

I found him in 1839, and still more so in 1842, weak and really
ill. The Senator was dead, the desolation about him was greater than
ever and he even had a different valet; but he himself was just the
same: only his physical powers were changed; there was the same
spiteful intelligence, the same tenacious memory, he still persecuted
everyone over trifles, and Sonnenberg, still unchanged, had his
nomad's camp in the old house as before, and ran errands.

Only then did I appreciate all the cheerlessness of his life; I looked
with an aching heart at the melancholy significance of this lonely,
abandoned existence, dying out in the arid, harsh, stony wilderness
which he had created about himself, but which he had not the will

---

[20] This book is not by Bourrienne but by E. de Las Cases (Paris. 1823-4). (*A.S.*)

E*

to change; he knew this; he saw death approaching and, overcoming weakness and infirmity, he jealously and obstinately controlled himself. I was dreadfully sorry for the old man, but there was nothing to be done: he was unapproachable.

Sometimes I passed softly by his study where, sitting in a hard, uncomfortable, deep armchair, surrounded by his dogs, he was playing all alone with my three-year-old son. It seemed as though the clenched hands and numbed nerves of the old man relaxed at the sight of the child, and he found rest from the incessant agitation, conflict, and vexation in which he had kept himself, as his dying hand touched the cradle.

Chapter 6

The University

'*Oh, years of boundless ecstasies,*
Of visions bright and free!
Where now your mirth untouched by spite,
Your hopeful toil and noisy glee?'

N. P. Ogarëv: Humorous Verse.

IN spite of the lame general's sinister predictions my father nevertheless put my name down with Prince N. B. Yusupov for employment
in the Kremlin Department. I signed a paper and there the matter
ended; I heard nothing more of the service, except that about three
years later Yusupov sent the Palace architect, who always shouted
as though he were standing on the scaffolding of the fifth storey
and there giving orders to workmen in the basement, to announce
that I had received the first officer's grade. All these miracles, I may
remark in passing, were unnecessary, for I rose at one jump, with
the grades I received in the service, by passing the examination
for my degree—it was not worthwhile giving oneself much trouble
for the sake of two or three years' seniority. And meanwhile this
supposed post in the service almost prevented me from entering the
university. The Council, seeing that I was reckoned as in the office
of the Kremlin Department, refused me the right to take the
examination.

For those in the government service there were special after-dinner
courses of study, extremely limited in scope and qualifying one for
entrance into the so-called 'committee examinations'.* All the
wealthy idlers, the young noblemen's sons who had learnt nothing,
all those who did not want to serve in the army and were in a hurry
to get the rank of assessor took the 'committee examinations'; they
were by way of being gold mines presented to the old profes-

sors, who coached them *privatissime* for twenty roubles a lesson.

To begin my life with such a disaster of the Caudine Forks of learning was far from suiting my ideas. I told my father resolutely that if he could not find some other means I should resign from the service.

My father was angry, said that with my caprices I was preventing him from organising a career for me, and abused the teachers who had stuffed me with this nonsense; but, seeing that all this had very little effect upon me, he made up his mind to go to Yusupov.

Yusupov settled the matter in a trice, partly like a lord and partly like a Tatar. He called his secretary and told him to write me a leave of absence for three years. The secretary hesitated and hesitated, and at last, with some apprehension, submitted that leave of absence for longer than four months could not be given without the sanction of His Majesty.

'What nonsense, my man,' the prince said to him. 'Where is the difficulty? Well, if leave of absence is impossible, write that I commission him to attend the university course, to perfect himself in the sciences.'

His secretary wrote this and next day I was sitting in the amphitheatre of the Physico-Mathematical auditorium.

The University of Moscow and the Lycée of Tsarkoye Selo play a significant part in the history of Russian education and in the life of the last two generations.

Moscow University grew in importance together with the city itself after 1812. Degraded by the Emperor Peter from being the capital of the Tsars, Moscow was promoted by the Emperor Napoleon (partly intentionally, but twice as much unintentionally) to being the capital of the Russian people. The people realised their ties of blood with Moscow from the pain they felt at the news of its occupation by the enemy. From that time a new epoch began for the city. Its university became more and more the centre of Russian culture. All the conditions necessary for its development were combined—historical importance, geographical position, and the absence of the Tsar.

The intensified mental activity of Petersburg after the death of Paul came to a gloomy close on the Fourteenth of December (1825). Nicholas appeared with his five gibbets, with penal servitude, with the white strap and the light blue uniform of Benckendorf.[1]

[1] The uniform of the gendarmes of the Third Division, the political police, of which Benckendorf was head, was light blue with a white strap. (*Tr.*)

Everything ran backwards: the blood rushed to the heart, the activity that was outwardly concealed boiled inwardly in secret. Moscow University remained firm and was the foremost to stand out in sharp relief from the general fog. The Tsar began to hate it from the time of the Polezhayev affair.[2] He sent A. Pisarev, the major-general of the *'Evenings at Kaluga'*,[3] as director, commanded the students to be dressed in uniform, ordered them to wear a sword, then forbade them to wear a sword, condemned Polezhayev to be a common soldier for his verses and Kostenetsky and his comrades for their prose, destroyed the Kritskys[4] for a bust, sentenced us to exile for Saint-Simonism, then made Prince Sergey Mikhaylovich Golitsyn Director, and took no further notice of that 'hot-bed of depravity', piously advising young men who had finished their studies at the Lyceum or at the School of Jurisprudence not to enter it.

Golitsyn was an astonishing person: it was long before he could accustom himself to the irregularity of there being no lecture when a professor was ill; he thought the next on the list ought to take his place, so that Father Ternovsky sometimes had to lecture in the clinic on women's diseases and Richter, the gynæcologist, to discourse on the Immaculate Conception.

But in spite of that the university that had fallen into disgrace grew in influence; the youthful strength of Russia streamed to it from all sides, from all classes of society, as into a common reservoir; in its halls they were purified from the prejudices they had picked up at the domestic hearth, reached a common level, became like brothers and dispersed again to all parts of Russia and among all classes of its people.

Until 1848 the organisation of our universities was purely democratic. Their doors were open to everyone who could pass the examination, who was neither a serf, a peasant, nor a man excluded from his commune. Nicholas spoilt all this; he restricted the admission of students, increased the fees of those who paid their own expenses, and permitted none to be relieved of payment but poor

---

[2] See below pp. 153ff. for a full account of this. (*Tr.*)

[3] A collection of the works of various authors published in two parts by A. A. Pisarev in 1825. See *The Complete Works and Letters of A. I. Herzen*, ed. M. K. Lemke (22 vols., Petrograd, 1919-25), Vol. XII, p. 99, note 2 (*R.*)

[4] It was a young man called Zubov who was put in a madhouse for hacking a bust of the Tsar. The Kritsky brothers were punished for addressing insulting words to his portraits. (*A.S.*)

noblemen.[5] All these belonged to the series of senseless measures
which will disappear with the last breath of that drag on the Russian
wheel, together with the law about passports,* about religious intolerance* and so on.[6]

Young men of all sorts and conditions coming from above and
from below, from the south and from the north, were quickly fused
into a compact mass of comrades. Social distinctions had not among
us the offensive influence which we find in English schools and
barracks; I am not speaking of the English universities: they exist
exclusively for the aristocracy and for the rich. A student who
thought fit to boast among us of his blue blood or his wealth would
have been excluded from 'fire and water' and made the butt of his
comrades.

The external distinctions—and they did not go very deep—that
divided the students arose from other causes. Thus, for instance, the
medical section which was on the other side of the garden was not
so closely united with us as the other faculties; moreover, the majority

[5] See footnote on p. 24.

[6] By the way, here is another of the fatherly measures of the 'never to be
forgotten' Nicholas. Foundling hospitals and the regulations for their public inspection are among the best monuments of the reign of Catherine. The very idea of
setting up hospitals, almshouses, and foundling hospitals on part of the percentage
made by the loan banks from the investment of their capital is remarkably intelligent.
These institutions were accepted, the banks and government departments enriched
them, the foundling hospitals and pious institutions flourished so far as the universal
thievishness of officials permitted them. Of the children brought into a foundling
hospital some remained in it, while others were put out to be brought up by
peasant-women in the country; the latter remained peasants, while the former were
brought up in the institution itself. The more gifted among them were picked
out to continue the high-school course, while the less promising were taught trades
or sent to the Institute of Technology. It was the same with the girls. Some were
trained in handicrafts, others as children's nurses, while the cleverest became school-
mistresses and governesses. It all went as well as could be. But Nicholas dealt a
terrible blow to this institution, too. It is said that the Empress on one occasion,
meeting in the house of one of her friends the children's governess, entered into
conversation with her and, being very much pleased with her, inquired where she
had been brought up, to which the young woman answered that she had been a
boarder at a foundling hospital. Anyone would suppose that the Empress would
have thanked the authorities. No—it gave her occasion to reflect on the *impropriety*
of giving such an education to abandoned children.

A few months later Nicholas promoted the higher classes of the foundling hospitals to the Officers' Institute, i.e. commanded that the foundlings should no longer
be put in these classes, but replaced them with the children of officers. He even
thought of a more radical measure: he forbade the provincial institutions in their
regulations to accept new-born infants. The best commentary on this intelligent
measure is to be found in the records of the Minister of Justice under the heading
'Infanticide'.

of the medical students consisted of seminarists and Germans.* The Germans kept a little apart and were deeply imbued with the Western bourgeois spirit. All the education of the luckless seminarists, all their ideas, were utterly different from ours; we spoke different languages. Brought up under the oppression of monastic despotism, stuffed with rhetoric and theology, they envied us our ease of manner; we were vexed by their Christian meekness.[7]

I entered the Faculty of Physics and Mathematics in spite of the fact that I had never had a marked ability nor much liking for mathematics. Nick and I had been taught mathematics together by a teacher[8] whom we loved for his anecdotes and stories; interesting as he was, he can hardly have developed any particular passion for his subject. His knowledge of mathematics extended only to conic sections, that is, exactly as far as was necessary for preparing high-school boys for the university; a real philosopher, he never had the curiosity to glance at the 'university' branches of mathematics. What was particularly remarkable, too, was that he never read more than one book, and that book, Francoeur's *Course*, he read constantly for ten years; but, being abstemious by temperament and having no love for luxury, he never went beyond a certain page.

I chose the Faculty of Physics and Mathematics because the natural sciences were taught in that Faculty, and just at that time I developed a great passion for natural science.

A rather strange meeting had led me to these studies.

After the famous division of the family property in 1822,[9] which I have described, my father's 'eldest brother'[10] went to live in Petersburg. For a long time nothing was heard of him; then suddenly a rumour spread that he was getting married. He was at that time over sixty, and everyone knew that besides a grown-up son he had other children. He did in fact marry the mother of his eldest son; the 'young woman', too, was over fifty. With this marriage he legitimised, as they said in the old days, his son. Why not all the children? It would be hard to say why, if we had not known his main purpose

---

[7] Immense progress has been made in this respect. All that I have heard of late of the theological academies, and even of the seminaries, confirms it. I need hardly say that it is not the ecclesiastical authorities but the spirit of the pupils that is responsible for this improvement.

[8] I. F. Volkov. (*A.S.*)

[9] The division of the property actually took place in the summer of 1821. (*A.S.*)

[10] That is Alexander, his eldest surviving brother; Pëtr, the eldest son of all, had died in 1813. (*R.*)

in doing what he did; his one desire was to deprive his brothers of the inheritance, and this he completely attained by legitimising the son. In the famous inundation of Petersburg in 1824 the old man was drenched with water in his carriage. He caught cold, took to his bed, and at the beginning of 1825 he died.

Of the son there were strange rumours. It was said that he was unsociable, refused to make acquaintances, sat alone for ever absorbed in chemistry, spent his life at his microscope, read even at dinner and hated feminine society. Of him it had been said in *Woe from Wit*,[11]

> *'He is a chemist, he is a botanist,*
> *Our nephew, Prince Fëdor,*
> *He flies from women and even from me.'*

His uncles, who transferred to him the rancour they had felt for his father, never spoke of him except as 'the Chemist', using this word as a term of disparagement, and assuming that chemistry was a subject that could by no means be studied by a gentleman.

Before his death the father used to persecute his son dreadfully, not merely affronting him with the spectacle of his grey-headed father's cynical debauchery, but actually being jealous of him as a possible rival in his seraglio. The Chemist on one occasion tried to escape from this ignoble existence by means of laudanum. He happened to be rescued by a comrade, with whom he used to work at chemistry. His father was thoroughly frightened, and before his death had begun to treat his son better.

After his father's death the Chemist released the luckless odalisques, halved the heavy *obrok* laid by his father on the peasants, forgave all arrears and presented them gratis with the army receipts for the full quota of recruits, which the old man had used to sell when he sent his house-serfs for soldiers.

A year and a half later he came to Moscow. I wanted to see him, for I liked him for the way he treated his peasants and because of the undeserved ill-will his uncles bore him.

---

[11] Griboyedov's famous comedy, which appeared and had a large circulation in manuscript copies in 1824, its performance and publication being prevented by the censorship. When performed later it was in a very mutilated form. It was a lively satire on Moscow society and full of references to well-known persons, such as Izmaylov and Tolstoy 'the American'. Griboyedov was imprisoned in 1825 in connection with the Fourteenth of December. (*Tr.*)

This passage, not entirely accurately quoted, is from Act III, Scene 2. (*A.S.*)

One morning a small man in gold spectacles, with a big nose, who had lost half his hair, and whose fingers were burnt by chemical reagents, called upon my father. My father met him coldly, sarcastically; his nephew responded in the same coin and gave him quite as good as he got: after taking each other's measure they began speaking of extraneous matters with external indifference, and parted politely but with concealed dislike. My father saw that here was a fighter who would not give in to him.

They did not become more intimate later. The Chemist very rarely visited his uncles; the last time he saw my father was after the Senator's death, when he came to ask him for a loan of thirty thousand roubles for the purchase of some land. My father would not lend it. The Chemist was moved to anger and, rubbing his nose, observed with a smile, 'There is no risk whatever in it; my estate is entailed; I am borrowing money for its improvement. I have no children and we are each other's heirs.' The old man of seventy-five never forgave his nephew for this sally.

I took to visiting the Chemist from time to time. He lived in a way that was very much his own. In his big house on the Tverskoy Boulevard he used one tiny room for himself and one as a laboratory. His old mother occupied another little room on the other side of the corridor; the rest of the house was neglected and remained exactly as it had been when his father left it to go to Petersburg. The blackened candelabra, the unusual furniture, all sorts of rarities, a clock said to have been bought by Peter I in Amsterdam, an armchair said to have come from the house of Stanislas Leszczynski,[12] frames without pictures in them, pictures turned to the wall, were all left anyhow, filling up three big, unheated and unlighted rooms. Servants were usually playing the *torban* and smoking in the hall, where in old days they had scarcely dared to breathe or say their prayers. A man-servant would light a candle and escort one through this arsenal, observing every time that I had better not take my cloak off for it was very cold in the big rooms. Thick layers of dust covered the horned trophies and various curios, the reflections of which moved together with the candle in the elaborate mirrors; straw left from packing lay undisturbed here and there together with scraps of paper and bits of string.

Through a row of these rooms one reached at last a door hung

[12] Stanislas Leszczynski, king of Poland from 1702 to 1709. His daughter Maria was married to Louis XV of France. (*Tr.*)

with a rug, which led to the terribly overheated study. In this the
Chemist, in a soiled dressing-gown lined with squirrel fur, was invariably sitting, surrounded by piles of books, and rows of phials,
retorts, crucibles, and other apparatus. In that study where Chevalier's
microscope now reigned supreme and there was always a smell of
chlorine, and where a few years before terrible piteous deeds had
been perpetrated—in that study I was born. My father, on his return
from foreign parts, before his quarrel with his brother, stayed for
some months in his house, and in the same house my wife was born
in 1817. The Chemist sold the house two years later, and it chanced
that I was in the house again at evening parties of Sverbeyev's,[13]
arguing there about Pan-Slavism and getting angry with Khomyakov, who never lost his temper about anything. The rooms had been
altered, but the front entrance, the vestibule, the stairs, the hall were
all left as before, and so was the little study.

The Chemist's housekeeping was even less complicated, especially
when his mother had gone away for the summer to their estate near
Moscow and with her the cook. His valet used to appear at four
o'clock with a coffee-pot, pour into it a little strong broth and, taking
advantage of the chemical furnace, would set it there to warm, along
with various poisons. Then he would bring bread and half a hazel-
hen from an eating-house, and that made up the whole dinner. When
it was over the valet would wash the coffee-pot and it would return to
its natural duties. In the evening the valet would appear again, take
from the sofa a heap of books, and a tiger-skin that had come down
to the Chemist from his father, spread a sheet and bring pillows and
a blanket, and the study was as easily transformed into a bedroom as
it had been into a kitchen and a dining-room.

From the very beginning of our acquaintance the Chemist saw
that I was interested in earnest, and began to try to persuade me to
give up the 'empty' study of literature and the 'dangerous and quite
useless pursuit of politics', and take to natural science. He gave me
Cuvier's speech on geological revolutions and Candolle's *Plant
Morphology*.* Seeing that these were not thrown away upon me he
offered me the use of his excellent collections, apparatus, herbariums,
and even his guidance. He was very interesting on his own ground,
extremely learned, witty and even amiable; but for this one had to
go no further than the apes; from the rocks to the orang-utan every-

[13] Sverbeyev, Dmitry Nikolayevich (1799-1876). Representatives of the 'Slavophils'
and Westerners' used to meet in his house in Moscow. (*A.S.*)

thing interested him, but he did not care to be drawn beyond them, particularly into philosophy, which he regarded as twaddle. He was neither a conservative nor a reactionary: he simply did not believe in people, that is, he believed that egoism is the sole source of all actions, and thought that it was restrained merely by the senselessness of some and the ignorance of others.

I was revolted by his materialism. The superficial Voltairianism of our fathers, which they were half afraid of, was not in the least like the Chemist's materialism. His outlook was calm, consistent, complete. He reminded me of the celebrated answer made by Lalande[14] to Napoleon. 'Kant accepts the hypothesis of God,' Bonaparte said to him. 'Sire,' replied the astronomer, 'in my studies I have never had occasion to make use of that hypothesis.'

The Chemist's atheism went far beyond the sphere of theology. He considered Geoffroy Saint-Hilaire[15] a mystic and Oken[16] simply deranged. He closed the works of the natural philosophers with the same contempt with which my father had put aside Karamzin's *History*. 'They themselves invented first causes and spiritual forces, and then are surprised that they can neither find them nor understand them,' he said. This was a second edition of my father, in a different age and differently educated.

His views became still more comfortless on all the problems of life. He thought that there was as little responsibility for good and evil in man as in the beasts; that it was all a matter of organisation, circumstances, and condition of the nervous system in general, of which he said *more was expected than it was capable of giving.* He did not like family life, spoke with horror of marriage, and naïvely acknowledged that in the thirty years of his life he had never loved one woman. However, there remained one current of warmth in this frigid man and it could be seen in his attitude to his old mother; they had suffered a great deal together at the hands of his father, and their troubles had welded them firmly together;

---

[14] Lalande, Joseph-Jérôme de (1732-1807), a French astronomer. (*Tr.*) This remark is usually attributed to Pierre Simon, Marquis de Laplace (1749-1827). (*R.*)

[15] Geoffroy Saint-Hilaire (1772-1844), French naturalist and author of many books on zoology and biology, in which, in opposition to Cuvier, he advanced the theory of the variation of species under the influence of environment. (*Tr.*)

[16] Oken, Lorenz (1779-1851), a German naturalist, who aimed at deducing a system of natural philosophy from *a priori* propositions, and incidentally threw off some valuable and suggestive ideas. (*Tr.*)

he touchingly surrounded her solitary and infirm old age, so far as he could, with tranquillity and attention.

He never advocated his theories, except those that concerned chemistry; they came out casually, evoked by me. He even showed reluctance in answering my romantic and philosophic objections; his answers were brief, and he made them with a smile and with the considerateness with which a big, old mastiff plays with a puppy, allowing him to tousle him and only gently pushing him away with his paw. But it was just that which provoked me most, and I would return to the charge without weariness—never gaining an inch of ground, however. Later on, twelve years afterwards, that is, I frequently recalled the Chemist's, just as I recalled my father's observations. Of course, he had been right in three-quarters of everything that I had objected to; but I had been right too, you know. There are truths (we have spoken of this already) which like political rights are not given to those under a certain age.

The Chemist's influence made me choose the Faculty of Physics and Mathematics; perhaps I should have done still better to enter the Medical Faculty, but there was no great harm in my first acquiring some degree of knowledge of the differential and integral calculus, and then completely forgetting it.

Without the natural sciences there is no salvation for modern man. Without that wholesome food, without that strict training of the mind by facts, without that closeness to the life surrounding us, without humility before its independence, the monastic cell remains hidden somewhere in the soul, and in it the drop of mysticism which might have flooded the whole understanding with its dark waters.

Before I completed my studies the Chemist had gone away to Petersburg, and I did not see him again until I came back from Vyatka. Some months after my marriage I went half secretly for a few days to the estate near Moscow where my father was then living. The object of this journey was to effect a final reconciliation with him, for he was still angry with me for my marriage.

On the way I halted at Perkhushkovo where we had so many times broken our journey in old days. The Chemist was expecting me there and had actually got a dinner and two bottles of champagne ready for me. In those four or five years he had not changed at all except for being a little older. Before dinner he asked me quite seriously:

'Tell me, please, frankly, how do you find married life: is it a good thing? or not very?'

I laughed.

'How venturesome of you,' he went on. 'I wonder at you; in a normal condition a man can never determine on such a terrible step. Two or three very good matches have been proposed to me, but when I imagine a woman taking up her abode in my room, setting everything in order according to her ideas, perhaps forbidding me to smoke my tobacco (he used to smoke rootlets from Nezhin),[17] making a fuss and an upset, I am so frightened that I prefer to die in solitude.'

'Shall I stay the night with you or go on to Pokrovskoye?' I asked him after dinner.

'I have no lack of room here,' he answered, 'but for you I think it would be better to go on; you will reach your father at ten o'clock. You know, of course, that he is still angry with you; well—in the evening before going to bed old people's nerves are usually relaxed and drowsy—he will probably receive you much better to-day than he would to-morrow; in the morning you would find him quite ready for battle.'

'Ha, ha, ha! I recognise my teacher in physiology and materialism,' said I, laughing heartily. 'How your remark recalls those blissful days when I used to go to you like Goethe's Wagner to weary you with my idealism and listen with some indignation to your chilling opinions.'

'Since then,' he answered, laughing too,' 'you have lived enough to know that all human affairs depend simply on the nerves and the chemical composition.'

Later on we had a difference: probably we were both wrong. . . . Nevertheless in 1846 he wrote me a letter. I was then beginning to be the fashion after the publication of the first part of *Who Is At Fault?* The Chemist wrote to me that he saw with grief that I was wasting my talent on idle pursuits.

'I became reconciled to you for the sake of your *Letters on the Study of Nature.* In them I understood German philosophy (so far as it is possible for the mind of man to do so)—why then instead of going on with serious work are you writing fairy-tales?' I sent him a few friendly lines in reply, and with that our intercourse ended.

[17] *Makhorka*, a strong, cheap tobacco produced, among other places, at Nezhin in the Ukraine. (R.)

If the Chemist's own eyes ever rest upon these lines, I would beg him to read them just after going to bed at night when his nerves are relaxed, and then I am sure he will forgive me this affectionate gossip, the more so since I retain a very genuine, kind memory of him.

And so at last the seclusion of the parental home was over. I was *au large*. Instead of solitude in our little room, instead of quiet, half-concealed meetings with Ogarëv alone, I was surrounded by a noisy family, seven hundred in number. I was more at home in it in a fortnight than I had been in my father's house from the day of my birth.

But the paternal home pursued me even at the university, in the shape of a footman whom my father ordered to accompany me, particularly when I went on foot. For a whole year I tried to get rid of my escort and only with difficulty succeeded in doing so officially. I say 'officially', because my valet Pëtr Fëdorovich, upon whom the duty was laid, very quickly grasped, first, that I disliked being accompanied, and, secondly, that it was a great deal more pleasant for him in various places of entertainment than in the hall of the Faculty of Physics and Mathematics, where the only pleasures open to him were conversation with the two porters and the three of them treating each other and themselves to snuff.

What was the object of sending an escort to walk after me? Could Pëtr, who from his youth had been given to getting drunk for several days at a time, have prevented me from doing anything? I imagine that my father did not even suppose so, but his own peace of mind took steps, which were ineffective but were still steps, like people who do not believe but take the sacrament. It was part of the old-fashioned education of landowners. Up to seven years old, orders had been given that I should be led by the hand on the staircase, which was rather steep; up to eleven I was washed in my bath by Vera Artamonovna; therefore, very consistently, a servant was sent to walk behind me when I was a student; and until I was twenty-one, I was not allowed to be out after half-past ten. In practice I found myself at liberty, standing on my own feet, when I was in exile; had I not been exiled, probably the same régime would have continued up to twenty-five or even thirty-five.

Like the majority of lively boys brought up in solitude, I flung myself on everyone's neck with such sincerity and impulsiveness, built myself up with such senseless imprudence, and was so candidly fond of everyone, that I could not fail to call forth a warm response from my hearers, who consisted of lads of about my own age. (I was then in my seventeenth year.)

The sage rules—to be courteous to all, intimate with no one and to trust no one—did as much to promote this readiness to make friends as the ever-present thought with which we entered the university, the thought that here our dreams would be accomplished, that here we should sow the seeds and lay the foundation of a league. We were persuaded that out of this lecture-room would come the company which would follow in the footsteps of Pestel and Ryleyev, and that we should be in it.

They were a splendid set of young men in our year. It was just at that time that theoretical tendencies were becoming more and more marked among us. The scholastic method of learning and aristocratic indolence were alike disappearing, and had not yet been replaced by that German utilitarianism which enriches men's minds with science, as the fields with manure, for the sake of an increased crop. A tolerably large group of students no longer regarded science as a necessary but wearisome short-cut by which they would come to be collegiate assessors. The problems that were arising amongst us had no reference whatever to the Table of Ranks.[18]

On the other hand the interest in science had not yet had time to degenerate into doctrinarianism; science did not draw us away from the life and suffering around us. Our sympathy with it raised the *social* morality of the students to an unusual extent. We said openly in the lecture-room everything that came into our heads; manuscript copies of *prohibited* poems passed from hand to hand, prohibited books were read with commentaries, but for all that I do not remember a single case of tale-bearing from the lecture-room or of betrayal. There were timid young men who turned away and held aloof, but they too were silent.[19]

One silly boy, questioned by his mother on the Malov affair,[20] under threat of the birch, did tell her something. The fond mother—an aristocrat and a princess—flew to the rector and passed on her son's information as proof of his penitence. We heard of this and

---

[18] See p. 25, fn. (R.)

[19] At that time there were none of the inspectors and sub-inspectors who played the part of my Pëtr Fëdorovich in the lecture-rooms.

[20] The Malov affair happened on 16th March, 1831. (A.S.)

tormented him so that he did not stay till the end of the course.

This affair, for which I too was imprisoned, deserves to be described.

Malov was a stupid, coarse, and uncultured professor in the Political Faculty. The students despised him and laughed at him.

'How many professors have you in your faculty?' the Director one day asked a student in the Politic lecture-room.

'Nine, not counting Malov,' answered the student.[21]

Well, this professor, who had to be left out of the reckoning in order that nine should remain, began to be more and more insolent in his treatment of the students; the latter made up their minds to drive him out of the lecture-room. After deliberating together they sent two delegates to our faculty to invite me to come with an auxiliary force. I at once proclaimed a declaration of war on Malov, and several students went with me; when we went into the Politics lecture-room Malov was present and saw us.

On the faces of all the students was written the same fear: that on that day he might say nothing rude to them. This fear soon passed. The overflowing lecture-room was restless and a vague subdued hum rose from it. Malov made some observation; there began a scraping of feet.

'You express your thoughts like horses, with your feet,' observed Malov, probably imagining that horses think at a gallop or a trot; and a storm arose, whistling, hisses, shouts; 'Out with him, *pereat!*' Malov, white as a sheet, made a desperate effort to control the uproar but could not; the students jumped on to the benches. Malov quietly left the dais and, cowering down, tried to slip through to the door; his audience followed, saw him through the university court into the street and flung his goloshes after him. The last circumstance was important, for in the street the case at once assumed a very different character; but where in the world are there lads of seventeen or eighteen who would consider that?

The University Council was alarmed and persuaded the Director to present the affair as disposed of, and for that purpose to put the culprits, or somebody anyhow, in prison. This was prudent; it might otherwise easily have happened that the Tsar would have sent an aide-de-camp who, with a view to gaining a cross, would have turned the affair into a conspiracy, a rising, a rebellion,

---

[21] A pun on the name—the phrase meaning also 'Nine all but a little'. (*Tr.*)

and would have proposed sending everyone to penal servitude, which the Tsar would graciously have commuted to service as common soldiers. Seeing that vice was punished and virtue triumphant, the Tsar confined himself to giving His Majesty's sanction to the confirmation of the wishes of the students, and dismissed the professor. We had driven Malov out as far as the university gates and he turned him out of them. It was *vae victis* with Nicholas, but this time we had no cause to reproach him.

And so the affair went merrily on; after dinner next day the watchman from the head office shuffled up to me, a grey-headed old man, who conscientiously assumed that the students' tips (given *na vodku*) were for vodka and therefore kept himself continually in a condition approximating more to drunkenness than sobriety. In the cuff of his greatcoat he brought a note from the rector; I was ordered to present myself before him at seven o'clock that evening. When he had gone a pale and frightened student appeared, a baron from the Baltic provinces, who had received a similar invitation and was one of the luckless victims led on by me. He began showering reproaches upon me and then asked advice as to what he was to say.

'Lie desperately, deny everything, except that there was an uproar and that you were in the lecture-room.'

'But the rector will ask why I was in the Politics lecture-room and not in ours.'

'What of it? Why, don't you know that Rodion Heyman[22] did not come to give his lecture, so you, not wishing to waste your time, went to hear another.'

'He won't believe it.'

'Well, that's his affair.'

As we were going into the university courtyard I looked at my baron: his plump little cheeks were very pale and altogether he was in a bad way.

'Listen,' I said, 'you may be sure that the rector will begin with me and not with you, so you say exactly the same with variations. You did not do anything in particular, as a matter of fact. Don't forget one thing: for making an uproar and for telling lies ever so many of you will be put in prison, but if you blab, and implicate anyone in front of me, I'll tell the others and we'll poison your existence for you.'

[22] Heyman, Rodion Grigorevich (1802-65), professor of chemistry at Moscow University from 1833. Herzen attended his lectures. (*A.S.*)

The baron promised and kept his word honourably.

The rector at that time was Dvigubsky, one of the relics and patterns of the professors before the flood, or to be more accurate, before the fire, that is, before 1812. They are extinct now; with the directorship of Prince Obolensky the patriarchal period of Moscow University comes to an end. In those days the government did not trouble itself about the university; the professors lectured or did not lecture, the students attended or did not attend; besides, if they did attend, it was not in uniform jackets *ad instar* of light-cavalry officers, but in all sorts of outrageous and eccentric garments, in tiny little forage-caps that would scarcely stay on their virginal locks. The professors consisted of two camps or strata who quietly hated each other. One group was composed exclusively of Germans, the other of non-Germans. The Germans, among whom were good-natured and learned men such as Loder,[23] Fischer,[24] Hildebrandt,[25] and Heym[26] himself, were as a rule distinguished by their ignorance of the Russian language and their disinclination to learn it, their indifference to the students, their spirit of Western favouritism and uninspired routine, their immoderate smoking of cigars and the immense quantity of decorations which they never took off. The non-Germans for their part knew not a single (living) language except Russian, were servile in their patriotism, as uncouth as seminarists, were sat upon, with the exception of Merzlyakov,[27] and instead of an immoderate consumption of cigars indulged in an immoderate consumption of liquor. The Germans for the most part hailed from Göttingen and the non-Germans were sons of priests.

Dvigubsky[28] was one of the non-Germans: his appearance was so edifying that a student from a seminary, who came in for a list of classes, went up to kiss his hand and ask for his blessing, and always

[23] Loder Just-Christian Ivanovich (1753-1832), anatomist and physician to the Tsar; instructed at Moscow University 1818-31. (*A.S.*)

[24] Fischer von Waldheim, Grigory Ivanovich (1771-1853), professor of zoology at Moscow University, 1804-35. Herzen attended his lectures. (*A.S.*)

[25] Hildebrandt, Fëdor Andreyevich (1773-1845), professor of surgery at the Moscow Academy of Medicine and Surgery, 1808-39, and at Moscow University, 1804-30. (*A.S.*)

[26] Heym, Ivan Andreyevich (1758-1821), professor of history, statistics and geography at Moscow University from 1784, and Rector 1808-18. (*A.S.*)

[27] Merzlyakov, Alexey Fëdorovich (1778-1830), poet, critic, translator; professor of Russian literature at Moscow University from 1807. (*A.S.*)

[28] Dvigubsky, Ivan Alexeyevich (1771-1839), natural philosopher; professor at Moscow University from 1807 and Rector 1826-33. Herzen attended his lectures. (*A.S.*)

called him 'Father Rector'. At the same time he was awfully like an owl with an Anna ribbon round its neck, in which form another student, who had received a more worldly education, drew his portrait. When he came into our lecture-room either with the dean, Chumakov, or with Kotelnitsky, who had charge of a cupboard inscribed *Materia Medica*, kept for some unknown reason in the mathematical lecture-room—or with Reiss, who had been bespoken from Germany because his uncle was a very good chemist, and who, when he read French, used to call a lamp-wick a *béton de coton,* and poison, *poisson,* and pronounced the word for 'lightning' so unfortunately that many people supposed he was swearing—we looked at them with round eyes as at a collection of fossils, as at the last of the Abencerrages,[29] representatives of a different age, not so near to us as to Tredyakovsky[30] and Kostrov;[31] the age in which Kheraskov[32] and Knyazhnin[33] were still read, the times of the good-natured Professor Diltey,[34] who had two little dogs, one which always barked and the other which never barked, for which reason he very appropriately called one Bavardka and the other Prudentka.

But Dvigubsky was not at all a good-natured professor; he received us extremely curtly and was rude. I reeled off a fearful rigmarole and was disrespectful; the baron served the same story warmed up. The rector, irritated, told us to present ourselves next morning before the council; and there for half an hour they questioned, condemned and sentenced us and sent the sentence to Prince Golitsyn for confirmation.

I had scarcely had time to give an imitation of the trial and the

[29] Abencerrages, a Moorish family, on the legend of whose tragic fate in Granada Chateaubriand founded his romance *Les Aventures du Dernier des Abencérages.* (*Tr.*)

[30] Tredyakovsky, Vasily Kirillovich (1703-69), son of a priest at Astrakhan, is said, like Lomonosov, to have walked to Moscow in pursuit of learning. He was the author of inferior poems, but did great service to Russian culture by his numerous translations. He was the first to write Russian as it was spoken. (*Tr.*)

[31] Kostrov, Yermil Ivanovich (1750-96), a peasant's son and a seminarist, wrote in imitation of Derzhavin, but is better known for his translations of the *Iliad,* Apuleius and Ossian. (*Tr.*)

[32] Kheraskov, Mikhail Matveyevich (1733-1807), author of an immense number of poems in pseudo-classic style. Wiener says 'they now appal us with their inane voluminousness'. But readers of Turgenev will remember how greatly they were admired by Punin. The best known of his epics is the *Rossiad,* dealing with Ivan the Terrible. (*Tr.*)

[33] Knyazhnin, Yakov Borisovich (1742-91) wrote numerous tragedies and comedies, chiefly adaptations from the French or Italian, and of no literary merit. (*Tr.*)

[34] Diltey, Philipp Genrikh (d. 1781), first professor of law at Moscow University (from 1756). (*R.*)

sentence of the University Senate to the students five or six times in the lecture-room when all at once, at the beginning of a lecture, the inspector, who was a major in the Russian army and a French dancing-master, made his appearance with a non-commissioned officer, bringing an order to take me and conduct me to the university prison. Some of the students came to see me on my way, and in the courtyard, too, there was a crowd of young men, so evidently I was not the first taken; as we passed they all waved their caps and their hands; the university soldiers tried to move them back but the students would not go.

In the dirty cellar which served as a prison I found two of the arrested men, Arapetov and Orlov; Prince Andrey Obolensky and Rosenheim had been put in another room; in all, there were six of us punished for the Malov affair. Orders were given that we should be kept on bread and water; the rector sent some sort of soup, which we refused, and it was well we did so. As soon as it got dark and the university grew empty, our comrades brought us cheese, game, cigars, wine, and liqueurs. The soldier in charge was angry and started grumbling, but accepted twenty kopecks and carried in the provisions. After midnight he went further and let several visitors come in to us; so we spent our time feasting by night and going to bed by day.

On one occasion it happened that the assistant-director, Panin, the brother of the Minister of Justice, faithful to his Horse-Guard habits, took it into his head to go the round of the State prison in the university cellar by night. We had only just lit a candle and put it under a chair so that the light could not be seen from outside, and were beginning on our nocturnal luncheon, when we heard a knock at the outer door; not the sort of knock that meekly begs a soldier to open, which is more afraid of being heard than of not being heard; no, this was a peremptory knock, a knock of authority. The soldier was petrified; we hid the bottles and our visitors in a little cupboard, blew out the candle and threw ourselves on our pallets. Panin came in.

'*I believe* you are smoking?' he said, so lost in thick clouds of smoke that we could hardly distinguish him from the inspector who was carrying a lantern. 'Where do they get a light? Do you give it to them?'

The soldier swore that he did not. We answered that we had tinder with us. The inspector undertook to remove it and to take away the cigars, and Panin withdrew without noticing that the number of caps in the room was double the number of heads.

On Saturday evening the inspector made his appearance and announced that I and one other of us might go home, but that the rest would remain until Monday. This proposal seemed to me insulting and I asked the inspector whether I might remain; he drew back a step, looked at me with that menacingly graceful air with which tsars and heroes in a ballet depict anger in a dance, and saying, 'Stay by all means,' went away. I got into more trouble at home for this last escapade than for the whole business.

And so the first nights I slept away from home were spent in prison. Not long afterwards it was my lot to have experience of a different prison, and there I stayed not eight days* but nine months, after which I went not home but into exile. All that comes later, however.

From that time forward I enjoyed the greatest popularity in the lecture-room. From the first I had been accepted as a good comrade. After the Malov affair I became, like Gogol's famous lady, a comrade 'agreeable in all respects'.

Did we learn anything with all this going on? Could we study? I suppose we did. The teaching was more meagre and its scope narrower than in the 'forties. It is not the function of a university, however, to give a complete training in any branch of knowledge; its business is to put a man in a position to continue to study on his own account; its work is to provoke inquiry, to teach men to ask questions. And this was certainly done by such professors as M. G. Pavlov, and on the other hand by such as Kachenovsky. But contact with other young men in the lecture-rooms and the exchange of ideas and of what they had been reading did more to develop the students than lectures and professors. . . . Moscow University did its work; the professors whose lectures contributed to the development of Lermontov, Belinsky,[35] Turgenev, Kavelin,[36] and Pirogov[37] may play their

---

[35] Belinsky, Vissarion Grigorevich (1810-48), was the greatest of Russian critics. See below chapter 25 and index. (R.)

[36] Kavelin, Konstantin Dmitriyevich (1818-85), a writer of brilliant articles on political and economic questions. A friend of Turgenev. (Tr.)

[37] Pirogov, Nikolay Ivanovich (1810-81), the great surgeon and medical authority, was the first in Russia to investigate disease by experiments on animals, and to use anæsthetics for operations. He took an active part in education and the reforms of the early years of Alexander II's reign, and published many treatises on medical subjects. To his genius and influence as Professor of Medicine in Petersburg University is largely due the very high standard of medical training in Russia. (Tr.)

game of boston in tranquillity and still more tranquilly lie under the earth.

And what originals, what prodigies, there were among them—from Fëdor Ivanovich Chumakov, who adjusted formulas to those in Poinsot's course with the perfect liberty of a privileged landowner, adding letters and taking them away, taking squares for roots and x for the known quantity, to Gavriil Myagkov, who lectured on military tactics, the *toughest* science in the world. From perpetually dealing with heroic subjects Myagkov's very appearance had acquired a military mien; buttoned up to the throat and wearing a cravat that was quite unbending, he delivered his lectures as though giving words of command.

'Gentlemen!' he would shout; 'Into the field!—*Artillery!*'

This did not mean that cannon were advancing into the field of battle, but simply that such was the heading in the margin. What a pity Nicholas avoided visiting the university! If he had seen Myagkov, he would certainly have made him Director.

And Fëdor Fëdorovich Reiss, who in his chemistry lectures never went beyond the second person of the chemical divinity, i.e. hydrogen! Reiss, who had actually been made Professor of Chemistry because not he, but his uncle, had at one time studied that science! Towards the end of the reign of Catherine, the old uncle had been invited to Russia; he did not want to come, so sent his nephew instead. . . .

Among the exceptional incidents of my course, which lasted four years (for the university was closed for a whole academic year during the cholera), were the cholera itself, the arrival of Humboldt[38] and the visit of Uvarov.[39]

Humboldt on his return from the Urals, was greeted in Moscow at a solemn session of the Society of Natural Scientists at the university, the members of which were various senators and governors—people, on the whole, who took no interest in the sciences, natural or unnatural. The fame of Humboldt, a privy councillor of His Prussian Majesty, on whom the Tsar had graciously bestowed the Anna, and to whom he had also commanded that the insignia and diploma should be presented free of charge, had reached even them. They were determined to keep up their dignity before a man who had been on Chimborazo and had lived at Sans-Souci.

[38] On 26th October, 1829. (*A.S.*)
[39] In the autumn of 1832. (*A.S.*)

To this day we look upon Europeans and upon Europe in the same way as provincials look upon those who live in the capital, with deference and a feeling of our own inferiority, knuckling under and imitating them, taking everything in which we are different for a defect, blushing for our peculiarities and concealing them. The fact is that we were intimidated, and had not recovered from the jeers of Peter I, from Biron's insults, from the arrogance of Germans in the services and of French instructors. They talk in Western Europe of our duplicity and wily cunning; they mistake the desire to show off and swagger a bit for the desire to deceive. Among us the same man is ready to be naïvely Liberal with a Liberal or to pretend to agree with a Legitimist, and this with no ulterior motive, simply from politeness and a desire to please; the bump *de l'approbativité* is strongly developed on our skulls.

'Prince Dmitry Golitsyn,' observed Lord Durham, 'is a true Whig, a Whig in soul!'

Prince D. V. Golitsyn was a respectable Russian gentleman, but why he was a Whig and in what way he was a Whig I do not understand. You may be certain that in his old age the prince wanted to please Durham and so played the Whig.

The reception of Humboldt in Moscow and in the university was no jesting matter. The Governor-General, various military and civic chiefs, and the members of the Senate, all turned up with ribbons across their shoulders, in full uniform, and the professors wore swords like warriors and carried three-cornered hats under their arms. Humboldt, suspecting nothing, came in a dark-blue dress-coat with gold buttons, and, of course, was overwhelmed with confusion. From the vestibule to the great hall of the Society of Natural Scientists ambushes were prepared for him on all sides: here stood the rector, there a dean, here a budding professor, there a veteran whose career was over and who for that reason spoke very slowly; everyone welcomed him in Latin, in German, in French, and all this took place in those awful stone tubes, called corridors, in which one cannot stop for a minute without being laid up with a cold for a month. Humboldt, hat in hand, listened to everything and replied to everything—I feel certain that all the savages among whom he had been, red-skinned and copper-coloured, caused him less trouble than his Moscow reception.

As soon as he reached the hall and sat down, he had to get up again. The Director, Pisarev, thought it necessary, in brief but vigorous language, to issue an *order of the day* in Russian concerning the services of his Excellency, the celebrated traveller; after which Sergey Glinka,[40] 'the officer', with an 1812 voice, deep and hoarse, recited his poem which began:

> *'Humboldt—Prométhée de nos jours!'*

While Humboldt wanted to talk about his observation on the magnetic needle* and to compare his meteorological records on the Urals with those of Moscow, the rector came up to show him instead something plaited of the imperial hair of Peter I . . . and Ehrenberg and Rose had difficulty in finding a chance to tell him something about their discoveries.[41]

Things are not much better among us in the non-official world: ten years later Liszt* was received in Moscow society in much the same way. Enough silly things were done in his honour in Germany, but here his reception was of quite a different quality. In Germany it was all old-maidish exaltation, sentimentality, all *Blumenstreuen*, while with us it was all servility, homage paid to power, rigid standing at attention; with us it was all 'I have the honour to present myself to your Excellency'. And here, unfortunately, there was also Liszt's fame as a celebrated Lovelace to add to it all. The ladies flocked round him, as peasant-boys on country roads flock round a traveller while his horses are being harnessed, inquisitively examining himself, his carriage, his cap. . . . No one listened to anybody but Liszt, no one spoke to anybody else, nor answered anybody else. I remember that at one evening party Khomyakov,[42] blushing for the honourable company, said to me,

---

[40] S. N. Glinka, author of patriotic verses of no merit. Referred to as 'the officer' by Pushkin in a poem. (*Tr.*)

[41] How diversely Humboldt's travels were understood in Russia may be gathered from the account of a Ural Cossack who served in the office of the Governor of Perm; he liked to describe how he had escorted the mad Prussian Prince, Gumplot. What did he do? 'Well, the silliest things, collecting grasses, looking at the sand; in the saltings he says to me, through the interpreter, "Get into the water and fetch what's at the bottom"; well, I got just what is usually at the bottom, and he asks, "Is the water very cold at the bottom?" No, my lad, I thought, you won't catch me. So I drew myself up at attention, and answered, "When it's our duty, your Highness, it's of no consequence: we are glad to do our best." ' ('We are glad, etc.,' was the formula which soldiers were expected to shout when addressed on parade by a senior officer. (*R.*))

[42] Khomyakov. See later, for Herzen's account of this leader of the Slavophil movement. (*Tr.*)

'Please let us argue about something, that Liszt may see that there are people in the room not exclusively occupied with him.'

For the consolation of our ladies I can only say one thing, that in just the same way Englishwomen dashed about, crowded round, pestered and obstructed other celebrities such as Kossuth and afterwards Garibaldi and others. But alas for those who want to learn good manners from Englishwomen and their husbands!

Our second 'famous' traveller was also in a certain sense 'the Prometheus of our day', only he stole the light not from Jupiter but from men. This Prometheus, sung not by Glinka but by Pushkin himself in his 'Epistle to Lucullus', was the Minister of Public Instruction, S. S. (not yet Count) Uvarov.[43] He amazed us by the multitude of languages and the heterogeneous hotch-potch which he knew; a veritable shopman behind the counter of enlightenment, he preserved in his memory samples of all the sciences, the concluding summaries, or, better, the rudiments. In the reign of Alexander, he wrote Liberal brochures in French; later on he corresponded on Greek subjects with Goethe in German. When he became Minister he discoursed on Slavonic poetry of the fourth century, upon which Kachenovsky observed to him that in those days our forefathers had enough to do to fight the bears, let alone singing ballads about the gods of Samothrace and the mercy of tyrants. He used to carry in his pocket, by way of a testimonial, a letter from Goethe, in which the latter paid him an extremely odd compliment, saying: 'There is no need for you to apologise for your style—you have succeeded in what I never could succeed in doing—forgetting German grammar.'

So this actual privy Pic de Mirandole[44] introduced a new kind of examination. He ordered that the best students should be selected to deliver a lecture, each on his own subject, instead of the professor. Of course the deans selected the liveliest.

These lectures went on for a whole week. The students had to prepare themselves in all the subjects of their course, and the dean picked out the student's name by lot. Uvarov assembled all the distinguished people of Moscow. Archimandrites and senators, the Governor-General and Ivan Ivanovich Dmitriyev—all were present.

I had to lecture on mineralogy in Lovetsky's lecture-room—and already he is dead!

[43] At this time Uvarov was the Assistant Minister. (*A.S.*)

[44] Giovanni Pico della Mirandola (1463-94), a learned Italian who was the most famous of all infant prodigies, a mediæval 'Admirable Crichton'. (*Tr.*)

F

'Where's our old comrade Langeron![45]
Where's our old comrade Benigson!
You, too, are nowhere to be seen,
And you, too, might have never been!'

Alexey Leontevich Lovetsky was a tall, roughly-hewn, heavily-moving man with a big mouth and a large face entirely devoid of expression. Removing in the corridor his pea-green overcoat adorned with a number of collars of varying size, such as was worn during the First Consulate, he would begin, before entering the lecture-room, in an even, passionless voice (which was in perfect keeping with his stony subject): 'We concluded in the last lecture all that is necessary to say concerning siliceous earth.' Then he would sit down and go on: 'The alumina. . . .' He had created an invariable system for formulating the qualities of each mineral, from which he never departed; so that it happened that the characteristics of some would be defined in the negative:

'Crystallisation—does not crystallise.
'Employment—is not employed for any purpose.
'Usefulness—injury to the organism. . . .'

He did not, however, avoid poetry, nor moral reflections, and every time he showed us artificial stones and told us how they were made, he added: 'Gentlemen, it's a fraud!' In dealing with husbandry, he found *moral* qualities in a good cock if he 'liked crowing and was attentive to the hens', and a distinct virtue in an aristocratic ram if he had 'bald knees'. He could also tell us touching tales in which flies described how on a fine summer evening they walked about a tree and were covered with resin which turned into amber, and he always added: 'That, gentlemen, is prosopopœia!'

When the dean summoned me, the audience was rather exhausted; two mathematical lectures had reduced the listeners, who did not understand a single word, to apathy and depression. Uvarov asked for something a little livelier and for a student with 'his tongue well hung'. Shchepkin indicated me.

I mounted the platform. Lovetsky was sitting near, motionless, with his arms on his knees like a Memnon or Osiris, and was apprehensive. I whispered to him,

---

[45] An incorrect quotation from V. A. Zhukovsky's *Anniversary of Borodino*. (*A.S.*)

'What luck that I have to lecture in your room. I shan't let you down.'

'Don't boast when you are going into action,' the worthy professor responded, scarcely moving his lips and not looking at me.

I almost burst out laughing; but when I looked before me, there was a mist before my eyes, I felt that I was turning pale and a dryness covered my tongue. I had never spoken in public before, the lecture-room was full of students—they relied upon me; at the table below were 'the powers of this world' and all the professors of our faculty. I picked up the question and read in an unnatural voice, 'Crystallisation, its contributing factors, laws and forms.'

While I was thinking how to begin, the happy thought occurred to me, that if I made a mistake the professors might notice it, but they would not say a word, while the rest of the audience knew nothing about the subject themselves, and the students would be satisfied so long as I did not break down in the middle, because I was a favourite. And so in the name of Haüy, Werner, and Mitscherlich, I delivered my lecture, concluding it with philosophic reflections, and all the time addressing myself to the students and not to the Minister. The students and the professors shook hands with me and thanked me. Uvarov led me off to be introduced to Prince Golitsyn and the latter said something, of which I could catch nothing but the vowel sounds. Uvarov promised me a book as a souvenir of the occasion, but never sent it.

The second and third occasions of my appearance on a stage were very different. In 1836 I played the part of 'Ugar' in the old Russian farce,[46] while the wife of the colonel of gendarmes was 'Marfa', before all the beau-monde of Vyatka, including Tyufyayev. We had been rehearsing for a month, but yet my heart beat violently and my hands trembled, when a deathly silence followed the overture and the curtain began rising with a sort of frightful shudder; Marfa and I were waiting behind the scenes. She was so sorry for me, or else so afraid that I should spoil the performance, that she gave me an immense glass of champagne, but even with that I was half dead.

After making my début under the auspices of a Minister of Education and a colonel of gendarmes, I appeared without any symptoms of nervousness or self-conscious shyness at a Polish meeting in London, and that was my third public appearance. The place of the ex-

---

[46] 'Marfa and Ugar, or The Lackeys' War . . . adapted from the French of Dubois', by A. A. Korsakov. (A.S.)

Minister Uvarov was on that occasion filled by the ex-Minister, Ledru-Rollin.[47]

But is not this enough of student reminiscences? I am afraid it may be a sign of senility to linger over them so long; I shall only add a few details about the cholera of 1831.

Cholera—the word so familiar now in Europe and so thoroughly at home in Russia that a patriotic poet calls the cholera the one faithful ally of Nicholas—rang out then for the first time in the North. Everyone trembled before the terrible infection that was moving up the Volga towards Moscow. Exaggerated rumours filled the imagination with horror. The disease advanced capriciously, halted, skipped over places, and seemed to have missed Moscow, when suddenly the dread news, 'The cholera is in Moscow!' was all over the city.

In the morning a student in the Political Faculty felt ill; next day he died in the university hospital. We rushed to look at his body. He was emaciated, as though after a long illness, the eyes were sunk, the features were distorted; beside him lay a watchman who had been taken ill in the night.

We were informed that an order had been given for the university to be closed. This order was read to our faculty by Denisov, the professor of technology; he was melancholy, perhaps frightened. He too was dead by the next evening.

We assembled together from all faculties in the big university courtyard; there was something touching in this crowd of young people bidden to disperse before the infection. Their faces were pale and particularly animated; many were thinking of friends and relations. We said good-bye to the State scholars, who were being separated from us by the quarantine measures and distributed in small numbers in different houses. And at home we were all met by the stench of chloride of lime, 'Four Robbers' vinegar and a diet such as might well have laid a man up, apart from chloride and cholera.

Strange to say those sad days have remained as it were a time of ceremonial solemnity in my memory.

Moscow assumed quite a different aspect. An easiness of intercourse, unknown at ordinary times, gave it a new life. There were fewer carriages in the streets, and gloomy crowds of people stood at

[47] Ledru-Rollin, Alexandre-Auguste (1808-74), member of the French Provisional Government of 1848, and one of the earliest advocates of universal adult suffrage. (Tr.)

the cross-roads and talked about poisoners. The conveyances that were taking the sick moved at a walking pace, escorted by police; people drew aside from the black hearses with corpses. Bulletins concerning the disease were printed twice a day. The town was cordoned off as in time of war, and the soldiers shot a poor sacristan who was making his way across the river. All this absorbed men's minds, and fear of the plague ousted fear of the authorities; the people murmured, and then there came one piece of news upon another, that so-and-so had been taken ill, that so-and-so had died. . . .

The Metropolitan, Filaret, arranged a universal service of prayer. On the same day and at the same hour the priests made the round of their parishes in procession with banners. The frightened inhabitants came out of their houses and fell on their knees, as the procession passed, praying with tears for the remission of sins. Even the priests, accustomed to address God on familiar terms, were grave and moved. Some of them went to the Kremlin. There in the open air, surrounded by the higher clergy, the Metropolitan genuflected and prayed that this cup might pass. On the same spot six years before he had held a thanksgiving for the killing of the Decembrists.

Filaret was by way of being a high priest in opposition; on behalf of what he was in opposition, I never could make out: perhaps on behalf of his own personality. He was an intelligent and learned man, and a master of the Russian language, successfully introducing Church Slavonic into it; but all this gave him no right to be in opposition. The common people did not like him and called him a freemason, because he was closely associated with Prince A. N. Golitsyn and was preaching in Petersburg in the most flourishing days of the Bible Society. The Synod forbade his catechism being used in teaching. The clergy under his sway went in terror of his despotism; possibly it was as rivals that Nicholas and he hated each other.

Filaret was very clever and ingenious in humiliating the temporal power; in his sermons there was the light of that vague Christian socialism which beamed from Lacordaire[48] and other far-sighted Catholics. From his exalted Primate's tribune Filaret declared that a man can never *lawfully* be the tool of another, that there can be nothing between men but an exchange of services; and this he said in a state in which half the population were slaves.

He used to say to the fettered convicts in the transit prison on the

[48] Lacordaire, Jean-Baptiste Henri (1802-61), French Roman Catholic preacher. He sided with the Republic in 1848; editor of the *Ère nouvelle*. (*A.S.*)

Sparrow Hills: 'The civil law has condemned you and drives you away, but the Church hastens after you, longing to say one more word, one more prayer for you and to give you her blessing for your journey.' Then, seeking to comfort them, he would add 'that they had been punished and had finished with their past, that a new life lay before them, while among others (probably there were no others except officials present) there were still greater criminals,' and he quoted the example of the robber who was crucified with Christ.

Filaret's sermon at the service on the occasion of the cholera surpassed all his others; he took as his text how the angel offered David the choice of war, famine or plague as a punishment; David chose the plague. The Tsar came to Moscow in a fury, sent the Court Minister, Prince Volkonsky, to give Filaret a good dressing down and threatened to send him to be Metropolitan in Georgia. The Metropolitan meekly submitted and sent out a new message to all the churches, in which he explained that they would be wrong to look in the text of his first sermon for any reference to the most pious Emperor; that David was ourselves, defiled by sin. Then, of course, the first sermon was understood even by those who had not grasped its meaning at first.

This was how the Metropolitan of Moscow played the game of opposition.

The service helped as little with the infection as the chloride of lime did; the sickness increased.

I was in Paris for the whole of its severest visitation by the cholera, in 1849. The ferocity of the sickness was frightening. The hot days of June helped to spread it: the poor died like flies, the tradespeople fled from Paris, while others stayed behind locked doors. The government, exclusively occupied with its struggles against the revolutionaries, did not think of taking active measures. The scanty collections raised were not commensurate with the demands. The poor working people were left to their fate; the hospitals had not beds enough, the police had not coffins enough; and in the houses, packed to overflowing with different families, the bodies remained two or three days in inner rooms.

In Moscow it was not like that.

Prince D. V. Golitsyn, at that time Governor-General, a weak but honourable man, cultured and much respected, aroused the enthusiasm of Moscow society, and somehow everything was arranged in a family way, that is, without special interference by the government. A committee was formed of citizens of standing—wealthy land-owners and merchants. Every member undertook one quarter of Moscow. Within a few days twenty hospitals had been opened; they did not cost the government a farthing, for everything was done by private subscription. Shopkeepers gave gratis everything needed for the hospitals, bedclothes, linen, and warm clothing for the convales-cent. Young men volunteered as superintendents of the hospitals to ensure that half of the contributions should not be stolen by the attendants.

The university did not lag behind. The whole Medical Faculty, students and doctors *en masse*, put themselves at the disposal of the cholera committee; they were assigned to the different hospitals and stayed there continuously until the cholera was over. For three or four months these marvellous young people lived in the hospitals as orderlies, assistants, nurses, secretaries, and all this without any re-muneration and at a time when there was such an exaggerated fear of the infection. I remember one student, a Little Russian, I think called Fitskhelaurov, who at the beginning of the cholera had asked for leave of absence on account of important family affairs. Leave is rarely given in term-time, but at last he obtained it; just as he was about to set off, the students went to the hospitals. The Little Russian put his leave in his pocket and went with them. When he came out of the hospital his leave had long expired and he was the first to laugh heartily over his trip.

Moscow, apparently so drowsy and apathetic, so absorbed in scan-dal and piety, weddings, and nothing at all, always wakes up when it is necessary, and is equal to the occasion when a storm breaks over Russia.

In 1612 she was joined in blood-stained nuptials with Russia, and their union was welded in fire in 1812.

She bowed her head before Peter because the future of Russia lay in his brutal grip. But with murmurs and disdain Moscow received within her walls the woman scarlet with her husband's blood, that impenitent Lady Macbeth, that Lucretia Borgia without her Italian blood, the Russian Tsaritsa of German birth[49]—and scowling and pouting, she quietly withdrew from Moscow.

---

[49] Catherine II, born a German princess, rose to be Empress of Russia through the murder—by her orders or with her connivance—of her husband, Peter III, to the great advantage of the country. (*Tr.*)

Scowling and pouting, Napoleon waited for the keys of Moscow at the Dragomilovsky Gate, impatiently playing with his curb-reins and tugging at his glove. He was not accustomed to enter foreign towns unescorted.

'But my Moscow came not forth,'[50]

as Pushkin says; but set fire to herself.

The cholera came and again the people's city showed itself full of heart and energy!

In August 1830 we went to Vasilevskoye, stopped, as we usually did, at the Radcliffian castle of Perkhushkovo and, after feeding ourselves and our horses, were preparing to continue our journey. Bakay, with a towel round his waist like a belt, had already shouted: 'Off!' when a man galloped up on horseback, signalling to us to stop, and one of the Senator's postillions, covered with dust and sweat, leapt off his horse and handed my father an envelope. In the envelope was the news of the Revolution of July! There were two pages of the *Journal des Débats* which he had brought with the letter; I read them over a hundred times and got to know them by heart, and for the first time I found the country dull.

It was a glorious time; events came quickly. Scarcely had the meagre figure of Charles X had time to disappear into the mists of Holyrood, when Belgium flared up, the throne of the Citizen King tottered, and a hot, revolutionary breeze began to blow in debates and literature. Novels, plays, poems, all once more became propaganda and conflict.

At that time we knew nothing of the artificial stage-setting of the Revolution in France, and we took it all for honest cash.

Anyone who cares to see how strongly the news of the July Revolution affected the younger generation should read Heine's description of how he heard in Heligoland 'that the great pagan Pan was dead'. There was no sham ardour there: Heine at thirty was as enthusiastic, as childishly excited, as we were at eighteen.

We followed step by step every word, every event, the bold questions and abrupt answers, the doings of General Lafayette, and of General Lamarque; we not only knew every detail concerning them but loved all the leading men (the Radicals, of course) and kept their

---

[50] *Yevgeny Onegin*, VII, 37 (not quite accurately quoted). (*A.S.*)

portraits, from Manuel[51] and Benjamin Constant to Dupont de l'Eure[52] and Armand Carrel.[53]

In the midst of this ferment all at once, like a bomb exploding close by, the news of the rising in Warsaw stunned us. This was not far away: this was at home, and we looked at each other with tears in our eyes, repeating our favourite line:

'Nein! es sind keine leere Träume!'[54]

We rejoiced at every defeat of Dibich; refused to believe in the failures of the Poles, and I at once add to my ikonostasis the portrait of Thaddeus Kosciuszko.

It was just then that I saw Nicholas for the second time and his face was still more strongly engraved on my memory. The nobility and gentry were giving a ball in his honour. I was in the gallery of the Assembly Hall and could stare at him to my heart's content. He had not yet begun to wear a moustache. His face was still young, but I was struck by the change in it since the time of the coronation. He stood morosely by a column, staring coldly and grimly before him, without looking at anyone. He had grown thinner. In those features, in those pewtery eyes one distinctly could read the fate of Poland, and indeed of Russia as well. He was shaken, *frightened*; he doubted[55] the security of his throne and was ready to avenge

---

[51] Manuel, Jacques-Antoine (1775-1827), a man of great independence and honesty, was expelled from the Chambre des Députés for his opposition to the war with Spain in 1823. (*Tr.*)

[52] Dupont de l'Eure, Jacques-Charles (1767-1855), a leader in the Revolution of 1830, was afterwards president of the Provisional Government in 1848. (*Tr.*)

[53] Carrel, Armand (1800-36), as editor of *Le National* he offered spirited opposition to Charles X, as well as to aggressive acts of the government of Louis-Philippe. (*Tr.*)

[54] From J. W. von Goethe's *Hoffnung*. (For *keine* read *nicht*.) (*A.S.*)

[55] Here is what Denis Davydov† tells in his Memoirs: 'The Tsar said one day to A. P. Yermolov: "I was once in a very terrible situation during the Polish War. My wife was expecting her confinement; rebellion had broken out in Novgorod; I had only two squadrons of the Horse Guards left me; the news from the army was only reaching me through Königsberg. I was forced to surround myself with soldiers discharged from hospital." '

The Memoirs of this partisan leave no room for doubt that Nicholas, like Arakcheyev, like all cold-hearted, cruel and vindictive people was a *coward*. Here is what General Chechensky told Davydov: 'You know that I can appreciate manliness and so you will believe my words. I was near the Tsar on the 14th December, and I watched him all the time. I can assure you on my honour that the Tsar, who was very *pale* all the time, *had his heart in his boots.*'

And Davydov himself tells us: 'During the riot in the Haymarket the Tsar only visited the capital on the second day, when order was restored. The Tsar was at

F*

himself for what he had suffered, for his fear and his doubts. With the subjection of Poland all the restrained malignancy of the man was let loose. Soon we felt it, too.

The network of espionage cast about the university from the beginning of the reign began to be drawn tighter. In 1832[56] a Pole who was a student in our faculty disappeared. Sent to the university as a government scholar, not at his own initiative, he had been put in our course; I made friends with him; he was discreet and melancholy in his behaviour; we never heard a bitter word from him, but we never heard a word of weakness either. One morning he was missing from the lectures; next day he was missing still. We began to make inquiries; the government scholars told us in secret that he had been fetched away at night, that he had been summoned before the authorities, and then people had come for his papers and belongings and had ordered them not to speak of it. There the matter ended: *we never heard anything of the fate of this unfortunate young man.*[57]

A few months passed when suddenly there was a rumour in the lecture-room that several students had been seized in the night; among them were Kostenetsky, Kohlreif, Antonovich and others; we knew them well: they were all excellent fellows. Kohlreif, the son of a Protestant pastor, was an extremely gifted musician. A *court-martial* was appointed to try them; this meant in plain language that they were doomed to perish. We were all in a fever of suspense to know what would happen to them,[58] but from the first they too

---

Peterhof, and himself once observed casually, "Volkonsky and I were standing all day on a mound in the garden, listening for the sound of cannon-shot from the direction of Petersburg." Instead of anxiously listening in the garden, and continually sending couriers to Petersburg,' Davydov adds, 'he ought to have hastened there himself; anyone of the slightest manliness would have done so. On the following day (when everything was quiet) the Tsar drove in his carriage into the crowd which filled the square, and shouted to it, "On your knees!" and the crowd hurriedly obeyed the order. The Tsar, seeing several people dressed in civilian clothes (among those following the carriage), imagined that they were suspicious characters, and ordered the poor wretches to be taken to the lock-up and, turning to the people, began shouting: "They are all vile Poles; they have egged you on." Such an ill-timed sally completely ruined the effect, in my opinion.'

A strange sort of bird was this Nicholas!

† Davydov (see Tolstoy's *War and Peace*) and Yermolov were both leaders of the partisan or guerilla warfare against the French in 1812. (*Tr.*)

[56] The *A.S.* note gives reasons for believing that this happened in 1831. The man was probably Gaspar Stefanovich Shanyavsky. (*R.*)

[57] And where are the Kritskys? What had they done? Who tried them? For what were they condemned? (See p. 95. (*R.*))

[58] They were made to serve in the army as privates. (*A.S.*)

vanished without trace. The storm that was crushing the sprouts was close at hand. We no longer had a foreboding of its approach: we heard it, we saw it, and we huddled closer and closer together.

The danger strung up our exasperated nerves even tighter, made our hearts beat faster and made us love each other with greater fervour. There were five of us at first[59] and now we met Passek.

In Vadim there was a great deal that was new to us. With slight variations we had all developed in similar ways: that is, we knew nothing but Moscow and our country estates, we had all learned out of the same books, had lessons from the same tutors, and been educated at home or at a boarding-school preparatory for the university. Vadim had been born in Siberia during his father's exile, in the midst of want and privations. His father had been himself his teacher. He had grown up in a large family of brothers and sisters, under a crushing weight of poverty but in complete freedom. Siberia sets its own imprint on a man, which is quite unlike our provincial stamp; it is far from being so vulgar and petty; it displays more healthiness and better tempering. Vadim was a savage in comparison with us. His daring was of another kind, unlike ours, more that of the *bogatyr*,[60] and sometimes arrogant; the aristocracy of misfortune had developed in him a peculiar self-esteem; but he knew how to love others too, and gave himself to them without stint. He was bold, even reckless to excess—a man born in Siberia, and in an exiled family too, has an advantage over us in not being afraid of Siberia.

Vadim from family tradition hated the autocracy* with his whole soul, and he took us to his heart as soon as we met. We made friends very quickly—though, indeed, at that time, there was neither ceremony nor reasonable precaution, nothing like it, to be seen in our circle.

'Would you like to make the acquaintance of Ketscher, of whom you have heard so much?' Vadim said to me.

'I certainly should.'

'Come to-morrow evening, then, at seven o'clock; don't be late: he'll be at my place.'

I went—Vadim was not at home. A tall man with an expressive face and a good-naturedly menacing look behind his spectacles was waiting for him. I took up a book: he took up a book.

[59] Herzen, Ogarëv, N. I. Sazonov, N. M. Satin, A. N. Savich. (*A.S.*)
[60] Legendary hero. (*R.*)

'But perhaps you,' he said as he opened it, 'perhaps you are Herzen?'

'Yes; and you're Ketscher?'

A conversation began and grew more and more lively. . . .

'Allow me,' Ketscher interrupted me roughly. 'Allow me: do me the kindness to use "thou" to me.'

'Let us use "thou".'

And from that minute (which may have been at the end of 1831) we were inseparable friends; from that minute the anger and kindness, the laugh and the shout of Ketscher have resounded at all the stages, in all the adventures of our life.

Our meeting with Vadim introduced a new element into our Cossack brotherhood.

As before we met most frequently at Ogarëv's. His invalid father had gone to live on his estate in Penza. Ogarëv lived alone on the ground floor of their house at the Nikitsky Gate. It was not far from the university, and all were particularly drawn towards it. There was in Ogarëv that magnetic attraction which forms the first traceable line of the process of crystallisation in every mass of chaotically colliding atoms, if only they have some affinity towards each other. Scattered about wherever it may be, they grow imperceptibly into the heart of the organism.

But besides his bright, cheerful room, furnished with red hangings striped with gold, with the perpetual smoke of cigars and smell of punch and other—I was going to say food and drink, but I stopped because there was seldom anything to eat except cheese—well, besides Ogarëv's ultra-student-like abode where we argued for whole nights together, and sometimes caroused for whole nights too, another house, in which almost for the first time we learnt to respect family life, became more and more our favourite resort.

Vadim often left our talks and went home; he missed his mother and sisters if he did not see them for a long time. To us who lived heart and soul in comradeship, it was strange that he could prefer his family to our company.

He introduced us to it. In that family everything bore traces of the Tsar's *visitation*; only yesterday it had come from Siberia, it was ruined, harassed, and at the same time full of that dignity which misfortune lays, not upon every sufferer, but on the foreheads of those who have known how to bear it.

Their father had been seized in the reign of Paul in consequence of some political denunciation, flung into the Schlüsselburg and then deported to Siberia. Alexander brought back thousands of those exiled by his insane father, but Passek was *forgotten*. He was the nephew of that Passek who took part in the murder of Peter III, who was afterwards Governor-General in the Polish provinces, and he might have claimed part of an inheritence which had already passed into other hands, and it was those 'other hands' which kept him in Siberia.

While confined in the Schlüsselburg Passek had married the daughter of one of the officers in the garrison there. The young girl knew that things would go hard with her, but she was not deterred by fear of exile. At first they struggled on somehow in Siberia, selling the last of their belongings, but their fearful poverty grew more and more irresistibly, and the more rapidly so as their family increased. Needy, toiling, deprived of warm clothing and at times even of their daily bread, they yet succeeded in coming through and in bringing up a whole family of young lions; the father transmitted to them his proud, indomitable spirit and faith in himself, the mystery of great misfortunes; he educated them by his example, the mother by her self-sacrifice and bitter tears. The sisters were in no way inferior to the brothers in heroic fortitude. Yes—why be afraid of words—they were a family of heroes. What they had all borne for one another, what they had done for the family was incredible, and always with head erect, not in the least subdued.

In Siberia the three sisters once had only one pair of shoes; they used to keep them for going for walks, that strangers might not see the extremity of their need.

At the beginning of 1826[61] Passek received permission to return to Russia. It was winter, and it was no joke to move with such a family, without fur-coats, without money, from the province of Tobolsk, while on the other hand the heart yearned for Russia: exile is more than ever insufferable when it is over. Our martyrs trudged back somehow; a peasant woman, who had wet-nursed one of the children during the mother's illness, brought them for the journey some money that she had somehow scraped up, asking only that they would take her too; drivers brought them to the Russian frontier for a trifle, or for nothing; some of the family walked while others were driven, and the young people took turns; so they made the long

---

[61] In fact the permission was received at the end of 1824; the family returned in 1825. (*A.S.*)

winter journey from the Urals to Moscow. Moscow was the dream of the young ones, their hope—and there hunger awaited them.

The government pardoned Passek, and never thought of restoring to him some part of his property. Wasted by exertions and privations, the old man took to his bed; they did not know what they should dine on the next day.

At this time Nicholas was celebrating his coronation: [62] banquet followed banquet, and Moscow was like a heavily decorated ballroom, everywhere lights, escutcheons and gay attire. . . . The two elder sisters, without consulting anyone, wrote a petition to Nicholas, describing the situation of the family, and begged him to review the case and restore their property. They left the house secretly in the morning and went to the Kremlin, elbowed their way to the front, and awaited the Tsar, 'crowned and exalted on high'. When Nicholas came down the steps of the Red Staircase, the two girls quietly stepped forward and held up the petition. He passed by, pretending not to notice them; an aide-de-camp took the paper and the police led them away to the police station.

Nicholas was about thirty at the time and already was capable of such heartlessness. This coldness, this intransigence is characteristic of slight commonplace natures, cashiers, and tipstaffs. I have often noticed this unshakable firmness of character in postal officials, salesmen of theatre and railway tickets, and people who are continually bothered and interrupted at every minute. They learn to look at a man without seeing him, and not to listen to him, although they are standing side by side. But how did this autocratic clerk train himself not to see, and what need had he not to be a minute late for a parade?

The girls were kept in custody until evening. Frightened and shocked, they besought the police superintendent with tears to let them go home, where their absence must have alarmed the whole family. Nothing was done about the petition.

The father could endure no more: he had had enough; he died. The children were left with their mother, struggling on somehow from day to day. The greater the need, the harder the sons worked; all three passed their university course brilliantly and took their degrees. The two elder ones went off to Petersburg; there, being excellent mathematicians, they gave lessons in addition to their work in the service (one in the Navy and the other in the Engineers) and,

---

[62] On 22nd August, 1826. (A.S.)

denying themselves everything, sent the money they earned home to the family.

I vividly remember the old mother in her dark gown and white cap. Her thin, pale face was covered with wrinkles, and she looked far older than she was; only her eyes retained something of her youth: so much gentleness, love, anxiety, and so many past tears could be seen in them. She adored her children; she was rich, famous, young in them . . . she read and re-read to us their letters; with deep and devout feeling she spoke of them in her weak voice, which sometimes broke and quivered with suppressed tears.

When they were all gathered together in Moscow and sitting at their simple meal, the old woman was beside herself with joy; she walked round the table, looked after their wants, and, suddenly stopping, would gaze at her young people with such pride, with such happiness, and then lift her eyes to me as though asking: 'They really are fine, aren't they?' At such times I wanted to throw myself on her neck and kiss her hand; and, moreover, they all really were very handsome, too.

She was happy then. . . . Why did she not die at one of those dinners? . . .

In two years, she had lost the three eldest sons. One died gloriously, amid the esteem of his enemies, victory, and glory, though it was not for his own cause he laid down his life. He was the young general killed by the Circassians at Dargo. Laurels do not heal a mother's heart. . . . The others did not have so happy an end; the hardness of Russian life weighed upon them, weighed upon them till it crushed them.

Poor mother! and poor Russia!

Vadim died in February 1843.[63] I was with him at the end, and for the first time looked upon the death of a man dear to me, and at the same time on death in its full, ruthless horror, in all its meaningless fortuitousness, in all its blind, immoral injustice.

Ten years before his death Vadim married my cousin[64] and I was a groomsman at his wedding. Married life and the change in his habits parted us somewhat. He was happy in his private life, but unfortunate in his outward circumstances, and unsuccessful in his undertakings. Not long before our arrest he went to Kharkov, where he had been promised a lecturer's chair at the university. His going

[63] October, 1842. (*A.S.*)
[64] i.e., Tatyana Kuchin, the 'cousin from Korcheva', mentioned in Chapter 3. (*Tr.*)

there saved him indeed from prison, but his name did not slip the attention of the police. Vadim was refused the post. The assistant director admitted to him that they had received a document by which they were forbidden to give him the chair, on account of his connections with *evilly-disposed persons*, of which the government had knowledge.

Vadim was left without a post, that is, without bread—that was his Vyatka.

We were exiled. Intercourse with us was dangerous. Black years of poverty followed for him; in seven years of struggle to get a bare living, in mortifying contact with coarse and heartless people, far from friends and from all possibility of calling to them and being answered, his healthy muscles wore out.

'Once we had spent all our money to the last farthing,' his wife told me afterwards; 'on the previous evening I had tried to get hold somewhere of ten roubles, but I couldn't get them anywhere. I had already borrowed from everyone from whom it was possible to borrow a little. In the shops they refused to give us provisions except for cash; we thought only of one thing: What would the children have to eat next day? Vadim sat gloomily by the window; then he got up, took his hat and said he wanted to go for a walk. I saw that he was very much depressed; I felt frightened, but still I was glad that he should distract his mind a little. When he was gone I flung myself on the bed and wept very bitterly; then I began thinking what to do— everything we had of the slightest value, our rings and our spoons, had long ago been pawned; I saw no recourse left but to apply to *my* people and beg their reluctant assistance. Meanwhile Vadim wandered aimlessly about the streets and so reached Petrovsky Boulevard. As he passed by Shiryayev's shop it occurred to him to inquire whether the bookseller had sold even one copy of his book; he had been in five days before, but had found nothing for him; he walked apprehensively into the shop. "Very glad to see you," Shiryayev said to him. "There is a letter from our Petersburg agent: he has sold three hundred roubles' worth of your book; would you like to have the money?" And Shiryayev counted him out fifteen gold roubles. Vadim lost his head in his delight, rushed into the first eating-house for provisions, bought a bottle of wine and fruit and dashed home in a cab in triumph. At the moment I was watering the remainder of some broth for the children, and was meaning to put a little aside for him and to assure him that I had already had some, when he suddenly came in with the parcel and the bottle, gay and joyous as he used to be.'

And she sobbed and could not utter another word.

After my exile I met him for a moment in Petersburg and found him very much changed. He kept his convictions, but he kept them like a warrior who will not let the sword drop out of his hand, though he feels that he has been pierced through. He was by then melancholy and exhausted and looked coldly towards the future. So, too, I found him in Moscow in 1842. His circumstances had somewhat improved; his work had begun to be appreciated; but all this came too late—it was like the epaulettes of Polezhayev[65] or the pardon of Kohlreif[66]—granted not by the Russian Tsar but by Russian life.

Vadim was wasting away; in the autumn of 1842 tuberculosis was discovered, that terrible disease which I was destined to see once again.

A month before his death I began to notice with horror that his mental faculties were growing dimmer and weaker, like guttering candles; the room was becoming darker and uneasier. Soon it was with difficulty and effort that he could find the words for his incoherent speech, and he would dwell on external assonances; then he scarcely spoke at all, but only inquired anxiously for his medicines and whether it was not time to take them.

At three o'clock one night in February Vadim's wife sent for me; the sick man was very bad, and was asking for me. I went in to him and gently took his hand; his wife mentioned my name; he gazed long and wearily at me but did not recognise me and closed his eyes. The children were brought in; he looked at them but I think did not recognise them either. His moaning became more painful; he would be quiet for minutes and then suddenly give a prolonged sigh and cry out; then a bell pealed in a neighbouring church: Vadim listened and said, 'That's matins.' After that he did not utter another word. . . . His wife knelt sobbing by the dead man's bedside; a good, kind lad, one of their university comrades, who had been looking after him of late, bustled about, moving back the medicine table, raising the blinds. . . . I went away—it was bright and frosty; the rising sun shone brilliantly on the snow as though something good had happened; I went to order the coffin.

When I went back a deathlike stillness reigned in the little house:

[65] Polezhayev was made an officer only just before he died. (*A.S.*)
[66] Kohlreif was recalled from banishment not long before his death. (*A.S.*)

the dead man lay in accordance with Russian custom on a table in the drawing-room; at a little distance from it sat his friend, the artist Rabus, making a pencil sketch of him through his tears; beside the dead man stood a tall woman, silent, with folded arms and an expression of infinite sorrow; no artist could have moulded a nobler, more profound, figure of grief. The woman was not young, but retained traces of a stern, majestic beauty; she stood motionless, wrapped in a long black velvet cloak lined with ermine fur.

I stopped in the doorway.

Two or three minutes passed in the same stillness, when all at once she bent down, warmly kissed the dead man on the forehead, and said, 'Farewell! farewell, friend Vadim,' and with resolute steps walked into the inner rooms. Rabus went on drawing. He nodded to me; we had no inclination to speak. I sat down by the window in silence.

That woman was Madame E. Chertkov, the sister of Count Zakhar Chernyshev, exiled for the Fourteenth of December.

The Simonovsky archimandrite, Melkhisedek, of his own accord offered a grave within the precincts of his monastery. Melkhisedek had once been a humble carpenter and a desperate schismatic; he had afterwards turned to orthodoxy, become a monk, been made abbot and finally archimandrite. With all that he remained a carpenter: that is, he kept his heart and his broad shoulders and his red, healthy face. He knew Vadim and respected him for his historical researches concerning Moscow.

When the dead man's body arrived before the monastery gates they were opened and Melkhisedek came out with all the monks to meet the sufferer's poor coffin with soft, mournful chanting, and to accompany it to the grave. Not far from Vadim's grave lie the ashes of another dear friend, Venevitinov,[67] with the inscription 'How well he knew life, how little he lived!' How well Vadim, too, knew life!

This was not enough for fate. Why did the old mother live so long? She had seen the end of their exile, had seen her children in all the beauty of their youth, in all the brilliance of their talent: what more had she to live for? Who prizes happiness should seek an early death. Lasting happiness is no more to be found than ice that never melts.

Vadim's eldest brother[68] died a few months after the third, Diomid,

---

[67] Venevitinov, Dmitri Vladimirovich (1805-27), a young poet. (A.S.)
[68] Yevgeny Vasilevich Passek. (A.S.)

was killed; he caught cold, neglected his illness, and his undermined organism succumbed. He was barely forty and he was the eldest.

These three graves of three friends cast long, dark shadows over the past; the last months of my youth are seen through funeral crape and the smoke of incense. . . .

A year passed, the trial of my arrested comrades was over. They were found guilty (just as we were later on, and later still the Petrashevsky group)[69] *of a design* to form a secret society, and of criminal conversations; for this they were sent as common soldiers to Orenburg. Nicholas made an exception of one of them, Sungurov.[70] He had completed his studies, and was in the service, married and had children. He was condemned to be deprived of his rights of status and to be exiled to Siberia.

'What could a handful of young students do? They destroyed themselves for nothing!' All that is very sensible, and people who argue in that way ought to be gratified at the *good sense* of the younger generation of Russians that followed us. After our affair, which followed that of Sungurov, *fifteen years* passed in tranquillity before the Petrashevsky affair, and it was those fifteen years from which Russia is only just beginning to recover and by which two generations were broken, the elder smothered in violence, and the younger poisoned from childhood, whose sickly representatives we are seeing to-day.

After the Decembrists all attempts to form societies were, in effect, unsuccessful; the scantiness of our forces and the vagueness of our aims pointed to the necessity for another kind of work—for preliminary work upon ourselves. All that is true.

But what would young men be made of who could wait for theoretical solutions while calmly looking on at what was being done round them, at the hundreds of Poles clanking their fetters on the Vladimir Road, at serfdom, at the soldiers flogged in the Khodynsky Field by some General Lashkevich, at fellow-students who disappeared and were never heard of again? For the moral purification of the generation, as a pledge of the future, they were bound to be so

[69] The members of the Petrashevsky group, of whom Dostoyevsky was one, were condemned to death, and led out to the scaffold. At the last moment their sentence was commuted to penal servitude in Siberia. (*Tr.*)

[70] Sungurov, Nikolay Petrovich (b. 1805), head of a secret society in Moscow at the end of the 1820's, arrested in 1831 and sentenced to hard labour. He died in Siberia. (*A.S.*)

indignant as to be senseless in their attempts and disdainful of danger. The savage punishments inflicted on boys of sixteen or seventeen served as a stern lesson and a kind of hardening process; the paw of the beast hung over every one of us, proceeding from a breast without a heart, and dispelled for good all rosy hopes of indulgence for youth. It was dangerous to play at Liberalism, and no one could dream of playing at conspiracy. For one badly concealed tear over Poland, for one boldly uttered word, there were years of exile, of the white strap,[71] and sometimes even the fortress; that was why it was important that those words were uttered and those tears were shed. Young people sometimes perished but they perished without checking the mental activity that was trying to solve the sphinx riddle of Russian life; indeed they even justified its hopes.

Our turn came now. Our names were already on the lists of the secret police.* The first play of the light-blue cat with the mouse began as follows.

When the young men who had been condemned were being sent off to Orenburg on foot under escort without sufficient warm clothing, Ogarëv in our circle, I. Kireyevsky in his, got up subscriptions. All the condemned men were without money. Kireyevsky brought the money collected to the commander, Staal, a good-natured old man of whom I shall have more to say later. Staal promised to remit the money and asked Kireyevsky,

'But what are these papers?'

'The names of those who subscribed,' answered Kireyevsky, 'and the amounts.'

'You do believe that I shall remit the money?' asked the old man.

'There's no doubt of that.'

'And I imagine that those who have given it to you trust you. And so what is the use *of our keeping their names?*' With these words Staal threw the list into the fire, and of course it was an excellent thing to do.

Ogarëv himself took the money to the barracks, and this went off without a hitch; but the young men took it into their heads to send their thanks from Orenburg to their comrades, and, as a government official was going to Moscow, they seized the opportunity and asked him to take a letter, which they were afraid to trust to the post. The official did not fail to take advantage of this rare chance to prove all

---

[71] i.e., of supervision by the political police, whose light-blue uniform was worn with a white strap. (*Tr.*)

the ardour of his loyal sentiments, and presented the letter to the general of gendarmes in Moscow.

The general of gendarmes at this time was Lesovsky, who was appointed to the post when A. A. Volkov went out of his mind, imagining that the Poles wanted to offer him the crown of Poland (an ironical trick of destiny to send a general of gendarmes mad over the crown of the Jagellons![72]). Lesovsky, himself a Pole, was not a bad man, and was no fool: having wasted his property over cards and a French actress, he philosophically preferred the place of general of gendarmes in Moscow to a place in the debtors' prison of the same city.

Lesovsky summoned Ogarëv, Ketscher, Satin, Vadim, I. Obolensky and the others, and charged them with being in communication with political criminals. On Ogarëv's observing that he had not written to anyone, and that if anyone had written to him he could not be responsible for it, and that, moreover, no letter had reached him, Lesovsky answered:

'You got up a subscription for them, *that's still worse.* For the first time the Sovereign is *so merciful* as to *pardon* you; only I warn you, gentlemen, a strict supervision will be kept over you: be careful.'

Lesovsky looked round at them all with a significant glance and, his eyes resting upon Ketscher, who was taller and a little older than the rest and who raised his eyebrows so fiercely, he added:

'You, my good sir, ought to be ashamed, in your station in life.'

It might have been supposed that Ketscher was vice-chancellor of the Russian Heraldry Office, while as a matter of fact he was only a humble district doctor.

I was not sent for: probably my name was not in the letter.

This threat was like a promotion, a consecration, a winning of our spurs. Lesovsky's advice threw oil on the fire, and as though to make their future task easier for the police we put on velvet bérets à la Karl Sand[73] and tied identical tricolour scarves round our necks.

Colonel Shubinsky, who was quietly and softly creeping with velvet steps into Lesovsky's place, pounced upon his *weakness* with us; we were to serve as one of the steps in his promotion—and we did.

But first I shall add a few words about the fate of Sungurov and his companions.

---

[72] The dynasty of kings of Poland from 1386 to 1572. (*Tr.*)

[73] Karl Sand, a student of Jena University, who in 1819 assassinated the German dramatist Kotzebue, because he ridiculed the *Burschenschaft* movement. (*Tr.*)

Nicholas let Kohlreif return *ten years* later from Orenburg, where his regiment was stationed. He pardoned him because he was in consumption, just as, because he was in consumption, Polezhayev was promoted to be an officer, and because he was dead Bestuzhev was given a cross. Kohlreif returned to Moscow and died in the arms of his old, grief-stricken father.

Kostenetsky distinguished himself in the Caucasus and was promoted to the rank of officer. It was the same with Antonovich.

The fate of the luckless Sungurov was incomparably more fearful. On reaching the end of the first stage on the Sparrow Hills, Sungurov asked leave from the officer in charge to go out into the fresh air, as the hut, packed to overflowing with exiles, was suffocating. The officer, a young man of twenty, went out himself on to the road with him. Sungurov, choosing a favourable moment, turned off the road and disappeared. Probably he knew the locality well. He succeeded in getting away from the officer, but next day the gendarmes got on his track. When Sungurov saw that it was impossible to escape, he cut his throat. The gendarmes took him to Moscow unconscious and losing blood.

The unfortunate officer was reduced to the ranks.

Sungurov did not die. He was tried again, this time not as a political criminal, but as a runaway exile: half his head was shaved: it is a peculiar method (probably inherited from the Tatars) used to forestall escapes, and it shows even more than corporal punishment the complete contempt for human dignity of the Russian legislature. To this external ignominy the sentence added *one* stroke of the lash within the walls of the prison. Whether this sentence was carried out I do not know. After that, Sungurov was sent to the mines at Nerchinsk.

I heard his name pronounced once more and then it vanished for ever.

In Vyatka I once met in the street a young doctor, a fellow-student at the university, who was on his way to some post in a factory. We talked of old days and common acquaintances.

'My God!' said the doctor, 'do you know whom I saw on my way here in Nizhny Novgorod Province? I was sitting in the posting station waiting for horses. It was very nasty weather. A staging officer, in charge of a party of prisoners, came in to get warm. We got into conversation; hearing that I was a doctor, he asked me to go to the halting-place to look at one of the exiles and see whether he was shamming or really was seriously ill. I went, of course with the intention of declaring in any case that the convict was ill. In the small halting-place there were about eighty people in chains, shaven and unshaven, women and children; they all moved apart as the officer went in, and we saw, lying on straw in a corner on the dirty floor, a figure wrapped in an exile's *caftan*.

' "This is the sick man," said the officer.

'I had no need to lie, for the poor wretch was in a high fever; emaciated and exhausted by prison and the journey, with half his head shaven and his beard uncut, he looked terrible as he stared about senselessly, and continually asked for water.

' "Well, brother, is it bad?" I said to the sick man, and added to the officer: "it is impossible for him to go on."

'The sick man fixed his eyes upon me and muttered "Is that you?" —he mentioned my name. "You don't know me?" he added in a voice which went to my heart like a knife.

' "Forgive me," I said, taking his dry, burning hand, "I can't recall you."

' "I am Sungurov," he answered.

'Poor Sungurov!' repeated the doctor, shaking his head.

'Well, did they let him stay?' I asked.

'No, but they got a cart for him.'

After I had written this I learned that Sungurov died at Nerchinsk. His property, which consisted of two hundred and fifty souls in the Bronnitsky district near Moscow, and four hundred souls in the Arzamas district of Nizhny Novgorod Province, *went to pay for the keep of him and his comrades in prison during the investigation.*

His family was ruined; the first care of the authorities, however, was to diminish it. *Sungurov's wife was seized with her two children, and spent six months* in the Prechistensky prison, and her unweaned baby died there. May the reign of Nicholas be damned for ever and ever! Amen!

Chapter 7

After the University

BEFORE the storm broke over our heads my time at the university was coming to an end. The ordinary anxieties, the nights without sleep spent in useless mnemonic tortures, the superficial study in a hurry and the thought of the examination overcoming all interest in science—all that was as it always is. I wrote a dissertation on *astronomy* for the gold medal, and got the silver one. I am certain that I am incapable of understanding now what I wrote then, and that it was worth its weight—in silver.

It has sometimes happened to me to dream that I am a student going in for an examination—I think with horror how much I have forgotten and feel that I shall be plucked—and I have woken up rejoicing from the bottom of my heart that the sea and passports, and years and visas cut me off from the university, that no one is going to torture me, and no one will dare to give me a horrid 'one'.[1] And, indeed, the professors would be surprised that I should have gone so far back in so few years. Indeed, this did once happen to me.[2]

After the final examination the professors shut themselves up to reckon the marks, while we, excited by hopes and doubts, hung about the corridors and entrance in little groups. Sometimes someone would come out of the council-room. We rushed to learn our fate,

[1] Marks in Russian educational establishments range from one to five. (*R.*)

[2] In 1844 I met Perevoshchikov at Shchepkin's and sat beside him at dinner. Towards the end he could not resist saying: 'It is a pity, a very great pity, that circumstances prevented you from taking up work. You had excellent abilities.'

'But you know it's not for everyone to climb up to heaven behind you. We are busy here on earth at work of some sort.'

'Upon my word, to be sure that may be work of a sort. Hegelian philosophy perhaps. I have read your articles, and there is no understanding them: bird's language, that's queer sort of work. No, indeed!'

For a long while I was amused at this verdict, that is, for a long while I could not understand that our language really was poor; if it was a bird's it must have been the bird that was Minerva's favourite.

138

but for a long time there was still nothing settled. At last Heyman came out.

'I congratulate you,' he said to me, 'you are a graduate.'

'Who else, who else?'

'So-and-so, and So-and-so.'

I felt at once sad and gay; as I went out at the university gates I thought that I was not going out at them again as I had yesterday and every day; I was becoming estranged from the university, from that parental home where I had spent four years, so youthfully and so well; on the other hand I was comforted by the feeling of being accepted as completely grown-up, and, why not admit it? by the title of graduate I had gained all at once.[3]

Alma Mater! I am so greatly indebted to the university, and lived its life and with it so long after I had finished my studies, that I cannot think of it without love and respect. It will not charge me with ingratitude, though at least as regards the university gratitude is easy; it is inseparable from the love and bright memories of youth . . . and I send it my blessing from this far-off foreign land!

The year we spent after taking our degrees made a triumphant end to our early youth. It was one prolonged feast of friendship, exchange of ideas, inspiration, carousing. . . .

The little group of university friends who had survived the course did not part, but went on living in their common sympathies and fancies, and no one thought of his material situation or of arranging his future. I should not think well of this in men of mature age, but I prize it in the young. Youth, if only it has not been desiccated by the moral corruption of *petit bourgeois* ideas, is everywhere impractical, and is especially bound to be so in a young country which is full of strivings and has attained so little. Moreover, to be impractical is far from implying anything false: everything turned towards the future is bound to have a share of idealism. If it were not for

[3] Among the papers sent me from Moscow I found a note in which I informed my *cousin* who was then in the country with the princess that I had taken my degree. 'The examination is over, and I am a graduate! You cannot imagine the sweet feeling of freedom after four years of work. Did you think of me on Thursday? It was a stifling day, and the torture lasted from nine in the morning till nine in the evening.' (26th June, 1833). I fancy I added two hours for effect or to round off the sentence. But for all my satisfaction my vanity was stung by another student's (Alexander Drashusov) winning the gold medal. In a second letter of the 6th July, I find: 'To-day was the prizegiving, but I was not there. I did not care to be the *second* to receive a medal.'

the impractical characters, all the practical people would remain at the same dull stage of perpetual repetition.

Some enthusiasm preserves a man from *real* spills far more than any moral admonitions. I remember youthful orgies, moments of revelry that sometimes went beyond bounds, but I do not remember one really immoral affair in our circle, nothing of which a man would have to feel *seriously* ashamed, which he would try to forget and conceal. Everything was done openly, and what is bad is rarely done openly. Half, more than half, of the heart was turned away from idle sensuality and morbid egoism, which concentrate on impure thoughts and accentuate vices.

I consider it a great misfortune for a nation when their young generation has no youth; we have already observed that for this being young is not enough by itself. The most grotesque period of German student life is a hundred times better than the *petit bourgeois* maturity of young men in France and England. To my mind the *elderly* Americans of fifteen are simply repulsive.

In France there was at one time a brilliant aristocratic youth, and later on a revolutionary youth. All the Saint-Justs[4] and Hoches,[5] Marceaux and Desmoulins,[6] the heroic children who grew up on the gloomy poetry of Jean-Jacques, were real youths. The Revolution was the work of young men: neither Danton nor Robespierre nor Louis XVI himself outlived their thirty-fifth year. With Napoleon the young men were turned into orderlies; with the Restoration, 'the revival of old age'—youth was utterly incompatible—everything became mature, businesslike, that is, *petit bourgeois*.

The last youth of France were the Saint-Simonists and the Fourierists. The few exceptions cannot alter the prosaically dull character of French youth. Escousse and Lebras[7] shot themselves because they

---

[4] Louis de Saint-Just (1767-94) was a member of the Convention and the Committee of Public Safety, a follower of Robespierre and beheaded with him at the age of twenty-seven. (*Tr.*)

[5] Lazare Hoche (1768-97) and François-Séverin Marceau (1769-96), were generals of the French Revolutionary Army. Both were engaged in the pacification of La Vendée. Both perished before reaching the age of thirty. (*Tr.*)

[6] Camille Desmoulins (1760-94) was one of the early leaders of the French Revolution, and headed the attack on the Bastille; he was afterwards accused of being a Moderate and beheaded together with Danton at the age of thirty-four. (*Tr.*)

[7] Victor Escousse (b. 1813) and Auguste Lebras (b. 1816) were poets who wrote in collaboration a successful play, *Farruck le Maure*, followed by an unsuccessful one called *Raymond*. On the failure of the latter they committed suicide in 1832. Béranger wrote a poem on them. (*Tr.*)

were young in a society of old men. Others struggled like fish thrown out of the water on to the muddy bank, till some were caught on the barricades and others on the hooks of the Jesuits.

But, since youth asserts its rights, the greater number of young Frenchmen work off their youth in a Bohemian period; that is, if they have no money, they live in little cafés with little *grisettes* in the Quartier Latin, and in grand cafés with grand *lorettes*, if they have money. Instead of a Schiller period, they have a Paul de Kock period; in this strength, energy, everything young is rapidly and rather wretchedly wasted and the man is ready—for a *commis* in a commercial house. The Bohemian period leaves at the bottom of the soul one passion only—the thirst for money, and the whole future is sacrificed to it—there are no other interests; these practical people laugh at theoretical questions and despise women (the result of numerous conquests over those whose trade it is *to be conquered*). As a rule the Bohemian period is passed under the guidance of some worn-out sinner, a faded celebrity, *d'un vieux prostitué*, living at someone else's expense, an actor who has lost his voice, or a painter whose hands tremble, and he is the model who is imitated in accent, in dress, and above all in a haughty view of human affairs and a profound understanding of good fare.

In England the Bohemian period is replaced by a paroxysm of pleasing originalities and amiable eccentricities. For instance, senseless tricks, absurd squandering of money, ponderous practical jokes, heavy, but carefully concealed vice, profitless trips to Calabria or Quito, to the North and to the South—with horses, dogs, races, and stuffy dinners by the way, and then a wife and an incredible number of fat, rosy babies; business transactions, *The Times*, Parliament, and the old port which weighs them to the earth.

We played pranks too and we caroused, but the fundamental tone was not the same, the diapason was too elevated. Mischief and dissipation never became our goal. Our goal was faith in our vocation; supposing that we were mistaken, still, believing it as a fact, we respected in ourselves and in each other the instruments of the common cause.

And in what did our feasts and orgies consist? Suddenly it would occur to us that in another two days it would be the sixth of December, St Nicholas's day. The supply of Nikolays was terrific, Nikolay Ogarëv, Nikolay Satin, Nikolay Ketscher, Nikolay Sazonov. . . .

'Gentlemen, who is going to celebrate the name-day?'

'I! I! . . .'

'I shall the next day then.'

'That's all nonsense, what's the good of the next day? We will keep it in common—club together! And what a feast it will be!'

'Yes! yes! At whose rooms are we to meet?'

'Satin is ill, so obviously it must be at his.'

And so plans and calculations are made, and it is incredibly absorbing for the future guests and hosts. One Nikolay drives off to the Yar to order supper, another to Materne's for cheese and salami. Wine, of course, is bought in the Petrovka from Depré's, on whose price-list Ogarëv wrote the epigram:

'De près ou de loin,
Mais je fournis toujours.'

Our inexperienced taste went no further than champagne, and was so young that we sometimes even exchanged *Rivesaltes mousseux* for champagne. I once saw the name on a wine-list in Paris, remembered 1833 and ordered a bottle, but, alas, even my memories did not help me to drink more than one glass.

Before the festive day the wines would be tried, and so it would be necessary to send a messenger for more, for clearly the samples were liked.

While we are on the subject, I cannot refrain from describing what happened to Sokolovsky. He was perpetually without money and immediately spent everything he received. A year before his arrest he arrived in Moscow and stayed with Satin. He had just succeeded in selling the manuscript of *Khever,** and so resolved to give a feast not only for us but also *pour les gros bonnets*, that is, he invited Polevoy, Maximovich, and others. On the morning of the previous day he set out with Polezhayev, who was at that time in Moscow with his regiment, to make purchases, bought cups and even a samovar and all sorts of unnecessary things and finally wines and eatables, that is, pasties, stuffed turkeys, and so on. In the evening we arrived at Satin's. Sokolovsky suggested uncorking one bottle, and then another; there were five of us, and by the end of the evening, that is, by the beginning of the next morning, it appeared that Sokolovsky had no more wine and no more money. He had spent everything he had left over after paying some small debts.

Sokolovsky was mortified, but controlled his feeling; he thought and thought, then wrote to all the *gros bonnets* that he had been taken seriously ill and was putting off the feast.

For the celebration of the *four name-days* I wrote out a complete programme, which was deemed worthy of the special attention of the inquisitor Golitsyn, who asked me at the enquiry whether the programme had been carried out exactly.

'À la lettre,' I replied. He shrugged his shoulders as though he had spent his whole life in the Smolny Convent or keeping Good Friday.

After supper as a rule a *vital* question arose; a question that aroused controversy, i.e. how to prepare the punch. Other things were usually eaten and drunk *in good faith, like the voting in Parliament, without dispute*, but in this everyone must have a hand and, moreover, it was after supper.

'Light it—don't light it yet—light it how?—put it out with champagne or Sauternes?—put the fruit and pineapple in while it is burning or afterwards?'

'Obviously when it is burning, and then the whole aroma will go into the punch.'

'But, I say, pineapples float, the edges will be scorched, simply a calamity.'

'That's all nonsense,' Ketscher would shout louder than all, 'but what's not nonsense is that you must put out the candles.'

The candles were put out; all the faces looked blue, and the features seemed to quiver with the movement of the flame. And meantime the temperature in the little room was becoming tropical from the hot rum. Everyone was thirsty and the punch was not ready. But Joseph, the Frenchman sent from the Yar, was ready; he had prepared something, the antithesis of punch, an iced beverage of various wines *à la base de cognac*. A genuine son of the *'grand peuple'*, he explained to us, as he put in the French wine, that it was so good because it had twice passed the Equator. *'Oui, oui, messieurs; deux fois l'équateur, messieurs!'*

When the beverage remarkable for its arctic iciness had been finished and in fact there was no need of more drink, Ketscher shouted, stirring the fiery lake in the soup-tureen and making the last lumps of sugar melt with a hiss and a wail,

'It's time to put it out! time to put it out!'

The flame blushes from the champagne, and runs along the surface of the punch, with a kind of anguish and foreboding.

Then comes a voice of despair:

'But I say, old man, you're mad: don't you see the wax is melting right into the punch?'

'Well, you try holding the bottle yourself in such heat so that the wax does not melt.'

'Well, something ought to have been wrapped round it first,' the distressed voice continues.

'Cups, cups, have you enough? How many are there of us? Nine, ten, fourteen, yes, yes!'

'Where's one to find fourteen cups?'

'Well anyone who hasn't got a cup must use a glass.'

'The glasses will crack.'

'Never, never; you've only to put a spoon in them.'

Candles are brought, the last flicker of flame runs across the middle, makes a pirouette and vanishes.

'The punch is a success!'

'It is a great success!' is said on all sides.

Next day my head aches—I feel sick. That's evidently from the punch, too mixed! And on the spot I make a sincere resolution never to drink punch for the future; it is a poison.

Pëtr Fëdorovich comes in.

'You came home in somebody else's hat, sir: our hat is a better one.'

'The devil take it entirely.'

'Should I run to Nikolay Mikhaylovich's[8] Kuzma?'

'Why, do you imagine someone went home without a hat?'

'It won't hurt to go just in case.'

At this point I guess that the hat is only a pretext, and that Kuzma has invited Pëtr Fëdorovich to the field of battle.

'You go and see Kuzma; only first ask the cook to let me have some sour cabbage.'

'So, Lexandr Ivanych, the gentlemen kept their name-days in fine style?'

'Yes, indeed: there hasn't been such a supper in our time.'

'So we shan't be going to the university to-day?'

My conscience pricks me and I make no answer.

'Your papa was asking me, "How is it," says he, "he is not up yet?" I was pretty smart. I said, "His honour's head aches; he

---

[8] N. M. Satin. Kuzma was his servant. (*A.S.*)

complained of it from early morning, so I did not even pull up the blinds." "Well," said he, "you did right there." '

'But do let me go to sleep, for Christ's sake. You wanted to go and see Kuzma, so go.'

'This minute, this minute, sir; first I'll run for the cabbage.'

A heavy sleep closes my eyes again; two or three hours later I wake up much refreshed. What can they be doing there? Ketscher and Ogarëv stayed the night. It's annoying that punch has such an effect on the head, for it must be owned it's very nice. It is a mistake to drink punch by the glass; henceforth and for ever I will certainly drink no more than a small cupful.

Meantime my father has already finished interviewing the cook and reading the newspapers.

'You have a headache to-day?'

'Yes, a bad one.'

'Perhaps you have been working too hard?' And as he asks the question I can see that he has his doubts already.

'I forgot, though: I believe you were with Nikolasha[9] and Ogarëv yesterday.'

'Of course.'

'They treated you, I expect . . . for the name-day? Madeira in the soup again? Ah, I don't like all that. Nikolasha is too fond of wine at the wrong time, and where he gets that from I don't understand. Poor Pavel Ivanovich . . . why, on the twenty-ninth of June, his name-day, he would invite all the relations and have a dinner in the regular way, quiet and proper. But the fashion nowadays, champagne and sardines in oil, it's a disgusting sight. As for that luckless young Ogarëv, I say nothing about him: he is alone and abandoned! Moscow . . . with plenty of money, his coachman Yeremy: "go and fetch some wine!" The coachman's glad to: he gets ten kopecks at the shop for it.'

'Yes, I lunched with Nikolay Pavlovich. But I don't think that that's why my head aches. I shall go for a little walk; that always does me good.'

'By all means; you will dine at home, I hope.'

'Of course; I am only going out for a little.'

To explain the *Madeira in the soup*, it must be said that a year or more before the famous celebration of the four name-days, Ogarëv

[9] i.e. Nikolay Pavlovich Golokhvastov, the younger of the two sons of a sister of Herzen's father. These two sons are fully described later. (*Tr.*)

and I had gone off for a spree in Easter Week and, to get out of dining at home, I had said that I had been invited to dinner by Ogarëv's father.

My father disliked my friends as a rule; he used to call them by the wrong surnames, invariably making the same mistake: thus he never failed to call Satin Saken and Sazonov, Snazin. He liked Ogarëv least of all, both because he wore his hair long and because he smoked without asking his leave. On the other hand, he regarded him as a distant cousin and so could not distort the name of a relation. Moreover, his father, Platon Bogdanovich, belonged both by family and by fortune to the little circle of persons recognised by my father, and he liked my being intimate with the family. He would have liked it better still if Platon Bogdanovich had had no son.

And so to refuse his invitation was considered unseemly.

Instead of settling ourselves in Platon Bogdanovich's respectable dining-room, we set off first to the Prices' booth (I was delighted later on to meet this family of acrobats in Geneva and in London). There was a little girl there, by whom we were enraptured and whom we had named Mignon.

After looking at Mignon and resolving to come and see her again in the evening, we set off to dine at the Yar. I had a gold piece and Ogarëv about the same. We were at that time complete novices and so, after long consultation, we ordered fish soup with champagne in it, a bottle of Rhine-wine, and some small bird, so that when we got up from the dinner, which was frightfully expensive, we were quite hungry and so went off to look at Mignon again.

When my father said good-night to me, he observed that he thought I smelt of wine.

'That must be because there was Madeira in the soup,' I said.

'*Au madère*—that must be Platon Bogdanovich's son-in-law's idea; *cela sent les casernes de la garde.*'

From that time until I was exiled, if my father fancied that I had been drinking, that my face was red, he would be sure to say to me,

'I suppose you have had Madeira in your soup to-day!'

And so I hastened off to Satin's.

Ogarëv and Ketscher, of course, were on the spot. Ketscher, looking tousled, was displeased with some of the arrangements and was criticising them severely. Ogarëv, on the homeopathic system of driving out one nail with another, was drinking up what was left, not merely after the supper but after the foraging of Pëtr Fëdorovich, who was already singing, whistling, and playing a tattoo in Satin's kitchen.

Recalling the days of our youth, of all our circle, I do not remember a single incident which would weigh on the conscience, which one would be ashamed to think of. And that applies to all our friends without exception.

There were, of course, Platonic dreamers among us, and disillusioned youths of seventeen. Vadim even wrote a drama in which he tried to depict 'the terrible ordeal of his spent heart'. The drama began like this: 'A garden—house in distance—windows lighted—storm—no one in sight—garden gate not fastened, it flaps to and fro and creaks.'

'Are there any characters in the drama besides the gate and the garden?' I asked Vadim.

And Vadim, rather nettled, said,

'You're always playing the fool! It's not a jest, it's the record of my heart; if you go on like that I shan't read it'—and proceeded to read it.

There were follies, too, that were not at all Platonic; even some that ended not in writing plays but in the chemist's shop. But there were no vulgar intrigues ruining the woman and humiliating the man; there were no *kept women* (indeed that vulgar word for them did not exist among us). Tranquil, secure, prosaic, *petit bourgeois* vice, vice by contract, passed our circle by.

'Then you do admit the worse form of vice, prostitution?' I shall be asked.

Not I, but you do! that is, not you individually, but all of you. It reposes so firmly on the social structure that it asks for no sanction from me.

Social enthusiasm, general theories, were our salvation; and not they alone but also a high development of scientific and artistic interest. Like flaming paper, they burnt out the grease spots. I have preserved some of Ogarëv's letters of that period, and the keynote of our lives can be easily judged from them. On 7th June, 1833, for instance, Ogarëv wrote to me:

'I believe we know each other, I believe we can be frank. You will not show my letter to anyone else. And so tell me—for some

G

time past I have been so absolutely brimming over, suffocated, I may
say, with sensations and thoughts, that I fancy, it's more than fancy,
the idea sticks in my head, that it is my vocation to be a poet, or
a musician, *alles eins*, but I feel that I must live in that thought,
for I have a feeling in myself that I am a poet; granted that I still
write rubbish, yet the fire in my soul, the exuberance of my feelings,
gives me the hope that I shall write decently (excuse the vulgar
expression). Tell me, friend, am I to believe in my vocation? You
know me, perhaps, better than I know myself, and will not make
a mistake.'—*June* 7, 1833.

'You write: *Yes, you are a poet, a true poet!** Friend, can you
conceive all that those words do for me? And so all that I feel, to
which I strive, in which I live, is not fallacious! It is not fallacious!
Are you telling the truth? It is not the delirium of fever—that I feel.
You know me better than anyone, don't you? I certainly feel that
you do. No, this exalted life is not the delirium of fever, not the
illusion of imagination, it is too exalted for deception, it is real, I
live in it, I cannot imagine myself with any other life. Why don't
I understand music? What a symphony would soar out of my soul
now! One can catch the stately *adagio*, but I have no power to
express myself; I want to say more than has been said; *presto,
presto,* I need a tempestuous, indomitable *presto. Adagio* and *presto,*
the two extremes. Away with that mediocrity, *andante* or
allegro moderato; they are stammerers or feeble-minded: they can
neither speak vigorously nor feel intensely.'—Chertkovo, *Aug.* 18,
1833.

We have grown out of the habit of this enthusiastic babble of
youth and it is strange to us, but in these lines of a young man not
yet twenty it can clearly be seen that he is insured against vulgar
vice and vulgar virtue, and that even if he is not saved from the mire,
he will come out of it unsullied.

It is not lack of self-confidence; it is the misgiving of faith, it is
the passionate desire for confirmation, for the superfluous word of
love, so precious to us. Yes, it is the uneasiness of creative conception,
it is the anxious searchings of a soul *in travail*.

'I cannot yet,' he writes in the same letter, 'catch the notes which
sound in my soul: physical incapacity limits the imagination. But,
devil take it! I am a poet, and poetry whispers the truth to me

where I could not have grasped it with cold reason. This is the philosophy of revelation.'

So ends the first part of our youth; the second begins with prison. But before we enter upon it I must say something of the tendencies, of the ideas, with which it found us.

The period that followed the suppression of the Polish insurrection educated us rapidly. We were not tormented only by the fact that Nicholas had grown to his full stature and was firmly established in severity; we began with inward horror to perceive that in Europe, too, and especially in France, to which we looked for our political watchword and battle-cry, things were not going well; we began to look upon our theories with suspicion.

The childish liberalism of 1826, which gradually passed into the French political view preached by the Lafayettes and Benjamin Constant and sung by Béranger, lost its magic power over us after the ruin of Poland.

Then some of the young people, and Vadim among them, threw themselves into a profound, earnest study of Russian history.

Others took to the study of German philosophy.

Ogarëv and I belonged to neither of these sets. We had grown too closely attached to other ideas to part with them readily. Our faith in revolution of the festive Béranger stamp was shaken, but we looked for something else which we could find neither in the *Chronicle* of Nestor[10] nor in the transcendental idealism of Schelling.

In the midst of this ferment, in the midst of surmises, of confused efforts to understand the doubts which frightened us, the pamphlets of Saint-Simon and his followers, their tracts and their trial came into our hands. They impressed us.

Critics, superficial and not superficial, have laughed enough at Father Enfantin[11] and his apostles; the time has now come for some recognition of these forerunners of socialism.

These enthusiastic youths with their terry waistcoats and their budding beards made a triumphant and poetic appearance in the midst of the *petit bourgeois* world. They heralded a new faith; they

[10] This is the earliest record of Russian history. It begins with the Deluge and continues in leisurely fashion up to the year 1110. Nestor, of whom nothing is really known, is assumed to have been a monk of the twelfth century. (*Tr.*)

[11] B.-P. Enfantin (1796-1864), a French engineer, was one of the founders of Saint-Simonism. (*Tr.*)

had something to say; they had something in the name of which to summon the old order of things before their court of judgment, fain to judge them by the Code Napoléon* and the religion of Orléans.*

On the one hand came the *emancipation of woman*, the call to her to join in common labour, the giving of her destiny into her own hands, alliance with her as with an equal.

On the other hand the justification, the *redemption of the flesh, réhabilitation de la chair!*

Grand words, involving a whole world of new relations between human beings; a world of health, a world of spirit, a world of beauty, the world of natural morality, and therefore of moral purity. Many scoffed at the emancipated woman and at the recognition of the rights of the flesh, giving to those words a filthy and vulgar meaning; our monastically depraved imagination fears the flesh, fears woman. Sensible people grasped that the purifying *baptism of the flesh* is the death-knell of Christianity; the religion of life had come to replace the religion of death, the religion of beauty to replace the religion of flagellation and mortification by prayer and fasting. The crucified body had risen again in its turn and was no longer ashamed of itself; man attained a harmonious unity and divined that he was a whole being and not made up like a pendulum of two different metals restraining each other, that the enemy that had been welded to him had disappeared.

What courage was needed in France to proclaim in the hearing of all those words of deliverance from the spirituality which is so strong in the notions of the French and so completely absent from their conduct!

The old world, ridiculed by Voltaire, undermined by the Revolution, but strengthened, patched up and made secure by the *petit bourgeois* for their own personal convenience, had never experienced this before. It wanted to judge the apostates on the basis of its secret conspiracy of hypocrisy, but these young men unmasked it. They were accused of being backsliders from Christianity, and they pointed above their judge's head to the holy picture that had been veiled after the Revolution of 1830. They were charged with justifying sensuality, and they asked their judge, was his life chaste?

The new world was pushing at the door, and our hearts and souls opened wide to meet it. Saint-Simonism lay at the foundation of our convictions and remained so in its essentials unalterably.

Impressionable, genuinely youthful, we were easily caught up in its mighty current and passed early over that boundary at which whole crowds of people remain standing with their arms folded, go back or look to the side for a ford—to cross the ocean!

But not everyone ventured with us. Socialism and realism remain to this day the touchstones flung on the paths of revolution and science. Groups of swimmers, tossed up against these rocks by the current of events or by process of reasoning, immediately divide and make two everlasting parties which, in various disguises, cut across the whole of history, across all upheavals, across innumerable political parties and even circles of no more than a dozen youths. One stands for logic, the other for history; one for dialectics, the other for embryogeny. One is more *correct*, the other more *practical*.

There can be no talk of choice; it is harder to bridle thought than any passion, it leads one on involuntarily; anyone who can check it by emotion, by a dream, by fear of consequences, will check it, but not all can. If thought gets the upper hand in anyone, he does not inquire about its applicability, or whether it will make things easier or harder; he seeks the truth, and inexorably, impartially sets out his principles, as the Saint-Simonists did at one time, as Proudhon does to this day.

Our circle drew in still closer. Even then, in 1833, the Liberals looked at us askance, as having strayed from the true path. Just before we went to prison Saint-Simonism set up a barrier between N. A. Polevoy[12] and me. Polevoy was a man of an unusually ingenious and active mind, which readily assimilated every kind of nutriment; he was born to be a journalist, a chronicler of successes, of discoveries, of political and learned controversies. I made his acquaintance at the end of my time at the university—and was sometimes in his house and at his brother Ksenofont's. This was the time when his reputation was at its highest, the period just before the prohibition of the *Telegraph*.

This man who lived in the most recent discovery, in the question of the hour, in the latest novelty in theories and in events, and who changed like a chameleon, could not, for all the liveliness of his mind, understand Saint-Simonism. For us Saint-Simonism was a revelation, for him it was insanity, a vain Utopia, hindering social

[12] Polevoy, Nikolay Alexeyevich (1796-1846), author, journalist and historian. (*A.S.*)

development. To all my rhetoric, my expositions and arguments, Polevoy was deaf; he lost his temper and grew splenetic. Opposition from a student was particularly annoying to him, for he greatly prized his influence on the young, and saw in this dispute that it was slipping away from him.

On one occasion, affronted by the absurdity of his objections, I observed that he was just as old-fashioned a Conservative as those against whom he had been fighting all his life. Polevoy was deeply offended by my words and, shaking his head, said to me:

'The time will come when you will be rewarded for a whole lifetime of toil and effort by some young man's saying with a smile, "Be off, you are behind the times." '

I felt sorry for him and ashamed of having hurt his feelings, but at the same time I felt that his sentence could be heard in his melancholy words. They were no longer those of a mighty champion, but of a superannuated gladiator who has served his time. I realised then that he would not advance, and would be incapable of standing still at the same point with a mind so active and on such unstable footing.

You know what happened to him afterwards: he set to work upon his *Parasha, the Siberian*.[13]

What luck a timely death is for a man who can neither leave the stage at the right moment nor move forward. I have thought that looking at Polevoy, looking at Pius IX, and at many others!

---

[13] Familiar to all English schoolgirls of the last generation in the French as *La Jeune Sibérienne* by Xavier de Maistre. I cannot discover whether the Russian version is the original and the French the translation or *vice versa*. (*Tr.*)

Appendix

A. Polezhayev

To complete the gloomy record of that period, I ought to add a few details about A. Polezhayev.

As a student, Polezhayev was renowned for his excellent verses. Amongst other things he wrote a humorous parody of *Onegin* called *Sashka* in which, regardless of proprieties, he tilted at many things in a jesting tone, in very pleasant verses.

In the autumn of 1826 Nicholas, after hanging Pestel, Muravëv, and their friends, celebrated his coronation in Moscow. For other sovereigns these ceremonies are occasions for amnesties and pardons: Nicholas, after celebrating his apotheosis, proceeded again to 'strike down the foes of the father-land', like Robespierre after his *Fête-Dieu*.

The secret police brought him Polezhayev's poem.

And so at three o'clock one night the Rector woke Polezhayev, told him to put on his uniform and go to the office. There the Director was awaiting him. After looking to see that all the necessary buttons were on his uniform and no unnecessary ones, he invited Polezhayev without any explanation to get into his carriage and drove off with him.

He conducted him to the Minister of Public Instruction. The latter put Polezhayev into his carriage and he too drove him off—but this time straight to the Tsar.

Prince Lieven[1] left Polezhayev in the great room—where several courtiers and higher officials were already waiting although it was only between five and six in the morning—and went into the inner apartments. The courtiers imagined that the young man had distinguished himself in some way and at once entered into conversa-

---

[1] The Minister of Public Instruction at this time was not K. A. Lieven but A. S. Shishkov. (*A.S.*)

153

tion with him. A senator suggested that he might give lessons to his son.

Polezhayev was summoned to the study. The Tsar was standing leaning on his desk and talking to Lieven. He flung an angry, searching glance at the newcomer; there was a manuscript-book in his hand.

'Did you write these verses?' he inquired.

'Yes,' answered Polezhayev.

'Here, prince,' the Tsar continued, 'I will give you a specimen of of university education. I will show you what young men learn there. Read the manuscript aloud,' he added, addressing Polezhayev again.

The agitation of Polezhayev was so great that he could not read. Nicholas's eyes were fixed immovably upon him. I know them and know nothing so terrifying, so hopeless, as those greyish, colourless, cold, pewtery eyes.

'I cannot,' said Polezhayev.

'Read!' shouted the imperial sergeant-major.

That shout restored Polezhayev's faculties; he opened the book. Never, he told us, had he seen *Sashka* so carefully copied and on such splendid paper.

At first it was hard for him to read; then as he got more and more into the spirit of the thing, he read the poem to the end in a loud and lively voice. At particularly cutting passages the Tsar made a sign with his hand to the Minister and the latter covered his eyes with horror.

'What do you say to that?' Nicholas inquired at the end of the reading. 'I shall put a stop to this corruption; these are the *last traces, the last remnants*; I shall root them out. What has his conduct been?'

The Minister, of course, knew nothing of his conduct, but some human feeling must have stirred in him, for he said:

'His conduct has been excellent, your Majesty.'

'That testimonial has saved you, but you must be punished, as an example to others. Would you like to go into the army?'

Polezhayev was silent.

'I give you a means of purging yourself by service in the army. Well?'

'I must obey,' answered Polezhayev.

The Tsar went up to him, laid his hand on his shoulder, and saying to him,

'Your fate is in your own hands; if I forget you you may *write* to me,' *kissed him on the forehead.*

I made Polezhayev repeat the story of the kiss a dozen times, it seemed to me so incredible. He swore that it was true.

From the Tsar he was led off to Dibich, who lived on the spot in the palace. Dibich was asleep; he was awakened, came out yawning, and, after reading the paper, asked the aide-de-camp:

'Is this he?'

'Yes, your Excellency.'

'Well! it's a capital thing; you will serve in the army. I have always been in the army, and you see what I've risen to, and maybe you'll be a field-marshal.'

This misplaced, feeble, German joke was Dibich's equivalent of a kiss. Polezhayev was led off to the camp and enlisted.

Three years passed. Polezhayev remembered the Tsar's words and wrote him a letter. No answer came. A few months later he wrote a second; again there was no answer. Convinced that his letters did not reach the Tsar, he ran away, and ran away in order to present his petition in person. He behaved carelessly, saw his old friends in Moscow and was entertained by them; of course, that could not be kept secret. In Tver he was seized and sent back to his regiment as a deserter, on foot and in chains. The court-martial condemned him to run the gauntlet; the sentence was despatched to the Tsar for confirmation.

Polezhayev wanted to kill himself before the punishment. After searching in vain in his prison for a sharp instrument, he confided in an old soldier who liked him. The soldier understood him and respected his wishes. When the old man learned that the answer had come, he brought him a bayonet and, as he gave him it, said through his tears:

'I have sharpened it myself.'

The Tsar ordered Polezhayev not to be punished.

Then it was that he wrote his fine poem beginning:

> *'I perished lonely,*
> *No help was nigh.*
> *My evil genius*
> *Passed mocking by.'* [2]

[2] Translated by Juliet Soskice.

G*

Polezhayev was sent to the Caucasus. There for distinguished service he was promoted to be a non-commissioned officer. Years and years passed; his inescapable, dreary situation broke him down; become a police poet and sing the glories of Nicholas he could not, and that was the only way of getting rid of the knapsack.

There was, however, another means of escape, and he preferred it; he drank to win forgetfulness. There is a frightening poem of his, 'To Corn-spirit'.

He succeeded in getting transferred to a regiment of the Carabineers stationed in Moscow. This was a considerable alleviation of his lot, but a malignant consumption was already eating away his chest. It was at this period that I made his acquaintance, about 1833. He languished for another four years and died in a military hospital.

When one of his friends appeared to ask for the body for burial, no one knew where it was; a military hospital traffics in corpses—sells them to the university and to the Medical Academy, boils them down to skeletons, and so on. At last he found poor Polezhayev's body in a cellar; it was lying under a heap of others and the rats had gnawed off one foot.

After his death his poems were published, and his portrait in a private's uniform was to have been included in the edition. The censor thought this unseemly, and the poor martyr was portrayed with the epaulettes of an officer—he had been promoted in the hospital.

PART II

PRISON AND EXILE
(1834—1838)

Chapter 8

Ogarëv's Arrest

ONE day in the spring of 1834 I arrived at Vadim's in the morning and found neither him nor any of his brothers and sisters at home. I went upstairs to his little room and sat down to write.

The door opened softly and Vadim's old mother came in; her footsteps were barely audible; looking weary and ill she went up to an armchair and said to me, as she sat down:

'Go on writing, go on writing. I came to see whether Vadya had come back; the children have gone for a walk and downstairs it is so empty, I felt sad and frightened. I'll stay here a little: I won't hinder you; go on with what you're doing.'

Her face was pensive and I could see in it even more clearly than usual the reflection of what she had suffered in the past and that suspicious timidity of the future, that distrust of life, which is always left after numerous great and prolonged misfortunes.

We began to talk. She told me something about Siberia:

'I have had very many troubles to bear and I shall have to see more yet,' she added, shaking her head; 'my heart bodes nothing good.'

I thought how sometimes, after hearing our bold talk and demagogic conversation, the old lady would turn pale, sigh softly, go out of the room and for a long time not utter a word.

'You and your friends,' she went on, 'you are going the sure road to ruin. You will destroy Vadya, yourself, and all of them; I love you, too, you know, like a son.'

A tear ran down her wasted cheek.

I did not speak. She took my hand and, trying to smile, added:

'Don't be angry: my nerves are overwrought. I understand it all; go your own way: there is no other for you, and, if there were, you would none of you be the same. I know that, but I cannot overcome my fears; I have been through so many troubles that I have no strength to face fresh ones. Mind you don't say a word to Vadya about this: he would be distressed; he would try to talk me over. . . . Here he is,' she added, hurriedly wiping away her tears and once more asking me with her eyes to say nothing.

Poor mother! A great, a sainted woman!

It is as fine as Corneille's 'qu'il mourût!'[1]

Her prediction was soon fulfilled; happily this time the storm passed over the heads of her family, but it brought the poor woman much sorrow and alarm.

'Taken? What do you mean?' I asked, jumping out of bed and feeling my head to make sure that I was awake.

'The *politsmeyster*[2] came in the night with the district policeman and Cossacks, about two hours after you left, seized all the papers and took Nikolay Platonovich away.'

It was Ogarëv's valet speaking. I could not imagine what pretext the police had invented: of late everything had been quiet. Ogarëv had arrived only a day or two before . . . and why had they taken him and not me?

It was impossible to fold my arms and do nothing; I dressed and went out of the house with no definite purpose. This was the first misfortune that had befallen me. I felt dreadful: I was tortured by my impotence.

As I wandered about the streets I thought, at last, of one friend whose social position made it possible for him to find out what was the matter and, perhaps, to help. He lived terribly far away, in a summer villa beyond the Vorontsov Field; I got into the first cab I came across and galloped off to him. It was before seven in the morning.

I had made the acquaintance of V——[3] about eighteen months before; in his way he was a lion in Moscow. He had been educated in Paris, was wealthy, intelligent, cultured, witty, free-thinking, had been in the Peter-Paul fortress over the affair of the Fourteenth of December and was among those set free; he had had no experience of exile, but the glory of the affair clung to him. He was in the government service and had great influence with the Governor-General, Prince Golitsyn, who was fond of men of a liberal way of

---

[1] From Corneille's *Horace*, Act III, Scene 6. (*A.S.*)

[2] *Politsmeyster* or *politseymeyster* (*Polizeimeister*), the chief of police of a town. (*R.*)

[3] V. P. Zubkov. (*A.S.*)

thinking, particularly if they expressed their views fluently in French.
The prince was not strong in Russian.

V—— was ten years older than we were, and surprised us by his
practical remarks, his knowledge of political affairs, his French
eloquence and the ardour of his Liberalism. He knew so much and
in such detail, talked so pleasantly and so easily; his opinions were
so firmly traced; he had answers, good advice, solutions for everything. He read everything, new novels, treatises, magazines, and
poetry, was moreover a devoted student of zoology, wrote out
schemes of reform for Prince Golitsyn and drew up plans for children's books.

His Liberalism was of the purest, trebly-distilled essence, of the
left wing between that of Mauguin[4] and of General Lamarque.[5]

His study was hung with portraits of all the revolutionary celebrities from Hampden and Bailly[6] to Fieschi[7] and Armand Carrel.[8] A
whole library of prohibited books was to be found under this
revolutionary ikonostasis. A skeleton, a few stuffed birds, some dried
amphibians and entrails preserved in spirit, gave a serious tone of
study and reflection to the too inflammatory character of the room.

We used to regard with envy his experience and knowledge of
men; his delicate, ironical manner of arguing had a great influence
on us. We looked upon him as a capable revolutionary, as a statesman *in spe.*

I did not find V—— at home : he had gone to town overnight for
an interview with Prince Golitsyn. His valet told me he would
certainly be home within an hour and a half. I waited.

V——'s summer villa was a splendid one. The study in which I
sat waiting was a lofty, spacious room on the ground floor, and an
immense door led to the verandah and into the garden. It was a
hot day; the fragrance of trees and flowers came in from the garden
and children were playing in front of the house with ringing laughter. Wealth, abundance, space, sunshine and shadow, flowers and

---

[4] François Mauguin (1785-1854), lawyer and politician. (*R.*)

[5] Jean Maximilien Lamarque (1770-1832), general and man of politics. He distinguished himself as a speaker for the opposition in the Chambre des Députés. (*R.*)

[6] J. S. Bailly (1736-93), one of the early leaders of the French Revolution, and an
astronomer and literary man of some distinction, was Mayor of Paris after the
taking of the Bastille, and executed in 1793. (*Tr.*)

[7] Fieschi, the celebrated conspirator, executed in 1836 for the attempt with an
'infernal machine' on the life of Louis-Philippe. (*Tr.*)

[8] Armand Carrel (1800-36), French publicist; founded *Le National.* (*R.*)

greenery . . . while in prison it is cramped, stifling, dark. I do not know how long I had been sitting there absorbed in bitter thoughts, when suddenly the valet called me from the verandah with a peculiar animation.

'What is it?' I inquired.

'Oh, please, come here and look.'

I went out to the verandah, not to wound him by a refusal, and stood petrified. A whole semi-circle of houses were blazing, as though they had caught fire at the same moment. The fire was spreading with incredible rapidity.

I remained on the verandah; the valet gazed with a sort of nervous pleasure at the fire, saying:

'It's going finely—look, that house on the right will catch fire: it will certainly catch.'

A fire has something revolutionary about it; it laughs at property and levels ranks. The valet understood that instinctively.

Half an hour later half the horizon was covered with smoke, red below and greyish-black above. That day Lefortovo was burned down. This was the beginning of a series of cases of incendiarism, which went on for five months; we shall speak of them again.

At last V—— arrived. He was in high spirits, pleasant and cordial; he told me about the fire by which he had driven and about the general belief that it was a case of arson, and added, half in jest:

'It's Pugachëvshchina. You look: you and I won't escape; they'll stick us on a stake.'

'Before they put us on a stake,' I answered, 'I am afraid they will put us on a chain. Do you know that last night the police arrested Ogarëv?'

'The police—what are you saying?'

'That's what I have come to you about. Something must be done; go to Prince Golitsyn, find out what it's about and ask permission for me to see him.'

Receiving no answer, I glanced at V——, but where he had been it seemed as though an elder brother of his were sitting with a yellowish face and sunken features; he was groaning and greatly alarmed.

'What's the matter?'

'There, I told you; I always said what it would lead to. . . . Yes, yes, we ought to have expected it. There it is. I am not to blame in thought nor in act, but very likely they will put me in prison too, and that is no joking matter; I know what a fortress is like.'

'Will you go to the prince?'

'Goodness gracious me, whatever for? I advise you as a friend, don't even speak of Ogarëv; keep as quiet as you can, or it will be the worse for you. You don't know how dangerous these things are; my sincere advice is, keep out of it; do your utmost and you won't help Ogarëv, but you will ruin yourself. That's what autocracy means —no rights, no defence; are the lawyers and judges any use?'

On this occasion I was not disposed to listen to his bold opinions and cutting criticisms. I took my hat and went away.

At home I found everything in a turmoil. Already my father was angry with me on account of Ogarëv's arrest. Already the Senator was on the spot, rummaging among my books, taking away what he thought dangerous, and in a very bad humour.

On the table I found a note from M. F. Orlov inviting me to dinner. Could he not do something for us? I was beginning to be discouraged by experience: still, there was no harm in trying and the worst I could get was a refusal.

Mikhail Fëdorovich Orlov was one of the founders of the celebrated League of Welfare,[9] and that he had not found himself in Siberia was not his own fault, but was due to his brother, who enjoyed the special friendship of Nicholas and had been the first to gallop with his Horse Guards to the defence of the Winter Palace on December the Fourteenth. Orlov was sent to his estate in the country, and a few years later was allowed to live in Moscow. During his solitary life in the country he studied political economy and chemistry. The first time I met him he talked of his new system of nomenclature in chemistry. All energetic people who begin studying a science late in life show an inclination to move the furniture about and rearrange it to suit themselves. His nomenclature was more complicated than the generally accepted French system. I wanted to attract his attention, and by way of *captatio benevolentiæ*

[9] The League of Public Welfare was formed in the reign of Alexander I to support philanthropic undertakings and education, to improve the administration of justice, and to promote the economic welfare of the country. The best men in Russia belonged to it. At first approved by Alexander, it was afterwards repressed, and it split into the 'Union of the North', which aimed at establishing constitutional government, and the 'Union of the South' led by Pestel, which aimed at republicanism. The two Unions combined in the attempt of December the Fourteenth, 1825. (*Tr.*)

began to try to prove to him that his system was good, but the old one was better.

Orlov contested the point and then agreed.

My effort to please succeeded: from that time we were on intimate terms. He saw in me a rising possibility; I saw in him a veteran of our views, a friend of our heroes, a noble figure in our life.

Poor Orlov was like a lion in a cage. Everywhere he knocked himself against the bars; he had neither space to move nor work to do and was consumed by a thirst for activity.

After the fall of France I more than once met people of the same sort, people who were disintegrated by the craving for public activity and incapable of finding their true selves within the four walls of their study or in home life. They do not know how to be alone; in solitude they are attacked by the spleen, they become capricious, quarrel with their last friends, see intrigues against them on all hands, and themselves intrigue to reveal all these non-existent plots.

A stage and spectators are as necessary to them as the air they breathe; in the public view they really are heroes and will endure the unendurable. They have to be surrounded by noise, clamour and clash, they want to make speeches, to hear their enemies' replies, they crave the stimulus of struggle, the fever of danger, and without these tonics they are miserable, they pine, let themselves go and grow heavy, have an urge to break out, and make mistakes. Ledru-Rollin is one such, who, by the way, has a look of Orlov, particularly since he has grown moustaches.

Orlov was very handsome; his tall figure, fine carriage, handsome, manly features and completely bare skull, altogether gave an irresistible attractiveness to his appearance. The upper half of his body was a match to that of A. P. Yermolov, whose frowning, quadrangular brow, thick thatch of grey hair, and eyes piercing the distance gave him that beauty of the warrior chieftain, grown old in battles, which won Maria Kochubey's heart in *Mazeppa*.

Orlov was so bored that he did not know what to begin upon. He tried founding a glass factory, in which mediæval stained glass was made, costing him more than he sold it for; and began writing a book 'On Credit'—no, that was not the way his heart yearned to go, and yet it was the only way open to him. The lion was condemned to wander idly between the Arbat and Basmannaya Street, not even daring to let his tongue run freely.

It was a mortal pity to see Orlov endeavouring to become a learned man, a theorist. His intelligence was clear and brilliant, but not at all speculative, and he got confused among newly invented systems for long-familiar subjects—like his chemical nomenclature. He was a complete failure in everything abstract, but went in for metaphysics with intense obstinacy.

Careless and incontinent of speech, he was continually making mistakes; carried away by his first impression, which was always chivalrously lofty, he would suddenly remember his position and turn back half way. He was an even greater failure in these diplomatic countermarches than in metaphysics and nomenclature; and, having got his legs tangled in the traces once, he would do it two or three times more in trying to get clear. He was blamed for this; people are so superficial and inattentive that they look more to words than to actions, and attach more weight to separate mistakes than to the combination of the whole character. What is the use of blaming, from the rigorous viewpoint of a Regulus, a man? One must blame the sorry environment in which any noble feeling must be communicated, like contraband, under ground, and behind locked doors; and, if one says a word aloud, one is wondering all day how soon the police will come. . . .

There was a large party at the dinner. I happened to sit beside General Rayevsky, the brother of Orlov's wife. He too had been in disgrace since the Fourteenth of December; the son of the celebrated N. N. Rayevsky,[10] he had as a boy of fourteen been with his brother at Borodino by his father's side; later on he died of wounds in the Caucasus.[11] I told him about Ogarëv, and asked him whether Orlov could do anything and whether he would care to.

A cloud came over Rayevsky's face: it was not the look of tearful self-preservation which I had seen in the morning, but a mixture of bitter memories and repulsion.

'There is no question here of caring or not caring,' he answered, 'only I doubt whether Orlov can do much; after dinner go to the study and I will bring him to you. So then,' he added after a pause, 'your turn has come, too; everyone will be dragged down into that slough.'

[10] Rayevsky, Nikolay Nikolayevich (1771-1829). General; a hero of the war of 1812. (*A.S.*)

[11] In fact N. N. Rayevsky, the younger, died in 1843 on his estate in Voronezh Province. (*A.S.*)

After questioning me, Orlov wrote a letter to Prince Golitsyn asking for an interview.

'The prince,' he told me, 'is a very decent man; if he doesn't do anything, he will at least tell us the truth.'

Next day I went for an answer. Prince Golitsyn said that Ogarëv had been arrested by order of the Tsar, that a committee of inquiry had been appointed, and that the material occasion had been some supper on the 24th June, at which seditious songs had been sung. I could make nothing of it. That day was my father's name-day; I had spent the whole day at home and Ogarëv had been with us.

It was with a heavy heart that I left Orlov; he, too, was troubled; when I gave him my hand he stood up, embraced me, pressed me warmly to his broad chest and kissed me.

It was as though he felt that we were parting for long years.

I only saw him once afterwards, exactly six years later.* His light was flickering out. The look of illness on his face, the melancholy and a sort of new angularity in it struck me; he was gloomy, was conscious that he was breaking up, knew things were all going wrong—and saw no way out. Two months later he died—the blood congealed in his veins.

. . . There is a wonderful monument[12] at Lucerne; carved by Thorwaldsen in the living rock. A dying lion is lying in a hollow: he is wounded to death; the blood is streaming from a wound in which the fragment of an arrow is sticking; he has laid his gallant head upon his paw, he is moaning, there is a look in his eyes of unbearable pain; all round it is empty, with a pond below, all this shut in by mountains, trees, and greenery; people pass by without seeing that here a royal beast is dying.

Once after sitting some time on a seat facing the stone agony, I was suddenly reminded of my last visit to Orlov. . . .

Driving home from Orlov's, I passed the house of the *oberpolitsmeyster*,[13] and the idea occurred to me of asking him openly for permission to see Ogarëv.

I had never in my life been in the house of a police official. I was kept waiting a long time; at last the *oberpolitsmeyster* came in.

My request surprised him.

---

[12] The monument was raised in 1821 to the memory of the Swiss Guards who fell in the defence of the Tuileries in 1792. (*A.S.*)

[13] *Oberpolits(ey)meyster* (*Oberpolizeimeister*), the senior police officer in Petersburg or Moscow. (*R.*)

'What grounds have you for asking this permission?'

'Ogarëv is my kinsman.'

'Your kinsman?' he asked, looking straight into my face.

I did not answer, but I, too, looked straight into his Excellency's face.

'I cannot give you permission,' he said; 'your kinsman is *au secret*. Very sorry!'

Uncertainty and inactivity were killing me. Hardly any of my friends were in town; I could find out absolutely nothing. It seemed as though the police had forgotten or overlooked me. It was very, very dreary. But just when the whole sky was overcast with grey storm-clouds and the long night of exile and prison was approaching, a ray of light shone down on me.

A few words of deep sympathy uttered by a girl of seventeen whom I had looked upon as a child, brought me to life again.

For the first time in my story a woman's figure[14] appears . . . and properly one single woman's figure appears throughout my life.

The passing fancies of youth and spring that had troubled my soul paled and vanished before it, like pictures in the mist; and no fresh ones came.

We met in a graveyard. She stood leaning against a tombstone and spoke of Ogarëv, and my grief was put away.

'Till to-morrow,' she said and gave me her hand, smiling through her tears.

'Till to-morrow,' I answered . . . and stood a long time looking after her disappearing figure.

That was the nineteenth of July 1834.

[14] Natalya Alexandrovna Zakharin, Herzen's first cousin and wife. (*R*.)

Chapter 9

My Arrest

'T<small>ILL</small> to-morrow,' I repeated, as I fell asleep. . . . I felt uncommonly light-hearted and happy.

Between one and two in the morning[1] my father's valet woke me; he was not dressed and was frightened.

'An officer is asking for you.'

'What officer?'

'I don't know.'

'Well, I do,' I told him and threw on my dressing-gown.

In the doorway of the great hall a figure was standing wrapped in a military greatcoat; by the window I saw a white plume, and there were other persons behind—I made out the cap of a Cossack.

It was the *politsmeyster*, Miller.

He told me that by an order of the military Governor-General, which he held in his hand, he must look through my papers. Candles were brought. The *politsmeyster* took my keys; the district police superintendent and his lieutenant began rummaging among my books and my linen. The *politsmeyster* busied himself among my papers; everything seemed suspicious to him; he laid everything on one side and suddenly turned to me and said:

'I must ask you to dress meanwhile; you'll come along with me.'

'Where to?' I asked.

'To the Prechistensky police station,' answered the *politsmeyster* in a soothing voice.

'And then?'

'There is nothing more in the Governor-General's order.'

I began to dress.

Meanwhile the frightened servants had woken my mother. She rushed out of her bedroom and was coming to my room, but was

[1] Of 21st July, 1834. (*A.S.*)

stopped by a Cossack at the doors between the drawing-room and the *salon*. She uttered a shriek: I shuddered and ran to her. The *politsmeyster* left the papers and came with me to the *salon*. He apologised to my mother, let her pass, swore at the Cossack, who was not to blame, and went back to the papers.

Then my father came up. He was pale but tried to maintain his studied indifference. The scene was becoming painful. My mother sat in the corner, weeping. My old father spoke of indifferent matters with the *politsmeyster*, but his voice shook. I was afraid that I could not stand this for long and did not want to afford the local police superintendent the satisfaction of seeing me in tears.

I pulled the *politsmeyster* by the sleeve,

'Let us go!'

'Let us go,' he said gladly.

My father went out of the room and returned a minute later. He brought a little ikon and put it round my neck, saying that his father had given it to him with his blessing on his deathbed. I was touched: this *religious* gift showed me the degree of fear and shock in the old man's heart. I knelt down while he was putting it on; he helped me up, embraced me and blessed me.

The ikon was a picture in enamel of the head of John the Baptist on a charger. What this was—example, advice, or prophecy?—I do not know, but the significance of the ikon struck me.

My mother was almost unconscious.

All the servants accompanied me down the staircase weeping and rushing to kiss my cheek or my hands. I felt as though I were present at my own funeral. The *politsmeyster* scowled and hurried me on.

When we went out at the gate he collected his detachment; he had with him four Cossacks, two police superintendents and two ordinary policemen.

'Allow me to go home,' a man with a beard who was sitting in front of the gate asked the *politsmeyster*.

'You can go,' said Miller.

'What man is that?' I asked, getting into the drozhki.

'The impartial witness; you know that without an impartial witness the police cannot enter a house.'

'Then why did you leave him outside the gate?'

'It's a mere form! It's simply keeping the man out of bed for nothing,' observed Miller.

We drove off accompanied by two Cossacks on horseback.

There was no special room for me in the police station. The *polits-meyster* directed that I should be put in the office until morning. He took me there himself; he flung himself in an easy chair and, yawning wearily, muttered:

'It's a damnable service. I've been on the jump since three o'clock in the afternoon, and here I've been bothered with you till morning. I bet it's past three already and to-morrow I must go with the report at nine.

'Good-bye,' he added a minute later, and went out.

A non-commissioned officer locked me in, observing that if I needed anything I could knock at the door.

I opened the window. The day was already beginning and the morning wind was rising; I asked the non-commissioned officer for water and drank off a whole jugful. There was no thinking of sleep. Besides, there was nowhere to lie down; apart from the dirty leather chairs and one easy chair, there was nothing in the office but a big table heaped up with papers and in the corner a little table with still more heaped up on it. A poor night-light did not light the room, but made a flickering patch of light on the ceiling that grew paler and paler with the dawn.

I sat down in the place of the police superintendent and took up the first paper that was lying on the table, a document relating to the funeral of a serf of Prince Gagarin's and a medical certificate that he had died according to all the rules of science. I picked up another— it was a set of police regulations. I ran through it and found a paragraph which stated that 'Every arrested man has the right within three days after his arrest to know the reason for it or to be released.' I noted this paragraph for my own benefit.

An hour later I saw through the window our major domo bringing me a pillow, bedclothes, and a greatcoat. He asked the non-commissioned officer something, probably permission to come in to me; he was a grey-headed old man, to two or three of whose children I had stood godfather as a small boy. The non-commissioned officer gave him a rough and abrupt refusal; one of our coachmen was standing near; I shouted to them from the window. The non-commissioned officer fussed about and told them to take themselves off. The old man bowed to the waist to me and shed tears; the coachman, as he whipped up the horse, took off his hat and wiped his eyes, the drozhki rattled away and my tears fell in streams. My heart was brimming over; these were the first and last tears I shed while I was in prison.

Towards morning the office began to fill up; the clerk arrived still drunk from the day before, a consumptive-looking individual with red hair, a look of brutal vice on his pimply face. He wore a very dirty, badly-cut, shiny, brick-red dress-coat. After him another extremely free-and-easy individual arrived, in a non-commissioned officer's greatcoat. He at once addressed me with the question:

'Were you taken at the theatre, sir, or what?'

'I was arrested at home.'

'Did Fëdor Ivanovich himself arrest you?'

'Who's Fëdor Ivanovich?'

'Colonel Miller.'

'Yes.'

'I understand, sir.' He winked to the red-haired man who showed no interest whatever. The cantonist[2] did not continue the conversation —he saw that I had been taken neither for disorderly conduct nor drunkenness, and so lost all interest in me; or perhaps was afraid to enter into conversation with a *dangerous* prisoner.

Not long afterwards various sleepy-looking police officials made their appearance and then came petitioners and litigants.

The keeper of a brothel brought a complaint against the owner of a beer-shop, that he had publicly abused her in his shop in such language as, being a woman, she could not bring herself to utter before the police. The shopkeeper swore that he had never used such language. The madam swore that he had uttered the words more than once and very loudly, and added that he had raised his hand against her and that, if she had not ducked, he would have laid her whole face open. The shopkeeper declared that, in the first place, she had not paid what she owed him, and, in the second, had insulted him in his own shop and, what was more, threatened that he should be thrashed within an inch of his life by her followers.

The brothel-keeper, a tall, untidy woman with puffy eyes, screamed in a loud, piercing voice and was extremely garrulous. The man made more use of mimicry and gesture than of words.

The police Solomon, instead of judging between them, cursed them both like a trooper.

'The dogs are too well fed, that's why they run mad,' he said; 'they should sit quiet at home, the beasts, seeing we say nothing and leave them in peace. What an opinion they have of themselves! They quarrel and run at once to trouble the police. And you're a fine lady! as though it were the first time—what's one to call you if not a bad word, with the trade you follow?'

The shopkeeper shook his head and shrugged his shoulders to express his profound gratification. The police officer at once pounced upon him and said:

'What do you go barking from behind your counter for, you dog? Do you want to go to the lock-up? You're a foul-tongued brute! Raise your paw any more—do you want a taste of the birch, eh?'

For me this scene had all the charm of novelty and it remained imprinted on my memory for ever; it was the first case of patriarchal Russian justice I had seen.

The brothel-keeper and the police officer continued shouting until the police superintendent came in. Without inquiring why these people were there or what they wanted, he shouted in a still more savage voice:

'Get out, be off! This isn't a public bath or a pot-house!'

Having driven 'the scum' out he turned to the police officer:

'You ought to be ashamed to allow such a disturbance! How many times I have told you? Respect for the place is being lost. After this every sort of riff-raff will turn it into a perfect Sodom. You are too easy-going with these scoundrels. What man is this?' he asked about me.

'A prisoner brought in by Fëdor Ivanovich, sir. Here is the document.'

The superintendent ran through the document, looked at me, met with disapproval the direct and unflinching gaze which I fixed upon him, prepared at the first word to give as good as I got, and said 'Excuse me.'

The affair of the brothel-keeper and the beer-shop man began again. She insisted on making a deposition on oath. A priest arrived. I believe they both made sworn statements; I did not see the end of it. I was taken away to the *oberpolitsmeyster's*. I do not know why; no one said a word to me; then I was brought back again to the police station, where a room had been prepared for me under the watch tower. The non-commissioned officer observed that if I wanted anything to eat I must send out to buy it, that my government ration had not been allotted yet and that it would not be for another two days or so; moreover, that it consisted of three or four kopecks of silver and that the *better-class* prisoners did not claim it.

There was a dirty sofa standing by the wall; it was past midday: I felt fearfully tired, flung myself on the sofa and slept like the dead. When I woke up, all was quiet and serene in my heart. I had been worn out recently by uncertainty about Ogarëv; now my turn too had come. The danger was no longer far off, but was all about me; the storm-cloud was overhead. This first persecution was to be our consecration.

Chapter 10

Imprisonment

A MAN soon becomes used to prison, if only he has some inner resources. One quickly becomes used to the peace and complete freedom in one's cage—no anxieties, no distractions.

At first, I was not allowed any books; the superintendent assured me that it was forbidden to get books from home. I asked him to buy me some. 'Something instructive, a grammar now, I might get, perhaps, but for anything else you must ask the general.' The suggestion that I should while away the time by reading a grammar was immensely funny, nevertheless I seized it with both hands, and asked the superintendent to buy me an Italian grammar and lexicon. I had two red twenty-five rouble notes with me, and I gave him one; he at once sent an officer for the books and gave him a letter to the *ober-politsmeyster* in which, on the strength of the paragraph I had read, I asked him to let me know the reason for my arrest or to release me.

The local superintendent, in whose presence I wrote the letter, tried to persuade me not to send it.

'It's a mistake, sir, upon my soul, it's a mistake to trouble the general; he'll say "they are restless people," it will do you harm and be no use whatever.'

In the evening the policeman appeared and told me that the *ober-politsmeyster* had bidden him tell me verbally that I should know the reason for my arrest in due time. Then he pulled out of his pocket a greasy Italian grammar, and added, smiling, 'It luckily happened that there was a vocabulary in it so there was no need to buy a lexicon.' Not a word was said about the change. I should have liked to write to the *oberpolitsmeyster* again, but the role of a miniature Hampden at the Prechistensky police station struck me as too funny.

Ten days after my arrest a little swarthy, pock-marked policeman appeared some time after nine in the evening with an order for me to dress and set off to the commission of inquiry.

While I was dressing the following ludicrously vexatious incident occurred. My dinner was being sent me from home. A servant gave it to the non-commissioned officer on duty below and he sent it up to me by a soldier. It was permitted to let in for me from home half a bottle to a whole bottle of wine a day. N. Sazonov took advantage of this permission to send me a bottle of excellent Johannisberg. The soldier and I ingeniously uncorked the bottle with two nails; one could smell the *bouquet* some distance away. I looked forward to enjoying it for the next three or four days.

One must be in prison to know how much childishness remains in a man and what comfort can be found in trifles, from a bottle of wine to a trick at the expense of one's guard.

The pock-marked policeman sniffed out my bottle and turning to me asked permission to taste a little. I was vexed; however, I said that I should be delighted. I had no wine-glass. The monster took a tumbler, filled it incredibly full and drank it down without taking breath; this way of pouring down spirits and wine only exists among Russians and Poles; in the whole of Europe I have seen no other people empty a tumbler at a gulp, or who could toss off a wine-glassful. To make the loss of the wine still more bitter, the pock-marked policeman wiped his lips with a snuffy blue handkerchief, adding 'First-class Madeira'. I looked at him with hatred and spitefully rejoiced that he had not been vaccinated and nature had not spared him the smallpox.

This connoisseur of wines conducted me to the *oberpolitsmeyster's* house in Tverskoy Boulevard, showed me into a side-room and left me there alone. Half an hour later a stout man* with a lazy, good-natured air came into the room from the inner apartments; he threw a portfolio of papers on to a chair and sent the gendarme standing at the door away on some errand.

'I suppose,' he said to me, 'you are concerned with the case of Ogarëv and the other young men who have lately been arrested?'

I said I was.

'I happened to hear about it,' he went on; 'it's an odd business: I don't understand it at all.'

'I've been a fortnight in prison in connection with the affair and I don't understand it at all, and, what's more, I simply know nothing about it.'

'A good thing, too,' he said, looking intently at me; 'and mind you don't know anything about it. You must forgive me if I give you a bit of advice; you're young, your blood is still hot, you long to speak out: that's the trouble. Don't forget that you know nothing about it: that's the only way to safety.'

I looked at him in surprise: his face expressed nothing evil; he guessed what I felt and said with a smile,

'I was a Moscow student myself twelve years ago.'

A clerk of some sort came in; the stout man addressed him and, after giving him his orders, went out with a friendly nod to me, putting his finger on his lips. I never met the gentleman afterwards and I do not know who he was, but I found out the genuineness of his advice.

Then a *politsmeyster* came in, not Miller, but another, called Tsynsky, and summoned me to the commission. In a large, rather handsome room five men were sitting at a table, all in military uniform, with the exception of one decrepit old man. They were smoking cigars and gaily talking together, lolling in easy chairs, with their uniforms unbuttoned. The *oberpolitsmeyster* presided.

When I went in, he turned to a figure sitting meekly in a corner, and said,

'If you please, Father.'

Only then I noticed that there was sitting in a corner an old priest with a grey beard and a reddish-blue face. The priest was half-asleep and yawning with his hand over his mouth; his mind was far away and he was longing to get home. In a drawling, somewhat chanting voice he began *admonishing* me, talking of the sin of concealing the truth before the persons appointed by the Tsar, and of the uselessness of such dissimulation considering the all-hearing ear of God; he did not even forget to refer to the eternal texts, that 'there is no power but of God' and 'to Cæsar the things that are Cæsar's.' In conclusion he said that I must put my lips to the Gospel and the *honourable* Cross in confirmation of the oath (which, however, I had not given, and he did not require) sincerely and candidly to reveal the whole truth.

When he had finished he began hurriedly wrapping up the Gospel and the Cross. Tsynsky, barely rising from his seat, told him that he could go. After this he turned to me and translated the spiritual speech into secular language:

'I will add only one thing to the priest's words—it is impossible for you to deny the charge, even if you wanted to.'

He pointed to the heaps of papers, letters, and portraits which were intentionally scattered about the table.

'Only a frank admission can mitigate your lot; to be at liberty, or Bobruysk, or in the Caucasus, depends on yourself.'

The questions were put to me in writing: the naïveté of some of them was striking: 'Do you not know of the existence of some secret society? Do you not belong to any society, literary *or other*? Who are its members? Where do they meet?'

To all this it was extremely easy to answer by the single word: 'No.'

'I see you know nothing,' said Tsynsky after looking through the answers. 'I have warned you, you are making your position more complicated.'

With that the first examination ended.

. . . Eight years later, in a different part of the very house in which this took place, there was living the sister of the new *oberpolitsmeyster*, a woman who had once been very handsome, and whose daughter was a beauty.

I used to visit them; and every time I passed through the room in which Tsynsky and Co. had examined us, very competently, as they thought; then and afterwards there hung in it the portrait of Paul, whether as a reminder of the depths of degradation to which a man may be brought by lack of restraint and the abuse of power, or as an incitement of the police to every sort of brutality, I do not know, but there he was, walking-stick in hand, snub-nosed and scowling. I stopped every time before that portrait, in old days as a prisoner, later on as a visitor. The little drawing-room close by, full of the fragrance of beauty and femininity, seemed somehow out of place in this stern house of strict discipline and police examinations; I felt unwell there, and somehow regretful that the blossom that was unfolding so beautifully should have lighted upon the gloomy brick wall of a police station. The things that we said and that were said by the little circle of friends that gathered round them sounded so ironical, so surprising to the ear, within those walls that were accustomed to listen to interrogations, secret information, and reports of general perquisitions— within those walls which separated us from the whisper of policemen, the sighs of prisoners, the clank of gendarmes' spurs and Ural Cossacks' sabres. . . .

A week or two later the pock-marked policeman came and took me to Tsynsky again. In the lobby several men in fetters were sitting or lying down, surrounded by soldiers with rifles; in the ante-room also there were several men of different classes, not chained but strictly guarded. The policemen told me that they were all incendiaries. Tsynsky was out at the fire and we had to await his return. We had arrived between nine and ten in the evening; no one had asked for me by one o'clock in the morning, and I was still sitting very quietly in the ante-room with the incendiaries. First one and then another of them was sent for, the police ran backwards and forwards, chains clanked, and the soldiers were so bored that they rattled their rifles and did arms-drill. About one o'clock Tsynsky arrived, sooty and grimy, and hurried straight through to his study without stopping. Half an hour passed and my policeman was sent for; he came back looking pale and out of countenance, with his face twitching convulsively. Tsynsky poked his head out of the door after him and said:

'The whole commission has been waiting for you all the evening, Monsieur Herzen; this *blockhead* brought you here when you were wanted at Prince Golitsyn's. I am very sorry you have had to wait here so long, but it is not my fault. What is one to do with such subordinates? I believe he has been fifty years in the service and he is still an idiot. Come, be off home now,' he added, changing to a much ruder tone as he addressed the policeman.

The little man repeated all the way:

'O Lord, what a calamity! a man has no thought, no notion what will happen to him. He will be the death of me now. He wouldn't care a bit if you had not been expected there, but since you were of course it is a disgrace to him. O Lord, how unlucky!'

I forgave him my wine, particularly when he told me that he had not been nearly so frightened when he had been almost drowned near Lisbon as he was now. This last circumstance was so unexpected that I was overcome with senseless laughter.

'Good lord, how very strange! However did you get to Lisbon?'

The old man had been a ship's officer for twenty-five years or so. One cannot but agree with the minister who assured Captain Kopeykin[1] that: 'It has never happened yet among us in Russia that a man who has deserved well of his country should be left a reward of some sort.' Fate had saved him at Lisbon only to be abused by Tsynsky like a boy, after forty years' service.

He was scarcely to blame, either.

The commission of inquiry formed by the Governor-General did

---

[1] See Gogol's *Dead Souls*. (Tr.)

not please the Tsar; he appointed a new one presided over by Prince Sergey Mikhaylovich Golitsyn. The members of this commission were Staal, the Commandant of Moscow, the other Prince Golitsyn, Shubinsky, a colonel of gendarmes, and Oransky, an ex-auditor.

In the instructions from the *oberpolitsmeyster* nothing was said about the commission's having been changed; it was very natural that the policeman from Lisbon took me to Tsynsky. . . .

There was great alarm at the police station, too; there had been three fires in one evening—and the commission had sent twice to inquire what had become of me, and whether I had not escaped. Anything that Tsynsky had left unsaid in his abuse the police station superintendent made up now to the man from Lisbon; which, indeed, was only to be expected, since the superintendent was himself partly to blame, not having inquired where I was to be sent. In a corner of the office someone was lying on some chairs, groaning; I looked: it was a young man of handsome appearance, neatly dressed, who was spitting blood and sighing. The police doctor advised his being taken to the hospital as early as possible in the morning.

When the non-commissioned officer took me to my room, I extracted from him the story of the wounded man. He was an ex-officer of the Guards, who had an intrigue with some maid-servant and had been with her when a wing of the house caught fire. This was the time of the greatest fright over arson; indeed, not a day passed without my hearing the bell ring the alarm three or four times; from my window I saw the glare of two or three fires every night. The police and the residents sought for the incendiaries with great persistence. To avoid compromising the girl the officer climbed over the fence as soon as the alarm was sounded, and hid in the stable of the next house, waiting for an opportunity to get away. A little girl who was in the yard saw him and told the first policeman who galloped up that the incendiary had hidden in the stable; they rushed in with a crowd of people and dragged the officer out in triumph. He was so thoroughly knocked about that he died next morning.

The people who had been captured began to be sorted out; about half were released, the others detained on suspicion. The *politsmeyster*, Bryanchaninov, used to come over every morning and cross-examine them for three or four hours. Sometimes the victims were thrashed or beaten; then their wailing, screams, entreaties and howls, and the moaning of women reached me, together with the harsh voice of the *politsmeyster* and the monotonous reading of the clerk.

H

It was awful, intolerable. At night I dreamed of those sounds and woke in a frenzy at the thought that the victims were lying on straw only a few paces from me, in chains, with lacerated wounds on their backs, and in all probability quite innocent.

To know what the Russian prisons, the Russian lawcourts and the Russian police are like, one must be a peasant, a house-serf, an artisan or a town workman. Political prisoners, who for the most part belong to the upper class, are kept in close custody and punished savagely, but their fate bears no comparison with the fate of the poor. With them the police do not stand on ceremony. To whom can the peasant or the workman go afterwards to complain? Where can he find justice?

So terrible is the confusion, the brutality, the arbitrariness and the corruption of Russian justice and of the Russian police that a man of the humbler class who falls into the hands of the law is more afraid of the process of law itself than of any legal punishment. He looks forward with impatience to the time when he will be sent to Siberia; his martyrdom ends with the beginning of his punishment. And now let us remember that three-quarters of the people taken up by the police on suspicion are released by the courts, and that they have passed through the same tortures as the guilty.

Peter III abolished torture and the Secret Chamber.

Catherine II abolished torture.

Alexander I abolished it *again*.

Answers given 'under intimidation' are not recognised by law. The official who tortures an accused man renders himself liable to trial and severe punishment.

And yet all over Russia, from the Bering Straits to Taurogen, men are tortured; where it is dangerous to torture by flogging, they are tortured by insufferable heat, thirst, and salted food. In Moscow the police put an accused prisoner with bare feet on a metal floor at a temperature of ten degrees of frost; he sickened, and died in a hospital which was under the supervision of Prince Meschchersky, who told the story with indignation. The government knows all this, the governors conceal it, the Senate connives at it, the ministers say nothing; the Tsar, and the synod, the landowners and the police all agree with Selifan: [2] 'Why not thrash a peasant? A peasant sometimes needs a thrashing!'

[2] A character in Gogol's *Dead Souls*. (*Tr.*)

The committee appointed to investigate the cases of incendiarism was investigating, that is, thrashing, for six months in a row, and had thrashed out nothing in the end. The Tsar was annoyed and ordered that the thing was to be finished in three days. The thing was finished in three days. Culprits were found and condemned to punishment by the knout, by branding, and by exile to penal servitude. The porters from all the houses were assembled to watch the terrible punishment of 'the incendiaries'. By then it was winter and at that time I was being held at the Krutitsky Barracks. The captain of gendarmes, a good-natured old man who had been present at the punishment, told me the details, which I pass on. The first man condemned to the knout told the crowd in a loud voice that he swore he was innocent, that he did not know himself what the pain had forced him to answer; then taking off his shirt he turned his back to the crowd and said: 'Look, good Christians!'

A groan of horror ran through the crowd: his back was a dark-blue striped wound, and on that wound he was to be beaten with the knout. The murmurs and gloomy aspect of the assembled people made the police hurry. The executioners dealt the legal number of blows, while others did the branding and others riveted fetters, and the business seemed to be finished. But this scene had impressed the inhabitants; in every circle in Moscow people were talking about it. The Governor-General reported upon it to the Tsar. The Tsar ordered a *new* trial to be held, and the case of the incendiary who had protested before his punishment to be particularly inquired into.

Several months afterwards, I read in the papers that the Tsar, wishing to compensate two men who had been punished by the knout, though innocent, ordered them to be given two hundred roubles a lash, and to be provided with a special passport testifying to their innocence in spite of the branding. These two were the incendiary who had spoken to the crowd and one of his companions.

The affair of the fires in Moscow in 1834, cases similar to which occurred ten years later in various provinces, remains a mystery. That the fires were caused by arson there is no doubt; fire, 'the red cock', is in general a very national means of revenge among us. One is continually hearing of the burning by peasants of their owners' houses, barns, and granaries, but what was the cause of the incendiarism in Moscow in 1834 no one knows, and least of all the members of the commission of inquiry.

Before 22nd August, Coronation Day, some practical jokers dropped letters in various places in which they informed the inhabitants that they need not bother about illuminations, that the place would be lit up.

The cowardly Moscow authorities were in a great fluster. The police station was filled with soldiers from early morning and a squadron of Uhlans were stationed in the yard. In the evening patrols on horseback and on foot were incessantly moving about the streets. Artillery was kept in readiness in the drill-shed. *Politsmeysters* galloped up and down with Cossacks and gendarmes. Prince Golitsyn himself rode about the town with his aides-de-camp. This military look of modest Moscow was odd, and affected the nerves. Till late at night I lay by the window under my watch tower and looked into the yard. . . . The Uhlans who had been hurried to the place were sitting in groups, near their horses, and others were mounting. Officers were walking about, looking disdainfully at the police; aides-de-camp with yellow collars arrived continually, looking anxious and, after doing nothing, rode away again.

There were no fires.

After this the Tsar himself came to Moscow. He was displeased with the inquiry into our case which was only beginning, was displeased that we were left in the hands of the ordinary police, was displeased that the incendiaries had not been found—in a word, he was displeased with everything and everyone.

We soon felt His Majesty's proximity.

Chapter 11

Krutitsky Barracks

THREE days after the Tsar's arrival, late in the evening—all these things are done in darkness to avoid disturbing the public—a police officer came to me with orders to collect my belongings and go with him.

'Where to?' I asked.

'You will see,' was the policeman's witty and polite reply. After this, of course, I did not continue the conversation, but collected my things and set off.

We drove on and on for an hour and a half, and at length we passed the Simonov Monastery and stopped at a heavy stone gate, before which two gendarmes with carbines were pacing up and down. This was the Krutitsky Monastery, converted into a barracks for gendarmes.

I was led into a small office. The clerks, the adjutants, the officers were all in light blue. The officer on duty, in a helmet and full uniform, asked me to wait a little and even suggested that I should light the pipe I held in my hand. After this he proceeded to write a receipt of having received a prisoner; giving it to the policeman he went away and returned with another officer.

'Your room is ready,' said the latter, 'let us go.'

A gendarme held a candle for us, and we went down some stairs and took a few steps across the courtyard and passed through a small door into a long corridor lit by a single lantern; on both sides were little doors, one of which the officer on duty opened; it led into a tiny guardroom beyond which was a small, damp, cold room that smelt like a cellar. The officer with an aiguillette who had conducted me then turned to me, saying in French that he was '*désolé d'être dans la nécessité*' of searching my pockets, but military service, duty, obedience. . . . After this eloquent introduction, he very simply turned to the gendarme and indicated me with his eyes. The gendarme at once thrust an incredibly large and hairy hand into my pocket. I observed to the courteous officer that this was quite unnecessary, and that I would myself, if he liked, turn my pockets inside out without such violent measures; moreover, what could I have after six weeks' imprisonment?

'We know,' said the polite officer with an aiguillette, with a smile of inimitable self-complacency, 'how things are done at police stations.'

The officer on duty also smiled sarcastically. However, they told the gendarme he need only look. I pulled out everything I had.

'Pour your tobacco out on the table,' said the officer who was *désolé*.

In my tobacco pouch I had a penknife and a pencil wrapped up in paper; from the very beginning I had been thinking about them and, as I talked to the officer, I played with the tobacco pouch, until I got the penknife into my hand. I held it through the material of the pouch, and boldly shook the tobacco out on the table. The gendarme poured it in again. The penknife and pencil were saved; so there was a lesson for the gendarme with the aiguillette for his proud disdain of the ordinary police.

This incident put me in the best of humours and I began gaily scrutinising my new domain.

Some of the monks' cells, built three hundred years before and sunk into the earth, had been turned into secular cells for political prisoners.

In my room there was a bedstead without a mattress, and a little table, with a jug of water on it, and a chair beside it. A thin tallow candle was burning in a big copper candlestick. The damp and cold pierced to one's bones; the officer ordered the stove to be lit, and then they all went away. A soldier promised to bring some hay; meanwhile, putting my greatcoat under my head, I lay down on the bare bedstead and lit my pipe.

A minute later I noticed that the ceiling was covered with 'Prussian' beetles. They had seen no candle for a long time and were running from all directions to where the light fell, bustling about, jostling each other, falling on to the table, and then racing headlong, backwards and forwards, along the edge of it.

I disliked black beetles, as I did every sort of uninvited guest; my neighbours seemed to me horribly nasty, but there was nothing to be done: I could not begin by complaining about the black beetles and my nerves had to submit. Two or three days later, however, all the 'Prussians' had moved beyond the partition to the soldier's room, where it was warmer; only occasionally a stray beetle would some-times run in, prick up his whiskers and scurry back to get warm.

Though I continually asked the gendarme, he still kept the stove closed. I began to feel unwell and giddy; I tried to get up and knock for the soldier; I did actually get up, but with this all that I remember comes to an end. . . .

When I came to myself I was lying on the floor with a splitting headache. A tall grey-haired gendarme was standing with his arms folded, staring at me blankly, as in the well-known bronze statuettes a dog stares at a tortoise.

'You have been finely suffocated, your honour,' he said, seeing that I had recovered consciousness. 'I've brought you horse-radish with salt and kvas; I have already made you sniff it, now you must drink it up.'

I drank it, he lifted me up and laid me on the bed. I felt very ill; there were double windows and no pane in them that opened; the soldier went to the office to ask permission for me to go into the yard; the officer on duty told him to say that neither the colonel nor the adjutant was there, and that he could not take the responsibility. I had to remain in the room full of charcoal fumes.

I got used even to the Krutitsky Barracks, conjugating the Italian verbs and reading some wretched little books. At first my confinement was rather strict: at nine o'clock in the evening, at the last note of the bugle, a soldier came into my room, put out the candle and locked the door. From nine o'clock in the evening until eight next morning I had to remain in darkness. I have never been a great sleeper, and in prison, where I had no exercise, four hours' sleep was quite enough for me; and not to have a candle was a real punishment. Moreover, every quarter of an hour from each end of the corridor the sentries uttered a loud, prolonged shout, to show that they were awake.

A few weeks later Colonel Seménov (brother of the celebrated actress, afterwards Princess Gagarin) allowed them to leave me a candle, forbade anything to be hung over the window, which was below the level of the courtyard, so that the sentry could see everything that was being done in the cell, and gave orders that the sentries should not shout in the corridor.

Then the commandant gave us permission to have ink and to walk in the courtyard. Paper was given in a fixed amount on condition that none of the leaves should be torn. I was allowed once in twenty-four hours to walk, accompanied by a soldier and the officer on duty, in the yard, which was enclosed by a fence and surrounded by a cordon of sentries.

Life passed quietly and monotonously; the military punctuality gave it a mechanical regularity like the cæsura in verse. In the morning, with the assistance of the gendarme, I prepared coffee on the stove; about ten o'clock the officer on duty appeared in gauntlets with enormous cuffs, in a helmet and a greatcoat, clanking his sabre and bringing in with him several cubic feet of frost. At one the gendarme brought a dirty napkin and a bowl of soup, which he always held by the edge, so that his two thumbs were perceptibly cleaner than his fingers. We were tolerably well fed, but it must not be forgotten that we were charged two paper roubles a day for our keep, which in the course of nine months' imprisonment ran up to a considerable sum for persons of no means. The father of one prisoner said quite simply that he had no money; he received the cool reply that it would be stopped out of his salary. If he had not been receiving a salary, it is extremely probable that he would have been put in prison.

I ought to add that a rouble and a half was sent to Colonel Semënov at the barracks for our board from the commandant's office. There was almost a row about this; but the adjutants, who got the benefit of it, presented the gendarmes' division with boxes for first performances and benefit nights, and with that the matter ended.

After sunset there followed a complete stillness, which was not disturbed at all by the footsteps of the soldier crunching over the snow just outside the window, nor by the far-away calls of the sentries. As a rule I read until one o'clock and then put out my candle. Sleep carried me into freedom; sometimes it seemed as though I woke up feeling—Ough, what horrible dreams I have had— prison and gendarmes—and I would rejoice that it was all a dream; and then there would suddenly be the clank of a sabre in the corridor, or the officer on duty would open the door, accompanied by a soldier with a lantern, or the sentry would shout in a voice that did not sound human, 'Who goes there?' or a bugle under my very window would rend the morning air with its shrill reveille. . . .

In moments of dullness, when I was disinclined to read, I would talk with the gendarmes who guarded me, particularly with the old fellow who had looked after me when I was overcome by the charcoal fumes. The colonel used, as a sign of favour, to free his old

soldiers from regular discipline, and detach them for the easy duty
of guarding a prisoner; a corporal, who was a spy and a rogue, was
set over them. Five or six gendarmes made up the whole staff.

The old man, of whom I am speaking, was a simple, good-hearted
creature, devotedly grateful for any kind action, of which he had
probably not had many in his life. He had been in the campaign
of 1812 and his chest was covered with medals; he had served his
full time and remained in the army of his own free will, not knowing
where to go.

'Twice,' he told me, 'I wrote to my home in Mogilëv province,
but I got no answer, so it seems as though there were none of my
people left: and so it would be painful to go home; one would stay
there a bit and then wander off like a lost soul, following one's nose
to beg one's bread.'

How barbarously and mercilessly the army is organised in Russia
with its monstrous term of service![1] A man's personality is everywhere sacrificed without the slightest mercy and with no reward.

Old Filimonov had pretensions to a knowledge of German which
he had studied in winter quarters after the taking of Paris. He very
felicitously adapted German words to the Russian spirit, calling a
horse, *fert*, eggs, *yery*, fish, *pish*, oats, *ober*, pancakes, *pankukhi*.

There was a naïveté about his stories which made me sad and
thoughtful. In Moldavia during the Turkish campaign of 1805 he
had been in the company of a captain, the most good-natured man
in the world, who looked after every soldier as though he were his
own son and was always foremost in action.

'A Moldavian girl captivated him and then we saw our captain
was worried, for, do you know, he noticed that the girl was making
up to another officer. So one day he called me and a comrade—a
splendid soldier, he had both his legs blown off afterwards at Maly-
Yaroslavets—and began telling us how the Moldavian girl had
wronged him and asked would we care to help him and give her a
lesson. "To be sure, sir," we said, "we are always glad to do our best[2]
for your honour." He thanked us and pointed out the house in which
the officer lived, and he says, "You wait on the bridge at night;

---

[1] Service in the Russian army at this time, for those who were not officers, was for
twenty-five years, and soldiers with bad records might be made to serve for life. Conscription was not general, and exemption could be bought (see p. 98). Under Alexander II, in 1874, the term was reduced to seven years; conscription became general and
exemption could not be purchased. All recruits must start in the ranks. (*R.*)

[2] See p. 114, n. 41.

H*

she will certainly go to him. You seize her without any noise and drop her in the river." "We can do that, your honour," we tell him, and my comrade and I got a sack ready. We were sitting there, when towards midnight there's the Moldavian girl running up. "Why, are you in a hurry, madam?" we say, and we give her one on the head. She never uttered a squeal, poor dear, and we popped her into the sack and over into the river; and next day our captain goes to the other officer and says: "Don't you be angry with your Moldavian girl: we detained her a little, and now she is in the river, and I am ready to take a turn with you," he says, "with the sabre or with pistols, which you like." So they hacked at each other. The officer gave our captain a great stab in the chest, and the poor, dear man wasted away and a few months later gave up his soul to God.'

'And the Moldavian girl was drowned, then?' I asked.

'Yes, sir, she was drowned,' answered the soldier.

I looked with surprise at the childish unconcern with which the old gendarme told me this story. And he, as though guessing what I felt, or thinking about it for the first time, added, to soothe me and conciliate his conscience:

'A heathen woman, sir, as good as not christened, that sort of people.'

On every Imperial holiday the gendarmes are given a glass of vodka. The sergeant allowed Filimonov to refuse his share for five or six times and to receive them all at once. Filimonov scored on a wooden tally-stick how many glasses he had missed, and on the most important holidays he would go for them. He would pour this vodka into a bowl, crumble bread into it and eat it with a spoon. After this dish he would light a big pipe with a tiny mouthpiece, filled with tobacco of incredible strength which he used to cut up himself, and therefore rather wittily called 'sans-cracher'. As he smoked he would fold himself up on a little window-seat, bent double—there were no chairs in the soldiers' rooms—and sing this song:

> 'The maids came out into the meadow,
> Where was an anthill and a flower.'

As he got more drunk the words would become more inarticulate until he fell asleep. Imagine the health of a man who had been twice wounded and at over sixty could still survive such carousals!

Before I leave these Flemish barrack scenes *à la* Wouverman[3] and *à la* Callot,[4] and this prison gossip, which is like the reminiscences of all prisoners, I shall say a few more words about the officers.

The greater number among them were quite decent men, by no means spies, but men who had come by chance into the gendarmes' division. Young gentlemen with little or no education and no fortune, who did not know where to lay their heads, they were gendarmes because they had found no other job. They performed their duties with military exactitude, but I never observed a shadow of zeal in any of them, except the adjutant, but that, of course, is why he was the adjutant.

When the officers had got to know me, they did all such little things as they could to alleviate my lot, and it would be a sin to complain of them.

One young officer told me that in 1831 he had been sent to find and arrest a Polish landowner, who was in hiding somewhere in the neighbourhood of his estate. He was charged with having relations with emissaries.[5] From evidence that the officer collected he found out where the landowner must be hidden, went there with his company, put a cordon round the house and entered it with two gendarmes. The house was empty—they walked through the rooms, peeping into everything and found no one anywhere, but yet a few trifles showed clearly that there had recently been people in the house. Leaving the gendarmes below, the young man went a second time up to the attic; looking round attentively he saw a little door which led to a closet or some small room; the door was fastened on the inside; he pushed it with his foot, it opened, and a tall, handsome woman stood before it. She pointed in silence to a man who held in his arms a girl of about twelve, who was almost unconscious. This was the Pole with his wife and child. The officer was embarrassed. The tall woman noticed this and asked him:

'And will you have the cruelty to destroy them?'

The officer apologised, saying the usual commonplaces about the inviolability of his military oath, and his duty, and, at last, in despair, seeing that his words had no effect, ended with the question:

'What am I to do?'

---

[3] Philip Wouverman (1619-68), a Dutch master who excelled in drinking and hunting scenes. (*Tr.*)

[4] Jacques Callot (1592-1635), a French painter and engraver. (*Tr.*)

[5] Of the Polish government formed at the time of the rising of 1830-31. (*A.S.*)

The woman looked proudly at him and said, pointing to the door:
'Go down and say there is no one here.'

'Upon my word, I don't know how it happened,' said the officer,
'or what was the matter with me, but I went down from the attic
and told the corporal to collect the men. A couple of hours later we
were diligently looking for him on another estate, while he was
making his way over the frontier. Well—woman! I admit it!'

Nothing in the world can be more narrow-minded and more inhuman than wholesale condemnation of whole classes of people by a
label, by a moral card-index, by the leading characteristics of their
trade. Names are dreadful things. Jean-Paul Richter says with extraordinary certainty: 'If a child tells a lie, frighten him with his
bad conduct, tell him he has told a lie, but don't tell him he is a
liar. You destroy his moral confidence in himself by defining him
as a liar. "That is a murderer," we are told, and at once we fancy
a hidden dagger, a brutal expression, black designs, as though murder were a permanent employment, the trade of the man who has
happened once in his life to kill someone. One cannot be a spy or
trade in the vice of others and remain an honest man, but one
may be an officer in the gendarmes without losing all human dignity;
just as one may very often find womanliness, a tender heart and even
nobility of character in the unhappy victims of "public incontin-
ence".'

I have an aversion for people who cannot, or will not, or do not
take the trouble to go beyond the name, to step over the barrier of
crime, over a confused, false position, but either modestly turn aside,
or harshly thrust it all away from them. This is usually done by
dry, abstract natures, egoistic and revolting in their purity, or base,
vulgar natures who have not yet managed, or have not needed, to
exhibit themselves in practice. In sympathy they are at home in the
dirty depths into which others have sunk.

Chapter 12

Investigation and Sentence

But with all this what of our *case*, what of the investigation and the trial?

They were no more successful in the new commission than in the old. The police had been on our track for a long time, but in their zeal and impatience could not wait to find a sensible occasion, and did something silly. They had sent a retired officer called Skaryatka to lead us on and expose us; he made acquaintance with almost all of our circle, but we very soon guessed what he was and held aloof from him. Other young men, for the most part students, had not been so cautious, but these others had no serious connection with us.

One student, on completing his studies, had given a lunch-party to his friends on 24th June, 1834. Not one of us was at the festivity: indeed none of us had been invited. The young men drank too much, played the fool, danced the mazurka, and among other things sang Sokolovsky's[1] well-known song on the accession of Nicholas:

> 'The Emperor of Russia
> Has gone to realms above,
> The operating surgeon
> Slit his belly open.
>
> 'The Government is weeping
> And all the people weep;
> There's coming to rule over us
> Constantine the freak.
>
> 'But to the King of Heaven,
> Almighty God above,
> Our Tsar of blessed memory
> Has handed a petition.

[1] It is probable that A. I. Polezhayev was the author of this song. (*A.S.*)

'When He read the paper,
Moved to pity, God
Gave us Nicholas instead,
The blackguard, the . . . [2]

In the evening[3] Skaryatka *suddenly* remembered that it was his name-day, told a tale of how he had made a profit on the sale of a horse, and invited the students to his quarters, promising them a dozen of champagne. They all went; the champagne appeared, and the host, staggering, proposed that they should once more sing Sokolovsky's song. In the middle of the singing the door opened and Tsynsky with the police walked in. All this was crude, stupid, clumsy, and at the same time unsuccessful.

The police wanted to catch *us*; they were looking for external evidence to involve in the case some five or six men whom they had already marked, and only succeeded in catching twenty innocent persons.

It is not easy, however, to disconcert the Russian police. Within a fortnight they arrested us as *implicated* in the supper case. In Sokolovsky's possession they found letters from Satin, in Satin's possession letters from Ogarëv, and in Ogarëv's possession my letters. Nevertheless, nothing was discovered. The first investigation failed. For the greater success of the second commission, the Tsar sent from Petersburg the choicest of the inquisitors, A. F. Golitsyn.

This breed of person is rare in Russia. It is represented among us by Mordvinov, the famous head of the Third Division, Pelikan, the rector of Vilna, and a few accommodating Baltic Germans and Poles[4] who have ratted.

But unluckily for the inquisition Staal, the Commandant of Moscow, was appointed the first member. Staal, a straightforward military man, a gallant old general, went into the case and found that it consisted of two circumstances that had no connection with each other: the affair of the supper party, which ought to have been punished by law, and the arrest, God knew why, of persons whose

---

[2] The epithet in the last line is left to the imagination in Russian also. (*Tr.*) The word is probably *svoloch* ('off-scourings', 'scum'. The Russian word is most opprobrious.) (*R.*)

[3] In fact Skaryatka's party took place on 8th July, 1834. (*A.S.*)

[4] Among those who have distinguished themselves in this line of late years is the famous Liprandi, who drew up a scheme for founding an Academy of Espionage (1858).

only guilt, so far as could be seen, lay in certain half-expressed opinions, for which it would be both difficult and absurd to try them.

Staal's opinion did not please Golitsyn junior. The dispute between them became caustic; the old warrior flared up, struck the floor with his sabre and said:

'Instead of ruining people, you had better draw up a report on the advisability of closing all the schools and universities; that would warn other unfortunates; however, you can do what you like, but you must do it without me. I shan't set foot in the commission again.'

With these words the old gentleman hastened out of the room.

The Tsar was informed of this the same day.

In the morning when the commandant appeared with his report, the Tsar asked him why he would not attend the commission; Staal told him why.

'What nonsense!' replied the Tsar, 'to quarrel with Golitsyn, for shame! I trust you will attend the commission as before.'

'Sire,' answered Staal, 'spare my grey hairs. I have lived to reach them without the slightest stain on my honour. My zeal is known to your Majesty, my blood, the remnant of my days are yours, but this is a question of my honour—my conscience revolts against what is being done in the commission.'

The Tsar frowned. Staal bowed himself out, and from that time was not once present in the commission.

This anecdote, the truth of which is not open to the slightest doubt, throws great light on the character of Nicholas. How was it that it did not enter his head that if a man whom he could not but respect, a brave warrior, an old man full of merit, so obstinately besought him to spare his honour, the business could not be quite clean? He should have done no less than require Golitsyn to present himself and insist on Staal's explaining the matter before him. He did not do this, but gave orders that we should be confined more strictly.

When Staal had gone there were only enemies of the accused in the committee, presided over by a simple-hearted old man, Prince S. M. Golitsyn, who after nine months knew as little about the case as he had nine months before it began. He preserved a dignified silence, very rarely put in a word, and at the end of an examination invariably asked:

'May we let him go?'

'We may,' Golitsyn junior would answer, and the senior would say with dignity to the prisoner,

'You may go.'

My first examination lasted four hours.

The questions were of two kinds. The object of the first was to discover a manner of thinking 'not akin to the spirit of the government, revolutionary opinions, imbued with the pernicious doctrines of Saint-Simon', as Golitsyn junior and the auditor Oransky expressed it.

These questions were easy, but they were hardly questions. In the papers and letters that had been seized the opinions were fairly simply expressed; the questions could properly only relate to the material fact of whether a man had or had not written the words in question. The committee thought it necessary to add to every written phrase, 'How do you explain the following passage in your letter?'

Of course it was useless to explain; I wrote evasive and empty phrases in reply. In one letter the auditor discovered the phrase: 'All constitutional charters lead to nothing: they are contracts between a master and his slaves; the task is not to make things better for the slaves, but that there should be no slaves.' When I had to explain this phrase I observed that I saw no obligation to defend constitutional government, and that, if I had defended it, it would have been charged against me.

'A constitutional form of government may be attacked from two sides,' Golitsyn junior observed in his nervous, hissing voice; 'you do not attack it from the monarchical point of view, or you would not talk about slaves.'

'In that I err in company with the Empress Catherine II, who ordered that her subjects should not be called *slaves*.'

Golitsyn, breathless with anger at this ironical reply, said:

'You seem to imagine that we are assembled here to conduct scholastic arguments, that you are defending a thesis in the university.'

'With what object, then, do you ask for explanations?'

'You appear not to understand what is wanted of you.'

'I don't understand.'

'What obstinacy there is in *all of them*,' Golitsyn senior, the president, added, shrugging his shoulders and glancing at Shubinsky, the colonel of gendarmes. I smiled.

'Just like Ogarëv,' the good-hearted president wound up.

A pause followed. The commission was assembled in Golitsyn senior's library, and I turned to the bookshelves and began examining the books. Among others there was an edition in many volumes of the memoirs of the Duc de Saint-Simon.

'Here,' I said, turning to the president, 'is it not unjust? I am being tried on account of Saint-Simonism, while you, prince, have twenty volumes of his works.'

As the good old man had never read anything in his life, he could not think what to answer. But Golitsyn junior looked at me with the eyes of a viper and asked:

'Don't you see that those are the memoirs of the Duc de Saint-Simon at the time of Louis XIV?'

The president with a smile gave me a nod that signified, 'Well, my boy, a bit flashy, that remark of yours, wasn't it?' and said,

'You may go.'

While I was in the doorway the president asked:

'Is he the one who wrote about Peter I, that thing you were showing me?'

'Yes,' answered Shubinsky.

I stopped.

'*Il a des moyens,*' observed the president.

'So much the worse. Poison in clever hands is all the more dangerous,' added the inquisitor; 'a very pernicious and quite incorrigible young man.'

My sentence lay in those words.

A propos Saint-Simon. When the *politsmeyster* seized Ogarëv's books and papers, he laid aside a volume of Thiers' *History of the French Revolution*, then found a second volume . . . a third . . . an eighth. At last he could bear it no longer, and said: 'Good Lord! what a number of revolutionary books . . . and here is another,' he added, giving the policeman Cuvier's *Discours sur les révolutions du globe terrestre*.

The second kind of question was more confusing. In them various police traps and inquisitional tricks were made use of to confuse, entangle, and involve one in contradictions. Hints of information given by others and different moral torments were employed. It is not worth while to tell them: it is enough to say that all their devices could not produce a single adequate confrontation among the four of us.[5]

[5] A. I. Herzen, N. P. Ogarëv, N. M. Satin and I. A. Obolensky. (*A.S.*)

After I had received my last question, I was sitting alone in the little room in which we wrote. All at once the door opened and Golitsyn junior walked in with a gloomy and anxious face.

'I have come,' he said, 'to have a few words with you before your evidence is completed. My late father's long connection with yours makes me take a special interest in you. You are young and may still make a career; to do so you must clear yourself of this affair . . . and fortunately it depends on yourself. Your father has taken your arrest deeply to heart and is living now in the hope that you will be released: Prince Sergey Mikhaylovich and I have just been speaking about it and we are genuinely ready to do all we can; give us the means of assisting you.'

I saw the drift of his words; the blood rushed to my head; I gnawed my pen with vexation.

He went on:

'You are going straight under the white strap, or to the fortress; on the way you will kill your father; he will not survive the day when he sees you in the grey overcoat of a soldier.'

I tried to say something but he interrupted me:

'I know what you want to say. Have a little patience! That you had designs against the government is evident. To merit the mercy of the Monarch you must give proofs of your penitence. You are obstinate, you give evasive answers and from a false sense of honour you spare men of whom we know more than you do and *who have not been so discreet as you*;[6] you will not help them, and they will drag you down with them to ruin. Write a letter to the commission, simply, frankly; say that you feel your guilt, that you were led away by your youth, name the unfortunate, misguided men who have led you astray. . . . Are you willing at this easy price to redeem your future and your father's life?'

'I know nothing and have not a word to add to my evidence,' I replied.

Golitsyn got up and said coldly:

'Ah, so you won't: it is not our fault!'

With that the examination ended.

In the January or February of 1835 I was before the commission for the last time. I was summoned to read through my answers, to add to them if I wished, and to sign them. Only Shubinsky was

---

[6] I need not say that this was a barefaced lie, a shameful police trap.

present. When I had finished reading them over I said to him:

'I should like to know what charge can be made against a man upon these questions and upon these answers? What article of the Code are you applying to me?'

'*The Code of laws is drawn up for crimes of a different kind,*' observed the light-blue colonel.

'That's a different point. After reading over all these literary exercises, I cannot believe that that makes up the whole business for which I have been in prison over six months.'

'But do you really imagine,' replied Shubinsky, 'that we believed you, that you have not formed a secret society?'

'Where is the society?'

'It is your luck that no traces have been found, that you have not succeeded in achieving anything. We stopped you in time, that is, to speak plainly, we have saved you.'

It was the story of the locksmith's wife and her husband in Gogol's *Inspector General* over again.

When I had signed, Shubinsky rang the bell and told them to summon the priest. The priest came up and wrote below my signature that all the evidence had been given by me voluntarily and without any compulsion. I need hardly say that he had not been present at the examination, and that he had not even the decency to ask me how it had been. (It was my impartial witness outside the gate again!)

At the end of the investigation, prison conditions were somewhat relaxed. Members of our families could obtain permits for interviews. So passed another two months.

In the middle of March our sentence was confirmed. No one knew what it was: some said we were being sent to the Caucasus, others that we should be taken to Bobruysk, others again hoped that we should all be released (this was the sentence which was proposed by Staal and sent separately by him to the Tsar; he advised that our imprisonment should be taken as equivalent to punishment).

At last, on 20th March, we were all assembled at Prince Golitsyn's to hear our sentence.[7] This was a gala day for us. We were seeing each other for the first time since our arrest.

Noisily, gaily embracing and shaking hands, we stood surrounded by a cordon of gendarme and garrison officers. This meeting cheered

[7] The sentence was pronounced on 31st March, 1835. (*R.*)

us all up; there was no end to the questions and the anecdotes. Sokolovsky was present, pale and somewhat thinner, but as brilliantly amusing as ever.

The author of *The Creation of the World* and of *Khever* and other rather good poems, had much poetic talent by nature, but was not wildly original enough to dispense with development, nor sufficiently well-educated to develop. A charming rake, a poet in life, he was not in the least a political man. He was amusing, likeable a merry companion in merry moments, a *bon vivant*, fond of having a good time—as we all were—perhaps rather more so.

Having dropped accidentally from a carousal into prison, Sokolovsky behaved extremely well; he grew up in confinement. The auditor of the commission, a pedant, a pietist, a detective, who had grown thin and grey-headed in envy, covetousness and slander, not daring from devotion to the throne and to religion to understand the last two verses of his poem in their grammatical sense, asked Sokolovsky,

'To whom do those insolent words at the end of the song refer?'

'Rest assured,' said Sokolovsky, 'not to the Tsar, and I would particularly draw your attention to that *extenuating* circumstance.'

The auditor shrugged his shoulders, lifted up his eyes unto the hills and after gazing a long time at Sokolovsky in silence took a pinch of snuff.

Sokolovsky was arrested in Petersburg and sent to Moscow without being told where he was being taken. Our police often perpetrate similar jests, and to no purpose at all. It is the form their poetical fancy takes. There is no occupation in the world so prosaic, so revolting that it has not its artistic yearnings for superfluous sumptuousness and decoration. Sokolovsky was taken straight to prison and put into a dark closet. Why was he put in prison while we were kept in various barracks?

He had two or three shirts with him and nothing else at all. In England every convict on being brought into prison is at once put into a bath, but with us they take every precaution against cleanliness.

If Dr Haas had not sent Sokolovsky a bundle of his own linen he would have been crusted with dirt.

Dr Haas was a very original eccentric. The memory of this 'crazy, deranged' man ought not to be choked among the weeds of the official necrologies describing the virtues of persons of the first two[8]

---

[8] In the Table of Ranks. See p. 25, fn. (R.)

grades, which are not discovered until their bodies have rotted away.

A thin little, waxen-looking old man, in a black swallow-tail coat, breeches, black silk stockings and buckled shoes, he looked as though he had just come out of some drama of the eighteenth century. In this *grand gala* fit for funerals and weddings, and in the agreeable climate of fifty-nine degrees north latitude, Haas used every week to drive to the stage-post on the Sparrow Hills when a batch of convicts were being sent off. In the capacity of prison doctor he had access to them; he used to go to inspect them and always brought with him a basket full of all manner of things, victuals and dainties of all sorts—walnuts, cakes, oranges and apples for the women. This aroused the wrath and indignation of the *philanthropic* ladies who were afraid of giving pleasure by their philanthropy, and afraid of being more charitable than was necessary to save the convicts from dying of hunger and the ringing frost.

But Haas was not easy to move, and after listening mildly to reproaches for his 'foolish spoiling of the female convicts', would rub his hands and say:

'Be so kind to see, gracious madam: a bit of bread, a copper every-one gives them; but a sweet or an orange for long they will not see; this no one gives them, that I can from your words deduce; I do them this pleasure for that it will not a long time be repeated.'

Haas lived in the hospital. A sick man came before dinner to consult him. Haas examined him and went into his study to write some prescription. On his return he found neither the patient nor the silver forks and spoons which had been lying on the table. Haas called the porter and asked him if anyone had come in besides the sick man. The porter grasped the situation, rushed out and returned a minute later with the spoons and the patient, whom he had stopped with the help of another hospital porter. The rascal fell at the doctor's feet and besought him for mercy. Haas was overcome with embarrassment.

'Go for the police,' he said to one of the porters, and to the other, 'and you send a clerk here at once.'

The porters, pleased at the discovery, at the victory and at their share in the business altogether, ran off, and Haas, taking advantage of their absence, said to the thief,

'You are a false man, you have deceived and tried to rob me. God will judge you . . . and now run quickly out of the back gate before the porters come back . . . but stop: perhaps you haven't a farthing: here is half a rouble, but try to reform your soul; from God you will not escape as from a watchman.'

At this even the members of his own household protested. But the incorrigible doctor maintained his point:

'Theft is a great vice; but I know the police, I know how they torment them—they will question him, they will flog him; to give up one's neighbour to the lash is a far worse crime; besides, how can one tell: perhaps what I have done may touch his heart!'

His domestics shook their heads and said, *'Er hat einen Raptus'*; the benevolent ladies said, *'C'est un brave homme, mais ce n'est pas tout à fait en règle, cela,'* and tapped their foreheads. But Haas rubbed his hands and went his own way.

. . . Sokolovsky had hardly finished his anecdotes, when several others at once began to tell theirs; it was as though we had all returned from a long journey—there was no end to the questions, jokes, and witticisms.

Physically, Satin had suffered more than the rest; he was thin and had lost part of his hair. He had been at his mother's in the country in the Tambov province when he heard that we had been arrested, and at once set off for Moscow, for fear that his mother should be alarmed by a visit of the gendarmes; but he caught cold on the way and reached home in a high fever. The police found him in bed, and it was impossible to move him to the police station. He was placed under arrest at home, a soldier from the police station was put on guard inside the bedroom and the local police superintendent was set to act as a male nurse by the patient's bedside, so that on coming to himself after his delirium he met the *attentive* gaze of the one, or the wizened phiz of the other.

At the beginning of the winter he was moved to the Lefortovsky Hospital; it appeared there was not a single empty *private* room for a prisoner, but such trifles were not deemed worth considering; a corner partitioned off, *with no stove*, was found, the sick man was put in this southern verandah and a sentry posted to watch him. What the temperature in this stone closet was like in winter may be judged from the fact that the sentry was so benumbed with cold at night that he would go into the corridor to warm himself at the stove, begging Satin not to tell the duty officer of it.

The hospital authorities themselves saw that such tropical quarters were impossible in a latitude so near the pole, and moved Satin to a room near the one in which frost-bitten patients were rubbed.

Before we had time to describe and listen to half our adventures, the adjutants began suddenly bustling about, the gendarme officers drew themselves up, and the policemen set themselves to rights: the door opened solemnly and little Prince Sergey Mikhaylovich Golitsyn walked in *en grande tenue* with a ribbon across his shoulder; Tsynsky was in court uniform, and even the auditor, Oransky, had put on some sort of pale-green civil-military uniform for the joyful occasion. The commandant, of course, had not come.

Meanwhile the noise and laughter had risen to such a pitch that the auditor came menacingly into the room and observed that loud conversation and, above all, laughter, showed a subversive disrespect to the will of His Majesty, which we were to hear.

The doors were opened. Officers divided us into three groups: in the first was Sokolovsky, the painter Utkin, and an officer called Ibayev; we were in the second; in the third, the *tutti frutti*.

The sentence regarding the first category was read separately. It was terrible; condemned for *lèse-majesté* they were sent to the Schlüsselburg for an indefinite period. All three listened to this savage sentence like heroes.

When Oransky, drawling to give himself importance, read, with pauses, that for '*lèse-majesté* and insulting the Most August Family, *et cetera*,' Sokolovsky observed:

'Well, I never insulted the family.'

Among his papers besides that poem were found some resolutions written in jest as though by the Grand Duke Mikhail Pavlovich, with intentional mistakes in spelling, and those orthographical errors helped to convict him.

Tsynsky, to show that he could be free and easy and affable, said to Sokolovsky after the sentence:

'I say, you've been in Schlüsselburg before?'

'Last year,' Sokolovsky answered promptly, 'as though I felt in my heart what was coming, I drank a bottle of Madeira there.'

Two years later Utkin died in the fortress. Sokolovsky, half dead, was released and sent to the Caucasus; he died at Pyatigorsk. Some remnant of shame and conscience led the government after the death of two to transfer the third to Perm. Ibayev's death was *sui generis*: he had become a mystic.*

Utkin, 'a free artist confined in prison', as he described himself in his signature to questionnaires, was a man of forty; he had never taken part in any kind of politics, but, being of a generous and impulsive temperament, he gave free rein to his tongue in the commission and was abrupt and rude to the members of it. For this he was *done to death* in a damp cell, in which the water trickled down the walls.

Ibayev's greater guilt lay in his epaulettes. Had he not been an officer, he would never have been so punished. The man had happened to be present at *some* supper party, had probably drunk and sung like all the rest, but certainly neither more nor louder than the others.

Our turn came. Oransky wiped his spectacles, cleared his throat, and began reverently announcing His Majesty's will. In this it was represented that the Tsar, after examining the report of the commission and taking into special consideration the youth of the criminals, *commanded that we should not be brought to trial*, but that we should be notified that by law we ought, as men convicted of *lèse-majesté* by singing seditious songs, to lose our lives or, in virtue of other laws, to be transported to penal servitude for life. Instead of this, the Tsar in his infinite mercy forgave the greater number of the guilty, leaving them in their present abode under the supervision of the police. The more guilty he commanded to be put under reformatory treatment, which consisted in being sent to civilian duty for an indefinite period in remote provinces, to live under the superintendence of the local authorities.

It appeared that there were six of the 'more guilty': Ogarëv, Satin, Lakhtin, Obolensky, Sorokin, and I. I was to be sent to Perm. Among those condemned was Lakhtin, who had not been arrested at all. When he was summoned to the commission to hear the sentence, he supposed that it was as a warning, to be punished by hearing how others were punished. The story was that someone of Prince Golitsyn's circle, being angry with Lakhtin's wife, had obliged him with this agreeable surprise. A man of delicate health, he died three years later in exile.

When Oransky had finished reading, Colonel Shubinsky made a speech. In choice language and in the style of Lomonosov he informed us that it was due to the good offices of the noble gentleman who had presided at the committee that the Tsar had been so merciful.

Shubinsky waited for all of us to thank Prince Golitsyn, but this did not come off.

Some of those who were pardoned nodded, stealing a stealthy glance at us as they did so.

We stood with folded arms, making not the slightest sign that our hearts were touched by the Imperial and princely mercy.

Then Shubinsky thought of another dodge and, addressing Ogarëv, said:

'You are going to Penza; do you imagine that that is by chance? Your father is lying paralysed at Penza and the prince besought the Tsar to designate that town for you, that your being near might to some extent alleviate for him the blow of your exile. Do you not think you have reason to thank the prince?'

There was no help for it: Ogarëv made a slight bow. This was what they were trying to get.

The good-natured old man was pleased at this, and next, I do not know why, he summoned me. I stepped forward with the devout intention of not thanking him, whatever he or Shubinsky might say; besides, I was being sent farther away than any and to the nastiest town.

'You are going to Perm,' said Prince Golitsyn.

I said nothing. He was disconcerted and, for the sake of saying something, he added,

'I have an estate there.'

'Would you care to send some commission through me to your steward?' I asked with a smile.

'I do not give commissions to people like you—*Carbonari*,' added the resourceful old man.

'Then what do you wish of me?'

'Nothing.'

'I thought you called me.'

'You may go,' Shubinsky interposed.

'Allow me,' I replied, 'since I am here, to remind you that you told me, Colonel, last time I was before the commission, that no one accused me of being connected with the supper-party affair. Yet in the sentence it is stated that I was one of those guilty in connection with that affair. There is some mistake here.'

'Do you wish to object to His Majesty's decision?' observed Shubinsky. 'You had better take care that Perm is not changed to something worse. I shall order your words to be taken down.'

'I meant to ask you to do so. In the sentence the words occur "on the report of the commission": I am protesting against your report and not against the will of His Majesty. I appeal to the prince: there was no question in my case of a supper party or of songs, was there?'

'As though you did not know,' said Shubinsky, beginning to turn pale with wrath, 'that you are ten times more guilty than those who were at the supper party. He, now'—he pointed to one of those who had been pardoned—'in a state of intoxication sang some filthy song, but afterwards he begged forgiveness on his knees with tears. But you are still far from any penitence.'

The gentleman at whom the colonel pointed said nothing, but hung his head and flushed crimson. . . . It was a good lesson: so he should, after behaving so vilely! . . .

'Excuse me, it is not the point whether my guilt is great or not,' I went on; 'but, if I am a murderer, I don't want to be considered a thief. I don't want it to be said of me, even in justification, that I did something in a "state of intoxication", as you expressed yourself just now.'

'If I had a son, my own son, who showed such stubbornness, I would myself beg the Tsar to send him to Siberia.'

At this point the *oberpolitsmeyster* interposed some incoherent nonsense. It is a pity that Golitsyn junior was not present, for it would have been an opportunity for his eloquence.

It all ended, of course, in nothing.

Lakhtin went up to Prince Golitsyn and asked that his departure might be deferred.

'My wife is with child,' he said.

'I am not responsible for that,' answered Golitsyn.

A wild beast, a mad dog when it bites, looks in earnest and puts its tail between its legs, but this crazy grandee, aristocrat, though he had the reputation of a good-natured man, was not ashamed to make this vulgar joke.

We stayed for a quarter of an hour more in the room, and, in spite of the zealous exhortations of the gendarme and police officers, embraced one another warmly and took a long farewell. Except Obolensky I saw none of them again until I came back from Vyatka.

Departure was before us.

Prison had been a continuation of our past; but our departure into the wilds was a complete break with it.

Our youthful existence in our circle of friends was over.

Our exile would probably last several years. Where and how should we meet, and should we ever meet? . . .

I regretted my old life, and I had to leave it so abruptly . . . without saying good-bye. I had no hope of seeing Ogarëv. Two of my friends had succeeded in seeing me during the last few days, but that was not enough for me.

If I could but once again see my youthful comforter and press her hand, as I had pressed it in the graveyard. . . . I longed both to take leave of my past and to greet my future in her person. . . .

We did see each other for a few minutes on the 9th of April, 1835, on the day before I was sent off into exile.

For years I kept that day sacred in my memory; it was one of the happiest moments in my life.

Why must the thought of that day and of all the bright days of my past bring back so much that is frightening? . . . The grave, the wreath of dark-red roses, two children holding my hand—torches, the crowd of exiles, the moon, the warm sea under the mountainside, the words that I did not understand and that wrung my heart. . . .

All is over![9]

[9] Herzen is recalling the burial of his wife in 1852. (*A.S.*)

Chapter 13

Perm

On the morning of the 10th of April an officer of gendarmes took me to the house of the Governor-General. There, in the private part of the building, my relations were allowed to come and say good-bye to me.

Of course all this was awkward, and it wrung the heart; the prying spies, the clerks, the reading of the instructions to the gendarme who was to take me away, the impossibility of saying anything without witnesses: in fact, more distressing and painful surroundings could not have been devised.

I heaved a sigh of relief when at last the carriage rolled off along the Vladimirka.

> '*Per me si va nella città dolente,*
> *Per me si va nel eterno dolore——*'

At a stage-post somewhere I wrote down those two lines, which apply equally well to the portals of Hell and the Siberian high-road.

Seven versts[1] from Moscow there is a restaurant called 'Perov's'; there one of my intimate friends had promised to wait for me. I suggested to the gendarme a drink of vodka, and he agreed: it was a long way from the town. We went in, but my friend was not there. I tried every device to linger in the tavern; the gendarme did not want to stay any longer, and the driver was starting the horses— when suddenly a troika dashed up straight to the restaurant. I flew to the door . . . two strangers, merchants' sons, out for a spree, noisily dismounted from the carriage. I looked into the distance—not one moving point, not one man could be seen on the road to Moscow. . . . It was bitter to get in and drive off. I gave the driver twenty kopecks, and we flew like an arrow from the bow.

We drove without stopping; the gendarme had been ordered to

[1] One *verst* = two-thirds of one British statute mile. (R.)

do not less than two hundred versts in the twenty-four hours. This would have been quite endurable at any time but the beginning of April. In places the road was covered with ice, in places with mud and water; moreover, as we drove towards Siberia it got worse and worse at every stage-post.

The first incident of my journey was at Pokrovo.

We had lost several hours owing to the ice which was floating down the river and cutting off all communication with the opposite bank. The gendarme was anxious to hurry on; all at once the superintendent of the posting station at Pokrovo announced that there were no horses. The gendarme pointed out that in the permit he was instructed to give couriers' horses if there were no post horses. The superintendent declared that the horses had been taken for the Deputy Minister of Home Affairs. I need hardly say that the gendarme began to argue and make a noise. The superintendent ran to try and get private horses and the gendarme went with him.

I got tired of waiting for them in the superintendent's dirty room. I went out at the gate and began walking in front of the house. It was my first walk unescorted by a soldier after nine months' imprisonment.

I had walked up and down for half an hour when suddenly I was met by a man wearing a uniform with no epaulettes and a blue *Pour le Mérite* ribbon round his neck. He looked at me with marked persistence, passed me, and at once turning back asked me with a fierce air:

'Is it you who are being taken by a gendarme to Perm?'

'Yes,' I answered without stopping.

'Excuse me, excuse me, but how dare he? . . .'

'With whom have I the honour to speak?'

'I am the mayor,' answered the stranger in a voice which betrayed a profound sense of the dignity of that public position. 'I beg your pardon, but I am expecting the Deputy Minister from hour to hour, and here are political prisoners strolling about the streets. What an ass your gendarme is!'

'Will you please address yourself to the gendarme in person.'

'It is not a matter of addressing myself: I'll arrest him. I'll order him a hundred strokes and send you on with a policeman.'

I nodded without waiting for him to finish his speech and strode rapidly back into the posting station. Through the window I could hear him fuming at the gendarme and threatening him. The gendarme apologised but did not seem much frightened. Three minutes later they both came in. I was sitting facing the window and did not look at them.

From the mayor's questions to the gendarme I saw at once that he was consumed by the desire to find out for what offence, how and why, I was being sent into exile. I remained obstinately silent. The mayor began addressing me and the gendarme indiscriminately:

'No one cares to enter into our position. Do you suppose it is pleasant for me to have to swear at a soldier and be unpleasant to a man whom I have never seen in my life? It is the responsibility! The mayor is in charge of the town. Whatever happens, I have to answer for it; if government funds are stolen, it is my fault; if the church is burnt down, it is my fault; if there are many men drunk in the street, it is my fault; if there is not enough liquor drunk, it is my fault;' (his last remark pleased him very much and he went on in a more cheerful tone). 'It's a good thing it was me you met, but if you had met the Minister and walked past him like that, he would have asked, How is this, a political prisoner out for a walk? Put the mayor under arrest. . . .'

At last I was weary of his eloquence, and I turned to him and said:

'Do what your duty requires, but I beg you to spare me your sermons. I see from what you say that you expected me to bow to you; it is not my habit to bow to strangers.'

The mayor was put out.

'It is always like that among us,' A—— A—— used to say; 'whichever shows his temper first, and begins to shout, always gets the best of it. If you allow an official to raise his voice, you are lost; hearing himself yelling, he becomes a wild beast. If at his first rude word you begin shouting, he is invariably scared and gives way, thinking you are a determined person and that such persons had better not be irritated too much.'

The mayor sent the gendarme to inquire about horses and, turning to me, observed by way of apology:

'I have acted like this more for the sake of the soldier; you don't know what our soldiers are like—one must not let pass the slightest slackness, but, believe me, I can discriminate—allow me to ask you what unlucky chance. . . .'

'At the conclusion of our trial we were forbidden to speak of it.'

'In that case. . . . Of course. . . . I do not venture. . . .' and the mayor's eyes expressed agonies of curiosity. He paused.

'I had a distant relative, he was a year in the Peter-Paul fortress. You know, contacts, too—permit me, it worries me. I believe you are still angry? I am a military man, strict, accustomed to the service; I went into the regiment at seventeen. I have a hasty temper, but it is all over in a minute. I won't touch your gendarme, the devil take him. . . .'

The gendarme came in with the reply that the horses could not be driven in from the grazing-ground in less than an hour.

The mayor informed him that he forgave him on my intercession. Then turning to me he added:

'And to show that you are not angry, you will not refuse my request. I live only two doors away: allow me to ask you to take pot-luck at lunch with me.'

This was so funny after our encounter that I went to the mayor's and ate his dried sturgeon and caviare and drank his vodka and Madeira.

He became so affable that he told me all his domestic affairs, even describing his wife's illness which had lasted seven years. After luncheon he took with proud satisfaction a letter from a vase standing on the table and gave me to read 'a poem' by his son, deemed worthy of being read in public at the examination for the Corps of Cadets. After obliging me with such marks of complete confidence, he adroitly passed to an indirect question about my case. This time I partly gratified his curiosity.

This mayor reminded me of the secretary of the district court of whom our friend Shchepkin used to tell: 'Nine police-captains came and went, but the secretary remained unchanged, and went on managing the district as before.

'How is it you get on with all of them?' Shchepkin asked him.

'Oh, it's all right; with God's help we manage somehow. Some certainly were hot-tempered at first, would stamp with their forelegs and their hindlegs, shout, swear, say they'd have me dismissed the service, and they'd report me to the governor—well, as you see, I know my place: one holds one's tongue and thinks: give him time, he'll be broken in! This is just first being in harness! And, really! how well they go afterwards.'

When we came near Kazan the Volga was in all the glory of the spring floods. The whole stage from Uslon to Kazan we had to travel by raft: the river had overflowed for fifteen versts or more.

It was a rainy day. The ferry had stopped, and a number of carts and conveyances of all sorts were waiting on the bank.

The gendarme went to the station-superintendent and asked for a raft. The man gave it reluctantly, saying it would be better to wait, there would be a better time to cross. The gendarme was in a hurry because he was drunk and because he wanted to show his power.

They put my carriage on a small raft and we set off. The weather seemed calmer. Half an hour later the Tatar put up a sail, when suddenly the storm began to rage again. We were carried along with such violence that, overtaking a log, we crashed against it so that the wretched raft was stove in and the water poured over the deck. It was an unpleasant situation; however, the Tatar succeeded in getting the raft on to a sandbank.

A merchant's barge came into sight. We shouted to it and asked them to send a boat; the bargeman heard us and sailed on without doing anything.

A peasant came up with his wife in a little dug-out canoe, asked us what was the matter, and, remarking, 'Well, what of it? Plug the hole and go your way rejoicing. What's there to mope about? It's because you are a Tatar, I suppose, you can't do anything,' he climbed on to our raft.

The Tatar certainly was very much alarmed. First, when the water had poured over the sleeping gendarme, the latter had leapt up and at once began beating the Tatar. Secondly, the boat was government property, and the Tatar kept repeating:

'It will go to the bottom! what will become of me! What will become of me!'

I comforted him by saying that if it went to the bottom he would go with it.

'It is all right, master, if I drown, but how if I don't?'

The peasant and the others plugged the hole with all sorts of things. The peasant struck it with his axe and knocked in some little plank; then, up to his waist in the water, he helped to drag the raft off the sandbank and we soon floated off into the channel of the Volga. The river rushed us along savagely. The wind and the sleet cut the face, the cold penetrated to the bone, but soon the monument of Ivan the Terrible began to stand out from the fog and the floods of water. It seemed as though the danger were over, when suddenly the Tatar shouted in a plaintive voice, 'A leak, a

leak!' and indeed water was pouring in hard at the hole that had
been plugged. We were in the deepest part of the channel, the raft
was moving more and more slowly: one could foresee that it would
soon sink altogether. The Tatar took off his cap and prayed. My
valet, out of his wits with terror, wept and said:

'Good-bye, mother, I shall never see you again.'

The gendarme swore and vowed to thrash them all as soon as we
got to the bank.

At first I too was frightened; besides, the wind and the rain
added confusion and uproar. But the thought that it was absurd
that I might perish without having *done anything*, and that youthful *'Quid times? Caesarem vehis!'* got the upper hand, and I calmly
awaited the end, convinced that I could not perish between Uslon
and Kazan. Later on life breaks us of this proud confidence and
punishes us for it; that is why youth is valiant and full of heroism,
but with the years a man grows cautious and is rarely carried away.

A quarter of an hour later we were ashore near the walls of the
Kazan Kremlin, drenched and shivering. I went into the nearest
tavern, drank off a glass of strong brandy, ate a fried egg, and set
off to the post-office.

In villages and little towns the superintendent of the posting-station
has a room for travellers; in big towns everyone puts up at hotels
and for travellers there is nothing at the posting-stations. I was taken
to the posting-station. The superintendent showed me his room; there
were women and children in it and a sick and bedridden old man;
there was absolutely not a corner where I could change my clothes.
I wrote a letter to the general of gendarmes and asked him to assign
a room to me somewhere that I might get warm and dry my clothes.

An hour later the gendarme returned and said that Count Apraxin
had ordered that a room should be given me. I waited a couple of
hours—no one came and I sent the gendarme off again. He came
back with the answer that Colonel Pol, to whom the general had
given the order to find me a room, was playing cards at the Gentleman's Club and that a room could not be allotted to me till next day.

This was barbarous; and I wrote a second letter to Count Apraxin
asking him to send me on immediately, saying that I might find
shelter at the next posting-station. The Count was graciously pleased
to be in bed, and the letter was left until the morning. There was
nothing for it. I took off my wet clothes and lay down on the
table of the post-office wrapped in the greatcoat of the 'elder';

I

for a pillow I took a thick book and laid some linen upon it.

In the morning I sent out for some breakfast. The post-office officials were by now assembling. The clerk in charge submitted to me that it really was not the right thing to have breakfast in a public office, that it did not matter to him personally, but that the postmaster might not like it.

I answered him jocosely that a man cannot be turned out who has no right to go, and if he has no right to go he is obliged to eat and drink where he is detained. . . .

Next day Count Apraxin gave me permission to remain three days in Kazan and to put up at an hotel.

I spent those three days wandering about the town with the gendarme. The Tatar women with their covered faces, their husbands with their prominent cheek-bones, mosques of the true faith side by side with orthodox churches, all was suggestive of Asia and the East. In Vladimir, in Nizhny Novgorod, there is a feeling of nearness to Moscow, here of remoteness from her.

In Perm I was taken straight to the governor. He was holding a great reception; his daughter was being married that day to an officer. He insisted on my going in, and I had to present myself to the whole society of Perm in a dirty travelling coat, covered with mud and dust. The governor, after talking all sorts of nonsense, forbade me to make acquaintance with the Polish exiles and ordered me to come to him in a few days, saying that then he would find me work in the office.

This governor was a Little Russian; he did not oppress the exiles, and altogether was a harmless person. He was improving his fortune somehow on the sly, like a mole working unseen underground; he was adding grain to grain and laying by a little something for a rainy day.

From some inexplicable idea of security and good order, he used to command all the exiles who lived in Perm to appear before him at ten o'clock in the morning on Saturdays. He would come out with his pipe and a list, verify whether we were all present, and, if anyone was not, send a policeman to find out the reason; then, after saying scarcely anything to anyone, he would dismiss us. In this way in his reception-room I became acquainted with all the Polish exiles, whose acquaintance he had warned me I must not make.

The day after my arrival the gendarme went away, and for the first time since my arrest I found myself at liberty.

At liberty . . . in a little town on the Siberian border, with no experience, with no conception of the environment in which I had to live.

From the nursery I had passed into the lecture-room, from the lecture-room to a circle of friends—it had all been theories, dreams, my own people, no active relationships. Then prison to let it all settle. Practical contact with life was beginning here near the Ural Mountains.

It manifested itself at once; the day after my arrival I went with a porter from the governor's office to look for a lodging and he took me to a big house of one storey. However much I explained that I was looking for a very small house or, still better, part of a house, he obstinately insisted on my going in.

The landlady made me sit down on her sofa and, learning that I came from Moscow, asked if I had seen Mr Kabrit in Moscow. I told her that I had never even heard the name.

'How is that?' observed the old woman; 'I mean Kabrit,' and she mentioned his Christian name and his father's name. 'Upon my word, sir, why, he was our Whist-Governor!'

'But I have been nine months in prison; perhaps that is why I have not heard of him,' I said, smiling.

'Maybe that is it. So you will take the house, my good sir?'

'It is too big, much too big; I told the man so.'

'You can't have too much of a good thing,' she said.

'That is so, but you will want more rent for so much of a good thing.'

'Ah, my good sir, but who has talked to you about my price? I have not said a word about it yet.'

'But I know that such a house cannot be let cheaply.'

'How much will you give?'

To get rid of her, I said that I would not give more than three hundred and fifty paper roubles.

'Well, I would be thankful for that. Bid the man bring your bits of trunks, my dear, and take a glass of Teneriffe.'

Her price seemed to me fabulously low. I took the house, and, just as I was on the point of going, she stopped me:

'I forgot to ask you: are you going to keep your own cow?'

'Good Heavens, no!' I answered, almost appalled by her question.

'Well, then, I will let you have cream.'

I went away thinking with horror where I was and what I was

that I could be considered capable of keeping my own cow. But before I had time to look round, the governor informed me that I was being transferred to Vyatka because another exile who had been allotted to Vyatka had asked to be transferred to Perm, where he had relations. The governor wanted me to leave the next day. This was impossible: thinking to remain some time in Perm, I had bought all sorts of things, and I had to sell them even at half-price. After various evasive answers, the governor gave me permission to remain forty-eight hours, exacting a promise that I would not seek an opportunity of seeing the other exiles.

I was preparing to sell my horse and all sorts of rubbish the next day when suddenly the *politsmeyster* appeared with an order to leave within twenty-four hours. I explained to him that the governor had given me an extension of time. The *politsmeyster* showed me the instructions, in which he certainly was directed to see me off within twenty-four hours. The document had been signed that very day and consequently after the conversation with me.

'Ah,' said the *politsmeyster*, 'I understand, I understand; our fine gentleman wants to throw the responsibility on me.'

'Let us go and confront him with it.'

'Let us!'

The governor said that he had forgotten the permission he had given me. The *politsmeyster* asked slyly whether he wished him to make a fresh copy of the instructions.

'Is it worth while?' the governor asked artlessly.

'We have caught him,' said the *politsmeyster*, gleefully rubbing his hands, 'the inky soul!'

The Perm *politsmeyster* belonged to a special type of military men turned officials. They are men who have had the luck in the army to come in contact with a bayonet or to be hit by a bullet, and so to be given mostly such posts as that of mayor or tipstaff.

In the regiment they have acquired certain habits of frankness, have learnt by heart various phrases about the inviolability of honour and nobility, and also sarcastic jeers at the 'scribblers'. The younger among them have read Marlinsky[2] and Zagoskin,[3] know

---

[2] A. Marlinsky (pseudonym for Bestuzhev—1797-1837), author of numerous tales, extremely romantic in style and subject. Readers of Turgenev will remember that he was the favourite author of the hero of *Knock, Knock, Knock. (Tr.)*

[3] M. N. Zagoskin (1789-1852), author of popular historical novels, sentimental and patriotic. (*Tr.*)

the beginning of the *Prisoner of the Caucasus* and *Voynarovsky*, and often repeat verses they have learnt by heart. Some, for instance, will say every time they see a man smoking:

> *'The amber smoked between his lips.'*

They are all without exception deeply and volubly conscious that their position is far inferior to their merits, that only poverty keeps them in this 'world of ink', that if it were not for their wounds and lack of means, they would be commanding army corps or have the rank of adjutants-general. Everyone of them will add a striking instance of some old comrade and say:

'Why, Kreyz, or Riediger—we were made cornets by the same warrant. We lodged together. Called each other Petrusha and Alësha —but there, I'm not a German, you see, and I had no backing—so I can stay a policeman. Do you imagine it's easy for an honourable man with our ideas to do police work?'

Their wives are even louder in their complaints, and with heavy hearts go to Moscow every year to put money into the bank, on the pretext that a mother or aunt is ill and wants to see them for the last time.

And so their life goes on for fifteen years or so. The husband, railing against destiny, thrashes his policeman, beats the workpeople, cringes to the governor, screens thieves, steals documents and repeats verses from the *Fountain of Bakhchisaray*.[4] The wife, railing against destiny and provincial life, grabs everything she can get, takes tribute from petitioners and shops, and raves over moonlit nights.

I have made this digression because at first I was taken in by these gentry and believed they really were rather better than the rest, which is far from being the case. . . .

I brought away from Perm one personal memory which is dear to me.

At one of the governor's inspections of the exiles a Polish priest invited me to go and see him. I found several Poles there. One of them sat in silence pensively smoking a little pipe; misery, hopeless misery, was apparent on every feature of his face. He was round-shouldered, even crooked; his face was of the irregular Polish-Lithuanian type which at first surprises and then attracts. The greatest of the Poles, Thaddeus Kosciuszko, had just such features.

---

[4] The *Prisoner of the Caucasus*, *Voynarovsky*, and the *Fountain of Bakhchisaray* are poems of Pushkin's. The line quoted is from the last of the three. (*Tr.*)

The clothes of this man, whose name was Tsekhanovich, gave evidence of fearful poverty.

A few days later I was walking along the deserted boulevard by which Perm is bounded on one side; it was in the second half of May, the young leaves were opening, the birches were in flower (I remember the whole avenue was of birches), and there was no one anywhere. Our provincials are not fond of *Platonic* walks. After wandering for a long time, I saw at last on the other side of the boulevard, that is, where the open country began, a man botanising, or perhaps simply gathering the scanty and monotonous flowers of that region. When he raised his head I recognised Tsekhanovich and went up to him.

Later on I saw a good deal of the victims of the Polish insurrection; their record is particularly rich in martyrs—Tsekhanovich was the first. When he told me how he had been persecuted by executioners in the uniform of adjutants-general—those tools with which the savage despot of the Winter Palace fought—then our misfortunes, our prison, and our trial seemed paltry to me.

At that time in Vilna the commanding officer *on the side of the victorious enemy* was the celebrated renegade Muravëv, who immortalised himself by the historic declaration that 'he belonged to the Muravëvs *who hang* and not the Muravëvs who are hanged'. For Nicholas' narrow, vindictive outlook, men of feverish ambition and coarse callousness were always the best fitted or, at any rate, the most sympathetic.

The generals who sat in the torture chamber and tormented the emissaries,[5] their friends or the friends of their friends, were blackguards in their treatment of the prisoners, with no breeding, no feeling of delicacy, and at the same time were very well aware that all their doings were covered by the military greatcoat of Nicholas, which was soaked in the blood of the Polish martyrs and the tears of Polish mothers. . . . This Passion Week of a whole people still awaits its Luke or its Matthew. . . . But let *them* know: one hangman after another will be disgraced at the bar of history and leave his name there. That will be the portrait gallery of the period of Nicholas, by way of pendant to the gallery of the generals of 1812.

Muravëv spoke to the prisoners as though they were of a lower class, and swore at them in the language of the market. Once he was so carried away by fury that he went up to Tsekhanovich and would have taken him by the breast of his coat and perhaps even have struck him, but met the fettered prisoner's eyes, was abashed, and went on in a different tone.

I guessed what those eyes must have looked like; when he told me the story three years after the event, they glowed, his features were convulsed and the veins in his forehead and throat were swollen with blood.

'What could you have done with chains on?'

'I could have torn him to pieces with my teeth, I could have beaten him to death with my skull, with my chains,' he said, trembling.

Tsekhanovich was sent at first to Verkhoturye, one of the remotest towns of the province of Perm, lost in the Ural Mountains, buried in snow and so far from every road that in winter there was scarcely any means of communication. I need hardly say that living in Verkhoturye was worse than in Omsk or Krasnoyarsk.[6] Being in complete solitude, Tsekhanovich occupied himself with the study of the natural sciences, collected the scanty flora of the Ural Mountains, and at last received permission to move to Perm; and for him this was already a great improvement. Once more he heard the sound of his own language and met with comrades in misfortune. His wife, who had remained in Lithuania, wrote that she was setting off to *walk* to him from the province of Vilna. . . . He was waiting for her.

When I was transferred so unexpectedly to Vyatka, I went to say good-bye to Tsekhanovich. The small room in which he lived was almost completely empty. A little, old trunk stood beside the wretched bed; a wooden table and one chair made up the rest of the furniture. To me it reeked of my cell in the Krutitsky Barracks.

The news of my departure grieved him, but he was so used to privations that a minute later he said to me with a smile that was almost bright:

'That's just what I love nature for; wherever a man may be, she cannot be taken from him.'

I wanted to leave him something as a souvenir. I took a little stud out of my shirt and asked him to accept it.

'It won't go with my shirt, but I shall keep your stud to the end of my days and I shall wear it at my funeral.'

Then he thought for a moment and suddenly began rapidly rummaging in his trunk. He found a little bag, drew out of it an iron

[6] Verkhoturye is not in Siberia: Omsk and Krasnoyarsk are. (R.)

chain made in a peculiar way and, tearing several links off, gave them to me with the words:

'That chain is very precious to me: my most sacred memories of a certain time are connected with it. I do not give you all, but take these links. I never thought that I, an exile from Lithuania, would present them to a Russian exile.'

I embraced him and said good-bye.

'When are you going?' he asked.

'To-morrow morning, but I shall not invite you; there is always a gendarme at my lodgings.'

'A good journey to you, then; may you be happier than I.'

By nine o'clock next morning the *politsmeyster* was already at my lodgings and hurrying me off. The Perm gendarme, a far more manageable person that the Krutitsky one, was busy about the carriage not concealing his joy at the hope of being able to be drunk for three hundred and fifty versts. Everything was ready. I glanced casually into the street; Tsekhanovich was passing: I rushed to the window.

'Well, thank God,' he said; 'this is the fourth time I have walked past to say good-bye to you, if only from a distance, and still you did not see me.'

With eyes full of tears I thanked him. This tender, womanly attention touched me deeply; but for this meeting I should have had nothing to regret in Perm!

On the day after we left Perm there was a heavy, unceasing downpour of rain ever since dawn, such as is common in forest districts, which lasted all day; about two o'clock we reached a very poor Votyak village. There was no house at the posting-station. Votyaks[7] (who could not read or write) performed the duties of overseers, looked through the permit for horses, saw whether there were two seals or one, shouted 'Ayda, ayda!' and harnessed the horses twice as quickly, I need hardly say, as it would have been done had there been a superintendent. I wanted to get dry and warm and to have something to eat. Before we reached the village the Perm gendarme had agreed to my suggestion that we should rest for a couple of hours. When I went into the stifling hut, without a chimney, and found that it was absolutely impossible to get anything, that there was not

[7] The Votyaks are a Mongolian tribe, found in Siberia and Eastern Russia; the geographical 'Vyatka' is a cognate noun. The people are known nowadays as Udmurty. (*Tr.*)

even a pot-house for five versts, I regretted our decision and was on
the point of asking for horses.

While I was thinking whether to go on or not to go on, a soldier
came in and reported that an escorting officer had sent to invite me to
a cup of tea.

'With the greatest pleasure. Where is your officer?'

'In the hut near by, your honour,' and the soldier made the familiar
left-about-turn.

I followed him.

A short, elderly officer with a face that bore traces of many anxieties,
petty necessities, and fear of his superiors, met me with all the genial
hospitality of deadly boredom. He was one of those unintelligent,
good-natured 'old' soldiers who pull at the collar for twenty-five years
in the service, and plod along without promotion and without reasoning about it, as old horses work, who probably suppose that it is their
duty to put on their harness at dawn and haul something.

'Whom are you taking, and where to?'

'Oh, don't ask; it'd even break your heart. Well, I suppose my
superiors know all about it; it is our duty to carry out orders and we are
not responsible, but, looking at it as a man, it is an ugly business.'

'Why, what is it?'

'You see, they have collected a crowd of cursed little Jew boys of
eight or nine years old. Whether they are taking them for the navy or
what, I can't say. *At first the orders were to drive them to Perm;
then there was a change and we are driving them to Kazan.* I took
them over a hundred versts farther back. The officer who handed
them over said, "It's dreadful, and that's all about it; a third were left
on the way" (and the officer pointed to the earth). Not half will
reach their destination,' he said.

'Have there been epidemics, or what?' I asked, deeply moved.

'No, not epidemics, but they just die off like flies. A Jew boy, you
know, is such a frail, weakly creature, like a skinned cat; he is not
used to tramping in the mud for ten hours a day and eating biscuit—
then again, being among strangers, no father nor mother nor petting;
well, they cough and cough until they cough themselves into their
graves. And I ask you, what use is it to them? What can they do
with little boys?'

I made no answer.

'When do you set off?' I asked.

'Well, we ought to have gone long ago, but it has been raining so
I*

heavily. . . . Hey, you there, soldier! tell them to get the small fry together.'

They brought the children and formed them into regular ranks: it was one of the most awful sights I have ever seen, those poor, poor children! Boys of twelve or thirteen might somehow have survived it, but little fellows of eight and ten. . . . Not even a brush full of black paint could put such horror on canvas.

Pale, exhausted, with frightened faces, they stood in thick, clumsy, soldiers' overcoats, with stand-up collars, fixing helpless, pitiful eyes on the garrison soldiers who were roughly getting them into ranks. The white lips, the blue rings under their eyes bore witness to fever or chill. And these sick children, without care or kindness, exposed to the icy wind that blows unobstructed from the Arctic Ocean, were going to their graves.

And note that they were being taken by a kind-hearted officer who was obviously sorry for the children. What if they had been taken by a military political economist?

What monstrous crimes are obscurely buried in the archives of the wicked, immoral reign of Nicholas! We are used to them, they were committed every day, committed as though nothing was wrong, unnoticed, lost in the terrible distance, noiselessly sunk in the silent sloughs of officialdom or kept back by the censorship of the police.

Have we not seen with our own eyes seven hungry peasants from Pskov, who were being forcibly removed to the province of Tobolsk, wandering, without food or lodging for the night, about Tverskoy Square in Moscow until Prince D. V. Golitsyn ordered them to be looked after at his own expense?

Chapter 14

Vyatka

THE Governor of Vyatka did not receive me, but sent word that I was to present myself next morning at ten o'clock.

I found in the room next morning the district police-captain, the *politsmeyster*, and two officials: they were all standing talking in whispers and looking uneasily at the door. The door opened and there walked in a short, broad-shouldered old man with a head set on his shoulders like a bull-dog's, and with big jaws, which completed his resemblance to that animal and moreover wore a carnivorous-looking smile; the elderly and at the same time priapic expression of his face, the quick little grey eyes, and the sparse, stiff hair made an incredibly disgusting impression.

To begin with he gave the district police-captain a good dressing-down for the state of the road on which he had driven the day before. The district police-captain stood with his head somewhat bowed in token of respect and submission, and replied to everything as servants used to do in the old days,

'I hear, your Excellency.'

When he had done with the district police-captain, he turned to me. He looked at me insolently and asked:

'Did you finish your studies at Moscow University?'

'I took my degree.'

'And then served?'

'In the Kremlin department.'

'Ha, ha, ha! a fine sort of service! Of course, you had plenty of time there for supper parties and singing songs. Alenitsyn!' he shouted.

A scrofulous young man walked in.

'Listen, my boy: here is a graduate of Moscow University. I expect he knows everything except his duties in the service; it is His Majesty's pleasure that he should learn them with us. Take him into your office and send me special reports on him. To-morrow you will come to the office at nine o'clock, and now you may go. But stay, I forgot to ask how you write.'

I did not at once understand.

'Come, your handwriting.'

'I have nothing with me.'

'Bring paper and pen,' and Alenitsyn handed me a pen.

'What am I to write?'

'What you like,' observed the secretary. 'Write, "On inquiry it appears—"'

'Well, you won't be corresponding with the Tsar,' the governor remarked, laughing ironically.

Before I left Perm I had heard a great deal about Tyufyayev, but he far surpassed all my expectations.

What does not Russian life produce!

Tyufyayev was born at Tobolsk. His father had nearly been exiled, and belonged to the poorest class of townsfolk. At thirteen young Tyufyayev joined a troupe of travelling acrobats who wandered from fair to fair, dancing on the tight-rope, turning somersaults and cart-wheels, and so on. With these he travelled from Tobolsk to the Polish provinces, entertaining good Christian people. There, I do not know why, he was arrested, and since he had no passport he was treated as a vagrant, and sent on foot with a party of prisoners back to Tobolsk. His mother was by then a widow and was living in great poverty. The son rebuilt the stove with his own hands when it was broken: he had to find some trade; the boy had learned to read and write, and he was engaged as a copying clerk in the local court. Being naturally of a free-and-easy character and having developed his abilities by a many-sided education in the troupe of acrobats and the parties of convicts with whom he had passed from one end of Russia to the other, he had made himself an enterprising, practical man.

At the beginning of the reign of Alexander some sort of inspector came to Tobolsk. He needed capable clerks, and someone recommended Tyufyayev. The inspector was so well satisfied with him that he suggested that he should go with him to Petersburg. Then Tyufyayev, whose ambition, in his own words, had never risen above the post of secretary in a district court, formed a higher opinion of himself, and with an iron will resolved to make a career.

And he did make it. Ten years later we find him the indefatigable secretary of Kankrin,[1] who was at that time a general in the commissariat. A year later still he was superintending a department in Arakcheyev's secretariat which administered the whole of Russia. He was with Arakcheyev in Paris at the time when it was occupied by the allied troops.

Tyufyayev spent the whole time sitting in the secretariat of the expeditionary army and literally did not see one street in Paris. He sat day and night collating and copying papers with his worthy colleague, Kleinmikhel.

Arakcheyev's secretariat was like those copper mines into which men are sent to work only for a few months, because if they stay longer they die. Even Tyufyayev was tired at last in that factory of orders and decrees, of regulations and institutions, and began asking for a quieter post. Arakcheyev could not fail to like a man like Tyufyayev, a man free from higher pretensions, from all interests and opinions, formally honest, devoured by ambition, and regarding obedience as the foremost human virtue. Arakcheyev rewarded Tyufyayev with the post of deputy governor. A few years later he made him governor of the Perm Province. The province, through which Tyufyayev had walked once on a rope and once tied to a rope, lay at his feet.

A governor's power generally increases in direct ratio to his distance from Petersburg, but it increases in geometrical progression in the provinces where there are no gentlefolk, as in Perm, Vyatka, and Siberia. Such a remote region was just what Tyufyayev needed.

He was an Oriental satrap, only an active, restless one, meddling in everything and for ever busy. Tyufyayev would have been a ferocious *Commissaire* of the Convention in 1794, a Carrier.[2]

Dissolute in his life, coarse by nature, intolerant of the slightest objection, his influence was extremely pernicious. He did not take bribes, though he did make his fortune, as it appeared after his death. He was strict with his subordinates, he punished without mercy those who were detected in wrongdoing, yet his officials stole more than ever. He carried the abuse of influence to an incredible point; for instance, when he sent an official on an inquiry he would (that is, if he was interested in the case) tell him that probably this or that

---

[1] Tyufyayev was not Kankrin's secretary. (*A.S.*)

[2] Jean-Baptiste Carrier (1756-94), was responsible for the *noyades* and massacre of hundreds of people at Nantes, while suppressing the counter-revolutionary rising of La Vendée. (*Tr.*)

would be discovered; and woe to the official of he discovered something else.

Perm was still full of the fame of Tyufyayev; there was a party of his adherents there, hostile to the new governor, who, of course, had surrounded himself with his own *coterie*.

On the other hand, there were people who hated him. One of them, a rather singular product of the warping influence of Russian life, particularly warned me what Tyufyayev was like. I am speaking of a doctor in one of the factories. This doctor, whose name was Chebotarëv, an intelligent, very nervous man, had made an unfortunate marriage soon after he completed his studies; then he was sent off to Yekaterinburg and without any experience stuck into the slough of provincial life. Though placed in a fairly independent position in these surroundings, none the less he was debased by them; all his activity took the form of a sarcastic persecution of the officials. He laughed at them to their faces, he said the most insulting things to them with leers and grimaces. Since no one was spared, no one particularly resented the doctor's spiteful tongue. He made a social position for himself by his attacks and forced a flabby set of people to put up with the lash with which he chastised them without resting.

I was warned that he was a good doctor, but crazy and extremely impertinent.

His gossip and jokes were neither coarse nor pointless; quite the contrary, they were full of humour and concentrated bile; they were his poetry, his revenge, his outcry of exasperation and, to some extent, perhaps, of despair as well. He had studied the circle of officials like an artist, and as a doctor he knew all their petty, concealed passions and, encouraged by their cowardice and lack of resource, took any liberty with them he liked.

At every word he would add, 'It won't make a ha'p'orth of difference to you.'

Once in joke I remarked upon his repeating this.

'Why are you surprised?' the doctor replied. 'The object of everything that is said is to convince. I hasten to add the strongest argument that exists. Convince a man that to kill his own father won't cost him a halfpenny, and he will kill him.'

Chebotarëv never refused to lend small sums of a hundred or two hundred paper roubles. When anyone asked him for a loan, he would take out his notebook and inquire the exact date when the borrower would return the money.

'Now,' he would say, 'allow me to make a bet of a silver rouble that you won't repay it then.'

'Upon my soul,' the other would object, 'what do you take me for?'

'It makes not a ha'p'orth of difference to you what I take you for,' the doctor would answer, 'but the fact is I have been keeping a record for six years, and not one person has paid me up to time yet, and hardly anyone has repaid me later either.'

The day fixed would pass and the doctor would very gravely ask for the silver rouble he had won.

A tax-farmer at Perm was selling a travelling coach. The doctor presented himself before him and made, without stopping, the following speech :

'You have a coach to sell, I need it; you are a wealthy man, you are a millionaire, everyone respects you for it and I have therefore come to pay you my respects also; as you are a wealthy man, it makes not a ha'p'orth of difference to you whether you sell the coach or not, while I need it very much and have very little money. You want to squeeze me, to take advantage of my necessity and ask fifteen hundred for the coach. I offer you seven hundred roubles. I shall be coming every day to bargain with you and in a week you will let me have it for seven-fifty or eight hundred; wouldn't it be better to begin with that? I am ready to give it.'

'Much better,' answered the astonished tax-farmer, and he let him have the coach.

Chebotarëv's anecdotes and mischievous tricks were endless. I will add two more.[3]

'Do you believe in magnetism?' a rather intelligent and cultured lady asked him in my presence.

'What do you mean by magnetism?'

The lady talked some vague nonsense in reply.

'It makes not a ha'p'orth of difference to you whether I believe in magnetism or not, but if you like I will tell you what I have seen in that way.'

'Please do.'

'Only listen attentively.'

After this he described in a very lively, witty and interesting way the experiments of a Kharkov doctor, an acquaintance of his.

[3] These two anecdotes were not in the first edition. I recollected them when I was revising the sheets.

In the middle of the conversation, a servant brought in some lunch on a tray.

As he was going out the lady said to him,

'You have forgotten to bring the mustard.'

Chebotarëv stopped.

'Go on, go on,' said the lady, a little scared already, 'I am listening.'

'Has he brought the salt?'

'So you are angry already,' said the lady, turning red.

'Not in the least, I assure you; I know that you were listening attentively. But I also know that, however intelligent a woman is and whatever is being talked about, she can never rise above the kitchen —so how could I dare to be angry with you personally?'

At Countess Polier's factory, where he also practised, he took a liking to a stout lad, and invited him to enter his service. The boy was willing, but the foreman said that he could not let him go without permission from the countess. Chebotarëv wrote to the lady. She told the foreman to let the lad have his passport on condition that the doctor paid five years' *obrok* in advance. The doctor promptly wrote to the countess that he agreed to her terms, but asked her as a preliminary to decide one point that troubled him: from whom could he recover the money if Encke's Comet should intersect the earth's orbit and knock it out of its course—which might occur a year and a half before the term fixed.

On the day of my departure for Vyatka the doctor appeared early in the morning and began with the following foolishness:

'Like Horace, once you sang, and to this day you are always being translated.'[4]

Then he took out his notecase and asked if I did not need some money for the journey. I thanked him and refused.

'Why won't you take any? It won't make a ha'p'orth of difference to you.'

'I have money.'

'That's bad,' he said; 'the end of the world must be at hand.' He opened his notebook and wrote down: 'After fifteen years of practice I have for the first time met a man who won't borrow, even though he is going away.'

Having finished playing the fool, he sat down on my bed and said gravely:

[4] Pun on the Russian word for 'translate', which also means 'transfer from one place to another'. (*Tr.*)

'You are going to a frightful man. Be on your guard against him and keep as far away from him as you can. If he likes you it will be a poor recommendation; if he dislikes you, he will finish you off by slander, chicanery, and I don't know what, but he will finish you, and it won't make a ha'p'orth of difference to him.'

With this he told me an incident the truth of which I had an opportunity of verifying afterwards from documents in the secretariat of the Minister of Home Affairs.

Tyufyayev carried on an open intrigue with the sister of a poor government clerk. The brother was made a laughing-stock and he tried to break the liaison, threatened to report it to the authorities, tried to write to Petersburg—in fact, he fretted and made such a to-do that on one occasion the police seized him and brought him before the provincial authorities to be certified as a lunatic.

The provincial authorities, the president of the court, and the inspector of the medical board, an old German who was very much liked by the working people and whom I knew personally, all found that Petrovsky, as the man was called, was mad.

Our doctor knew Petrovsky, who was a patient of his. He was asked too, as a matter of form. He told the inspector that Petrovsky was not mad at all, and that he proposed that they should make a fresh inquiry into the case, otherwise he would take the matter further. The local authorities were not at all opposed to this, but unluckily Petrovsky died in the madhouse without waiting for the day fixed for the second inquiry, although he was a robust young fellow.

The report of the case reached Petersburg. Petrovsky's sister was arrested (why not Tyufyayev?) and a secret investigation began. Tyufyayev dictated the answers; he surpassed himself on this occasion. To hush it up at once and to ward off the danger of a second involuntary journey to Siberia, Tyufyayev instructed the girl to say that her brother had been on bad terms with her ever since, carried away by youth and inexperience, she had been deprived of her innocence by the Emperor Alexander on his visit to Perm, for which she had received five thousand roubles through General Solomka.

Alexander's habits were such that there was nothing improbable in the story. To find out whether it was true was not easy, and in any case would have created a great deal of scandal. To Count Benckendorf's inquiry General Solomka answered that so much money passed through his hands that he could not remember the five thousand.

'La regina ne aveva molto!' says the *improvisatore* in Pushkin's
Egyptian Nights. . . .

So this estimable pupil of Arakcheyev's and worthy comrade of
Kleinmikhel's, the acrobat, vagrant, copying clerk, secretary, and
governor, this tender heart, and disinterested man who locked up the
sane in a madhouse and did them to death there, the man who slan-
dered the Emperor Alexander to divert the attention of the Emperor
Nicholas, was now undertaking to train me in the service.

I was almost completely dependent upon him. He had only to write
some nonsense to the minister and I should have been sent off to some
place in Irkutsk. And no need to write: indeed he had the right to
transfer me to any outlandish town, Kay or Tsarevo-Sanchursk, without any communications, without any resources. Tyufyayev despatched a young Pole to Glazov because the ladies preferred dancing
the mazurka with him to dancing it with his Excellency.

In this way Prince Dolgoruky[5] was sent from Perm to Verkhoturye. The latter place, lost in the mountains and the snows, is reckoned in the province of Perm, though it is as bad as Berëzov for
climate and worse for desolation.

Prince Dolgoruky was one of the aristocratic scamps of the wrong
sort such as are rarely met with in our day. He played all sorts of
pranks in Petersburg, pranks in Moscow, and pranks in Paris.

His life was spent in this way. He was an Izmaylov on a small
scale, a Prince E. Gruzinsky without his den of runaways at Lys-
kovo, that is, a spoilt, insolent, repulsive jester, a gentleman and a
buffoon at once. When his tricks went beyond all bounds, he was
ordered to live at Perm.

He arrived in two carriages; in one was himself with his dog, in
the other, his French cook with his parrots. The people of Perm were
delighted at the arrival of a wealthy visitor, and soon all the town
was hanging about in his dining-room. Dolgoruky got up an affair
with a young lady at Perm; the lady, suspecting some infidelity,
appeared unexpectedly at the prince's house one morning and found
him with his housemaid. This led to a scene which ended in the faith-
less lover's taking a riding-whip from the wall; the councillor's wife,
seeing his intention, took to flight; he went after her, negligently
dressed in no more than a dressing-gown; overtaking her in the little
square in which the battalion usually did its training, he gave the

jealous lady three or four lashes with the whip and calmly returned home as though he had done his duty.

Such nice pranks brought down upon him the censure of his friends at Perm, and the authorities decided to send this forty-years-old scamp to Verkhoturye. On the eve of his departure he gave a sumptuous dinner, and in spite of their differences the officials came to it. Dolgoruky promised to give them a rare kind of pie for dinner. The pie certainly was excellent and vanished with incredible rapidity. When nothing but scraps were left, Dolgoruky turned pathetically to his guests and said:

'Never let it be said that I grudged you anything at parting. I ordered my Gardi to be killed yesterday for the pie.'

The officials looked at one another in horror, and looked round them for the Great Dane they knew so well; it was not to be seen. The prince saw what they felt and bade the servant bring the mortal remains of Gardi, his skin; the contents of it were in the stomachs of the Perm officials. Half the town was taken ill from horror.

Meanwhile Dolgoruky, satisfied with the neat trick he had played on his friends, drove in triumph to Verkhoturye. A third conveyance carried a whole poultry yard—a poultry yard conveyed by post horses! On the way he carried off the ledgers from several posting-stations, mixed them up, altered the figures and almost drove the staffs out of their minds, for even with their books they were not always adroit enough to make their accounts balance.

The stifling emptiness and torpidity of Russian life, strangely combined with the liveliness and even turbulence of the Russian character, develops every sort of folly in us.

In Suvorov's habit of crowing like a cock, just as in Prince Dolgoruky's dog-pie, in the savage escapades of Izmaylov,[6] in the half-voluntary madness of Mamonov,[7] in the violent crimes of Tolstoy 'the American', I detect a kindred note, familiar to us all, though weakened in us by education, or directed to some other end.

---

[6] In 1802 Alexander I ordered a report to be sent him concerning the management by Major-General Izmaylov of the latter's estates in Tula, where serfs were tortured and imprisoned by their owner on the slightest provocation. By the connivance of the local authorities, Izmaylov was able to retain control and persist in his brutal practices till 1830. Even then he was only punished by being deprived of the management of his estates and interned in a small town. Both Izmaylov and Tolstoy 'the American' are referred to in Griboyedov's famous play, *Woe from Wit*. (*Tr.*)

[7] Mamonov was one of the lovers of Catherine II, declared insane for having married against her wishes. (*Tr.*)

I knew Tolstoy personally, just at the time when he lost his daughter Sarra, an exceptional girl with marked poetic gifts. One glance at the old man's exterior, at his forehead covered with grey curls, at his sparkling eyes and athletic frame revealed how much energy and vigour nature had bestowed on him. He had developed only turbulent passions and evil propensities, and this is not surprising; among us everything vicious is allowed to develop for a long time without hindrance, while for humane passions a man is sent to a garrison or Siberia at the first step. . . . He rioted, won at cards, fought, mutilated people and ruined families for twenty years on end, till at last he was sent to Siberia, from which he 'returned an Aleutian' as Griboyedov says, that is he made his way through Kamchatka to America, and thence obtained permission to return to Russia. Alexander pardoned him, and from the day after his arrival he carried on the same life as before. Married to a girl who had belonged to the Moscow gipsy camp and was famous for her voice, he turned his house into a gambling den, spent all his time in orgies, all his nights at cards, and wild scenes of cupidity and drunkenness took place beside the cradle of the little Sarra. The story goes that on one occasion, to prove the accuracy of his eye, he made his wife stand on the table and shot through the heel of her shoe.

His last prank almost sent him to Siberia again. He had long been angry with a certain workman; he caught him one day in his (Tolstoy's) house, bound him hand and foot, and pulled out one of his teeth. Will it be believed that this incident took place only ten or twelve years ago? The injured man lodged a complaint. Tolstoy bribed the police and the court, and the man was put in prison for making a false accusation. At that time a well-known Russian literary man, N. F. Pavlov, was serving on the prison commission. The workman told him his story, the inexperienced official took it up; Tolstoy was scared in earnest, for the case was clearly going to end in his condemnation; but great is the God of Russia. Count Orlov wrote a secret communication to Prince Shcherbatov, in which he advised him to hush up the case, so as not to allow the *open triumph of a man of inferior rank over a member of the higher classes*. As for Pavlov, Count Orlov advised that he should be removed from such a post. This is almost more incredible than the extraction of the tooth. I was in Moscow at the time and knew the imprudent official well. But let us return to Vyatka.

The government office was incomparably worse than prison. Not that the actual work was great, but the stifling atmosphere, as of the Dogs' Grotto,[8] of those musty surroundings, and the fearful, stupid waste of time made the office intolerable. Alenitsyn did not worry me: he was, indeed, more polite than I expected; he had been at the Kazan High School and consequently had a respect for a graduate of Moscow University.

There were some twenty clerks in the office. For the most part they were persons of no education and no moral conceptions; sons of clerks and secretaries, accustomed from their cradle to regard the service as a source of profit, and the peasants as soil that yielded revenue, they sold certificates, took twenty kopecks and quarter-roubles, cheated for a glass of wine, demeaned themselves and did all sorts of shabby things. My valet gave up going to the 'billiard room', saying that the officials cheated there worse than anybody, and one could not teach them a lesson because they were 'officers'.

So with these people, whom my servant did not thrash only on account of their rank, I had to sit every day from nine in the morning until two, and from five to eight in the evening.

Besides Alenitsyn, who was the head of the office, there was a head-clerk of the table at which I was put, who also was not an ill-natured creature, though drunken and illiterate. At the same table sat four clerks. I had to talk to and become acquainted with these, and, indeed, with all the others, too. Apart from the fact that these people would have paid me out sooner or later for being 'proud' if I had not, it is simply impossible to spend several hours of every day with the same people without making their acquaintance. Moreover it must not be forgotten that provincials make up to anyone from outside and particularly to anyone who comes from the capital, especially if there is some interesting story connected with him.

After spending the whole day in this galley, I would sometimes come home with all my faculties in a state of stupefaction and fling myself on the sofa, worn out, humiliated, and incapable of any work or occupation. I heartily regretted my Krutitsky cell with its charcoal fumes and black-beetles, with a gendarme on guard and a lock on the door. There I had freedom, I did what I liked and no one in-

---

[8] At Terme d'Agnano, west of Naples, there is a grotto, filled at the bottom with carbon dioxide, where dogs suffocated. F. L. Lucas: *The Search for Good Sense* (Collins, 1958), p. 244. (R.)

terfered with me; instead of these vulgar remarks, dirty people, mean ideas and coarse feelings, there had been the stillness of death and undisturbed leisure. And when I remembered that after dinner I had to go again, and again to-morrow, I was at times overcome by fury and despair and tried to find comfort in drinking wine and vodka.

And then, what is more, one of my fellow-clerks would look in 'on his way' and relieve his boredom by staying on talking until it was time to go back to the office.

Within a few months, however, the office became somewhat more bearable.

Prolonged, regular persecution is not in the Russian character unless a personal or mercenary element comes in; and this is not at all because the government does not want to stifle and crush a man, but is due to the Russian carelessness, to our *laissez-aller*. Russians in authority are as a rule ill-bred, audacious, and insolent; it is easy to provoke them to rudeness, but persistent knocking about is not in their line: they have not enough patience for it, perhaps because it brings them no profit.

In the first heat, in order to display, on the one hand their zeal, and on the other their power, they do all sorts of stupid and unnecessary things; then little by little they leave a man in peace.

So it was with the office. The Ministry of Home Affairs had at that time a craze for statistics: it had given orders for committees to be formed everywhere, and had issued programmes which could hardly have been carried out even in Belgium or Switzerland; at the same time there were to be all sorts of elaborate tables with maxima and minima, with averages and various deductions from the totals for periods of ten years (made up on evidence which had not been collected for *a year before*!), with moral remarks and meteorological observations. Not a farthing was assigned for the expenses of the committees and the collection of evidence; all this was to be done from love of statistics through the rural police and put into proper shape in the governor's office. The clerks, overwhelmed with work, and the rural police, who hate all peaceful and theoretical tasks, looked upon a statistics committee as a useless luxury, as a caprice of the ministry; however, the reports had to be sent in with tabulated results and deductions.

This business seemed immensely difficult to the whole office; it was simply impossible; but no one troubled about that: all they worried about was that there should be no occasion for reprimands. I promised Alenitsyn to prepare a preface and introduction, and to draw up summaries of the tables with eloquent remarks introducing foreign words, quotations, and striking deductions, if he would allow me to undertake this very hard work not at the office but at home. After parleying with Tyufyayev, Alenitsyn agreed.

The introduction to the record of the work of the committee, in which I discussed their hopes and their plans, for in reality nothing had been done at all, touched Alenitsyn to the depths of his soul. Tyufyayev himself thought it was written in masterly style. With that my labours in the statistical line ended, but they put the committee under my supervision. They no longer forced upon me the unpleasant task of copying papers, and the drunken head-clerk who had been my chief became almost my subordinate. Alenitsyn only required, from some consideration of propriety, that I should go to the office for a short time every day.

To show the complete impossibility of real statistics, I will quote the facts sent in from the unimportant town of Kay. There, among various absurdities, were for instance the entries: Drowned—2. Causes of drowning not known—2, and in the column of totals was set out the figure 4. Under the heading of extraordinary incidents was reckoned the following tragic anecdote: So-and-so, townsman, having deranged his intelligence by ardent beverages, hanged himself. Under the heading of the morality of the town's inhabitants was the entry: 'There have been no Jews in the town of Kay.' To the inquiry whether sums had been allotted for the building of a church, a stock exchange, or an almshouse, the answer ran thus: 'For the building of a stock exchange was assigned—nothing.'

The statistics that rescued me from work at the office had the unfortunate consequence of bringing me into personal relations with Tyufyayev.

There was a time when I hated that man; that time is long past and the man himself is past. He died on his Kazan estates about 1845. Now I think of him without anger, as of a peculiar beast met in the wilds of a forest which ought to have been studied, but with which one could not be angry for being a beast. At the time I could not help coming into conflict with him; that was inevitable for any decent man. Chance helped me or he would have done me great injury; to owe him a grudge for the harm he did not do me would be absurd and paltry.

Tyufyayev lived alone. His wife was separated from him. The governor's favourite, the wife of a cook who for no fault but being married to her had been sent away to the country, was, with an awkwardness which almost seemed intentional, kept out of sight in the back rooms of his house. She did not make her appearance officially, but officials who were particularly devoted to the governor—that is, particularly afraid of inquiries—formed a sort of court about the cook's wife 'who was in favour'. Their wives and daughters paid her stealthy visits in the evening and did not boast of doing so. This lady was possessed of the same sort of tact as distinguished one of her brilliant predecessors—Potëmkin; knowing the old man's disposition and afraid of being replaced, she herself sought out for him rivals who were no danger to her. The grateful old man repaid this indulgent love with his devotion and they got on well together.

All the morning Tyufyayev worked and was in the office of the secretariat. The poetry of life only began at three o'clock. Dinner was for him no jesting matter. He liked a good dinner and he liked to eat it in company. Preparations were always made in his kitchen for twelve at table; if the guests were fewer than half that number he was mortified; if there were no more than two visitors he was wretched; if there was no one at all, he would go off on the verge of despair to dine in his Dulcinea's apartments. To procure people in order to feed them till they felt sick was no difficult task, but his official position and the terror he inspired in his subordinates did not permit them to enjoy his hospitality freely, nor him to turn his house into a tavern. He had to confine himself to councillors, presidents (but with half of these he was on bad terms, that is, he would not condescend to them), travellers (who were rare), rich merchants, tax-farmers, and the few visitors to the town and 'oddities', who were something in the style of the *capacités* whom in the time of Louis-Philippe there was a wish to introduce as candidates at elections.* Of course I was an oddity of the first magnitude at Vyatka.

Persons exiled 'for their opinions' to remote towns are somewhat feared, but are never confounded with ordinary mortals. 'Dangerous people' have for provincials the same attraction that notorious Lovelaces have for women and courtesans for men. Dangerous people are far more shunned by Petersburg officials and Moscow big pots than by provincials, and especially by Siberians.

Those who were exiled in connection with the Fourteenth of December were looked upon with immense respect. Officials paid their first visit on New Year's Day to the widow of Yushnevsky. Senator Tolstoy, when taking a census of Siberia, was guided by evidence received from the exiled Decembrists in checking the facts furnished by the officials.

Münnich[9] from his tower in Pelym superintended the affairs of the Tobolsk Province. Governors used to go to consult him about matters of importance.

The working people are still less hostile to exiles: on the whole they are on the side of those who are punished. The word 'convict' disappears near the Siberian frontier and is replaced by the word 'unfortunate'. In the eyes of the Russian people a legal sentence is no disgrace to a man. The peasants of the Perm Province, living along the main road to Tobolsk, often put out kvas, milk, and bread in a little window in case an 'unfortunate' should be secretly slipping through that way from Siberia.

By the way, speaking of exiles, Polish exiles begin to be met beyond Nizhny Novgorod and their number increases rapidly after Kazan. In Perm there were forty, in Vyatka not fewer; there were several besides in every district town.

They lived quite apart from the Russians and avoided all contact with the inhabitants. There was great unanimity among them, and the rich shared with the poor like brothers.

On the part of the inhabitants I never saw signs of either hatred or special goodwill towards them. They looked upon them as outsiders—the more so, as scarcely a single Pole knew Russian.

One tough old Sarmatian, who had been an officer in the Uhlans in Poniatowski's time and had taken part in Napoleon's campaigns, received permission in 1837 to return to his Lithuanian domains. On the eve of his departure he invited me and several Poles to dinner. After dinner my cavalry officer came up to me, goblet in hand, embraced me, and with a warrior's simplicity whispered in my ear, 'Oh, why are you a Russian!' I did not answer a word, but this observation sank deeply into my heart. I realised that *this* generation could never set Poland free.

---

[9] Münnich (also spelt Minikh), Burchardt Christoph (Khristophor Antonovich) 1683-1767, was a minister and general prominent under Peter the Great and Anna. On the latter's death he brought about the downfall of Biron, was exiled by Elizabeth, and finally brought back from Siberia by Catherine. (*Tr.*)

From the time of Konarski,[10] the Poles have come to look quite differently upon the Russians.

As a rule Polish exiles are not oppressed, but the material situation is awful for those who have no private means. The government gives those who have nothing *fifteen paper roubles a month*; with that they must pay for lodging, food, clothes, and fuel. In fairly big towns, in Kazan and Tobolsk, it was possible to earn something by giving lessons or concerts, playing at balls, executing portraits and teaching dancing. In Perm and Vyatka they had no such resources. And in spite of that they would ask for nothing from Russians.

Tyufyayev's invitations to his greasy Siberian dinners were a real imposition on me. His dining-room was just like the office, but in another form, less dirty but more vulgar, because it had the appearance of free will and not of compulsion.

Tyufyayev knew his guests through and through, despised them, showed them his claws at times, and altogether treated them as a master treats his dogs: at one time with excessive familiarity, at another with a rudeness which was beyond all bounds—and yet he invited them to his dinners and they appeared before him in trembling and in joy, demeaning themselves, talking scandal, eavesdropping, trying to please, smiling, bowing.

I blushed for them and felt ashamed.

Our friendship did not last long. Tyufyayev soon guessed that I was not fit for 'high' Vyatka society.

A few months later he was dissatisfied with me, a few months later still he hated me, and I not only went no more to his dinners but even gave up going to him at all. The Heir's passage through Vyatka saved me from his persecution, as we shall see later on.

I must observe that I had done absolutely nothing to deserve first his attention and invitations, and afterwards his anger and disfavour. He could not endure to see in me a man who behaved independently, though not in the least insolently; I was always *en règle* with him, and he demanded obsequiousness.

[10] Simon Konarski, a Polish revolutionary, also active in the 'Young Europe' (afterwards 'Young Italy') movement, lived in disguise and with a false passport in Poland, founding a printing press and carrying on active propaganda till he was caught and shot at Vilna in 1839. His admirers cut the post to which he was tied into bits which they preserved, like the relics of a saint. (*Tr.*) An attempt to liberate Konarski from the prison at Vilna was made by a secret organisation of Russian officers headed by Kuzmin-Karayev. (*A.S.*)

He loved his power jealously. He had earned it the hard way, and he exacted not only obedience but an *appearance* of absolute submission. In this, unhappily he was typically native.

A landowner says to his servant, 'Hold your tongue; I won't put up with your answering me back!'

The head of a department, turning pale with anger, observes to a clerk who has made some objection, 'You forget yourself; do you know *to whom* you are speaking?'

The Tsar sends men to Siberia 'for opinions', does them to death in dungeons for *a poem*—and all these three are readier to forgive stealing and bribe-taking, murder and robbery, than the impudence of human dignity and the insolence of a plain-spoken word.

Tyufyayev was a true servant of the Tsar. He was highly thought of, but not highly enough. Byzantine servility was exceptionally well combined in him with official discipline. Obliteration of self, renunciation of will and thought before authority went inseparably with harsh oppression of subordinates. He might have been a civilian Kleinmikhel; his 'zeal' might in the same way have overcome everything,[11] and he might in the same way have plastered the walls with the dead human bodies, have used living men's lungs to dry the damp walls of his palace, and have flogged the young men of the engineering corps even more severely for not being informers.

Tyufyayev had an intense, secret hatred for everything aristocratic; he had kept this from his bitter experiences. The hard labour of Arakcheyev's secretariat had been his first refuge, his first deliverance. Till then his superiors had never offered him a chair, but had employed him on menial errands. When he served in the commissariat, the officers had persecuted him, as is the custom in the army, and one colonel had horsewhipped him in the street at Vilna. . . . All this had entered into the copying clerk's soul and rankled there; now he was governor and it was his turn to oppress, to keep men standing, to call people 'thou', to raise his voice more than was necessary, and sometimes to bring gentlemen of ancient lineage to trial.

From Perm Tyufyayev had been transferred to Tver. The gentry of the province, for all their submissiveness and servility, could not put up with him. They petitioned the minister, Bludov, to remove him. Bludov appointed him to Vyatka.

[11] 'The motto of the coat of arms granted by Nicholas I to Count Kleinmikhel was 'Zeal overcomes all'. (*A.S.*)

There he was quite at home again. Officials and contractors, factory-owners and government clerks—a free hand, and that was all about it. Everyone trembled before him, everyone stood up when he came in, everyone offered him drink and gave him dinners, everyone waited on his slightest wish; at weddings and name-day parties, the first toast was 'To the health of his Excellency!'

Chapter 15

Misgovernment in Siberia

ONE of the most melancholy results of the Petrine revolution was the development of the official class. An artificial, hungry, and un-cultivated class, capable of doing nothing but 'serving', knowing nothing but official forms, it constitutes a kind of civilian clergy, celebrating divine service in the courts and the police forces, and sucking the blood of the people with thousands of greedy, unclean mouths.

Gogol lifted one corner of the curtain and showed us Russian officialdom in all its ugliness; but Gogol cannot help conciliating one with his laughter; his enormous comic talent gets the upper hand of his indignation. Moreover, in the fetters of the Russian censorship he could scarcely touch upon the melancholy side of that foul underworld, in which the destinies of the miserable Russian people are forged.

There, somewhere in grimy offices which we make haste to pass through, shabby men write and write on grey paper, and copy on to stamped paper—and persons, families, whole villages are outraged, terrified, ruined. A father is sent into exile, a mother to prison, a son for a soldier—and all this breaks like a thunderclap upon them, unexpected, for the most part undeserved. And for the sake of what? For the sake of money. A contribution . . . or an inquiry will be held into the dead body of some drunkard, burnt up by spirits and frozen to death. And the head-man collects and the village elder collects, the peasants bring their last kopeck. The police-commissary must live; the police-captain must live and keep his wife too; the councillor must live and educate his children, for the councillor is an exemplary father.

Officialdom reigns supreme in the north-eastern provinces of Russia and in Siberia. There it has flourished unhindered, without look-ing back . . . it is a fearful long way, and everyone shares in the

profits, stealing becomes *res publica*. Even the Imperial power, which
strikes like grape-shot, cannot breach these boggy trenches, that are
dug in mud that sucks you down, and are hidden under the snow. All
the measures of government are enfeebled, all its intentions are
distorted; it is deceived, fooled, betrayed, sold, and all under cover
of loyal servility and with the observance of all the official forms.

Speransky[1] tried to improve the lot of the Siberian people. He
introduced everywhere the collegiate principle, as though it made
any difference whether the officials stole individually or in gangs. He
discharged the old rogues by hundreds and engaged new ones by
hundreds. At first he inspired such terror in the rural police that they
actually *bribed the peasants* not to lodge petitions against them.
Three years later the officials were making their fortunes by the new
forms as well as they had done by the old.

Another eccentric was General Velyaminov. For two years he
struggled at Tobolsk trying to check abuses, but, seeing his lack of
success, threw it all up and quite gave up attending to business.

Others, more judicious, did not make the attempt, but got rich
themselves and let others get rich.

'I shall eradicate bribe-taking,' said Senyavin, the Governor of
Moscow, to a grey-haired peasant who had lodged a complaint
against some obvious injustice. The old man smiled.

'What are you laughing at?' asked Senyavin.

'Why, you must forgive me, sir,' answered the peasant; 'it put me
in mind of one fine young fellow who boasted he would lift the
Tsar-pushka,[2] and he really did try, but he did not lift it for all that.'

Senyavin, who told the story himself, belonged to that class of
unpractical men in the Russian service who imagine that rhetorical
sallies on the subject of honesty, and the despotic persecution of two
or three rogues who happen to be there, can remedy so universal a
disease as Russian bribe-taking, which grows freely under the shadow
of the censorship.

There are only two remedies for it: publicity, and an entirely
different organisation of the whole machinery, the re-introduction of

---

[1] Speransky, Mikhail Mikhaylovich (1772-1839), a leading statesman of the early
period of the reign of Alexander I, banished in 1812 on a trumped-up charge of
treason, recalled by Nicholas. He was responsible for the codification of Russian
laws. (*Tr.*)

[2] A cannon, cast in the seventeenth century, which weighs forty tons. It is in the
Kremlin at Moscow and is said to be the biggest in the world. It has never been
fired. (*R.*)

the popular principle of the arbitration courts, verbal proceedings, sworn witnesses, and all that the Petersburg administration detests.

Pestel, the Governor-General of Western Siberia, father of the celebrated Pestel put to death by Nicholas, was a real Roman proconsul and one of the most violent. He carried on an open system of plunder in the whole region which was cut off from Russia by his spies. Not a single letter crossed the border without the seal being broken, and woe to the man who should dare to write anything about his government. He kept merchants of the first guild for a year at a time in prison in chains; he tortured them. He sent officials to the borders of Eastern Siberia and left them there for two or three years.

For a long time the people bore it; at last a working man of Tobolsk made up his mind to bring the condition of affairs to the knowledge of the Tsar. Afraid of the ordinary routes, he went to Kyakhta and from there made his way with a caravan of teas across the Siberian frontier. He found an opportunity at Tsarskoye Selo of giving Alexander his petition, beseeching him to read it. Alexander was amazed by the terrible things he read in it. He sent for the man, and after a long talk with him was convinced of the melancholy truth of his report. Mortified and somewhat embarrassed, he said to him:

'You go home now, my friend; the thing shall be inquired into.'

'Your Majesty,' answered the man, 'I shall not go home now. Better command me to be put in prison. My conversation with your Majesty will not remain a secret and I shall be killed.'

Alexander shuddered and said, turning to Miloradovich, who was at that time Governor-General in Petersburg:

'You will answer to me for him.'

'In that case,' observed Miloradovich, 'allow me to take him into my own house.'

And the man actually remained there until the case was ended.

Pestel almost always lived in Petersburg. You may remember that the proconsuls as a rule lived in Rome. By means of his presence and connections, and still more by the division of the spoils, he anticipated all sorts of unpleasant rumours and scandals.[3] The Imperial Council

[3] This gave Count Rostopchin occasion for a biting jest at Pestel's expense. They were both dining with the Tsar. The Tsar, who was standing at the window, asked: 'What's that on the church, the black thing on the cross?' 'I can't make out,' observed Count Rostopchin. 'You must ask Ivan Borisovich, he has wonderful eyes for he can see from here what is being done in Siberia.'

took advantage of Alexander's temporary absence at Verona or Aachen[4] to come to the intelligent and just decision that since the matter in a denunciation related to Siberia the case should be passed to Pestel to deal with, seeing that he was on the spot. Miloradovich, Mordvinov, and two others were opposed to this decision, and the case was brought before the Senate.

The Senate, with that outrageous injustice with which it constantly judges cases relating to higher officials, exculpated Pestel but exiled Treskin, the civilian governor of Tobolsk, and deprived him of his rank and privileges as a member of the gentry, and relegated him to somewhere or other. Pestel was only dismissed from the service.

After Pestel there appeared at Tobolsk Kaptsevich, a man of the school of Arakcheyev. Thin, bilious, a tyrant by nature and a tyrant because he had spent his whole life in the army, a man of restless activity, he brought outward discipline and order into everything, fixed maximum prices for goods, but left everyday affairs in the hands of robbers. In 1824 the Tsar wished to visit Tobolsk. Through the Perm province runs an excellent, broad high-road, which has been in use for ages and is probably good owing to the nature of the soil. Kaptsevich made a similar road to Tobolsk in a few months. In the spring, in the time of alternate thaw and frost, he forced thousands of workmen to make the road by levies from villages near and far; sickness broke out and half the workmen died, but 'zeal can overcome anything'—the road was made.

Eastern Siberia is still more negligently governed. It is so far away that news hardly reaches Petersburg. At Irkutsk, Bronevsky, the Governor-General, was fond of firing off cannon in the town when 'he was merry'. And another high official when he was drunk used to say mass in his house in full vestments and in the presence of the bishop. At least the noisiness of the one and the devoutness of the other were not so pernicious as Pestel's blockade and Kaptsevich's indefatigable activity.

It is a pity that Siberia is so rottenly governed. The choice of its governors-general has been particularly unfortunate. I do not know what Muravëv is like; he is well known for his intelligence and his abilities; the others were good for nothing. Siberia has a great future: it is looked upon merely as a cellar, in which there are great stores of gold, fur, and other goods, but which is cold, buried in snow,

---

[4] Congresses of the Holy Alliance were held at Aachen in 1818 and Verona in 1822. (*A.S.*)

poor in the means of life, without roads or population. This is not true.

The dead hand of the Russian government, that does everything by violence, everything with the stick, cannot give the vital impetus which would carry Siberia forward with American rapidity. We shall see what will happen when the mouths of the Amur are opened for navigation and America meets Siberia near China.

I said long ago that the *Pacific Ocean is the Mediterranean of the future*.[5] In that future the part played by Siberia, the land that lies between the Ocean, Southern Asia, and Russia, will be extremely important. Of course Siberia is bound to extend to the Chinese frontier. Why freeze and shiver in Berëzov and Yakutsk when there are Krasnoyarsk, Minusinsk, and other such places?

Even the Russian immigrants into Siberia have elements in their nature that suggest a different development. Generally speaking, the Siberian race is healthy, well-grown, intelligent, and extremely steady. The Siberian children of settlers know nothing of the land-owners' power. There is no upper class in Siberia and at the same time there is no aristocracy in the towns; the officials and the officers, who are the representatives of authority, are more like a hostile garrison stationed there by a victorious enemy than an aristocracy. The immense distances save the peasants from frequent contact with them; money saves the merchants, who in Siberia despise the officials and, though outwardly giving way to them, take them for what they are—their clerks employed in civil affairs.

The habit of using firearms, indispensable for a Siberian, is universal. The dangers and emergencies of his daily life have made the Siberian peasant more warlike, more resourceful, readier to offer resistance than the Great Russian. The remoteness of churches leaves his mind freer from fanaticism than in Russia; he is phlegmatic about religion and most often a schismatic. There are remote hamlets which the priest visits only three or four times a year and administers baptism wholesale, buries, marries, and hears confessions for the whole time since he was there last.

On this side of the Ural Mountains things are done more discreetly, and yet I could fill volumes with anecdotes of the abuse of power and the roguery of the officials, heard in the course of my service in the office and dining-room of the governor.

---

[5] I have seen with great pleasure that the New York papers have several times repeated this.

K

'Oh, he was a master at it, my predecessor,' the *politsmeyster* of Vyatka said to me in a moment of confidential conversation. 'Well, of course, that's the way to get on, only you have got to be born to it, sir; he was a regular Seslavin,[6] a Figner in his own way, I may say,' and the eyes of the lame major, promoted to be a *politsmeyster* for his wound, sparkled at the memory of his glorious predecessor.

'A gang of robbers turned up not far from the town, and once or twice news reached the authorities of merchants' goods being stolen, or money being seized from a contractor's steward. The governor was in a great taking and wrote off one order after another. Well, you know the rural police are cowards; they are equal to tying up a wretched little thief and bringing him to justice—but this was a gang and maybe with firearms. The rural police did nothing. The governor sends for the *politsmeyster* and says: "I know," he says, "that it's not your duty, but your efficiency makes me turn to you."

'The *politsmeyster* had information about the business beforehand. "General," said he, "I shall set off in an hour. The robbers must be at such and such a place; I'll take a squad of soldiers with me, I shall find them at such and such a place, and within a few days I shall bring them in chains to the prison."

'Why, it was like Suvorov with the Austrian Emperor! And indeed, no sooner said than done—he fairly pounced on them with the soldiers, they had no time to hide their money, the *politsmeyster* took it all and brought the robbers into town.

'The inquiry began. The *politsmeyster* asked them: "Where is the money?"

' "Why, we gave it to you, sir, into your very hands," two of the robbers answer.

' "Gave it to me?" says the *politsmeyster* in amazement.

' "Yes, to you, to you," shout the robbers.

' "What insolence!" says the *politsmeyster* to the inspector, turning pale with indignation. "Why, you scoundrels, you'll be saying next, I suppose, that I stole it with you. I'll teach you to try to tarnish my uniform; I'm a cornet of Uhlans and won't allow a slur on my honour!"

'He has them flogged, saying "Confess where you've put the

---

[6] For Seslavin and Figner see the index. (R.)

money, and have done with it." At first they stick to their story: only when he gives the order for them to be flogged *for two pipefuls* the leader shouts: "We are guilty, we blued the money."

' "You should have said so long ago," says the *politsmeyster,* "instead of talking such nonsense; you won't catch me very soon, my man."

' "Well, to be sure, we ought to come to your honour for a lesson and not you to us. We couldn't teach you anything!" muttered the old robber, looking with admiration at the *politsmeyster.*

'And do you know, he got the Vladimir ribbon for that business.'

'Excuse me,' I asked, interrupting the praises of the great *politsmeyster,* 'what is the meaning of "for two pipefuls"?'

'That's just a saying *among us.* It's a dreary business you know, flogging, so as you order it to begin you light your pipe and it is usually over by the time you have smoked it—but in exceptional cases we sometimes order our friends to be treated to two pipefuls. The police are used to it; they know pretty well how much to give.'

About that Figner there were regular legends current in Vyatka. He performed miracles. Once, I do not remember the occasion, some adjutant-general or minister arrived, and the *politsmeyster* wanted to show that he had not worn the uniform of an Uhlan for nothing and that he could spur his horse as smartly as anyone. To this end he applied to one of the Mashkovtsevs, rich merchants of that region, asking him to give him his valuable grey saddle-horse. Mashkovtsev would not give it.

'Very good,' said Figner, 'you won't do such a trifle for me of your own accord, so I'll take the horse without your permission.'

'Well, we shall see about that,' said Gold.

'Yes, you shall see,' said Steel.[7]

Mashkovtsev locked up the horse and put two men on guard. This time the *politsmeyster* would be unsuccessful.

But in the night, as though of design, some empty barns belonging to some tax-farmers, and adjoining Mashkovtsev's house, took fire. The *politsmeyster* and the police did their work admirably; to save Mashkovtsev's house, they even pulled down the wall of his stable and carried off the horse in dispute, without a hair of his tail or of

---

[7] An epigram of Pushkin's contains the two lines:
  ' "I'll buy all," said Gold.
   "I'll take all," said Steel.' (*Tr.*)

his mane singed. Two hours later the *politsmeyster*, parading on a white stallion, went to receive the thanks of the person of consequence for the exemplary way in which he had extinguished the fire. After this no one doubted that the *politsmeyster* could do anything.

The governor Rykhlevsky was driving from an assembly; at the moment when his carriage was moving off, the driver of a small sledge carelessly got between the traces of the wheelers and the leaders; this led to a minute's confusion, which did not, however, prevent Rykhlevsky from reaching home perfectly comfortably. Next day the governor asked the *politsmeyster* if he knew whose coachman it was who had driven into his traces, and said that he ought to be given a fright.

'That coachman, your Excellency, will never drive into traces again; I've had him given a good lesson,' the *politsmeyster* answered, smiling.

'But whose man is he?'

'Councillor Kulakov's, your Excellency.'

At that moment the old councillor, whom I found and left still a councillor of the provincial government, walked into the governor's.

'You must forgive us,' said the governor to him, 'for having given your coachman a lesson.'

The astonished councillor looked at him inquiringly, unable to understand.

'You see he drove into my traces yesterday. You see if he is allowed to. . . .'

'But, your Excellency, I was at home all day yesterday, and my wife too, and the coachman was at home.'

'What's the meaning of this?' asked the governor.

'I am very sorry, your Excellency. I was so busy yesterday, my head was in a whirl, I quite forgot about the coachman, and I confess I did not dare to report that to your Excellency. I meant to see about him at once.'

'Well, you are a regular *politsmeyster*, there is no doubt about it!' observed Rykhlevsky.

Side by side with this rapacious official, I shall describe another of the opposite breed—tame, gentle, compassionate.

Among my acquaintances was a venerable old man, a police-captain dismissed from his position by a senatorial committee of inspection. He spent his time drawing up petitions and getting up cases, which was just what he was forbidden to do. This man, who had been in the service from time immemorial, had stolen, doctored official documents, and collected false evidence in three provinces, been tried twice, and so on. This veteran of the rural police liked to tell amazing anecdotes about himself and his colleagues, not concealing his contempt for the degenerate officials of the younger generation.

'They're giddy-pates,' he said; 'of course they take what they can get, there is no living without it; but it is no use looking for cleverness or knowledge of the law in them. I'll tell you, for instance, about one friend of mine. He was a judge for twenty years and only died last year. There was a brain for you! And the peasants don't remember evil against him, though he has left his family a bit of bread. He had quite a special way of his own. If a peasant came along with a petition, the judge would admit him at once and be as friendly and pleasant as you please.

' "What is your name, uncle," says he, "and what was your father's?"

'The peasant would bow and say, "Yermolay, sir, and my father was called Grigory."

' "Well, good health to you, Yermolay Grigoryevich; from what parts is the Lord bringing you here?"

' "We are from Dubilovo."

' "I know, I know. You have a mill, I fancy, on the right from the road—the high road."

' "Yes, sir, the mill of our commune."

' "A well-to-do village; the land is good, black soil."

' "We don't complain against God, kind sir; He looks after us."

' "Well, that is as it should be. I'll be bound you have a good-sized family, Yermolay Grigoryevich?"

' "Three sons and two daughters, and I have married the elder to a young fellow who has been with us five years."

' "I dare say you have grandchildren by now?"

' "Yes, there are little ones, your honour."

' "And thank God for it! increase and multiply. Well, Yermolay Grigoryevich, it is a long way you have come, so let us have a glass of birch wine."

'The peasant makes a show of refusing. The judge fills a glass for him, saying,

"Nonsense, nonsense, my man, the holy Fathers don't forbid wine and oil to-day."

' "It's true it's not forbidden, but wine brings a man to every kind of trouble." Then he crosses himself, bows, and drinks the birch wine.

' "With such a family, Grigorych, I'll be bound life is hard? To feed and clothe every one of them you can't manage with one wretched nag or cow; there would not be enough milk."

' "Upon my word, sir, how could I manage with only one horse? I have three. I did have a fourth, a roan, but it was bewitched about St Peter's fast; the carpenter in our village, Dorofey, may God be his judge, hates to see another man well off and has the evil eye."

' "It does happen, it does happen. And you have big grazing lands, of course; I'll be bound you keep sheep?"

' "To be sure, we have sheep too."

' "Ah, I've been too long talking with you. It's the Tsar's service, Yermolay Grigorych; it is time I was in the court. Had you come about some little business, or what?"

' "Yes, your honour, that's it."

' "Well, what is it? some quarrel? Make haste and tell me, uncle! it is time I was going."

' "Well, kind sir, trouble has come upon me in my old age. Just at Assumption, we were in the tavern and came to high words with a peasant from a neighbouring village—ugly fellow: he's always stealing our wood. We had hardly said a word before he swung his fist and gave me a punch in the chest. 'Keep your blows for your own village,' I said to him, I said: and just to make an example, I would have given him a smack, but, being drunk perhaps, or else the devil was in it, hit him in the eye—and, well, I spoilt it, his eye, that is, and he is gone with the church elder straight to the inspector—'I want a trial,' he says, 'in proper shape.' "

'While he's telling this story, the judge—your Petersburg actors are nothing to him—grows graver and graver, puts on a terrifying expression, and does not say a word.

'The peasant sees this and turns pale, lays his hat at his feet and takes out a towel to wipe the sweat off. The judge still sits silent and turns over the leaves of a book.

' "So I have come here to you, kind sir," says the peasant, who has almost lost his voice.

' "What can I do in the matter? And what did you hit him right in the eye for?"

' "That's true indeed, sir, what for. . . . The evil one mixed me up."

' "It's a pity! a great pity! to think that a household must be ruined! Why, what will become of the family without you, all those young people and little grandchildren, and I am sorry for your old woman, too."

'The peasant's legs begin to tremble.

' "Well, kind sir, what have I brought on myself?"

' "Look here, Yermolay Grigorych, read for yourself . . . or perhaps you are no great reader? Well, here is the article. On Maiming and Mutilation . . . to be punished by flogging and exile to Siberia."

' "Don't let a man be ruined! Don't destroy a Christian! Can't it be managed like. . . ."

' "What a fellow! Can we go against the law? Of course, it is all in human hands. Well, instead of thirty we'll order five light ones."

' "But about Siberia? . . ."

' "That's not in our power to decide, my good man."

'The peasant pulls out of his bosom a little bag, takes out of the bag a bit of paper, out of the paper two and then three gold pieces, and with a low bow lays them on the table.

' "What's this, Yermolay Grigoryevich?"

' "Save me, kind sir."

' "That'll do, that'll do: what do you mean? Sinful man that I am, I do sometimes accept a token of gratitude. My salary is small, so one is forced to, but if one accepts it, it must be for something! How can I help you? It would be a different thing if it were a rib or a tooth, but right in the eye! Take your money back."

'The peasant is crushed.

' "I'll tell you what; shall I talk to my colleagues and write to the governor's office? Very likely the case will come into the court of justice: I have friends there, who can do anything; only they are a different sort of people: you won't get off for three gold pieces there."

'The peasant begins to recover his faculties.

' "You needn't give me anything. I am sorry for your family, but it is no use your offering them less than two grey notes."

' "But, kind sir, as God is above, I don't know where I am to turn to get such a regular Palestine of money—four hundred roubles —these are hard times."

' "Yes, I expect it's a bit difficult. We could diminish the punishment in view of your penitence, we'll say, and taking into consideration that you were not sober . . . and, there, you know, even in Siberia people do manage to live. There's no telling how far you may have to go. . . . Of course, if you were to sell a couple of horses and one of the cows, and the sheep, that might be enough. But it would take you time to scrape together that money again at your sort of work! On the other hand, if you do keep the horses, you'll have to make your way further than where Makar drove his calves to. Think it over, Grigorych; there is no hurry, we can wait till to-morrow; but it is time I was going," adds the judge, and puts the gold pieces he had refused into his pocket, saying, "This is quite unnecessary. I only take it so as not to offend you."

'Next morning you may be sure the old skinflint brings to the judge the worth of three hundred and fifty paper roubles in all sorts of old-fashioned coins.

'The judge promises to look after his interests: the peasant is tried and tried and properly scared and then let off with some light punishment, or with a warning to be careful in future, or with a note that he is to be kept under police supervision; and he remembers the judge in his prayers for the rest of his life.

'That's how it used to be in the old days,' the discharged police-inspector told me; 'they were plain dealers.'

The peasants of Vyatka are, generally speaking, not very long-suffering, and for that reason the officials consider them pettifogging and troublesome. The rural police find their real gold mine in the Votyaks, the Mordvins, and the Chuvashes; they are pitiful, timid, dull-witted people. Police-inspectors pay double to the governor for appointments in districts inhabited by these Finnish tribes.

The police and the officials do incredible things with these poor creatures.

If a land-surveyor passes through a Votyak village on some commission, he invariably halts in it, takes an astrolabe out of his cart, sticks a post into the ground and stretches out a chain. Within an hour the whole village is in a turmoil. 'The surveyors, the surveyors!' the peasants say with the expression with which in 1812 they used to say, 'The French, the French!'

The village head-man comes with the commune to make his bow. And the surveyor goes on measuring and writing things down. The elder entreats him not to measure wrongly and do them harm. The surveyor demands twenty or thirty roubles. The Votyaks are delighted, they collect the money—and the surveyor goes on to the next Votyak village.

If a dead body comes into the hands of the police, they take it about with them for a fortnight, if it is frosty weather, from one Votyak village to another, and in each one declare that they have just picked it up, and that an inquest and an inquiry are to be held in that village. The Votyaks buy them off.

A few years before I came to the district, a police-inspector who had acquired a taste for taking bribes brought a dead body into a big Russian village and demanded, I think it was, two hundred roubles. The village elder called the commune together. The commune refused to give more than a hundred. The police official would not give way. The peasants lost their tempers and shut him with his two clerks in the hut which serves as the parish office, and in their turn threatened to burn them. The police-inspector did not believe in the threat. The peasants laid straw round the hut and, as an ultimatum, passed a hundred-rouble note in at the window on a stake. The heroic police-inspector still insisted on another hundred. Then the peasants set fire to the straw on all four sides and the three Mucius Scaevolas of the rural police were burnt to death. This affair was afterwards brought before the senate.

The Votyak villages are as a rule much poorer than the Russian ones.

'You live poorly, brother,' I said to my Votyak host while I was waiting for horses in a stuffy, smoky little hut all on the slant with its windows looking out backwards, into the back-yard.

'Can't be helped, master! We are poor, we save money for a black day.'

'Well, it would be hard for a day to be blacker than this one, old man,' I said to him, pouring out a glass of rum. 'Drink, and forget your troubles.'

'We do not drink,' answered the Votyak, looking avidly at the glass and suspiciously at me.

'Nonsense! come, take it.'

'Drink yourself first.'

I drank and then the Votyak drank.

K*

'And what are you?' he asked. 'From the government on business?'

'No,' I answered, 'on a journey; I am going to Vyatka.'

This reassured him considerably and, looking round carefully, he added by way of explanation,

'It is a black day when the police-inspector and the *priest* come to us.'

I should like to add something concerning the latter. Our priests are being more and more transformed into clerical police, as might indeed be expected from the Byzantine meekness of our Church and the spiritual supremacy of the Tsar.

The Finnish tribes partly accepted baptism before the time of Peter I, and partly were baptised in the reign of Elizabeth, while some of them have remained heathen. A great number of those christened in Elizabeth's time secretly adhere to their savage, gloomy religion.[8]

Every two or three years the police-inspector or the rural police superintendent goes through the villages accompanied by a priest, to discover which of the Votyaks have made their communion, and which have not and why not. They are persecuted, thrown into prison, flogged and made to pay for church-services; and, above all, the priest and the police-inspector search for any proof that they have not given up their old rites. Then the spiritual detective and the police missionary raise a storm, exact an immense bribe, give them a 'black day', and so depart leaving everything as before, in order that they may come again with cross and rods a year or two later.

In 1835 the Most Holy Synod thought it needful to do apostolic work in the Vyatka Province and convert the Cheremis heathen to orthodoxy.

This conversion is a type of all the great reforms carried out

[8] All their prayers may be summed up as a materialistic petition for the continuance of their race, for their crops, and the preservation of their herds, and nothing more than that. 'Grant, Yumala, that from one sheep may be born two, that from one grain may come five, that my children may have children.' There is something miserable and gloomy, the survival from ancient times of oppression, in this lack of confidence in life on earth and daily bread. The devil (Shaitan) is regarded as equal with God. I saw a severe fire in a village, in which the inhabitants were mixed Russian and Votyak. The Russians were hard at work shouting and dragging out their things, the tavern-keeper being particularly conspicuous among them. It was impossible to check the fire, but at first it was easy to save things. The Votyaks had collected on a little hill, and were weeping and sobbing and doing nothing.

by the Russian government, a façade, scene-painting, *blague*, lies, a pompous report, while somebody steals and someone else is flogged.

The Metropolitan, Filaret, sent an energetic priest as a missionary. His name was Kurbanovsky.[9] Consumed by the Russian disease of ambition, Kurbanovsky set to work with ardour. He determined at all costs to force the grace of God upon the Cheremises. At first he tried preaching, but he soon got tired of that. And, indeed, does one make much way by that old method?

The Cheremises, realising what was up, sent their priests, wild, fanatical and shrewd. After a prolonged parleying, these men said to Kurbanovsky:

'In the forest are white birch-trees, tall pines and firs; there is also the little juniper. God suffers them all and bids not the juniper to be a pine-tree. And so are we among ourselves, like the forest. Be ye the white birch, we will remain the juniper; we will not trouble you, we will pray for the Tsar, will pay the taxes and furnish recruits, but we will not change our holy things.'[10]

Kurbanovsky saw that there was no making them hear reason, and that the portion of Cyril and Methodius[11] would not be vouchsafed to him. He appealed to the local police-captain. The latter could not have been more delighted. He had long been eager to display his devotion to the Church. He was an unbaptised Tatar, i.e. a Mahommedan of the true faith, by name Devlet Kildeyev.

The police-captain took a squad of soldiers and set off to besiege the Cheremises with the Word of God. Several villages were christened. The apostle Kurbanovsky performed a thanksgiving service and went meekly off to receive the *calotte*. To the Tatar apostle the government sent the Vladimir Cross for the propagation of Christianity.[12]

Unfortunately, the Tatar missionary was not on good terms with the mullah at Malmyzho. The mullah was not at all pleased that a son of the true faith of the Koran should preach the Gospel so

---

[9] Herzen has confused the priest Alexander Pokrovsky, who was sent by Filaret as a missionary to Vyatka Province, with the archpriest Nikolay Kurbanovsky. (*A.S.*)

[10] A similar reply (if Kurbanovsky did not invent this one) was made by peasants in Germany when an attempt was made to convert them to Catholicism.

[11] Cyril and Methodius were brothers who in the ninth century evangelised in Thrace, Moesia and Moravia, invented the Slav alphabet, and made a Slav translation of the Bible. They are saints of both the Greek and the Catholic Churches. (*Tr.*)

[12] Devlet Kildeyev's reward was a diamond ring. (*A.S.*)

successfully. In Ramadan the police-captain, heedlessly affixing the Cross to his button-hole, appeared in the mosque and of course took up his stand before all the rest. The mullah had only just begun reading the Koran through his nose, when he suddenly stopped, and said that he dared not continue in the presence of a Mussulman who had come into the mosque wearing a Christian emblem.

The Tatars raised a murmur, the police-captain was overcome with confusion and either withdrew or removed the Cross.

I read afterwards in the *Journal of the Ministry of Home Affairs* about this brilliant conversion of the Cheremises. The article referred to the zealous co-operation of Devlet Kildeyev. Unluckily they forgot to add that his zeal for the Church was the more disinterested, the more firmly he believed in Islam.

Before the end of my time at Vyatka the Department of Crown Property was stealing so impudently that a commission of inquiry was appointed over it, which sent inspectors about the provinces. With that began the introduction of the new administration of Crown peasants.

Governor Kornilov was to appoint two officials from his staff for this inspection. I was one of those appointed. What things it was my lot to read!—sad, funny and nasty. The very headings of the cases struck me with amazement.

'Relating to the disappearance of the house of the Parish Council, *no one knows where to*, and to the gnawing of the plan of it by mice.'

'Relating to the loss of twenty-two government quit-rent articles,' i.e. of fifteen versts of land.

'Relating to the registration of the peasant boy Vasily among the female sex.'

This last was so good that I at once read the case from cover to cover.

The father of this supposed Vasily wrote in his petition to the governor that fifteen years earlier he had a daughter born, whom he had wanted to call Vasilisa, but that the priest, being 'in liquor', christened the girl Vasily and so entered it in the register. The circumstance apparently troubled the peasant very little; but when he realised that it would soon come to his family to furnish a recruit and pay the poll tax, he reported on the matter to the mayor and the rural police superintendent. The case seemed very odd to the police. They began by refusing the peasant's request, saying that he

had let pass the ten-year limitation. The peasant went to the governor; the latter arranged a solemn examination of the boy of the
female sex by a doctor and a midwife. . . . At this point a correspondence suddenly sprang up with the Consistory, and a priest, the successor of the one who, when 'in liquor', had chastely failed to make
fleshly distinctions, appeared on the scene, and the case went on for
years and the girl was nearly left under the suspicion of being a
man.

Do not imagine that this is an absurd figment made up by me
for a joke; not at all: it is quite in harmony with the spirit of
Russian autocracy.

In the reign of Paul a colonel in the Guards in his monthly report
entered as dead an officer who was dying in the hospital. Paul struck
him off the list as dead. Unluckily the officer did not die, but recovered. The colonel persuaded him to withdraw to his country
estate for a year or two, hoping to find an opportunity to rectify
the error. The officer agreed, but unfortunately for the colonel the
heirs who had read of the kinsman's death in the Orders refused on
any consideration to acknowledge that he was alive and, inconsolable
at their loss, demanded possession of the property. When the living
corpse saw that he was likely to die a second time, not merely on
paper but from hunger, he went to Petersburg and sent in a petition
to Paul. The Tsar wrote with his own hand on the petition: 'Foras-
much as His Majesty's decree has been promulgated concerning this
gentleman, the petition is to be refused.'

This is even better than my Vasilisa-Vasily. Of what consequence
was the crude fact of life beside the decree of His Majesty? Paul was
the poet and dialectician of autocracy!

Foul and muddy as this morass of officialdom is, I must add a few
words more about it. To bring it into the light of day is the least
poor tribute one can pay to those who have suffered and perished,
unknown and uncomforted.

The government readily gives the higher officials uncultivated
lands by way of reward. There is no great harm in that, though it
would be more sensible to keep these reserves to provide for the
increase of population. The regulations that govern the fixing of
the boundaries of these lands are fairly detailed; forests containing
building timber, the banks of navigable rivers, indeed both the
banks of any river, must not be given away, nor under any circumstances may lands be so assigned that have been cultivated by

peasants, even though the peasants have no right to the land except that of long usage. . . .[13]

All these restrictions of course are only on paper. In reality the assignment of land to private owners is a fearful source of plunder to the Treasury and of oppression to the peasants.

Great noblemen in receipt of lands usually either sell their rights to merchants, or try through the provincial authorities to gain some special privilege contrary to the regulations. Even Count Orlov himself was *by chance* assigned a main road and lands on which flocks and herds are pastured in the Province of Saratov.

It is therefore no wonder that one fine morning the peasants of Darovsky *volost*[14] in Kotelnichesky district had their land cut away right up to their stackyards and houses and given as private property to merchants who had bought them from some kinsman of Count Kankrin. The merchants fixed a rent for the land. This led to a lawsuit. The Court of Justice, bribed by the merchants and afraid of Kankrin's kinsman, confused the issues of the case. But the peasants were determined to persist with it. They chose two hard-headed peasants from amongst themselves and sent them to Peters-burg. The case was brought before the Senate. The land-surveying department perceived that the peasants were in the right, but did not know what to do, so they asked Kankrin. He simply admitted that the land had been irregularly cut away, but considered that it would be difficult to restore it, because it *might* have changed hands since then, and its present owners *might* have made various improve-ments. His Excellency proposed, therefore, that advantage should be taken of the vast amount of Crown property available, and that the peasants should be assigned a full equivalent in another place. Everybody liked this except the peasants. In the first place, it is no light matter to bring fresh land under cultivation, and, in the second, the fresh land turned out to be swampy and unsuitable. Since the peasants of Darovsky *volost* were more interested in growing corn than in shooting snipe, they sent another petition.

Then the Court of Justice and the Ministry of Finance made a new case out of the old one and, finding a law in which it was said

[13] In the Province of Vyatka the peasants are particularly fond of moving to new settlements. Very often three or four *clearings* are suddenly discovered in the forest. The immense lands and forests (now half cut down) tempt the peasants to take this *res nullius* which is left unused. The Ministry of Finance has several times been obliged to confirm these squatters in possession of the land.

[14] An administrative district which included several villages. (R.)

that, if the land that was assigned turned out to be unsuitable, it was not to be cancelled, but another half of the amount was to be added to it, they ordered the Darovsky peasants to be given another half swamp in addition to the swamp they already had.

The peasants once more petitioned the Senate, but, before their case came up for investigation, the land-surveying department sent them plans of their new land, bound and coloured, as is usual, with the points of the compass in the form of a star and appropriate explanations for the lozenge marked R.R.Z., and the lozenge marked Z.Z.R., and, what was most important, a demand for so much rent per acre. The peasants, seeing that far from giving them land they were trying to squeeze money out of them for the bog, refused point-blank to pay.

The police-captain reported it to Tyufyayev, who sent a punitive expedition under the command of the Vyatka *politsmeyster*. This man arrived, seized a few persons, flogged them, restored order in the *volost*, took the money, handed over the *guilty parties* to the Criminal Court, and was hoarse for a week afterwards from shouting. Several men were punished with the lash and sent into exile.

Two years later, when the Heir to the Throne passed through the *volost*, the peasants handed him a petition; he ordered the case to be investigated. It was upon this occasion that I had to draw up a report on it. Whether any sense came of this re-investigation I do not know. I have heard that the exiles returned, but whether the land was returned I have not heard.

In conclusion, I must mention the celebrated story of the potato revolt[15] and how Nicholas tried to bring the blessings of Petersburg civilisation to the nomad gypsies.

Like the peasantry of all Europe at one time, the Russian peasants were not very keen on planting potatoes, as though an instinct told the people that this was a trashy kind of food which would give them neither health nor strength. However, on the estates of decent landowners and in many Crown villages 'earth apples' had been planted long before the potato terror. But anything that is done of itself is distasteful to the Russian Government. Everything must be done under threat of the stick and the drill-sergeant, and by numbers.

The peasants of the Kazan and of part of the Vyatka Province

---

[15] Herzen appears to be speaking of the 'potato revolt' of 1842; there had been an earlier one, less wide-spread, in 1834. (*A.S.*)

planted potatoes in their fields. When the potatoes were lifted, the idea occurred to the Ministry to set up a central potato-pit in each *volost*. Potato-pits were ratified, potato-pits were prescribed, potato-pits were dug; and at the beginning of winter the peasants, much against their will, took the potatoes to the central pits. But when in the following spring the authorities tried to make them plant *frozen* potatoes, they refused. There cannot, indeed, be a more flagrant insult to labour than a command to do something obviously absurd. This refusal was represented as a revolt. The Minister Kiselëv sent an official from Petersburg; he, being an intelligent and practical man, exacted a rouble apiece from the peasants of the first *volost* and allowed them not to plant the frozen potatoes.

He repeated this proceeding in the second *volost* and the third; but in the fourth the head-man told him point-blank that he would neither plant the potatoes nor pay him anything. 'You have let off these and those,' he told the official; 'it's clear you must let us off too.'

The official would have concluded the business with threats and thrashings, but the peasants snatched up stakes and drove the police away; the military governor sent Cossacks. The neighbouring *volosts* came in on their own people's side.

It is enough to say that it came to using grape-shot and bullets. The peasants left their homes and dispersed into the woods; the Cossacks drove them out of the thickets like wild beasts; then they were caught, put into irons, and sent to be court-martialled at Kosmodemyansk.

By an odd chance the old major in charge there was an honest, simple man; he good-naturedly said that the official sent from Petersburg was solely to blame. Everyone pounced upon him, his voice was stifled, he was suppressed; he was intimidated and even put to shame for 'trying to ruin an innocent man'.

And the inquiry followed the usual Russian routine: the peasants were flogged during the examination, flogged as a punishment, flogged as an example, flogged to extort money, and a whole crowd of them sent to Siberia.

It is worth noting that Kiselëv passed through Kosmodemyansk during the inquiry. He might, it may be thought, have looked in at the court-martial or have sent for the major.

He did not do so!

The famous Turgot, seeing the hatred of the peasants for the potatoes, distributed seed-potatoes among contractors, purveyors, and other persons under government control, strictly forbidding them to give them to the peasants. At the same time he gave them secret orders not to prevent the peasants from stealing them. In a few years a part of France was under potatoes.

Tout bien pris, is not that better than grape-shot, Pavel Dmitri-yevich?[16]

In 1836 a party of gypsies came to Vyatka and settled in a field. These gypsies had wandered as far as Tobolsk and Irbit and, accompanied by their eternal trained bear and entirely untrained children, had led their free, wandering existence from time immemorial, engaged in horse-doctoring, fortune-telling, and petty pilfering. They peacefully sang songs and robbed hen-roosts, but all at once the governor received instructions from His Majesty that if gypsies were found *without passports* (not a single gypsy had ever had a passport, and that Nicholas and his men knew perfectly well) they were to be given a fixed time within which they were to inscribe themselves as citizens of the village or town where the decree found them.

At the expiration of the time limit, it was ordained that those fit for military service should be taken for soldiers and the *rest* sent into exile, all but the children of the male sex.

This senseless decree, which recalled biblical accounts of the massacre and punishment of whole races and him that pisseth against the wall, disconcerted even Tyufyayev. He communicated the absurd *ukaz* to the gypsies and wrote to Petersburg that it was impossible to carry it out. To get themselves inscribed as citizens they would need both money for the officials and the consent of the town or village, which would also have been unwilling to accept the gypsies for nothing. It was necessary, too, to assume that the gypsies should themselves have been desirous of settling just there. Taking all this into consideration, Tyufyayev—and one must give him credit for it—asked the Ministry to grant postponements and exemptions.

The Minister answered by instructions that at the expiration of the time-limit this Nebuchadnezzar-like decree should be carried out. Most unwillingly Tyufyayev sent a squad of soldiers with orders to surround the gypsy camp; as soon as this was done, the police arrived with a garrison battalion, and what happened, I am told, was beyond all imagination. Women with streaming hair ran about in a frenzy, screaming and weeping, and falling at the feet of the police; grey-headed old mothers clung to their sons. But order triumphed and the lame[17] *politsmeyster* took the boys and took the recruits—while the rest were sent by stages somewhere into exile.

But when the children had been taken away, the question arose what was to be done with them and at whose expense they were to be kept.

There had formerly been foundling hospitals connected with the Charitable Board, which cost the government nothing. But the Prussian chastity of Nicholas abolished them as detrimental to morals. Tyufyayev advanced money of his own and asked the Minister for instructions. Ministers never stick at anything. They ordered that the boys, until further instructions, were to be put into the care of the old men and women maintained in the almshouses.

Think of lodging little children with moribund old men and women, making them breathe the atmosphere of death—and charging old people who need peace and quiet with looking after children for nothing.

What imagination!

While I am on the subject I must describe what happened some eighteen months later to the head-man of my father's village in the province of Vladimir. He was a peasant of intelligence and experience who carried on the trade of a carrier, had several teams of three horses each, and had been for twenty years the head-man of a little village that paid *obrok*[18] to my father.

Some time during the year I spent in Vladimir the neighbouring peasants asked him to hand over a recruit for them. Bringing the future defender of his country on a rope, he arrived in the town with great self-confidence as a man proficient in his business.

'This,' said he, combing with his fingers the fair, grizzled beard that framed his face, 'is all the work of men's hands, sir. The year before last we pitched on our lad, such a wretched, puny fellow he was—the peasants were fearfully afraid he wouldn't do. So I says, "And roughly how much, good Christians, will you go to? A wheel will not turn without it's greased." We talked it over and the *mir*[19] decided to give twenty-five gold pieces. I went to the town and after talking in the government office I went straight to the president—he

---

[17] See page 244. (R.)
[18] See page 29, fn. (R.)
[19] Village council. (R.)

was a sensible man, sir, and had known me for ages. He told them to call me into his study and he had something the matter with his leg, so he was lying on a sofa. I put it all before him and he answered me with a laugh, "All right, all right; you tell me how many *of them* you have brought—you are a skinflint, I know you." I put ten gold pieces on the table and made him a low bow—he took the money in his hand and kept playing with it. "But I say," he said, "I am not the only one you will have to pay; what more have you brought?" I reported that I'd got together another ten. "Well," he said, "you can reckon yourself what you must do with it. Two to the doctor, two to the army receiver, then the clerk . . . and any treating won't come to more than three—so you had better leave the rest with me and I will try to arrange the affair." '

'Well, did you give it to him?'

'To be sure I did—and they shaved the boy's head[20] all right.'

Trained in such a way of rounding off accounts, and accustomed to reckonings of this sort, and also, perhaps, to the five gold pieces about the fate of which he had been silent, the head-man was confident of success. But there may be many mishaps between the bribe and the hand that takes it. Count Essen, one of the Imperial adjutants, was sent to Vladimir for a levy of recruits. The head-man approached him with his gold pieces. Unfortunately the Count had, like the heroine of Pushkin's *Nulin,* been reared 'not in the traditions of his fathers', but in the school of the Baltic aristocracy, which instils a German devotion to the Russian Tsar. Essen lost his temper, shouted at him and, what was worse than anything, rang the bell; the clerk ran in and gendarmes made their appearance. The head-man, who had never suspected the existence of men in uniform who would not take bribes, lost his head so completely that he did not deny the charge, did not vow and swear that he had never offered money, did not protest, might God strike him blind and might another drop never pass his lips, if he had thought of such a thing! He let himself be caught like a sheep and led off to the police station, probably regretting that he had offered the general too little and so offended him.

But Essen, not satisfied with the purity of his own conscience, nor the terror of the luckless peasant, and probably wishing to eradicate bribery *in Russland*, to punish vice and set a salutary example, wrote

[20] Took him as a recruit. (*R.*)

to the police, wrote to the governor, wrote to the recruiting office about the head-man's wicked attempt. The peasant was put in prison and committed for trial. Thanks to the stupid and grotesque law which metes out the same punishment to the honest man who gives a bribe to an official and to the official himself who accepts the bribe, things looked black and the head-man had to be saved at all costs.

I rushed to the governor; he refused to intervene in the matter; the president and councillors of the Criminal Court shook their heads, terrified at the interference of the Imperial adjutant. The adjutant himself, relenting, was the first to declare that he 'wished the man no harm, that he only wanted to give him a lesson, that he ought *to be tried and then let off*'. When I told this to the *politsmeyster*, he observed: 'The fact is, none of these gentry know how things are done; he should have simply sent him to me. I would have given the fool a good drubbing—to teach him to look before he leaps—and would have sent him home. Everyone would have been satisfied, but now how are things to be patched up with the Criminal Court?'

These two comments express the Imperial Russian conception of law so neatly and strikingly that I cannot forget them.

Between these pillars of Hercules of the national jurisprudence, the head-man had fallen into the deepest slough, that is, into the Criminal Court. A few months later the verdict was prepared that the head-man after being punished with the lash should be exiled to Siberia. His son and all his family came to me, imploring me to save their father, the head of the family. I myself felt fearfully sorry for the peasant, ruined though perfectly innocent. I went again to the president and the councillors, and pointed out to them once more that they were doing themselves harm by punishing the elder so severely; that they knew very well themselves that no business was ever done without bribes; that, in fact, they would have nothing to eat if they did not, like true Christians, consider that every gift is perfect and every gift is good. Entreating, bowing, and sending the head-man's son to bow still lower, I succeeded in gaining half my object. The elder was condemned to a few strokes of the lash within the prison walls, was allowed to remain in his place of residence, but was forbidden to act as intermediary for the other peasants.

I sighed with relief when I saw the governor and the prosecutor had agreed to this, and went to the police to ask for some mitigation of the severity of the flogging; the police, partly because they were flattered at my coming myself to ask them a favour, partly through compassion for a man who was suffering for something that concerned them all so intimately, and knowing, moreover, that the man was well off, promised me to make it a pure formality.

One morning a few days later the head-man appeared, thinner and greyer than before. I saw that for all his delight he was sad about something and weighed down by some thought that oppressed him.

'What are you worrying about?' I asked him.

'Well, I wish they'd settle it once for all.'

'I don't understand.'

'I mean, when are they going to punish me?'

'Why, haven't they punished you?'

'No.'

'Then how is it they have let you go? You are going home, aren't you?'

'Home, yes; but you see I keep thinking about the punishment. The secretary did read it out.'

I could really make nothing of it, and at last asked him whether they had given him any sort of paper. He gave it me. The whole verdict was written in it, and at the end it was stated that, punishment with the lash having been inflicted within the prison walls in accordance with the sentence of the Criminal Court, 'he was to be given a certificate to that effect and set free'.

I burst out laughing.

'Well, you have been punished already, then!'

'No, sir, I haven't.'

'Well, if you are dissatisfied, go back and ask them to punish you; perhaps the police will put themselves in your place, and see your point.'

Seeing that I was laughing, the old man smiled too, shaking his head dubiously and adding: 'Go on with you! What strange doings!'

'How irregular!' many people will say; but they must remember that it is only through such irregularity that life in Russia is possible.

Chapter 16

Alexander Lavrentevich Vitberg

AMONG the grotesque and greasy, petty and loathsome people and scenes, files and titles, in this setting of official routine and red-tape, I recall the noble and melancholy features of an artist, who was crushed by the government with cold and callous cruelty.

The leaden hand of the Tsar not merely smothered a work of genius in its cradle, not merely destroyed the very creation of the artist, entangling him in judicial snares and the wiles of a police inquiry, but tried to snatch from him his honourable name altogether with his last crust of bread, and brand him as a taker of bribes and a pilferer of government funds.

After ruining and disgracing A. L. Vitberg, Nicholas exiled him to Vyatka. It was there that we met.

For two years and a half I lived with the great artist and saw the strong man, who had fallen a victim to the autocracy of red-tape officialdom and barrack-discipline, which blockishly measures everything in the world by the standard of the recruiting officer and the copying clerk's ruler, breaking down under the weight of persecution and misery.

It cannot be said that he succumbed easily; he struggled desperately for full ten years. He came into exile still hoping to confound his enemies and vindicate himself; he came, in a word, still ready for conflict, bringing plans and projects. But he soon discerned that all was over.

Perhaps he could have dealt even with this discovery, but he had at his side a wife and children and ahead of him years of exile, poverty, and privation; and Vitberg was turning grey, growing old, growing old not by the day but by the hour. When I left him in Vyatka at the end of two years he was ten years older.

Here is the story of this long martyrdom.

The Emperor Alexander did not believe it was *his* victory over

Napoleon: he was oppressed by the fame of it and genuinely gave the glory to God. Always disposed to mysticism and melancholy, in which many people saw the fretting of conscience, he gave way to it particularly after the series of victories over Napoleon.

When 'the last soldiers of the enemy had crossed the frontier', Alexander issued a proclamation in which he vowed to raise in Moscow a huge temple to the Saviour.

Plans were invited from all sides, and a great competition was instituted.

Vitberg was at that time a young artist who had just completed his studies and won a gold medal for painting. A Swede by origin, he was born in Russia and at first was educated in the Engineers' Cadet Corps. The artist was enthusiastic, eccentric, and given to mysticism: he read the proclamation, read the appeal for plans, and flung aside all other pursuits. For days and nights he wandered about the streets of Petersburg, tormented by a persistent idea; it was stronger than he was: he locked himself up in his room, took a pencil and set to work.

To no one in the world did he confide his design. After some months of work he went to Moscow to study the city and the surrounding country and set to work once more, shutting himself up for months together and keeping his design a secret.

The date of the competition arrived. The plans were numerous: there were designs from Italy and from Germany and our Academicians sent in theirs. And the unknown young man sent in his among the rest. Weeks passed before the Emperor examined the plans. These were the forty days in the wilderness, days of temptation, doubt, and agonising suspense.

Vitberg's colossal design, filled with religious poetry, impressed Alexander. He came to a stop before it, and it was the first of which he inquired the authorship. They broke open the sealed envelope and found the unknown name of an Academy pupil.

Alexander desired to see Vitberg. He had a long talk with the artist. His bold and fervent language, his genuine inspiration and the mystical tinge of his convictions impressed the Emperor. 'You speak in stones,' he observed, examining Vitberg's design again.

That very day his design was accepted and Vitberg was chosen to be the architect and the director of the building committee. Alexander did not know that with the laurel wreath he was putting a crown of thorns on the artist's head.

There is no art more akin to mysticism than architecture; abstract, geometrical, mutely musical, passionless, it lives in symbol, in emblem, in suggestion. Simple lines, their harmonious combination, rhythm, numerical relationships, make up something mysterious and at the same time incomplete. The building, the temple, is not its own object, as is a statue or a picture, a poem, or a symphony; a building requires an inmate; it is a place mapped and cleared for habitation, an environment, the cuirass of the tortoise, the shell of the mollusc; and the whole point of it is that the receptacle should correspond with its spirit, its object, its inmate, as the cuirass does with the tortoise. The walls of the temple, its vaults and columns, its portal and façade, its foundation and its cupola must bear the imprint of the divinity that dwells within it, just as the convolutions of the brain are imprinted on the bone of the skull.

The Egyptian temples were their holy books. The obelisks were sermons on the high-road.

Solomon's temple was the Bible turned into architecture; just as St Peter's in Rome is the architectural symbol of the escape from Catholicism, of the beginning of the lay world, of the beginning of the secularisation of mankind.

The very building of temples was so invariably accompanied by mystic rites, symbolical utterances, mysterious consecrations that the mediaeval builders looked upon themselves as something apart, a kind of priesthood, the heirs of the builders of Solomon's temple, and made up secret guilds of stonemasons, which afterwards passed into Freemasonry.

From the time of the Renaissance architecture loses its properly mystical character. The Christian faith is struggling with philosophic doubt, the Gothic arch with the Greek pediment, spiritual holiness with worldly beauty. What gives St Peter's its lofty significance is that in its colossal dimensions Christianity struggles towards life, the church becomes pagan and on the walls of the Sistine Chapel Michelangelo paints Jesus Christ as a broad-shouldered athlete, a Hercules in the flower of his age and strength.

After St Peter's basilica, church architecture deteriorated completely and was reduced at last to simple repetition, on a larger or smaller scale, of the ancient Greek peripteres or of St Peter's.

One Parthenon is called St Madeleine's church in Paris; the other, the Exchange in New York.

Without faith and without special circumstances, it was hard to create anything living: there is an air of artificiality, of hypocrisy, of anachronism, about all new churches, such as the five-domed cruet-stands with onions instead of corks in the Indo-Byzantine manner, which Nicholas builds, with Ton for architect, or the angular, Gothic churches, so offensive to the artistic eye, with which the English decorate their towns.

But the circumstances under which Vitberg created his design, his personality, and the state of mind of the Emperor were all exceptional.

The war of 1812 had caused a violent upheaval in men's minds in Russia; it was long after the deliverance of Moscow before the ferment of thought and nervous irritation could subside. Events outside Russia, the taking of Paris, the story of the Hundred Days, the suspense, the rumours, Waterloo, Napoleon sailing over the ocean, the mourning for fallen kinsmen, apprehension for the living, the returning troops, the soldiers going home, all had a violent effect on even the coarsest natures. Imagine a youthful artist, a mystic, gifted with creative power and at the same time a fanatic, under the influence of all that was happening, under the influence of the Tsar's challenge and his own genius.

Near Moscow, between the Mozhaysk and Kaluga roads, there is a slight eminence which dominates the whole city. These are the Sparrow Hills of which I have spoken in the first reminiscences of my youth. The city lies stretched at their foot, and one of the most picturesque views of Moscow is from the top of them. Here Ivan the Dread, at that time a young profligate, stood weeping and watching his capital burn; here the priest Sylvester appeared before him and with stern words transformed that monster of genius for twenty years.

Napoleon with his army skirted this hill, here his strength was broken, it was at the foot of the Sparrow Hills that his retreat began.

Could a better spot be found for a temple to commemorate the year 1812 than the furthest point which the enemy reached?

But this was not enough: the hill itself was to be turned into the lower part of the temple; the open ground down to the river was to be encircled by a colonnade, and on this base, built on three sides by nature itself, a second and a third temple were to be raised, making up a marvellous whole.

Vitberg's temple, like the chief dogma of Christianity, was three-fold and indivisible.

The lowest temple, carved out of the hill had the form of a paral-

lelogram, a coffin, a body: its exterior formed a heavy portal supported by almost Egyptian columns, and it merged into the hill, into
rough, unhewn nature. This temple was lit up by lamps in tall Etrus-
can candelabra, and the daylight filtered sparsely into it from the
second temple, passing through a transparent picture of the Nativity.
In this crypt all the heroes who had fallen in 1812 were to be laid to
rest. An eternal requiem was to be said for those slain on the field of
battle; the names of all of them, from generals to private soldiers,
were to be carved upon the walls.

Upon this tomb, upon this graveyard, the second temple—the
temple of outstretched hands, of life, of suffering, of labour—was
laid out in the form of a Greek cross with its four equal arms. The
colonnade leading to it was decorated with statues from figures of the
Old Testament. At the entrance stood the prophets: they stood outside the temple pointing the way which they were not destined to
tread. The whole story of the Gospels and of the Acts of the Apostles
was depicted within this temple.

Above it, crowning it and completing it, was a third temple in the
form of a dome. This temple, brightly lit, was the temple of the
spirit of untroubled peace, of eternity, expressed in its circular plan.
Here there were neither pictures nor sculpture, only on the outside it
was encircled by a ring of archangels and was covered by a colossal
cupola.

I am now giving from memory Vitberg's main idea. He had it
worked out to the minutest detail and everywhere perfectly in harmony with Christian theology and architectural beauty.

The amazing man spent his whole life over his design. During the
ten years that he was on his trial he was occupied with nothing else
and, though harassed by poverty and privation in exile, he devoted
several hours every day to his temple. He lived in it, he did not
believe that it would never be built; memories, consolations, glory, all
were in the artist's portfolio.

Perhaps one day some other artist, after the martyr's death, will
shake the dust off those sheets and with reverence publish that architectural martyrology, in which was spent and wasted a life full of
strength, for a moment illuminated by radiant light, then smudged
and crushed among a drill-sergeant Tsar, serf-senators, and pettifogging ministers.

The design was a work of genius, frightening, almost mad; that
was why Alexander chose it, that is why it ought to have been carried

out. It was said that the hill could not have borne the weight of the temple. I find that incredible, especially if we remember all the new resources of American and English engineers, the tunnels which a train takes eight minutes to pass through, the chain-bridges, and so on.

Miloradovich[1] advised Vitberg to make the thick columns of the lower temple of single blocks of granite. On this someone observed that it would be very expensive to bring the granite blocks from Finland.

'That is just why we ought to order them,' answered Miloradovich; 'if there were a granite-quarry on the river Moskva there would be nothing wonderful in putting them up.'

Miloradovich was a warrior poet and he understood poetry in general. Grand things are done by grand means.

Only nature does great things for nothing.

Even those who never had any doubt of Vitberg's honesty blame him most for having undertaken the duty of directing operations, though he was an inexperienced young artist who knew nothing of official business. He ought to have confined himself to the part of architect. That is true.

But it is easy to make such criticisms sitting at home in one's study. He undertook it just because he was young, inexperienced, and an artist; he undertook it because, when his design had been accepted, everything seemed easy to him; he undertook it because the Tsar himself had proposed it to him, encouraged him, supported him. Is there any man whose head would not have been turned? . . . Are there any so prudent, so sober, so restrained? Well, if there are, they do not design colossal temples nor do they make 'stones speak'!

It need hardly be said that Vitberg was surrounded by a crowd of rogues, men who look on Russia as a field for speculation, on the service as a profitable line of business, on a public post as a lucky chance to make a fortune. It was easy to understand that they would dig a pit under Vitberg's feet. But that, after falling into it, he should be unable to get out again, was due also to the envy of some and the wounded vanity of others.

Vitberg's colleagues on the committee were the metropolitan Filaret, the Governor-General of Moscow,[2] and Senator Kushnikov; they were all offended in advance by being associated with a young puppy,

---

[1] See this volume, p. 11, fn. (R.)
[2] Prince D. V. Golitsyn. (A.S.)

especially as he gave his opinion boldly and objected when he did not agree.

They helped to get him into trouble, they helped to slander him and with cold-blooded indifference completed his ruin afterwards.

They were helped in this first by the fall of the mystically-minded minister Prince A. N. Golitsyn, and afterwards by the death of Alexander.

With the fall of Golitsyn came the collapse of Freemasonry, of the Bible Societies, of Lutheran pietism, which in the persons of Magnitsky[3] at Kazan and of Runich[4] in Petersburg ran to grotesque extremes, to savage persecutions, to convulsive dances, to states of hysteria and God knows what strange doings.

Savage, coarse, ignorant orthodoxy had the upper hand. It was preached by Foty[5] the archimandrite of Novgorod, who lived on intimate terms (not physically, of course) with Countess Orlov. The daughter of the well known Alexey Grigorevich Orlov who smothered Peter III, she hoped to win redemption for her father's soul by devoting herself to frenzied fanaticism, by giving up to Fotiy and his monastery the greater part of her enormous estates, which had been forcibly seized from the monasteries by Catherine.

But the one thing in which the Petersburg government is persistent, the one thing in which it does not change, however its principles and religion may change, is its unjust oppression and persecution. The fury of the Runiches and the Magnitskys was turned against the Runiches and the Magnitskys. The Bible Society, only yesterday patronised and approved—the prop of morality and religion—was to-day closed and sealed, and its members put almost on the level of counterfeit coiners; the *Messenger of Zion*, only yesterday recommended to all fathers of families, was more severely prohibited than Voltaire and Diderot, and its editor, Labzin,[6] was exiled to Vologda.

Prince A. N. Golitsyn's downfall involved Vitberg; everyone fell upon him, the committee complained of him, the metropolitan was offended and the Governor-General was dissatisfied. His answers were 'insolent' ('insolence' is one of the principal charges in the in-

---

[3] Magnitsky, Mikhail Leontevich (1778-1855), reactionary official and mystic; Warden of Kazan educational district and University, 1820-26. (*A.S.*)

[4] Runich, Dmitry Pavlovich (1778-1860), reactionary official and mystic; Warden of Petersburg educational district, 1821-26. (*A.S.*)

[5] Foty (1792-1838), archimandrite of the Yurevsky monastery at Novgorod. He took part in Palace intrigues under Alexander I, and influenced his reactionary policy. (*A.S.*)

[6] See this volume, p. 45, fn.

dictment of him); his subordinates were *thieves*—as though there was anyone in the government service who was not a thief. Though indeed it is likely that there was more thieving among Vitberg's subordinates than among others; he had had no practice in superintending houses of correction and highly placed thieves.

Alexander commanded Arakcheyev to investigate the case. He was sorry for Vitberg; he let him know through one of his intimates that he believed in his rectitude.

But Alexander died and Arakcheyev fell. Under Nicholas Vitberg's case at once took a turn for the worse. It dragged on for *ten* years, with incredible absurdities. On the points on which he was found guilty by the Criminal Court he was acquitted by the Senate. On those on which he was acquitted by the Court he was found guilty by the Senate. The committee of ministers found him guilty on all the charges. The Tsar, taking advantage of the 'best privilege of monarchs, to show mercy and mitigate punishment', added exile to Vyatka to his sentence.

And so Vitberg was sent into exile, dismissed from the service 'for abuse of the confidence of the Emperor Alexander and causing loss to the treasury'. He was fined, I believe, a million roubles, all his property was seized and sold at public auction, and a rumour was circulated that he had transferred countless millions to America.

I lived in the same house with Vitberg for two years and remained on intimate terms with him up to the time I left Vyatka. He had not saved the barest crust of bread; his family lived in the most frightful poverty.

To give an idea of this case and of all similar ones in Russia, I will quote two small details which have remained specially in my memory.

Vitberg bought for timber for the temple a copse from a merchant called Lobanov; before the trees were felled Vitberg saw another wood, also Lobanov's, nearer to the river and asked him to exchange the one he had sold for the second one. The merchant agreed. The trees were felled and the timber floated down the river. Later on more timber was needed, and Vitberg bought the first wood again. This was the celebrated accusation of having bought the same copse twice over. Poor Lobanov was put in prison for it and died there.

The second instance came before my own eyes. Vitberg bought estates for the temple. His idea was that the peasants bought with the land for the temple should be bound to furnish a certain number of workmen for it, and by this means should obtain complete freedom for themselves and their village. It is amusing that our serf-owning Senators found a suggestion of slavery in this measure!

Among other things Vitberg wanted to buy my father's estates in the Ruzsky district on the bank of the Moskva. Marble had been found on it, and Vitberg asked permission to make a geological survey to discover how much of it there was. My father gave permission. Vitberg went off to Petersburg.

Three months later my father learnt that quarrying was going forward on an immense scale, and that the peasants' winter cornfields were heaped up with marble. He protested; no notice was taken. A protracted lawsuit began. At first they tried to throw all the blame on Vitberg, but unluckily it appeared that he had given no orders, and that it all had been done by the committee in his absence.

The case was taken before the Senate. To the *general surprise* the Senate's decision was not very far from *common sense*. The marble quarried was to remain the property of the landowner as compensation for the ruined cornfields. The government money spent on quarrying and labour, amounting to a hundred thousand paper roubles, was to be made good by those who signed the contract for the work. Those who signed were Prince Golitsyn, Filaret, and Kushnikov. There was of course a great clamour and outcry. The case was taken before the Tsar.

He had his own system of justice. He directed that the offenders should be excused payment because—he wrote it with his own hand, and it is also printed in the minutes of the Senate—'The members of the committee did not know what they were signing'. Even if we admit that the metropolitan was professionally bound to show a meek spirit, what are we to think of the other two grand gentlemen who accepted a favour which was granted from such a courteous and gracious motive.

But from whom was the hundred thousand to be taken? Government property, they say, is not burnt in the fire nor drowned in the water. It is only stolen, we might add. No trying to think it out here: an adjutant-general was sent off post-haste to Moscow to go into the matter.

Strekalov went into everything, set everything straight, arranged and settled it all in a few days: the marble was to be taken from the landowner to make good the sum paid for the quarrying; if, however, the landowner wished to retain the marble he was required to pay the hundred thousand. The landowner needed no special compensation, because the value of his property was increased by the discovery of a new form of wealth upon it (this was the *chef-d'œuvre*!), but for the damaged fields of the peasants so many kopecks per *desyatina*[7] were to be allotted in accordance with the law about flooded meadows and trampled hayfields passed by Peter I.

The person really punished in this case was my father. There is no need to add that the quarrying of this marble was nevertheless brought up against Vitberg in his indictment.

Two years after Vitberg's exile the merchants of Vyatka formed a project to build a new church.

Nicholas, being desirous of killing all spirit of independence, of individuality, of imagination, and of freedom, everywhere and in everything, published a whole volume of frontages for churches sanctioned by His Majesty. If anyone wanted to build a church he was absolutely obliged to select one of the government plans. He is said to have forbidden the writing of Russian operas, considering that even those written by the adjutant Lvov, in the Third Division of his own Chancellery, were good for nothing. But that was not enough: he ought to have published a collection of musical airs sanctioned by His Majesty!

The Vyatka merchants after turning over the 'approved' plans had the audacity to differ from the Tsar's taste. Nicholas marvelled at the design they sent in; he sanctioned it and sent instructions to the provincial authorities to see that the architect's ideas were faithfully carried out.

'Who made this design?' he asked the secretary.

'Vitberg, your Majesty.'

'What, the same Vitberg?'

'The same, your Majesty.'

And behold, like a bolt from the blue, comes permission for Vitberg to return to Moscow or Petersburg. The man had asked leave to clear his character and it had been refused; he made a successful design, and the Tsar bade him return—as though anyone had ever doubted his artistic ability. . . .

In Petersburg, almost perishing of want, he made one last effort to defend his honour. It was utterly unsuccessful. Vitberg asked the assistance of A. N. Golitsyn, but the latter thought it impossible to raise the case again, and advised Vitberg to write a plaintive letter to

---

[7] A *desyatina* (obs.) was equal to 2·7 acres. (*R*.)

the Heir with a request for financial assistance. He undertook to do his best for him with the assistance of Zhukovsky,[8] and promised to get him a thousand silver roubles.

Vitberg refused.

I was in Petersburg for the last time at the beginning of the winter of 1846 and there saw Vitberg. He was completely crushed. Even his old wrath against his enemies which I had liked so much had begun to die down; he had no more hope, he did nothing to escape from his situation, blank despair was bringing him to his end, all the components of his existence had broken down and he was waiting for death.

If this was what Nicholas Pavlovich wanted he may be satisfied. Whether the sufferer is still living I do not know, but I doubt it.

'If it were not for my family, my children,' he said at parting, 'I should tear myself away from Russia and go begging alms about the world. With the Vladimir Cross on my neck I would calmly hold out to passers-by the hand pressed by the Emperor Alexander and tell them of my design and the fate of an artist in Russia!'

'They shall hear in Europe of your fate, poor martyr,' I thought; 'I will answer for that.'

The society of Vitberg was a great solace to me in Vyatka. A grave serenity and a solemnity in his manner lent him something of a priestly air. He was a man of very pure morals and in general more disposed to asceticism than indulgence; but his severity did not detract from the wealth and luxuriance of his artistic nature. He could give to his mysticism so plastic a form and so exquisite a colouring that criticism died away on one's lips; one was sorry to analyse, to dissect the glittering images and misty pictures of his imagination.

Vitberg's mysticism was partly due to his Scandinavian blood; it was the same coldly-thought-out visionariness that we see in Swedenborg, and which in its turn is like the fiery reflection of sunbeams in the icy mountains and snows of Norway.

Vitberg's influence made me waver, but my realistic temperament nevertheless gained the upper hand. I was not destined to rise into the third heaven: I was born a quite earthly creature. No tables turn

---

[8] Zhukovsky, Vasily Andreyevich, (1783-1852), the well-known poet, was tutor to the Tsarevich, afterwards Alexander II. He was a man of fine and generous character. His original work is not of the first order, but as a translator from the European and classical languages he was of invaluable service in the development of Russian culture. (Tr.)

at the touch of my hands nor do rings swing at my glance. The daylight of thought is more akin to me than the moonlight of phantasy.

But I was more disposed to mysticism at the period when I was living with Vitberg than at any other time.

Separation, exile, the religious exaltation of the letters I was receiving, the love which was filling my heart more and more intensely, and at the same time the oppressive feeling of remorse,* all reinforced Vitberg's influence.

And for two years afterwards I was under the influence of ideas of a mystical socialist tinge, drawn from the Gospel and from Jean-Jacques, after the style of French thinkers like Pierre Leroux.[9]

Ogarëv plunged into the sea of mysticism even before I did. In 1833 he was beginning to write the words for Gebel's[10] oratorio, *The Lost Paradise*. 'In the idea of a "Lost Paradise", Ogarëv wrote to me 'there is the whole history of humanity'; so at that time, he too mistook the paradise of the ideal that we are seeking for a paradise we have lost.

In 1838 I wrote historical scenes in the religious socialist spirit, and at the time took them for dramas. In some I pictured the conflict of the pagan world with Christianity. In these Paul entering Rome raised a dead youth to a new life. In others I described the conflict of the official Church with the Quakers and the departure of William Penn to America, to the New World.[11]

---

[9] Leroux, Pierre (1797-1871), a follower of Saint-Simon, of the first half of the nineteenth century. (*Tr.*)

[10] Gebel, Franz (1787-1843), a well-known musical composer of the period. (*Tr.*)

[11] I thought fit, I don't understand why, to write these scenes *in verse*. Probably I thought that anybody could write unrhymed five-foot iambics, since even Pogodin† wrote them. In 1838 or 1840, I gave both the manuscripts to Belinsky to read and calmly awaited his praises. But next day Belinsky sent them back to me with a note in which he said: 'Do please have them copied to run on without being divided into lines, then I will read them with pleasure, but as it is I am bothered all the time by the idea that they are in verse.'

Belinsky killed both my dramatic efforts. It is always pleasant to pay one's debts. In 1841 Belinsky published a long dialogue upon literature in the *Notes of the Fatherland*. 'How do you like my last article;' he asked me, as we were dining together *en petit comité* at Dusseau's. 'Very much,' I answered. 'All that you say is excellent, but tell me, please, how could you go on struggling for two hours talking to that man without seeing at the first word that he was a fool?' 'That's perfectly true,' said Belinsky, dying with laughter. 'Well, my boy, that's killing! Why, he is a perfect fool!'

† Pogodin, Mikhail Petrovich (1800-75), chiefly known as a historian of a peculiar Slavophil tinge, was co-editor with Shevyrëv of the *Moskvityanin*, a reactionary journal, and wrote historical novels of little merit. (*Tr.*)

L

The mysticism of the Gospel was soon replaced in me by the mysticism of science; fortunately I rid myself of the second also.

But to return to our modest little town of Khlynov, the name of which was, I don't know why, perhaps from Finnish patriotism, changed by Catherine II to Vyatka.

In the loneliness of my exile at Vyatka, in the filthy environment of the government clerks, in that gloomy, remote place, separated from all that was dear to me and put defenceless in the power of the governor, I spent many exquisite sacred moments, and met many warm hearts and friendly hands.

Where are you? What has happened to you, my friends of that snowy region? It is twenty years since we met. I dare say you have grown old as I have, you are marrying your daughters, you don't now drink champagne by the bottle and liqueur by the wine-glass. Which of you has grown rich, which of you has come to ruin, who is high up in the service, who is paralysed? Above all, is the memory of our daring talks still living in you, and do those chords which vibrated so eagerly with love and *indignation* still vibrate?

I have remained the same, that you know; I dare say news of me reaches you from the banks of the Thames. Sometimes I think of you, always with love; I have some letters of that time, some of them are exceedingly dear to me and I like reading them over.

'I am not ashamed to own to you that I am passing through a very bitter time,' a young man wrote to me on the 26th January 1838. 'Help me for the sake of that life to which you called me; help me with your advice. *I want to learn* : indicate some books, prescribe anything you like, I shall use all my power; give me a course to steer; it will be a sin if you spurn me.'

'I bless you,' another wrote to me after I had gone away, 'as the husbandman blesses the rain that has quickened his unmanured soil.'

It is not from vanity that I have quoted these lines, but because they are very dear to me. For the sake of those youthful appeals and youthful love, for the sake of the yearnings aroused in those hearts, one could well resign oneself to nine months' imprisonment and to three years' exile at Vyatka.

And then twice a week the post from Moscow came in; with what excitement I waited by the post-office while the letters were sorted, with what a tremor I broke the seal and looked in the letter from home for a little note on thin paper written in a wonderfully fine and elegant hand.

I never read it in the post-office, but walked quietly home, putting off the minute of reading it, enjoying the mere thought that *there was* a letter.

Those letters were all kept. I left them in Moscow. I should fearfully like to read them over again, and I should be afraid to touch them. . . .

Letters are more than memories: the very blood of events is congealed in them; they are the very past just as it was, preserved and undecayed.

. . . Should one know it, see it all again? Should one touch with wrinkled hands one's wedding garment?

Chapter 17

The Tsarevich's Visit

THE Heir will visit Vyatka! The Heir is travelling about Russia to show himself and look at the country! This news interested everyone, but the governor, of course, more than any. He was harassed and did a number of incredibly stupid things: ordered the peasants along the high-road to be dressed in their holiday *caftans*, ordered the fences in the towns to be painted and the sidewalks to be repaired. At Orlov a poor widow who owned a small house told the mayor that she had no money to repair the sidewalk and he reported this to the governor. The latter ordered the floors in the house to be taken up (the sidewalks there are made of wood), and that, should they not be sufficient, the repairs should be made at the government expense and the money recovered from her afterwards, even if it were necessary to sell her house at public auction. Things did not go so far as a sale, but the widow's floors were broken up.

Fifty versts from Vyatka is the place at which the wonder-working ikon of St Nicholas of Khlynov appeared to the people of Novgorod. When emigrants from Novgorod settled at Khlynov (now Vyatka) they brought the ikon, but it disappeared and turned up again on the Great River fifty versts from Vyatka. They fetched it back again, and at the same time took a vow that if the ikon would stay they would carry it every year in a solemn procession to the Great River. This was the chief summer holiday in the Vyatka province; I believe it is on the 23rd of May. For twenty-four hours the ikon travels down the river on a magnificent raft with the bishop and all the clergy in full vestments accompanying it. Hundreds of all sorts of boats, rafts, and dug-out canoes filled with peasants, men and women, Votyaks, and artisans follow the sailing image in a motley throng, and foremost of all is the governor's decked boat covered with red cloth. This barbaric spectacle is very fine. Tens of thousands of people from districts near and far wait for the image on the banks of the Great River. They all camp in noisy crowds about a small village, and, what is strangest of all, crowds of unbaptised Votyaks, Cheremises, and even Tatars come to pray to the image; indeed, the festival has a thoroughly pagan appearance. Outside the monastery-wall Votyaks and Russians bring sheep and calves to be sacrificed; they are killed on the spot, a monk reads a service over them, and blesses and consecrates the meat, which is sold at a special window within the precincts. The meat is distributed in pieces to the people; in the old days it used to be given for nothing: now the monks charge a few kopecks for every piece; so that a peasant who has presented a whole calf has to pay something for a piece for his own consumption. In the monastery-yard sit whole crowds of beggars, the halt, the blind, the deformed of all sorts, who sing 'Lazar' in chorus.[1] Lads—priests' sons or boys from the town—sit on the tomb-stones near the church with inkpots[2] and cry: 'Who wants lists written? Who wants lists?' Peasant girls and women surround them, mentioning names, and the lads, deftly scratching with their pens, repeat: 'Marya, Marya, Akulina, Stepanida, Father Ioann, Matrëna. . . . Well, Auntie, you have got a lot; you've shelled out two kopecks, we can't take less than five; such a family—Ioann, Vasilisa, Iona, Marya, Yevpraxia, Baby Katerina. . . .'

In the church there is much jostling and strange preferences are shown; one peasant woman will hand her neighbour a candle with exact instructions to put it up 'for our guest', another gives one for 'our host'. The Vyatka monks and deacons are continually drunk during the whole time of this procession. They stop at the bigger villages on the way, and the peasants treat them to enough to kill them.

So this popular holiday, to which the peasants had been accustomed for ages, the governor proposed to move to an earlier date, wishing to entertain the Tsarevich who was to arrive on the 19th of May; he thought there would be no harm in St Nicholas, the *guest*, going on his visit to his *host* three days earlier. Of course the consent of the bishop was necessary; fortunately he was an amenable person, and found nothing to protest at in the governor's intention of celebrating the 23rd of May on the 19th.

The governor sent a list of his ingenious plans for the reception of

[1] A plaintive, wheedling song sung by beggars. (*R.*)

[2] The lists of names were sent up to the priest, who said a prayer for the owner of each name. (*R.*)

the Tsarevich to the Tsar—as though to say, 'See how we fête your son'. On reading this document the Tsar flew into a rage, and said to the Minister of Home Affairs: 'The governor and the bishop are fools; leave the holiday as it was.' The Minister gave the governor a good scolding, the Synod did the same to the bishop, and St Nicholas the guest kept to his old habits.

Among the various instructions from Petersburg, orders came that in every provincial town an exhibition should be held of the various natural products and handicrafts of the district, and that the things exhibited should be arranged according to the three natural kingdoms. This division into animal, vegetable and mineral greatly worried the officials, and even Tyufyayev to some extent. In order not to make a mistake he made up his mind in spite of his ill will to summon me to give advice.

'Now, for instance, honey,' he said, 'where would you put honey? or a gilt frame—how are you to decide where it is to go?'

Seeing from my answers that I had wonderfully precise information concerning the three natural kingdoms, he offered me the task of arranging the exhibition.

While I was busy arranging wooden vessels and Votyak dresses, honey and iron sieves, and Tyufyayev went on taking the most ferocious measures for the entertainment of his Imperial Highness at Vyatka, the Highness in question was graciously pleased to arrive at Orlov, and the news of the arrest of the mayor of Orlov burst like a clap of thunder on the town. Tyufyayev turned yellow, and there was an uncertainty apparent in his gait.

Five days before the Tsarevich arrived at Orlov, the mayor had written to Tyufyayev that the widow whose floor had been broken up to make the sidewalk was making a fuss, and that So-and-so, a wealthy merchant and a prominent person in the town, was boasting that he would tell the Tsarevich everything. Tyufyayev disposed of the man very cleverly; he told the mayor to have doubts of his sanity (the precedent of Petrovsky pleased him[3]), and to send him to Vyatka to be examined by the doctors; while the affair was going on the Tsarevich would have left the province of Vyatka, and that would be the end of it. The mayor did as he was bid; the merchant was in the hospital at Vyatka.

At last the Tsarevich arrived.[4] He gave Tyufyayev a frigid bow,

[3] See p. 227. (R.)
[4] 18th May, 1837. (A.S.)

did not invite him to visit him, but at once sent Dr Enokhin to examine the arrested merchant. He knew all about it. The Orlov widow had given him her petition; the other merchants and townsmen had told him all that was going on. Tyufyayev's face was more awry than ever. Things looked black for him. The mayor said straight out that he had had written instructions for everything from the governor.

Dr Enokhin declared that the merchant was perfectly sane. Tyufyayev was lost.

Between seven and eight in the evening the Tsarevich visited the exhibition with his suite. Tyufyayev conducted him, explaining things incoherently, getting into a muddle and speaking of a 'Tsar Tokhtamysh'.[5] Zhukovsky and Arsenev, seeing that things were not going well, asked me to show them the exhibition. I took them round.

The Tsarevich's expression had none of that narrow severity, that cold, merciless cruelty which was characteristic of his father; his features were more suggestive of good nature and listlessness. He was about twenty, but was already beginning to grow stout.

The few words he said to me were friendly and very different from the hoarse, abrupt tones of his uncle Constantine and without his father's custom of making his hearer almost faint with terror.

When he had gone away Zhukovsky and Arsenev began asking me how I had come to Vyatka. They were surprised to hear a Vyatka official speak like a gentleman. They at once offered to speak of my situation to the Tsarevich, and did in fact do all that they could for me. The Tsarevich approached the Tsar for permission for me to travel to Petersburg. The Tsar replied that that would be unfair to the other exiles, but, in consideration of the Tsarevich's representations, he ordered me to be transferred to Vladimir, which was geographically an improvement, being seven hundred versts nearer home. But of that later.

In the evening there was a ball at the Assembly Rooms. The musicians who had been sent for expressly from one of the factories had arrived dead drunk; the governor had arranged that they should be locked up for twenty-four hours before the ball, escorted straight from the police-station to their seats in the orchestra, which none of them should be allowed to leave till the ball was over.

[5] The Tatar khan of the Golden Horde, who in 1382 sacked the Kremlin at Moscow and massacred 24,000 people. (*R.*)

The ball was a stupid, awkward, extremely poor and extremely gaudy affair, as balls always are in little towns on exceptional occasions. Police officers fussed about, government officials in uniform huddled against the wall, ladies flocked round the Tsarevich as savages do round travellers. . . . *A propros* the ladies, in one little town a *goûter* was arranged after the exhibition. The Tsarevich took nothing but one peach, the stone of which he threw on the windowsill. Suddenly a tall figure saturated with spirits stepped out from the crowd of officials; it was the district assessor, notoriously a dissolute character, who with measured steps approached the window, picked up the stone and put it in his pocket.

After the ball or the *goûter*, he approached one of the ladies of most consequence and offered her the stone gnawed by royalty; the lady was in raptures. Then he approached a second, then a third: all were in ecstasies.

The assessor had bought five peaches, cut out the stones, and made six ladies happy. Which had the real one? Each was suspicious of the genuineness of her own stone. . . .

After the departure of the Tsarevich, Tyufyayev with a heavy heart prepared to exchange his *pashalik* for the chair of a senator; but worse than that happened.

Three weeks later the post brought from Petersburg papers addressed to 'the administrator of the province'. Everything was turned upside down in the secretariat; the registrar ran in to say that they had received an *ukaz*; the office manager rushed to Tyufyayev; Tyufyayev gave out that he was ill and did not go to the office.

Within an hour we learned that he had been dismissed *sans phrase*.

The whole town was delighted at the fall of the governor; there was something stifling, unclean, about his rule, a fetid odour of red tape, but for all that it was nasty to watch the rejoicings of the officials.

Yes, every ass gave a parting kick to this wounded boar. The meanness of men was just as apparent as at the fall of Napoleon, though the catastrophe was on a different scale. Of late I had been on terms of open hostility with him, and he would have certainly sent me off to some obscure little town such as Kay, if he had not been sent away himself. I had held aloof from him, and I had no reason to change my behaviour to him. But the others, who only the day before had been cap in hand to him, who had grudged him his carriage, eagerly anticipating his wishes, fawning on his dog and offering snuff to his valet, now barely greeted him and made an outcry all over the town against the irregularities, the guilt of which *they* shared with him. This is nothing new; it has been repeated so continually in every age and in every place that we must accept this meanness as a common trait of humanity and at any rate feel no surprise at it.

The new governor, Kornilov, arrived. He was a man of quite a different type: a tall, stout, lymphatic man about fifty with a pleasantly smiling face and a cultured manner. He expressed himself with unusual ordinary grammatical correctness, and at great length, with a precision and clarity calculated by their very excess to obscure the simplest subject. He had been at the Lyceum of Tsarskoye Selo, had been a schoolfellow of Pushkin's, had served in the Guards, bought the new French books, liked talking of important subjects, and gave me Tocqueville's book on democracy in America on the day after his arrival.

The change was very striking. The same rooms, the same furniture, but instead of a Tatar *baskak* (tax-collector), with the exterior of a Tungus and the habits of a Siberian—a doctrinaire, something of a pedant, but at the same time quite a decent man. The new governor was intelligent, but his intelligence seemed somehow to shed light without giving warmth, like a bright, winter day which is pleasant though one does not look for fruits from it. Moreover, he was a terrible formalist—not in a pettifogging way, but . . . how shall I express it? . . . it was formalism of the second degree, but just as tiresome as any other.

Since the new governor was really married, the house lost its ultra-bachelor and polygamous character. Of course this brought all the councillors back to their lawful spouses; bald old men no longer boasted of their conquests among the fair, but, on the contrary, alluded tenderly to their faded, stiff, angularly-bony, or monstrously fat wives.

Kornilov had some years before coming to Vyatka been promoted to be civil governor somewhere, straight from being a colonel in the Seménovsky or Izmaylovsky regiment. He went to his province knowing nothing of his duties. To begin with, like all novices, he set to work to read everything. One day a document came to him from another province which he could make nothing of, though he read it two or three times.

L*

He called the secretary and gave it to him to read. The secretary could not explain the business clearly either.

'What will you do with that document,' Kornilov asked him, 'if I pass it on to the office?'

'I shall hand it in to the third table, it's their job.'

'Then the head-clerk of the third table knows what to do?'

'To be sure he does, your Excellency, he has been in charge of that table for seven years.'

'Send him to me.'

The head-clerk came in. Kornilov handed him the paper and asked what was to be done. The head-clerk glanced through the file and informed him that they ought to make an inquiry in the palace of justice and send an order to the police-captain.

'But order what?'

The head-clerk was nonplussed, and at last admitted that it was difficult to express it in words, but that it was easy to write it.

'Here is a chair: please write the answer.'

The head-clerk took up the pen and without hesitation briskly scribbled off two documents.

The governor took them, read them once, read them twice, but could make nothing of them.

'I saw,' he told me, smiling, 'that it really was an answer to the document, and I thanked God and signed it. Nothing more was heard of the business—the answer was completely satisfactory.'

The news of my transfer to Vladimir came just before Christmas; I was soon ready and set off.

My parting with Vyatka society was very warm. In that remote town I had made two or three genuine friends among the young merchants.

Everyone vied in showing sympathy and kindness to the exile. Several sledges accompanied me as far as the first posting-station, and in spite of all my efforts to defend myself my sledge was filled up with a perfect load of provisions and wine. Next day I reached Yaransk.

From Yaransk the road goes through endless pine forests. It was moonlight and very frosty at night. The little sledge flew along the narrow road. I have never seen such forests since; they go on like that unbroken as far as Archangel, and sometimes reindeer come through them to the province of Vyatka. The forest is for the most part composed of large trees; the pines, extraordinarily straight, ran past the sledge like soldiers, tall and covered with snow from under which their black needles stuck out like bristles; one would drop asleep and wake up again and still the regiments of pines would be marching rapidly by, sometimes shaking off the snow. The horses are changed at little clearings; there is a tiny house lost among the trees, the horses are tied up to a trunk, the sledge-bells begin tinkling, and two or three Cheremis boys in embroidered shirts run out, looking sleepy. The Votyak driver swears at his companion in a husky alto, shouts 'Ayda', begins singing a song on two notes . . . and again pines and snow, snow and pines.

Just as I drove out of Vyatka province it was my lot to take my last farewell of the official world, and it showed itself in all its glory *pour la clôture*.

We stopped at a posting-station, and the driver had begun un-harnessing the horses, when a tall peasant appeared in the porch and asked:

'Who is travelling through?'

'What's that to do with you?'

'Why, the police-captain told me to inquire, and I am the messen-ger of the rural court.'

'Well then, go into the station hut; my travelling permit is there.'

The peasant went away and came back a minute later, saying to the driver,

'He is not to have horses.'

This was too much. I jumped out of the sledge and went into the hut. A half-tipsy police-captain was sitting on a bench, dictating to a half-tipsy clerk. A man with fetters on his hands and feet was sitting or rather lying on another bench in the corner. Several bottles, glasses, tobacco ash, and bundles of papers were scattered about.

'Where is the police-captain?' I asked in a loud voice as I went in.

'The police-captain's here,' answered the half-tipsy man whom I recognised as Lazarev, a man I had seen in Vyatka. As he spoke he fixed a rude and impudent stare upon me—and suddenly rushed at me with open arms.

I must explain that after Tyufyayev's dismissal the officials, seeing that I was on quite good terms with the new governor, had begun to be rather afraid of me.

I stopped him with my hand and asked him very gravely,

'How could you give orders that I shouldn't have horses? What nonsense is this, stopping travellers on the high-road?'

'Why, I was joking; upon my soul, aren't you ashamed to be angry? Here, horses, order the horses! Why are you standing there, you rascal?' he shouted to the messenger. 'Do me the favour of having a cup of tea with rum.'

'Thank you very much.'

'But haven't we any champagne? . . .' He hurried to the bottles; they were all empty.

'What are you doing here?'

'An inquiry, sir. This fine fellow here has killed his father and sister with an axe, in a quarrel, through jealousy.'

'So that's why you are drinking together?'

The police-captain was disconcerted. I glanced at the Cheremis; he was a young fellow of twenty, with nothing savage about his face, which was typically oriental, with shining, narrow eyes and black hair.

It was all so nasty that I went out into the yard again. The police-captain ran out after me with a glass in one hand and a bottle of rum in the other, and pressed me to have a drink.

To get rid of him I drank some; he caught hold of my hand and said:

'I am sorry, there, I am sorry! there it is, but I hope you won't speak of this to his Excellency; don't ruin an honourable man!'

With that the police-captain *seized my hand and kissed it*, repeating a dozen times over:

'For God's sake don't ruin an honourable man.'

I pulled away my hand in disgust and said to him:

'Oh get away; as though I were likely to tell him.'

'But how can I be of service to you?'

'See they make haste and harness the horses.'

'Look alive,' he shouted, 'Ayda, ayda!' and he himself began dragging at some ropes and straps of the harness.

This incident is vividly imprinted on my memory. In 1846, when I was in Petersburg for the last time, I had to go to the secretariat of the Minister of Home Affairs to try to get a passport. While I was talking to the head-clerk of the table, a gentleman passed . . . shaking hands familiarly with the magnates of the secretariat and bowing condescendingly to the head-clerks of the tables. 'Bah, devil take it,' I thought, 'can that be he!'

'Who is that?' I asked.

'Lazarev, a clerk of special commissions and of great influence with the Minister.'

'Was he once a police-captain in the Vyatka province?'

'Yes.'

'Well, I congratulate you, gentlemen: nine years ago he kissed my hand.'

Perovsky was a master hand at choosing men!

Chapter 18

The Beginning of my Life at Vladimir

WHEN I went out to get into my sledge at Kosmodemyansk it was harnessed in the Russian style, with three horses abreast: one between the shafts and two flanking it. The shaft horse, with its yoke, rang the bells gaily.

In Perm and Vyatka the horses are put in tandem, one before the other or two side by side and the third in front.

So my heart throbbed with delight when I saw the familiar troika.

'Come now, show us your mettle,' I said to the young lad who sat smartly in the driver's seat in a sheepskin coat, the bare side turned outwards, and stiff gauntlets which barely allowed his fingers to close enough to take fifteen kopecks from my hand.

'We'll do our best, sir, we'll do our best. Hey, darlings! Now, sir,' he said, turning suddenly to me, 'you just hold on; there is a hill yonder, so I'll let them go.'

It was a steep descent to the Volga; in the winter the way lay across the ice.

He certainly did let the horses go. The sledge did not so much run as bound from right to left, from left to right, as the horses whirled it down-hill; the driver was tremendously pleased, and indeed, sinful man that I am, so was I—it is the Russian temperament.

So my post-horses brought me into 1838—into the best, the brightest year of my life. I shall describe how we saw the New Year in.

Eighty versts from Nizhni Novgorod we, that is Matvey, my valet, and I, went into the station-superintendent's to warm ourselves. There was a very sharp frost, and it was windy too. The superintendent, a thin, sickly, pitiful-looking man, inscribed my travelling permit, dictating every letter to himself and yet making mistakes. I took off my fur-lined coat and walked up and down the room in my huge fur boots, Matvey was warming himself at the red-hot stove, the superintendent muttered, and a wooden clock ticked on a faint, cracked note.

'I say,' Matvey said to me, 'it will soon be twelve o'clock; it's the New Year, you know. I'll bring in something,' he added, looking at me half-inquiringly, 'from the stores they put in our sledge at Vyatka.' And without waiting for an answer he ran to fetch bottles and a bag with some food.

Matvey, of whom I shall have more to say later, was more than a servant: he was a friend, a younger brother to me. A man of Moscow, apprenticed to Sonnenberg, whose acquaintance we shall also make, to learn the art of bookbinding, in which Sonnenberg, however, was not very proficient, he passed into my hands.

I knew that if I refused it would disappoint Matvey, and besides I had nothing against celebrating the day at the posting-station. . . . The New Year is a station of a sort.

Matvey brought ham and champagne.

The champagne turned out to be frozen solid; the ham could have been chopped with an axe, and was all glistening with ice; but *à la guerre comme à la guerre.*

'May the New Year bring new happiness.' Yes indeed, new happiness. Was I not on the way back? Every hour was bringing me nearer to Moscow—my heart was full of hopes.

The frozen champagne did not exactly please the superintendent. I added half a glass of rum to his wine. This new 'half-and-half'[1] was very successful.

The driver, whom I had also invited to join us, was still more extreme in his views; he sprinkled pepper into his glass of foaming wine, stirred it with a spoon, drank it off at one gulp, uttered a painful sigh and almost with a moan added: 'It did scorch fine!'

The superintendent himself tucked me into the sledge, and was so zealous in his attentions that he dropped the lighted candle into the hay and could not find it afterwards. He was in great spirits and kept repeating:

'You've given me a New Year's Eve, too!'

The scorched driver started the horses off. . . .

---

[1] In English in the text. (R.)

At eight o'clock on the following evening I reached Vladimir and put up at the hotel, which is extremely faithfully described in V. A. Sollogub's *Tarantas* with its fowls in rice, its dough-like *pâtisserie*, and vinegar by way of Bordeaux.

'A man was asking for you this morning, he's probably waiting at the beer-shop,' the waiter told me after reading my name on my travel permit. He wore the rakish parting and dashing lovelocks, which in old days were only affected by Russian waiters, but now are also worn by Louis Napoleon.

I could not conceive who this could be.

'But here he is, sir,' added the waiter, moving aside. What I saw first, however, was not a man but a tray of terrific size, on which were piles of all sorts of good things, a cake and cracknels, oranges and apples, eggs, almonds, raisins . . . and behind the tray appeared the grey head and blue eyes of the village head-man, from my father's Vladimir estate.

'Gavrilo Semënych,' I cried, and rushed to embrace him. This was the first of our own people, the first figure out of my former life, whom I met after imprisonment and exile. I could not take my eyes off the intelligent old man, and felt as though I would never say all I had to say to him. He was the living proof of my nearness to Moscow, to my home, to my friends; only three days before he had seen them all, he brought me greetings from them all. . . . So it was not so far away!

The governor, who was a clever Greek called Kuruta, had a thorough knowledge of human nature, and had long become indifferent to good and evil. He grasped my situation at once and did not make the slightest attempt to be a nuisance to me. Official forms were not even referred to; he commissioned me and a master at the high school* to edit the *Vladimir Provincial News*—that was my only duty.

The work was familiar to me; in Vyatka I had put the unofficial part of the *Provincial News* on its feet,* and had published in it an article which almost got my successor into trouble. Describing the festival on the Great River, I said that the mutton sacrificed to St Nicholas of Khlynov used in old days to be distributed to the poor, but now was sold. The bishop was incensed and the governor had difficulty in persuading him to let the matter drop.

These provincial newspapers were introduced in 1837.* The very
original idea of training the inhabitants of the land of silence and
dumbness to express themselves in print occurred to Bludov, the
Minister of Home Affairs. This man, famous for being chosen to
continue Karamzin's *History*, though he never actually added a line
to it, and for being the author of the report of the committee of
investigation into the affair of the 14th of December, which it would
have been better not to write at all, belonged to the group of
doctrinaire statesmen who appeared on the scene at the end of the
reign of Alexander. They were intelligent, cultured, honourable old
'Arzamas geese'[2] who had risen and grown old in the service.
They could write Russian, were patriots, and were so zealously
engaged in the history of their native land that they had no time
to give serious attention to its present condition. They all cherished
the never-to-be-forgotten memory of N. M. Karamzin, loved Zhukovsky, knew Krylov by heart, and used to go to Moscow to converse
with I. I. Dmitriyev in his house in Sadovaya Street,* where I too
visited him as a student, armed with romantic prejudices, a personal
acquaintance with N. Polevoy, and a concealed disapproval of the
fact that Dmitriyev, who was a poet, should be Minister of Justice.
Great things were hoped of them, and like most doctrinaires of all
countries they did nothing. Perhaps they might have succeeded in
leaving more permanent traces under Alexander, but Alexander
died and they were left with nothing but their *desire* to do something
worth doing.

At Monaco there is an inscription on the tombstone of one of the
hereditary princes: 'Here lies the body of Florestan So-and-so—he
desired to do good to his subjects.'[3] Our doctrinaires also desired to
do good, not to their own subjects but to the subjects of Nicholas
Pavlovich, but they reckoned without their host. I do not know who
hindered that Florestan, but these were hindered by our Florestan.
They were drawn into complicity in all the measures detrimental to
Russia and had to restrict themselves to useless innovations, mere
alterations of name and form. Every head of a department among us
thinks it his highest duty to produce at intervals a project, an innova-
tion, usually for the worse but sometimes simply neutral. They

---

[2] The reference is to the 'Arzamas', a literary club of which Karamzin, Batyush-
kov, Uvarov, this Bludov and some others were members. The town Arzamas is
noted for its geese. (*Tr.*)
[3] *Il a voulu le bien de ses sujets.*

thought it necessary for instance to call the secretary in the governor's office by a name of purely Russian origin,[4] while they left the secretary of the provincial office untranslated into Russian.[5] I remember that the Minister of Justice brought forward a plan for essential changes in the uniforms of civil servants. This scheme opened in a majestic and solemn style: 'Taking into special consideration the lack of unity, of standard, in the make and pattern of certain uniforms in the civil department and adopting as a fundamental principle', and so on.

Possessed by the same mania for reform the Minister for Home Affairs replaced the rural assessors by police inspectors. The assessors lived in the towns and used to visit the villages. The police inspectors sometimes met together in the town but lived permanently in the country. In this way all the peasants were put under the supervision of the police and this was done with full knowledge of the predatory, carnivorous, corrupt character of our police officials. Bludov introduced the policeman into the secrets of the peasants' industry and wealth, into their family life, into the affairs of the *mir*, and in this way laid his hand on the last refuge of peasant life. Fortunately our villages are very many and there are only two police inspectors in a district.

Almost at the same time the same Bludov had the notion of establishing provincial newspapers. In Russia, although the government has no regard for popular education, it has great literary pretensions, and while in England, for instance, there are no official organs, every one of our departments has its own magazine, and so have the universities and the academy. We have journals relating to mining, to dry-salting, French and German ones, naval and military ones. All these are published at the government expense; contracts for literary articles are made in the ministries exactly as contracts are for fuel and candles, but without competition; there are plenty of statistics, invented figures and fantastic inferences from them. After monopolising everything else, the government has now taken the monopoly of talk and, imposing silence on everyone else, has begun chattering unceasingly. Continuing this system, Bludov commanded every provincial government to publish its own newspaper, which was to have an unofficial part for articles on historical, literary, and other subjects.

---

[4] '*Pravitel' del*' (lit. 'manager of affairs'). (R.)
[5] '*Sekretar*'. (R.)

No sooner said than done, and the officials in fifty provinces were tearing their hair over this unofficial part. Priests with a seminary education, doctors of medicine, high-school teachers, all who could be suspected of a tinge of culture and ability to spell correctly were requisitioned. After much reflection and reading over of the *Library of Good Reading* and the *Notes of the Fatherland*, with tremors and false starts they at last wrote the articles.

The desire to see one's name in print is one of the strongest artificial passions in a man who has been corrupted by this bookish age. Nevertheless it needs a special occasion to induce people to expose their efforts to public criticism. People who would never have dared to dream of their essays being printed in the *Moscow News* or in a Petersburg magazine, began to publish them at home. And, meanwhile, the fatal habit of having a newspaper, the habit of publicity, took root. And, indeed, it may not be amiss to have an instrument ready. The printing press, too, is an unruly member!

My colleague in the editorship was also a Moscow graduate and of the same faculty. I have not the heart to speak of him with a smile because of his sad end, and yet he was an absurd figure up to the end. Though far from being stupid, he was unusually clumsy and awkward. It would be hard to find an ugliness not merely so complete but so great, that is, on so large a scale. His face was half as big again as an ordinary face and somehow rugged-looking; a huge fish-like mouth reached to his ears, white eyelashes did not shade but rather emphasised his pale grey eyes, his skull was scantily covered with bristling hair, and at the same time he was a head taller than I was, round-shouldered, and very slovenly in his appearance.

Even his name was such that a sentry at Vladimir locked him up on account of it. Late one evening he was walking past the governor's house, wrapped up in his overcoat, carrying a pocket telescope; he stood still and took aim with it at some planet. This perplexed the sentry who probably regarded the stars as State property.

'Who goes there?' he shouted to the motionless star-gazer.

'Nebaba,'[6] answered my friend in his thick voice, without budging.

'Don't play the fool,' answered the sentry, offended; 'I am on duty.'

'But I tell you I am Nebaba.'

This was too much for the sentry and he rang his bell; a sergeant

[6] The name means 'not a woman'. (*Tr.*)

appeared and the sentry handed over the astronomer to be taken to the guardroom. 'There they'll find out whether you are a woman or not.' He would certainly have spent the night in custody if the officer on duty had not recognised him.

One morning Nebaba came to tell me that he was going to Moscow for a few days; he gave a sly, rather appealing smile as he told me this.

'I shall not return alone,' he said hesitatingly.

'What, you mean. . . ?'

'Yes, I am embarking on legal wedlock,' he said shyly.

I marvelled at the heroic courage of the woman who could bring herself to marry this good-hearted but monstrously ugly man. But when two or three weeks later I saw in his house a girl of eighteen, who was not exactly beautiful but quite pretty and with a lively expression in her eyes, I began to look upon him as the hero.

Six weeks later I began to notice that things were not going well with my Quasimodo. He was plunged in dejection, corrected his proofs badly, did not finish his article on migratory birds, and was gloomily preoccupied. Sometimes his eyes looked as though he had been weeping. It did not last long. One day as I was returning home through the Golden Gate I saw shopmen and boys running to the churchyard; policemen were bustling about. I went with them.

Nebaba's dead body was lying by the church wall and beside him a rifle. He had shot himself just opposite the window of his house; the string with which he had pulled the trigger was still round his foot. The inspector of the medical board, in well-rounded sentences, assured the bystanders that the dead man had felt no pain; the police were preparing to take the body to the police station.

How savage nature is to some people! What were the feelings in the heart of the victim before he brought himself to stop with his bit of string the pendulum that measured for him nothing but humiliations and misfortunes? And why? Because his father was scrofulous or his mother lymphatic? That may all be so. But what right have we to expect justice, to call to account, to ask for reasons from —whom? The whirling hurricane of life? . . .

At that very time a new chapter in my life was opening, a chapter full of purity, serenity, youth, earnestness, secluded and bathed in love. . . .

It belongs to another Part.

PART III

VLADIMIR
ON THE KLYAZMA

(1838—1839)

*Do not expect from me long accounts of my inner
life of that period. . . . Frightful events, woes of all
sorts, are yet more easily put upon paper than quite
bright and cloudless memories. . . . Can happiness be
described?*

*Fill in for yourselves what is lacking, divine it with
the heart—while I will tell of the external side, of the
setting, only rarely, rarely touching by hint or by word
on my ineffable secrets.*

A. I. HERZEN: *My Past and Thoughts*

Chapter 19

The Two Princesses

When I was five or six years old and was very naughty, Vera Artamonovna used to say: 'Very well, very well, you wait a bit, I'll tell the princess everything as soon as she comes.' I was at once subdued by this threat and begged her not to complain.

Princess Marya Alexeyevna Khovansky, my father's sister, was a stern, forbidding old lady, stout and dignified, with a birth-mark on her cheek and false curls under her cap; she used to screw up her eyes as she spoke, and to the end of her days, that is till she was eighty, used a little rouge and powder. Whenever she caught sight of me she persecuted me; there was no end to her lecturing and grumbling; she would scold me for anything, for a crumpled collar, or a stain on my jacket, would declare I had not gone up to kiss her hand properly, and make me go through the ceremony again. When she had finished lecturing me, she would sometimes say to my father, taking with her fingertips a pinch of snuff out of a tiny gold snuff-box: 'My dear, you should send your spoilt child to me to be corrected; he would be as soft as silk when he had been a month in my hands.' I knew that they would not give me up, but I shivered with horror at these words.

My fear of her passed off with the years, but I never liked the old princess's house; I could not breathe freely in it, I could not be myself, but like a trapped hare, looked uneasily from one side to the other to make my escape.

The old princess's household was not in the least like my father's or the Senator's. It was an old-fashioned, orthodox Russian house-hold in which they kept the fasts, went to the early service, put a cross on the doors on the eve of Epiphany, made marvellous pan-cakes at Shrove-tide, ate pickled pork with horse-radish, dined ex-actly two o'clock and supped at nine. The Western contagion which had infected her brothers and thrown them somewhat out of their native rut had not touched the life of the old princess; on the contrary, she disapproved of the way in which 'Vanyusha and Levushka', as she called my father and uncle, had been corrupted in 'that France'.

Princess Marya Alexeyevna lived in a wing of the house occupied by her aunt, Princess Anna Borisovna Meshchersky, a maiden lady of eighty.

This Princess Meshchersky was the living and almost the only link connecting all the seven ascending and descending branches of the family. At the chief holidays all the relations gathered about her. She reconciled those who were at variance and brought together those who had drifted apart. She was respected by all, and she deserved it. At her death family ties were loosened and lost their rallying-point, and the relations forgot each other.

She had seen the education of my father and his brothers through; after the death of their parents she looked after their property until they came of age. She put them into the Guards, and she made marriages for their sisters.[1] I do not know how far she was satisfied with the fruits of her bringing up, which with the help of a French engineer, a kinsman of Voltaire, had turned them into landowners and *esprits forts*, but she knew how to inspire esteem for herself, and her nephews, though not greatly disposed to feelings of obedience and reverence, respected the old lady and often obeyed her to the end of her life.

Princess Anna Borisovna's house, preserved by some miracle at the time of the fire of 1812, had not been repaired nor redecorated for fifty years: the silk hangings that covered the walls were faded and blackened; the lustres on the chandeliers, discoloured by heat and turned into smoky topazes by time, shook and tinkled, glittering and shining dimly when anyone walked across the room. The heavy, solid mahogany furniture, ornamented with florid carvings that had lost all their gilt, stood gloomily along the walls; chests of drawers with Chinese incrustations, tables with little copper trellis-work, rococo porcelain dolls—all recalled another age and different manners.

Grey-headed flunkeys sat in the outer hall, occupied with quiet dignity in various trifling tasks, or sometimes reading half aloud from a prayer-book or a psalter, the pages of which were darker

[1] M. A. Khovansky and Ye. A. Golokhvastov. (*A.S.*)

than its cover. Boys stood at the doors, but they were more like old dwarfs than children—they never laughed nor raised their voices.

A deathly silence reigned in the inner apartments; only, from time to time, there was the mournful cry of a cockatoo, its unhappy, faltering effort to repeat a human word, the bony tap of its beak against its perch, covered with tin, and the disgusting whimper of a little old monkey, shrunken and consumptive, that lived in the great hall, on a little shelf of the stove with its Dutch tiles. The monkey, dressed like a *débardeur*, in full, red trousers, gave the whole room a peculiar and extremely unpleasant smell. In another big room hung a multitude of family portraits of all sizes, shapes, periods, ages, and costumes. These portraits had a peculiar interest for me, especially from the contrast between the originals and their semblances. The young man of twenty with a powdered head, dressed in a light-green embroidered *caftan*, smiling courteously from the canvas, was my father. The little girl with dishevelled curls and a bouquet of roses, her face adorned with a patch, mercilessly tight-laced into the shape of a wine-glass, and thrust into enormous petticoats, was the formidable old Princess Marya Alexeyevna.

The stillness and the stiffness grew more marked as one approached the princess's room. Old maidservants in white caps with wide frills moved to and fro with little teapots, so softly that their footsteps were inaudible; from time to time a grey-headed manservant in a long coat of stout dark-blue cloth appeared in a doorway, but his footsteps too were as inaudible, and, when he gave some message to the head parlourmaid, his lips moved without making a sound.

The little, withered, wrinkled, but by no means ugly, old lady, Princess Anna Borisovna, was usually sitting or reclining on the big clumsy sofa, propped up with cushions. One could scarcely distinguish her; everything was white, her morning dress, her cap, the cushions, the covers on the sofa. Her waxen white face of lace-like fragility, together with her faint voice and white dress, gave her an air of something that had passed away, that was scarcely breathing.

The big English clock on the table with its loud, measured spondee —tick-tack, tick-tack—seemed marking off the last quarters of an hour of her life.

Between twelve and one Princess Marya Alexeyevna would enter and settle herself with dignity in a big easy-chair. She was dull in her empty apartments. She was a widow, and I still remember her husband, a little grey-headed old gentleman who, unknown to the princess, drank liqueurs and home-made beverages; he never played an important part in the house, and was accustomed to obey his wife implicitly—though he sometimes rebelled against her in word, especially after his secret potations, but never in deed. The princess would be surprised at the great effect produced on her spouse by the minute glass of vodka which he drank officially before dinner, and she used to leave him in peace to play the whole morning with his blackbirds, nightingales, and canaries, which trilled at the pitch of their throats in emulation of each other; he trained some of them with a little organ, others by whistling to them himself; he used to drive off very early to the bird-market to exchange, sell, and buy birds; he took an artistic delight in succeeding as he supposed, in cheating a dealer. . . . And so he continued his profitable life, until one morning, after whistling to his canaries, he fell forward on his face and two hours afterwards died.

His widow was left alone. She had had two daughters, both of whom married not for love but simply to escape from the maternal yoke. Both died in their first childbirth. The princess was really an unfortunate woman, but her troubles rather warped her character than softened it. The blows of fate made her not milder, not kinder, but harder and more forbidding.

Now she had no one left but her brothers and, most important, her aunt. The old lady, from whom she had scarcely parted all her life, drew her still closer to herself after her husband's death. The aunt had no say in the running of her household; the niece managed everything like an autocrat, and oppressed her aunt under the pretext of looking after her and caring for her wants.

There were always some old women of every sort, either *habituées* of the old princess's house, or encamped there temporarily, like nomads, ranged along the walls or sitting in various corners. Half saints and half vagrants, rather crazy and very devout, sickly and extraordinarily unclean, these old women trailed from one old-fashioned house to another: in one they were fed, in another presented with an old shawl; from one place they were sent groats and firewood, from another cloth and cabbage; and so they somehow made both ends meet. Everywhere they were a nuisance, everywhere they were passed over, everywhere put in the lowest seat, and everywhere received through boredom and emptiness and, most of all, through love of gossip. In the presence of other company these mournful figures were usually silent, looking with envious hatred at each other. . . . They sighed, shook their heads, made the sign of the cross, and muttered to themselves the number of their stitches, prayers, and perhaps even words of abuse. On the other hand, *tête à tête* with their *benefactresses* and *patronesses,* they rewarded themselves for their silence by the most treacherous gossip about all the other benefactresses who received them, fed them and made them presents.

They were continually begging from the old princess and, in return for her presents, often made without the knowledge of her niece, who did not like them to be indulged, brought her holy bread, hard as a stone, and unnecessary woollen and knitted articles of their own make, which the old lady afterwards sold for their benefit, regardless of whether the purchaser was willing or not.

Apart from birthdays, name-days, and other holidays the most solemn gathering of kinsmen and friends in Princess Anna Borisovna's house took place on New Year's Eve. On that day she 'elevated' the Iversky Madonna. The holy ikon was carried through all the apartments by chanting monks and priests. The old princess walked under it in front, crossing herself, and after her all the visitors, men and maid servants, old people and children. After this they all congratulated her on the approaching New Year, and made her all sorts of trifling presents such as are given to children. She would play with them for a few days and then give them away.

My father used to take me every year to this heathen ceremony; everything was repeated in exactly the same order, except that some old men and women were missing, and their names were intentionally avoided; only the old lady would say:

'Our Ilya Vasilyevich is no longer here, the Kingdom of Heaven be his! . . . Whom will the Lord summon in the coming year?'

And she would shake her head dubiously.

And the spondees of the English clock would go on measuring out the days, the hours, the minutes, and at last it reached the fatal second. The old lady felt unwell on getting up one day; she walked about the rooms and was no better; her nose began bleeding, and very violently; she was feeble and tired, and lay down fully dressed on her sofa, fell quietly asleep . . . and did not wake up. She was over ninety.

She left her house and the greater part of her property to her niece, but the inner significance of her life she did not hand on to her. Princess Marya Alexeyevna could not continue the—in its own way—elegant rôle of head of the family, of the patriarchal link connecting many threads. With the death of Princess Anna Boris-ovna everything at once took on an aspect of gloom, as in mountain-ous places at sunset; long, black shadows on everything. Princess Marya Alexeyevna shut up her aunt's house entirely and remained living in a wing; the yard was overgrown with grass, the walls and picture-frames grew blacker and blacker; the front hall, in which ungainly, yellowish dogs were for ever asleep, fell out of the perpendicular.

Friends and relations came less frequently, her house was deser-ted; she was distressed at it, but did not know how to put things right.

The only survivor of the whole family, she began to fear for her own useless life, and mercilessly repulsed everything that could disturb her physical or moral equilibrium and cause her uneasiness or annoyance. Afraid of the past and of memories, she removed every object that had belonged to her daughters, even their portraits. It was the same with her aunt's belongings—the cockatoo and the monkey were exiled to the servants' hall, and then turned out of the house. The monkey lived out its days in the coachman's quarters at the Senator's, suffocated by the rank tobacco and amusing the postillions.

The egoism of self-preservation has a fearfully hardening effect on the heart of the old. When her last surviving daughter's illness be-came quite hopeless, they tried to persuade the mother to go home, *and she went.* At home she at once ordered spirits of various sorts and cabbage leaves (she used to tie them on her head) to be got ready, that she might have everything necessary at hand when the *terrible news* should come. She did not take leave of her dead hus-band nor of her daughter, she did not see them after their death and was not at their funerals. When later on the Senator, her favourite brother, died, she guessed what had happened from a few words dropped by a nephew, and *begged him* not to tell her the sad news nor any details of the end. With these precautions against one's own heart, and such a compliant heart, one may well live to eighty or ninety in perfect health and with undisturbed digestion.

However, in defence of Princess Marya Alexeyevna I must say that this monstrous avoidance of everything sad was more in fashion with the spoilt aristocrats of last century than it is now. The celebrated Kaunitz[2] in his old age sternly forbade anyone's death, or the smallpox, of which he was very much afraid, to be mentioned before him. When Joseph II died, his secretary, not knowing how to announce it to Kaunitz, decided to say, 'The Emperor now reigning, Leopold.' Kaunitz understood and, turning pale, sank into an armchair, asking no questions. His gardener avoided the word 'grafting'[3] for fear of reminding him of smallpox. At length he heard of the death of his own son by chance from the Spanish ambassador. And people laugh at ostriches who hide their heads under their wings to escape danger!

To preserve her peace untroubled, the old princess established a special sort of police, and entrusted the command of it to skilled hands.

Besides the nomadic old women inherited from Princess Anna Borisovna, she had a permanent lady companion living with her. This post of honour was filled by the healthy, rosy-cheeked widow of a Zvenigorod government clerk, very proud of 'being a lady' and of her dead husband's rank of assessor; a bustling termagant who could never forgive Napoleon the premature death of her Zvenigorod cow, which had perished in the war of 1812. I remember how seriously troubled she was on the death of Alexander I about what width of crape weepers she should wear to conform with her *rank*.

This woman had played a very insignificant part in the household while Princess Anna Borisovna was alive, but afterwards she managed so adroitly to humour the younger princess's caprices and apprehensive anxiety about herself, that she obtained the same control over her as the princess herself had had over her aunt.

Draped in the weepers suited to her rank, this Marya Stepanovna Makashin bounced about the house like a ball from morning to night; she shouted and was noisy, gave the servants no peace, complained of them, held investigations into the doings of the maids, slapped the boys and pulled them by the ears, cast up the accounts, ran into the kitchen, rushed out to the stables, brushed away the flies, rubbed the princess's feet, and made her take her medicine. The members of the household no longer had access to their mistress; the woman was an Arakcheyev, a Biron, in a word, a Prime Minister.

---

[2] Kaunitz-Ritberg, Wencel Anton (1711-94), was for over forty years the leading statesman of Austria under Maria Theresa and Joseph II, and one of the most prominent figures in European politics. (*Tr.*)

[3] In Russian the same word as 'inoculation.' (*Tr.*) Cf. the German *Okulierung.* (*R.*)

The princess, a haughty and, although in the old-fashioned style, a well-bred woman, was often vexed, especially at first, by the Zvenigorod widow, by her scolding voice and market-woman's manners, but she gradually put more and more confidence in her, and saw with delight that Marya Stepanovna considerably diminished the household expenses, which had not been over-high before. For whom the princess was saving her money it is hard to say; she had no near relations except her brothers, who were twice as wealthy as she was.

For all that the princess was really bored after the death of her husband and daughters, and was glad when an old Frenchwoman, who had been her daughters' governess, came to spend a fortnight with her, or when her niece from Korcheva paid her a visit. But these were only passing, rare events, and the tedious *tête à tête* with her lady companion did not fill the intervals satisfactorily.

An occupation, a plaything, and a distraction had been provided for her in a quite natural way not long before her aunt's death.

Chapter 20

The Forlorn Child

In the middle of 1825 'the Chemist', who found his father's affairs in great confusion when he took them over, sent his brothers and sisters from Petersburg to the Shatskoye estate; he assigned them the house there and their keep, proposing to arrange for their education and their future later on. My aunt, Princess Marya Alexeyevna, drove over to look at them. A child of eight[1] caught her attention by her mournfully pensive face; my aunt put her in the carriage, took her home and kept her.

The mother was glad, and went off with the other children to Tambov.

The Chemist gave his consent—it did not matter to him.

'Remember all your life,' Marya Stepanovna kept saying to the little girl when they had reached home, 'remember that the princess is your *benefactress* and pray that her days may be long. What would you be without her?'

And so into this house which had ceased to live, which was gloomily oppressed by two restless old women, one full of whims and caprices, the other her indefatigable spy, devoid of all trace of delicacy or tact, a child was brought, torn away from everything familiar to her, strange to everything surrounding her, and adopted out of boredom, as people take a puppy, or as my aunt's husband had kept canaries.

The little girl with a face so pale that it had a bluish tinge was sitting at the window in a long, woollen mourning frock when my father brought me a few days later to visit the princess. She was sitting in silence, scared and bewildered, gazing out of the window, afraid to look at anything else.

My aunt called her over and presented her to my father. Always frigid and ungracious, he patted her carelessly on the shoulder, ob-

---

[1] Natalya Alexandrovna Zakharin, an illegitimate daughter of 'the Chemist's' father. (*R.*)

served that his late brother had not known what he was about, abused
'the Chemist', and began talking of something else.

The little girl had tears in her eyes; she sat down by the window
again and again began to look out of it.

A hard life was beginning for her. Not one warm word, not one
tender glance, not one caress; beside her, around her, were strangers,
wrinkled faces, yellowed cheeks, sickly creatures whose life was
smouldering out. Princess Marya Alexeyevna was always stern, exacting and impatient, and she kept the forlorn child at such a distance
that it could never enter her head to seek refuge with her, to find
warmth or comfort in being near her, or to shed tears. Visitors took
no notice of her. Marya Stepanovna put up with her as one of the
princess's whims, as something superfluous, but which could do her
no harm; she even made a show of protecting the child and interced-
ing for her with the princess, especially before outsiders.

The child did not grow used to her surroundings, and a year later
was as little at home as on the day of her arrival, and even more sorrowful. Even the princess was surprised at her 'seriousness', and
sometimes, seeing her sitting dejectedly for hours together at her little
embroidery frame, would say to her:

'How is it you don't play and run about?'

The little girl would smile, flush, and thank her, but stay where
she was.

And the old lady left her in peace, in reality caring nothing about
the child's sadness and doing nothing to distract her. Holidays came,
other children were given playthings, other children talked of treats,
of new clothes. . . . No presents were given to the little orphan. The
princess considered that she was doing enough for her in giving her
shelter; she had shoes—what did she want with dolls? And in fact
she did not need them, for she did not know how to play; besides,
she had no one to play with.

Only one creature realised the forlorn child's situation; an old
nurse had been put in charge of her, and she alone loved the child
simply and naïvely. Often in the evening when she undressed her she
would ask: 'But why is it you are so sad, my little lady?'

The child would throw herself on her neck and weep bitterly, and
the old woman would shed tears and shake her head as she went
away with the candlestick in her hand.

So the years passed. She did not complain, she did not murmur;
only, at twelve she longed for death. 'It always seemed to me,' she

wrote,[2] 'that I had come into this life by mistake, and that soon I should go home again—but where was my home? . . . When we drove out of Petersburg I saw a great mound of snow over my father's grave; when my mother left me in Moscow she vanished on the broad, endless road. . . . I wept bitterly and prayed God to take me home quickly. . . .

'My childhood was most mournful and bitter; how many tears I shed unseen, how many times, before I understood what prayer meant, I would get up secretly at night (hardly even daring to say my prayers except at the fixed time) and pray to God that someone might love me and make much of me. I had no amusement or plaything to interest or comfort me, for, if anything was given me, it was given reproachfully, and invariably with the words: "You don't deserve it." Every rag I received from them I paid for with tears: later on I got over that; I was almost suffocated by a craving for knowledge, and envied other children for nothing more than for their lessons. Many people praised me, thought I had ability, and said compassionately: "If only I could get to work on that child." "She would astonish the world," I finished the sentence in my thoughts, and my cheeks glowed; I was in a hurry to get away, somewhere—I had visions of my pictures, my pupils, and meanwhile they would not give me a piece of paper nor a pencil. . . . The longing to get out into another world grew stronger and stronger, and with it my disdain for my dark prison-house and its cruel sentinels; I was continually repeating the lines from "The Monk":

> *"A mystery this; already I know*
> *All the sorrow of life, in the spring of my days."*[3]

'Do you remember, we were once staying with you long ago, still in the other house, and you asked me if I had read Kozlov and recited just that passage from him? A shudder ran over me, I smiled, hardly able to keep from crying.'

There was always a strain of profound melancholy in her heart; it was never quite absent, and only sometimes did it fall silent, muted by some radiant moment of her life.

Two months before her death, going back once more to her childhood, she wrote:

'Around me all was old, bad, cold, dead, false; my education began

[2] The excerpts from Natalya's letters which H. quotes are often more or less edited by him. (R.)

[3] By I. I. Kozlov (1825). (A.S.)

with reproofs and taunts, and the result of this was estrangement
from everyone, distrust of their kindness, aversion for their sympathy, and absorption in my own self. . . .'

But to be able to be absorbed like this in one's own self one must have
not only a terrific depth of soul into which one can plunge untram-
melled, but a terrific strength of independence and self-sufficiency.
Very few can live their own life in hostile and vulgar surroundings
from the oppression of which there is no escape. Sometimes the spirit
is broken by it, sometimes the health gives way.

Loneliness and harsh treatment at the tenderest age left a black
trace on her soul, a wound which never fully closed.

'I do not remember,' she writes in 1837, 'any time when I could
utter the word "mother" freely and spontaneously, any person on
whose breast I could lay my head in security, forgetting everything.
I have been a stranger to everyone since I was eight years old; I love
my mother . . . but we do not know each other.'[4]

Looking at the pale face of the twelve-year-old girl, at her big eyes
with dark rings round them, at her tired listlessness and everlasting
sadness, many people thought she was one of the predestined, early
victims of consumption, those victims marked from childhood by the
finger of death with a special imprint of beauty and premature
thoughtfulness. 'Perhaps,' she says, 'I should not have survived this
struggle if I had not been saved by our meeting.'

And I was so slow to understand her and read her heart!

Till 1834 I failed to appreciate the richly gifted nature that was unfolding beside me, although nine years had passed since the old princess had presented her to my father in her long woollen dress. It is
not hard to explain. She was *farouche*, I was preoccupied; I was sorry
for the child who sat so solitary and sad in the window, but we saw
each other very seldom. It was only rarely and always unwillingly
that I went to the princess's; still more rarely did she bring her to see
us. Besides, my aunt's visits almost always left unpleasant impressions. She and my father usually quarrelled over trifles and, when
they had not seen each other for two months, they said barbed things
to each other, hiding them in affectionate turns of phrase, just as
nasty medicines are covered with a coating of sugar. 'My dear boy,'
the princess would say; 'My dear girl,' my father would answer, and
the quarrel would go its way. We were always glad when the prin-

---

[4] 'I love . . . each other.' These words are not in the original of the letter of 1st
December, 1837, from which Herzen is quoting. (*A.S.*)

cess drove away. Moreover, it must not be forgotten that at that time I was completely absorbed by my political dreams and my studies, and my life was in the university and my comrades.

But what had *she* to live in, besides her melancholy, during those long, dark *nine years*, surrounded by stupid bigots, haughty relations, tedious priests and fat priests' wives, hypocritically patronised by the 'lady companion', not allowed to go farther from the house than the gloomy courtyard overgrown with grass and the little garden at the back?

From the foregoing lines it may be seen that the princess was not particularly lavish in her expenditure on the education of her adopted child. Her moral training she undertook herself; it consisted in external observances and in inoculation with a complete system of hypocrisy. The child had from early morning to be laced up, standing at attention, with her hair properly dressed: this might be admissible so far as it was not injurious to health; but the princess put her soul in stays as well as her waist, suppressing every open, spontaneous feeling; she insisted on a smile and an air of gaiety when the child was sad, on amiable phrases when she wanted to cry, on an appearance of participation in subjects of no interest—in short, on continual duplicity.

At first the poor girl was taught nothing, on the pretext that learning things early was useless; later on, that is *three or four years later*, wearied by the observations made by the Senator and even by outsiders, the princess made up her mind to arrange for her to be taught, keeping in view the strictest economy.

For this purpose she availed herself of an old governess who considered herself under an obligation to the princess and sometimes was in need of her assistance. In this way the French language was brought down to the lowest price; but in return for that, it was taught *à bâtons rompus*.

But the Russian language, too, was equally cheapened; to teach it and *all other subjects,* the princess engaged the son of a priest's widow, to whom she had been a benefactress—of course, at no special expense to herself: through her good offices with the metropolitan the widow's two sons had been made priests in the cathedral. The instructor was their elder brother, the deacon of a poor parish, burdened with a large family. He was in the lowest depths of poverty, was glad of any payment, and dared not haggle over terms with his brothers' benefactress.

Nothing could have been more pitiful, more insufficient than such an education; and yet all went well, it all brought forth marvellous fruits, so little is needed for development if only there is something to develop.

The poor deacon, a tall, thin, bald man, was one of those enthusiasts whom neither years nor misfortunes can cure of their dreams; on the contrary, their troubles tend to keep them in a state of mystic contemplation. His faith, which approached fanaticism, was sincere and not without a shade of poetry. Between these two, the father of a hungry family and the forlorn child fed on alien bread, a good understanding sprang up at once.

The deacon was received in the princess's household as a defenceless, and at the same time mild-tempered pauper usually is received, with barely a nod, barely a condescending word. Even the 'lady companion' thought it necessary to show her disdain; while he scarcely noticed either them or their manners, taught his subjects with love, was touched by his pupil's readiness of understanding, and could move her to tears. This the old princess could not understand; she scolded the child for being a cry-baby and was greatly displeased, declaring that the deacon was upsetting her nerves. 'It's . . . I don't quite know what,' she said: 'it's not at all like a child!'

Meanwhile the old man's words were opening before the young creature another world, attractive in a very different way from that in which religion itself was turned into an affair of diet, reduced to keeping the fasts, and going to church at night, where fanaticism, nourished by fear, walked side by side with imposture, where everything was limited, artificial, and conventional, and oppressed the soul with its narrowness. The deacon put the Gospel into his pupil's hands—and it was long before she let it go again. The Gospel was the *first book* she read, and she read it over and over again, with her one friend, Sasha,[5] her old nurse's niece, now a young maid of the princess's.

Later on I knew Sasha very well. Where and how she had managed to develop I never could understand, born, as she was, between the coachman's quarters and the kitchen, and never leaving the maids' room, but developed she was, unusually so. She was one of those innocent victims who perish unnoticed in the servants' quarters, and more often then we suppose, are crushed by the state of being a serf.

---

[5] Vyrlin. (*A.S.*) Sasha is the affectionate diminutive form of both Alexander and Alexandra. (*R.*)

They perish not only without compensation, without commiseration, without an hour of brightness, without a joyful memory, but without knowing, without themselves suspecting, what is perishing in them and how much is dying with them.

Their mistress says with vexation: 'The wretched girl was just beginning to be trained to her work when she took to her bed and died.' . . . The seventy-year-old housekeeper grumbles: 'What are servants coming to nowadays? They are worse than any young lady,' and goes to the funeral dinner. The mother weeps and weeps and begins to drink—and that is the end of the business.

And we pass hurriedly by, seeing the terrible dramas enacted at our feet, thinking we have more important things to fill our time, and feeling that we have done our part with a few roubles and a kindly word. And then suddenly, astounded, we hear the heart-rending moan with which the broken spirit lets itself be heard of for all time, and as though awakening from sleep we ask ourselves whence came that spirit, that strength.

Princess Marya Alexeyevna killed her maid, unintentionally and unconsciously, of course; she worried her to death over trifles, broke her heart, oppressed her whole life, wore her out with humiliations and with rough churlish treatment. For several years she would not let her marry, and allowed it only when she could see consumption in her suffering face.

Poor Sasha, poor victim of the loathsome, accursed Russian life, defiled by serfdom, by death you escaped to freedom! And yet you were incomparably happier than others: in the harsh bondage of the princess's house you met a friend, and the affection of her whom you loved so immeasurably accompanied you invisibly to the grave. You cost her many tears; not long before her own death she still thought of you, and blessed your memory as the one bright image that had appeared in her childhood!

The two young girls (Sasha was a little the elder) used to get up early in the mornings when all the household was still asleep, read the Gospel and pray, going out into the courtyard under the open sky. They prayed for the princess and her lady-companion, besought God to soften their hearts; they invented ordeals for themselves, ate no meat for weeks together, dreamed of a nunnery and of the life beyond the grave.

Such mysticism is in keeping with adolescence, with the age in which everything is still a secret, still a religious mystery, when the awakening thought is still shining dimly through the mist of early morning, and the mist is not yet dissipated by experience or passion.

At quiet and gentle moments I loved in after years to hear of these childish prayers, with which one full life began and one unhappy existence ended. The image of the forlorn child outraged by coarse patronage, and of the *slave girl* outraged by the hopelessness of her situation, praying for their oppressors in the neglected courtyard, filled the heart with tenderness, and breathed a rare peace upon the spirit.

The pure and gracious being, whom none of her equals appreciated in the princess's senseless household, won, besides the devotion of the deacon and Sasha, a warm response and adoration from all the servants. These simple people saw in her more than a kind and affable young lady: they divined in her something higher for which they felt reverence; they had faith in her. The girls of the princess's household, when they were going to their weddings, would beg her to pin a ribbon on them with her own hands. One young maidservant—I remember her name was Yelena—was suddenly stricken with a stitch in the side; it turned out to be acute pleurisy; there was no hope of saving her, and the priest was sent for. The frightened girl kept asking her mother whether it was all over with her; the mother, sobbing, told her that God would soon summon her. Then the sick girl clung to her mother and besought her with bitter tears to fetch her young lady that she might come herself to bless her with the holy ikon for the other world. When she came the sick girl took her hand, laid it on her forehead, and repeated: 'Pray for me, pray for me!' The young girl, herself in tears, began praying in a low voice, and the sick girl died as she prayed. All in the room knelt round her, crossing themselves; Natalie closed the dead girl's eyes, kissed the cold forehead, and went out.[6]

---

[6] Among my papers are several letters of Sasha's* written between 1835 and 1836. Sasha had stayed in Moscow and her friend was in the country with the princess. I cannot read this simple, ecstatic babble of the heart without deep emotion. 'Can it be true,' she writes, 'that you are coming? Ah, if you really did come, I don't know what would happen to me. You would not believe how often I have thought of you, almost all my desires, all my thoughts, all, all, all are with you. . . . Ah, Natalya Alexandrovna, how beautiful you are, how sweet, how noble!—but I cannot express it. Truly, these are not studied words, they are straight from the heart. . . .'

In another letter she thanks her 'young lady' for writing so often. 'It is really too good, but there, that's you, you,' and she ends the letter with the words: 'They keep interrupting me, I embrace you, my angel, with true, immeasurable love. Give me your blessing!'

Only dry and ungifted natures know nothing of this romantic period; they are as much to be pitied as those frail and sickly beings in whom mysticism outlives youth and remains for ever. In our age this does not happen with realistic natures; but whence could the *secular* influence of the nineteenth century penetrate into the princess's house, where every crevice was so well caulked?

A crack was found, nevertheless.

My Korcheva cousin[7] used sometimes to come on a visit to the princess. She was fond of the 'little cousin', as one is fond of children, especially if they are unhappy, but she did not understand her. With amazement, almost with dread, she discovered later on her exceptional nature, and, impulsive in everything, at once determined to make up for her neglect. She begged from me Hugo, Balzac, or anything new I might have.

'The little cousin,' she said to me, 'is a genius, we ought to guide her onward!'

The 'big cousin'—and I cannot help smiling at this name for her, for she was a tiny creature—at once communicated to her protégée every stray thought in her own mind—Schiller's ideas and Rousseau's, revolutionary ideas picked up from me and the dreams of a girl in love picked up from herself. Then she secretly lent her French novels, verses, poems; they were for the most part books that had appeared since 1830. With all their defects, they stimulated thought, and baptised youthful hearts with the spirit and with fire. In the novels and stories, the poems and songs of that period, whether the author knew it or not, the vein of social feeling everywhere pulsed strongly: everywhere social sores were revealed and the groan of the hungry could be heard, the innocent galley-slaves of labour; even by that date their murmur and complaint was no longer feared as a crime.

I need hardly say that my cousin lent the books without any discrimination, without any explanations, and I think there was no harm in that; there are natures which never need help, support or guidance from others, who always walk most safely where there is no rail.

Another person who carried on the secular influence of my Korcheva cousin was soon added to the list. The princess at last made up her mind to engage a governess, and to avoid expense had taken on a young *Russian* girl[8] who had only just left a boarding-school.

Russian governesses are not thought much of with us; at any rate they were not in the 'thirties, yet for all their defects they are better than the majority of French girls from Switzerland, of courtesans on indefinite leave and retired actresses who catch at teaching in despair as a last means of earning their daily bread, a resource needing neither talent nor youth, nothing in fact but the ability to pronounce 'hrrra' and the manners *d'une dame de comptoir*, which in the provinces are often taken for 'good' manners. Russian governesses come from boarding-schools, or foundling hospitals, and so have had some sort of regular education, and are free from the *petit bourgeois* coating which the foreign women bring with them.

The French governesses of to-day must be distinguished from those who used to come to Russia before 1812. In those days France was less *bourgeois* and the women who came to Russia belonged to quite a different social stratum. To some extent they were the daughters of emigrants, of ruined noblemen, or widows of officers, often their deserted wives. Napoleon used to marry off his warriors in the way that our landowners marry their serfs, without much regard for love or inclination. He wanted, by these marriages, to unite his new gun-powder aristocracy with the old nobility; he wanted to knock his Skalozubs[9] into shape by means of their wives. Accustomed to blind obedience, they married without protest, but soon abandoned their wives, finding them too stiff for the festivities of the barracks and the bivouac. The poor women made their way to England, to Austria, to Russia. The old Frenchwoman who used to stay with the princess belonged to this earlier class of governess. She spoke with a smile in an exquisite style and never made use of a single strong expression. She was entirely made up of good manners and never forgot herself for a minute. I am convinced that even at night in her bed she was more preoccupied with teaching the proper way to sleep than with sleeping.

The young governess was an intelligent, alert, energetic girl with a good share of boarding-school enthusiasm and an innate feeling for what is fine. Active and high-spirited, she brought more life and movement into the existence of her pupil and friend.

---

[8] Emilia Aksberg. (*A.S.*)

[9] Skalozub, a character in Griboyedov's celebrated play, *Woe from Wit* (or perhaps better, 'Sorrow comes from having Sense'), is the typical coarse, ignorant, blustering military bully. (*Tr.*)

There had been a shade of mourning, of melancholy in the sad and depressing friendship with the wasting Sasha. Her company, together with the words of the deacon and the absence of every kind of diversion, was drawing the young girl away from the world and from people. The arrival of this third person was very timely, for she was young, full of life and gaiety, and at the same time sympathetic with everything visionary and romantic, and came in the nick of time: she drew her back to earth, to the true, the real soil.

At first the pupil to some extent adopted her Emilia's outward ways; a smile was more often to be seen on her face, and her conversation grew livelier; but within a year the natures of the two girls had occupied places that corresponded to the specific gravity of each. The nice, dreamy Emilia gave way before the stronger nature and was completely dominated by her pupil, saw with her eyes, thought her thoughts, lived in her smile and in her affection.

Before I had finished my studies at the university, I took to going more frequently to the princess's house. The younger girl seemed pleased when I came, and sometimes her cheeks glowed and her talk grew more animated, but she quickly withdrew into her usual pensive stillness, recalling the cold beauty of sculpture or Schiller's 'Mädchen aus der Fremde' who put a stop to every approach.

It was not unsociability or coldness, but an active inner life; not understood by others, she did not as yet understand herself, and had rather a presentiment than a knowledge of what was in her. In her lovely features there was still something incomplete, not fully expressed; they lacked a spark, a touch of the sculptor's chisel which would decide whether she was destined to pine and fade away in sandy soil, knowing neither herself nor life, or to reflect the glow of passion, to be enfolded by it, and to live, perhaps to suffer—certainly, indeed, to suffer, but *to live abundantly*.

I first saw the impress of life coming out on her half-childish face on the eve of our long separation.

Well I remember her eyes with quite a different light in them, and all her features with their significance transformed, as though penetrated by a new thought, a new fire . . . as though the secret had been guessed and the inner mist dissipated. This was[10] when I was in prison. A dozen times we said good-bye, and still we could not bear

---

[10] On 9th April, 1835. (*A.S.*)

M*

to part. At last my mother, who had come with Natalie[11] to the Krutitsky Barracks, resolutely got up to go. The young girl trembled, turned pale, squeezed my hand with unexpected strength, and repeated, turning away to hide her tears, 'Alexander, don't forget your sister.'

The gendarme saw them out and started his walking up and down. I flung myself on my bed and gazed long at the door behind which that bright apparition had vanished. 'No,' I thought, 'your brother will not forget you.'

The next day I was taken to Perm, but before I speak of our time of separation I shall tell of something else that prevented me, before my prison days, from understanding Natalie better and from being more friendly with her. I was in love!

Yes, I was in love, and the memory of that pure, youthful love is as dear to me as the memory of a spring day spent by the sea amid flowers and singing. It was a dream that wafted over me much that was lovely, and vanished as dreams usually do vanish!

I have mentioned already that there were few women in our circle, especially of the sort with whom I could have been on intimate terms: my affection for my Korcheva cousin, ardent at first, little by little became more even in tone. After her marriage we saw each other less often, and then she went away. A desire for a warmer, tenderer feeling than the affection of my men friends hovered undefined about my heart. Everything was ready, all that was lacking was 'she'. In one of the families of our acquaintance there was a young girl[12] with whom I quickly made friends. It was a strange chance that brought us together. She was engaged to be married, but some dissension suddenly arose and her fiancé abandoned her and went off to the other end of Russia. She was in despair, overcome with distress and morti-

---

[11] I know very well how affected the French translation of names sounds, but a name is a traditional thing and how is one to change it? Besides, all unSlavonic names are with us, as it were, truncated and less musical; we, educated to some extent, 'not in the law of our fathers',† in our youth 'romanticised' names, while the powers in authority 'Slavonicised' them. As a man is promoted and attains to influence at court, the letters in his name are changed—thus, for instance, Count Strogonov remained to the end of his days Sergey Grigorevich, but Prince Golitsyn was always called Sergiy Mikhaylovich. The last example of such a promotion we saw in General Rostovtsev, *so celebrated* in connection with the Fourteenth of December; throughout the reign of Nicholas Pavlovich he was Yakov, as was Yakov Dolgoruky, but with the accession of Alexander II he became Iakov, the same as the brother of our Lord!

† From *Graf Nulin*, by A. S. Pushkin. (*A.S.*)

[12] L. V. Passek. (*A.S.*)

fication. With deep and sincere sympathy I saw her being consumed by grief. Without daring to hint at the cause, I tried to comfort her and distract her mind, brought her novels, read them aloud to her, told her long stories, and sometimes neglected to prepare for my lectures at the university in order to stay longer with the distressed girl.

Little by little her tears fell less frequently, and from time to time a smile glimmered through them; her despair passed into a languid sadness. Soon she began to feel frightened for her past, she struggled with herself and defended it against the present, from a *point d'honneur* of the heart, as a soldier defends the flag, though he knows that the battle is lost. I saw these last clouds faintly lingering on the horizon and, myself carried away, with a beating heart, softly, softly drew the flag out of her hands, and when she ceased to cling to it I was in love. We believed in our love. She wrote verses to me, I wrote whole essays to her in prose, and then we dreamed together of the future, of exile, of prisons, for she was ready for anything. The external side of life never took a very clear shape in our imaginations; doomed to battle with a monstrous power, we felt success almost impossible. 'Be my Gaetana,' I said to her after reading Saintine's[13] 'The Mutilated Poet', and I used to fancy how she would accompany me to the Siberian mines.

'The Mutilated Poet' was the poet who wrote a lampoon upon Sixtus V and gave himself up when the Pope gave his word not to inflict the death penalty. Sixtus V ordered his tongue and hands to be cut off. The figure of the luckless victim, choked by the mass of ideas which swarmed in his brain and found no outlet, could not help attracting us in those days. The martyr's sad and exhausted eyes found peace when they rested with gratitude and some remnant of joy on the girl who had loved him before and did not abandon him in misfortune. Her name was Gaetana.

This first experience of love was soon over, but it was perfectly sincere. Perhaps, indeed, it was right for this love to pass, or it would have lost its finest, most fragrant worth, its innocent freshness, its nineteen-year-old charm. Lilies of the valley do not flower in winter.

And can it be, my Gaetana, that you do not recall our meeting with the same serene smile? Can it be that there is any bitterness mixed with your memory of me after twenty-two years? That would

---

[13] Xavier Saintine (1798-1865), a French writer of whose many plays and stories only *Picciola, or the Prisoner's Flower* is still well known. (*Tr.*)

be very grievous to me. And where are you, and how have you spent your life?

I have lived my life and now am trudging downhill, broken, and morally 'mutilated'. I seek no Gaetana, I go over the memories of the past and gladly meet your image among them. . . . Do you remember the window in the corner facing the little side street into which I had to turn, and how you always came to it to see me off, and how disappointed I was if you did not come, or moved away before it was time for me to turn?

But I should not want to meet you in reality; in my imagination you have remained with your youthful face, your *blond cendré* curls: remain as you were. And you, too, if you think of me, will remember a well-knit lad with sparkling eyes and fiery speech, and may you think of him like that and never know that the eyes have lost their lustre, that I have grown heavy, that my brow is furrowed, that long ago my face lost its former radiant, eager look which Ogarëv used to call 'the look of hope'. And, indeed, hope too is gone.

We ought to be for each other as we were then . . . neither Achilles nor Diana grows old. . . . I do not want to meet you as Larina met Princess Alina: [14]

> 'Do you remember Grandison?
> Cousin, how is Grandison?—
> Oh, Grandison! In Moscow, living at Semeon's.
> He visited me on Christmas Eve;
> A son of his was married lately.'

The last, flickering flame of love for a moment lit up the prison vault, warmed the heart with its old dreams, and then we each went our way. She went away to the Ukraine while I was setting off into exile. Since then I have had no news of her.

---

[14] From Pushkin's *Yevgeny Onegin*, Canto VII, Stanza 41. (*Tr.*)

Chapter 21

Separation

'Ah, people, wicked people,
You separated their . . .'

So my first letter to Natalie ended, and it is noteworthy that,
frightened by the word 'hearts', I did not write it, and signed
the letter 'your brother'.

How dear 'my sister' was then to me and how continually in my
thoughts is clear from the fact that I wrote to her from Nizhny,
from Kazan and from Perm on the very day after my arrival there.
The word 'sister' expressed all that was recognised in our affection;
I liked it immensely and I like it now, used not as the limit of the
feelings but, on the contrary, as the mingling of them all; in it are
united friendship, love, the tie of kinship, a common devotion, surroundings, family, and habitual association. I had called no one by
that name before, and it was so dear to me that in later years, too,
I often used it to Natalie.

Before I fully understood our relationship, and perhaps just because I did not understand it fully, a different temptation awaited
me which did not pass for me as such a luminous spell as was my
encounter with Gaetana; a temptation that humbled me and cost
me much regret and inner distress.

Having very little experience of life, and being flung into a world
completely alien to me, after nine months of prison, I lived carelessly at first and, without looking round; the new country, the new
surroundings dazzled me. My social position was transformed. In
Perm and in Vyatka I was regarded quite otherwise than I had
been in Moscow; there I had been a young man living in my
father's house, here in this slough I stood on my own feet, and was
accepted as a government official, although I was not quite one. It
was not hard for me to perceive that without much effort I might

319

play the part of a man of the world in the drawing-rooms beyond the Volga and the Kama, and be a lion in Vyatka society.

In Perm, before I had time to look about me, the landlady to whom I had gone to take lodgings asked me whether I wanted a kitchen garden and whether I was keeping a cow! It was a question by which I could, with horror, judge the depth of my descent from the academic heights of student life. But at Vyatka I made acquaintance with all the *monde*, especially with the younger people of the merchant class, which is much better educated in these remote provinces than in those nearer the centre, though they are no less given to dissipation. Turned aside from my usual pursuits by my work in the office, I led a restlessly idle life; owing to my peculiar impressionability, or perhaps mobility, of character and absence of experience, adventures of all sorts might well be expected.

From a coquettish passion *de l'approbativité* I tried to please right and left indiscriminately, forced my sympathies, made friends over a dozen words, became far more intimate than I need have, recognised my mistake a month or two later, said nothing, out of tact, and dragged a weary chain of false relationships until it was broken by an absurd quarrel in which I was blamed for capricious impatience, ingratitude, and inconstancy.

At Vyatka I did not live alone at first. A strange, comic figure, which from time to time appears at all the turning points of my life, at all its important events, the person who nearly gets drowned to make me acquainted with Ogarëv, and waves a handkerchief from Russia when I cross the frontier at Taurogen—K. I. Sonnenberg—lived with me at Vyatka; I forgot to mention this when I described my exile.

This was how it happened: at the moment when I was being sent to Perm, Sonnenberg was preparing to go to the Fair at Irbit. My father, who always liked to complicate anything simple, suggested to Sonnenberg that he should go to Perm and there *furnish my house*, undertaking in return to pay his travelling expenses.

At Perm Sonnenberg zealously set to work, that is, to purchasing unnecessary articles, all sorts of crockery, saucepans, cups, glass, and provisions. He went himself to Obva to procure a Vyatka horse *ex ipso fonte*. When everything was complete I was transferred to Vyatka. We sold, at half-price, the goods he had purchased and left Perm. Sonnenberg, conscientiously carrying out my father's wishes, thought it his duty to go to Vyatka too to furnish my house. My father was so well pleased with his devotion and self-sacrifice that he offered him a salary of a hundred roubles a month so long as he would stay with me. This was more profitable and more secure than Irbit—and he was in no hurry to leave me.

At Vyatka he bought not one but three horses, one of which belonged to himself, though it too was bought at my father's expense. These horses elevated us extraordinarily in the eyes of Vyatka society. Karl Ivanovich, as I have already said, was, in spite of his fifty years and of considerable defects in his looks, a great dangler after women, and was agreeably convinced that any girl or woman who came near him risked the fate of a moth flying near a lighted candle. Karl Ivanovich had no intention of wasting the effect produced by the horses, but tried to turn them to his advantage in the erotic department. Moreover, all our circumstances favoured his designs; we had a verandah looking out into a courtyard beyond which there was a garden. From ten o'clock in the morning Sonnenberg, arrayed in Kazan *ichigi*,[1] a gold embroidered *tyubiteyka*,[2] and a Caucasian *beshmet*,[3] with an immense amber mouthpiece between his lips, would sit on watch, pretending to be reading. The *tyubiteyka* and the amber mouthpiece were all aimed at three young ladies who lived in the next house. The young ladies for their part were interested in the new arrivals and gazed with curiosity at the oriental-looking doll smoking on the verandah. Karl Ivanovich knew when and how they secretly lifted their blind, thought that things were going successfully—and tenderly blew a gentle stream of smoke in the direction of the objects of his devotion.

Soon the garden gave us the opportunity of making our neighbours' acquaintance. Our landlord had three houses, and the garden was common to them all. Two of the houses were occupied: we lived in one of them, together with the landlord and his stepmother, a fat, flabby widow who looked after him so maternally and with such jealousy that it was only on the sly that he ventured to speak to the ladies of the garden. In the second house lived the young ladies and their parents, and the third house stood empty. Within a week Karl Ivanovich was quite at home with the female society of our garden. He constantly spent several hours a day swinging the young ladies in the swing and running to fetch their capes and

---

[1] Half-boots. (*R.*)
[2] Skull-cap. (*R.*)
[3] Under-tunic. (*R.*)

sunshades, in a word he was *aux petits soins*. The young ladies behaved more foolishly with him than with anybody else, just because he was more beyond suspicion than Caesar's wife: a mere glance at him was enough to check the most audacious piece of scandal.

In the evenings I used to walk into the garden, too, from that herd instinct which makes people do what others are doing, apart from any inclination. To the garden came, besides the lodgers, their acquaintances; the chief subject of talk and interest was flirtation and spying on one another. Karl Ivanovich devoted himself to sentimental espionage with the vigilance of a Vidocq[4], and always knew who walked with whom most often, and who looked meaningly at whom. I was a terrible stumbling-block for all the secret police in our garden; the ladies and the men wondered at my reserve, and for all their efforts could not discover whom I was making up to, and who particularly attracted me; and indeed it was not easy to do so, for I was not making up to anyone and I did not find any of the young ladies particularly attractive. In the end they were annoyed and offended by this, they began to consider me haughty and a quiz, and the friendliness of the young ladies grew noticeably cooler—though everyone of them tried her most deadly glances upon me when we were alone.

While things were like this, Karl Ivanovich informed me one morning that the landlady's cook had opened the shutters of the third house that morning and was cleaning the windows. The house had been taken by a family who had arrived in the town.

The garden was absorbed exclusively in details concerning the new arrivals. The unknown lady, who was either tired from the journey or had not yet had time to unpack, refused, as though to spite us, to show herself outside. Everyone tried to see her at a window or in the front hall, some succeeded, while others watched for days together in vain; those who saw her reported her to be pale and languid, interesting, in short, and good-looking. The young ladies said that she looked melancholy and sickly. A young clerk in the governor's office, a scamp and a quite intelligent fellow, was the only one who

---

[4] The reference is probably to Bulgarin, a journalist in close relations with Benckendorf (Chief of the Secret Police). This Bulgarin made many petty personal attacks on Pushkin, who in a well-known poem addresses him by the name Vidocq-Figlyarin. (*Tr.*) F.-E. Vidocq (1775-1859) was head of the Sûreté, after being himself a criminal. (*R.*)

knew the strangers. He had once served in the same province with them, and everyone besieged him with questions.

This sprightly clerk, pleased at knowing what other people did not, held forth endlessly upon the charms of their new neighbour. He praised her to the skies, and declared that you could see she was a lady from Petersburg or Moscow.

'She is intelligent,' he repeated, 'nice, cultured, but she won't look at fellows like us. Ah, upon my soul,' he added, suddenly turning to me, 'there's a happy thought; you must keep up the honour of Vyatka society and get up a flirtation with her. . . . Why, you are from Moscow, you know, and in exile; no doubt you write verses. She's a godsend for you.'

'What rot you're talking,' I said, laughing, but I flushed crimson : I longed to see her.

A few days later I did meet her in the garden and found that she really was a very attractive blonde. The gentleman who had talked about her introduced me. I was agitated and was as little able to hide it as my sponsor could his smile.

The shyness of vanity passed and I got to know her; she was very unhappy and, deceiving herself by an assumed composure, was pining away and languishing in a kind of inertia of the heart.

Madame R——[5] was one of those secretly passionate natures only to be met among women of a fair complexion. The ardour of their hearts is masked by the mildness and gentleness of their features; they turn pale with emotion, and their eyes do not flash but rather grow dim when feeling brims over. Her languid eyes looked exhausted with a vague craving, her unsatisfied breast heaved unevenly. There was something restless and electric in her whole being. Often when walking in the garden she would suddenly turn pale and, inwardly troubled or alarmed, would answer absent-mindedly and hurry into the house. It was just at those moments that I liked to look at her.

I soon saw what was passing within her. She did not love her husband and could not love him; she was twenty-five, he was over fifty, yet that disparity she might have got over, but the difference of education, of interests, of temperament, was too great.

Her husband scarcely ever came out of his room; he was a dry,

[5] P. P. Medvedev. (*A.S.*)

harsh, elderly man, an official with pretensions to being a landowner, irritable like all invalids and like most people who have lost their fortune. She had been sixteen when she married him and then he had some property, but afterwards he had lost everything at cards and was forced to go into the service for a living. Two years before he was transferred to Vyatka he began to fall into ill-health; a sore on his leg developed into caries. The old man became surly and ill-humoured, was afraid of his illness, and looked with alarmed, helpless suspicion at his wife. She waited upon him with mournful self-sacrifice, but she did this as her duty. Her children could not make amends for everything; her unoccupied heart longed for something more.

One evening, speaking of one thing and another, I said that I should very much like to send my cousin my portrait, but that I could not find a man in Vyatka who could hold a pencil.

'Let me try,' said the lady. 'I used to draw rather successful portraits in pencil.'

'I shall be delighted. When?'

'To-morrow before dinner, if you like.'

'Of course. I will come to-morrow at one o'clock.'

All this was in her husband's presence; he said not a word.

The next morning I got a note from Madame R——. It was the first I ever received from her. She very courteously and circumspectly informed me that her husband was displeased at her having offered to draw my portrait, begged me not to judge harshly of the whims of an invalid, said that he must not be worried, and, in conclusion, offered to make the sketch some other day, saying nothing about it to her husband, that he might not be upset by it.

I thanked her warmly, perhaps excessively warmly. I did not accept her offer to draw the portrait in secret, but nevertheless these two notes drew us much closer together. Her attitude to her husband, upon which I should never have touched, was openly expressed; a secret understanding, a league against him, was involuntarily formed between us.

In the evening I went to see them—not a word was said about the portrait. If her husband had been cleverer he must have guessed what had happened; but he was not clever. I thanked her with my eyes, and she answered with a smile.

Soon they moved into another part of the town. The first time

I went to see them I found her alone in a barely furnished drawing-room; she was sitting at the piano, and her eyes were tear-stained. I begged her to go on; but the music dragged, she played false notes, her hands trembled, the colour left her face.

'How stifling it is!' she said, getting up quickly from the piano.

In silence I took her hand, a weak, feverish hand; her head, like a flower grown too heavy, as though passively obeying some external force, sank on my breast, she pressed her forehead against me and instantly fled.

The next day I received a rather frightened note from her, trying to gloss over the evening before; she wrote of the fearfully nervous state in which she had been when I came in and of scarcely remembering what had happened. She apologised for her behaviour—but the thin veil of her words could not conceal the passion that blazed between the lines.

I went to see them; that day her husband was better, though he had not got up from his bed since they had been in their new quarters. I was excited, played the fool, fired off witty jokes, talked all sorts of nonsense, made the invalid almost die with laughter, and of course all this was to smother her embarrassment and my own. Moreover, I felt that the laughter was intoxicating and captivating her.

Two weeks went by.[6] Her husband was less and less well, and at half past nine he would ask visitors to leave. His weakness, emaciation and pain increased. One evening, about nine, I said good-night to the sick man, and Madame R—— came to see me out. In the drawing-room a full moon laid three oblique bands of pale mauve across the floor. I opened the window: the air was pure and fresh, and I was bathed in it.

'What an evening!' I said. 'And how I wish I weren't going.'

She came to the window.

'Stay here for a bit.'

'I can't. This is when I change his bandage.'

'Come back afterwards: I'll wait for you.'

She was silent, and I took her hand.

'Well, come, then. I beg you . . . you'll come?'

---

[6] The following is omitted from the Berlin edition of 1921, and therefore by Constance Garnett. In the Academy of Sciences' edition of H.'s complete works, Vol. IV (1956), pp. 339-41, and in the Moscow edition of *Byloye i Dumy*, (1958) Vol. I, pp. 334-5, it is restored to the text. (*R.*)

'I really can't. I put an overall on first.'

'Come in an overall. I've found you in an overall in the mornings, many times.'

'But if someone sees you?'

'Who? Your manservant is drunk: let him go to bed; and your Darya loves you more than she does your husband, truly. And she's a friend of mine. Anyhow, where's the harm? Goodness, it's only just after nine: you wanted to ask me to do something for you, and asked me to wait. . . .'

'In the dark. . . ?'

'Have some candles brought. Though this night is as good as day.' She still hesitated.

'Come, darling, come!' I whispered in her ear, calling her that for the first time.

She shivered.

'I'll come—but only for a minute.'

I waited for more than half an hour. All was quiet in the house: I could hear the old man sighing and coughing, his slow talk, a table being moved. The drunk servant was whistling as he prepared his bed on a chest in the hall; he swore, and in a minute began to snore. The heavy tread of the house-maid, as she left the bedroom, was the last sound I heard. Then silence, a groan from the sick man; and silence again. . . . Then a rustle, the floor creaked, light footsteps, and a white overall glimmered in the doorway.

She was so violently agitated that at first she could not pronounce a single word; her lips were cold and her hands like ice. I could feel how hard her heart was beating.

'I've carried out your[7] wish,' she said at last. 'Now let me go. . . . Good-bye . . . good-bye, for God's sake—and you go home,' she added in a voice of sad entreaty.

I embraced her and pressed her firmly to my breast.

'My dear . . . but go!'

That was impossible. *Troppo tardi.* . . . To leave her at a moment when her heart and mine were beating so—that would have been beyond human power, and very foolish. . . . I did not go: she remained. . . . The moon traced out its bands in a different direction. She sat in the window and wept bitterly. . . . I kissed her wet eyes and wiped them with the locks of her hair that fell on her dull, pale

---

[7] *i.e.* 'thy'. She now uses the more familiar form. (*R.*)

shoulder, into which the moonlight was absorbed and lost without reflection in the dim, tender lustre.

I was sorry to leave her in tears, and I gabbled some nonsense to her in a half whisper. She looked up at me, and so much happiness gleamed in her eyes through the tears that I smiled. She seemed to follow my thought, and covered her face with both hands and stood up. . . . Now it really was time for me to go: I seized her hands, kissed them and her face over and over again—and went.

The maid let me out quietly, and I went by her without daring to look her in the face. The moon, grown heavy, was setting in a great, red ball. The dawn was beginning. It was cool and fresh, and the wind blew right in my face: I breathed it in deeper and deeper, for I needed to cool myself. As I approached my house the sun came up, and the good people I met were surprised that I had got up so early 'to take advantage of the good weather'.[8]

This orgy of love lasted for a month; then my heart seemed to become tired, exhausted; I began to have moments of depression; I studiously concealed them, tried not to believe in them, wondered what was passing within me—while still love was cooling, cooling.

I began to feel constrained by the presence of the old man. I found his company uncomfortable and repellent. Not that I felt myself in the wrong as regards the man who had the civil and ecclesiastical rights of property in a woman who could not love him and whom he was incapable of loving, but my double part struck me as degrading; hypocrisy and duplicity are the vices most foreign to my nature. While burgeoning passion was in the ascendant I thought of nothing, but as soon as it was somewhat cooler I began to falter.

One morning Matvey came into my bedroom with the news that old R—— 'had passed away'. I was overcome by a strange feeling at this news; I turned on the other side and was in no hurry to dress. I did not want to see the dead man. Vitberg came in, quite ready to go out. 'What?' he said, 'you're still in bed! Haven't you heard what's happened? I expect poor Madame R—— is all alone, so let us go and make enquiries; hurry up and dress.' I dressed—and we went.

We found Madame R—— in a swoon or in a sort of nervous lethargy. There was no pretence about it: her husband's death had recalled her helpless situation; she was left alone with her children in a strange town, without money, without friends or relations. Besides, she had on previous occasions fallen into this cataleptic condition, which was brought on by some violent shock and lasted several hours. On these occasions she would lie pale as death, with her face cold and her eyes closed, from time to time giving a gasp, not breathing at all in the intervals.

Not one woman came to help her, to show her sympathy, or to look after the children or the house. Vitberg remained with her; the prophetic clerk and I set about seeing to things.

The old man, looking black and shrunken, lay in his uniform on the drawing-room table, frowning as though he was angry with me. We laid him in the coffin, and two days later lowered him into the grave. After the funeral we went back to the dead man's house; the children in their black frocks with crape weepers huddled in the corner, more surprised and frightened than grieved: they whispered to each other and walked on tiptoe. Madame R—— sat with her head leaning on her hands, as though pondering, and did not say a single word.

In that drawing-room, on that sofa I had waited for her, listened to the sick man's groans and the drunken servant's swearing. Now everything was so black. . . . In the midst of the funereal surroundings and the smell of incense, I was haunted by confused and gloomy recollections of words and minutes of which I still could not think without tenderness.

Little by little her grief subsided and she looked more resolutely at her situation; then, little by little, other thoughts, too, began to light up her careworn and despondent face. Her eyes rested upon me with a sort of agitated inquiry, as though she were waiting for something . . . a question . . . an answer. . . .

I said nothing—and she, frightened, alarmed, began to feel doubts.

Then I saw that her husband had in reality been an excuse for me in my own eyes—love had burnt itself out in me. It was not that I had no feeling for her, far from it, but the feeling was not what she needed. My thoughts were now occupied by ideas of a different order, and that outburst of passion seemed to have possessed me simply to make another feeling clear to myself. Only one thing can I say in my defence—I was perfectly sincere in my infatuation.

While I had lost my head and did not know what to do, while with cowardly weakness I was waiting for a change to be brought about by time or circumstance, time and circumstance complicated my situation still further.

Tyufyayev, seeing the helpless condition of a young, beautiful widow cast away without any support in a remote town in which she was a stranger, like the true 'father of the province', showed her the tenderest solicitude. At first we all thought that he felt real sympathy for her. But soon Madame R—— noticed with horror that his attentions were by no means so simple. Two or three dissolute governors before him had kept Vyatka ladies as mistresses, and Tyufyayev, being used to such women, lost no time but at once began making declarations of love to her. Madame R—— of course responded with cold disdain and mockery to his servile blandishments. Tyufyayev would not consider himself rebuffed, but persisted in his insolent attentions. Seeing, however, that he was making little progress, he gave her to understand that her children's future lay in his hands, that without his assistance she could not place them in schools at government expense, and that he on his side would not exert himself in her favour if she did not adopt a less chilly attitude to him. The insulted woman sprang up like a wounded wild beast. 'Kindly leave my house and don't dare to set foot in it again,' she said, pointing to the door.

'Ough, how angry you are!' said Tyufyayev, trying to turn things off with a jest.

'Pëtr, Pëtr,' she shouted into the hall, and the terrified Tyufyayev, fearing a public scandal fled to his carriage, abashed and humiliated, gasping with fury.

In the evening Madame R—— told Vitberg and me all that had happened. Vitberg realised at once that her gallant, put to flight and insulted, would not leave the poor woman in peace; Tyufyayev's character was pretty well known to us all. Vitberg resolved to save her at all costs.

Persecutions soon began. The petition with regard to the children was written in such a way that refusal was inevitable. The landlord and the shopkeepers demanded payment with particular insistence. God knows what might not be expected; the man who had done Petrovsky to death in a madhouse[9] was not to be trifled with.

Though burdened with an immense family and weighed down by poverty, Vitberg did not hesitate for one minute, but invited

[9] See p. 227. (R.)

Madame R—— to move with her children into his house two or three days after his wife's arrival at Vyatka. In his house Madame R—— was safe, so great was the moral power of this exile. His inflexible will, his noble appearance, his fearless words, his scornful smile were dreaded even by the Vyatka Shemyaka.[10]

I lived in a separate apartment in the same house and dined at Vitberg's table, so we two found ourselves under the same roof, just when we ought to have been oceans apart.

In this close proximity she saw that there was no bringing back the past.

Why had it been precisely I whom she met, when at that time I was so unstable? She might have been happy: she deserved to be happy. The sorrowful past was over; a new life of love and harmony was so possible for her! Poor woman! Was it my fault that this storm-cloud of love, which had swooped down upon me so irresistibly, had blown upon me with its fiery breath, had intoxicated me and carried me away—and had then dispersed?

I lived in a state of alarm. Perplexed, foreseeing misfortune, and dissatisfied with myself, again I turned to dissipation and sought distraction in noise, was vexed at finding it and vexed at not finding it, and waited for a few lines from Natalie in Moscow as for a breath of pure air in the midst of sultry heat. The gentle image of the child on the verge of womanhood rose brighter and brighter above all this ferment of passion. My outburst of passion for Madame R—— made my own heart clear to me and revealed its secret.

More and more absorbed by my feeling for my far-away cousin, I had not clearly analysed the sentiment that bound me to her. I was used to the feeling and did not watch closely to see whether it had changed or not.

My letters became more and more troubled; on the one hand I felt deeply not only the wrong I had done Madame R——, but the fresh wrong I did in the lying of which I was guilty by my silence. It seemed to me that I had fallen, that I was unworthy of any other love . . . while my love was growing and growing.

The name of *sister* began to fret me; affection now was not enough for me: that calm emotion seemed cold. Her love was apparent in every line of her letters, but now that did not satisfy me. I needed not only the love but the very word itself, and I wrote:

[10] Shemyaka, Dmitry Yurevich (1420-53), appanage prince of Zvenigorod. This name came to be used for an unjust, mercenary judge. (*A.S.*)

'I am going to put a strange question to you. Do you believe that the feeling you have for me is only affection? Do you believe that the feeling I have for you is only affection? *I don't believe it.*'

'You seem somewhat agitated,' she answered. 'I knew your letter frightened you more than it frightened me. Set your mind at rest, my dear, it has changed absolutely nothing in me; it could not make me love you either more or less.'

But the word had been uttered: 'The mist has vanished,' she writes; 'all is clear and bright again.'

With unclouded joy she gave herself up to the feeling that had been given its name; her letters are one youthful song of love rising from a childish lisp to lyrical heights.

'Perhaps at this moment,' she writes, 'you are sitting in your study, not writing, not reading, but pensively smoking a cigar, and your eyes are fixed on the vague distance and you have no answer for the greeting of anyone who comes in. Where are your thoughts? What are you seeking to see? Do not answer, let them come to me. . . .'

'Let us be children, let us fix an hour for both of us to be in the open air, an hour in which we can both be sure that nothing separates us but distance. At eight o'clock in the evening you, too, are surely free? Or else—what happened once before: I stepped out into the porch—and came back at once thinking that you were in the room.'

'Looking at your letters, at your portrait[11], thinking of my letters, of my bracelet[12], I have wished I could skip a hundred years and see what their fate would be. The things which have been for us holy relics, which have healed us, body and soul, with which we have talked and which have to some extent deputised for us to each other in absence; all these weapons with which we have defended ourselves from others, from the blows of fate, from ourselves, what will they be when we are gone? Will their virtue, their soul remain in them? Will they awaken, will they warm some other heart, will they tell the story of us, of our sufferings, of our love, will they win the reward of a single tear? How sad I feel when I imagine that your portrait will one day hang unknown in someone's study,

[11] A portrait of H. by A. L. Vitberg, commissioned for Natalya's birthday, 22nd October, 1836. (*A.S.*)
[12] Natalya had sent the bracelet to H. (*A.S.*)

or that a child perhaps will play with it, and break the glass and efface the features.'

My letters were not like this[13]; in the midst of complete, enraptured love there is a note of bitter vexation with myself and repentance; the dumb reproach of Madame R—— was gnawing at my heart and troubling the clear radiance of my feeling; I seemed to myself a liar, and yet I had not been lying.

How could I make my avowal? How was I to tell Madame R—— in January that in August I had been mistaken in telling her of my love? How could she believe in the truth of my story—a new love would have been easier to understand, betrayal would have been simpler. How the far-away image of her who was absent could enter into conflict with the present, how the stream of another love could have flowed through that furnace and have emerged stronger and more recognisable—all that I did not understand myself, but I felt that it was all true.

Finally Madame R—— herself with the elusive agility of a lizard swerved away from any serious explanation; she had an inkling of danger, was seeking an answer to the enigma, and at the same time was fending off the truth. It was as though she foresaw that my words would reveal terrible truths, after which everything would be finished, and she cut short all talk at the point where it became dangerous.

At first she looked about her, and for a few days thought she had found her rival in a nice, lively young German girl whom I liked as one likes a child, and with whom I was at ease just because it had never entered her head to flirt with me, nor mine to flirt with her. In a week she saw that Paulina was not at all dangerous. But I cannot go further without saying a word about the latter.

In the government dispensary at Vyatka there was a German chemist, and there was nothing surprising about that, but what was

---

[13] The difference between the style of Natalie's letters and mine is very great, especially in the early part of our correspondence; afterwards it was less unequal and in the end becomes similar. In my letters, together with genuine feeling there are affected expressions, far-fetched high-flown phrases; the influence of the school of Hugo and the new French novelists is apparent. There is nothing of the sort in her letters: her language is simple, poetic, and sincere, the only influence that can be discerned in it is the influence of the Gospel. At that time I was still trying to write in the grand style and wrote badly, because it was not my own language. A life in spheres cut off from practical experience, and too much reading, prevent a young man for years from speaking and writing naturally and simply. Intellectual maturity only begins when the style is established and has taken its final form.

surprising is that his assistant was Russian and was called Bolman. With this man I became acquainted; he was married to the daughter of a Vyatka government clerk, a lady who had the longest, thickest, and most beautiful hair I have ever seen. The dispenser himself, Ferdinand Rulkovius, was absent at first, and Bolman and I used to drink together various 'fizzing drinks' and artistic cordials compounded by the pharmacist. The dispenser was away in Reval; there he made the acquaintance of a young girl and offered her his hand; the girl, who hardly knew him, rushed into marriage with him, as generally happens to girls, and to German girls in particular; she had no notion even into what wilds he was taking her. But when after the wedding they had to start off, she was overcome by fear and despair. To comfort his bride, the dispenser invited a young girl of seventeen, a distant relation of his wife, to go with them to Vyatka. She, even more precipitately, and with no more idea of what was meant by Vyatka, consented. Neither of the German girls spoke a word of Russian, and in Vyatka there were not four men who spoke German. Even the teacher of that language in the high school did not know it, a fact which surprised me so much that I actually ventured to ask him how he managed to teach it.

'With the grammar,' he answered, 'and with dialogues.'

He further explained that he was really a teacher of mathematics, but that, since there was no post vacant, he was teaching German meanwhile, and that he received, however, only half the salary.[14] The German girls were dying of *ennui*, and seeing a man who, if he could not speak German well, could at least express himself intelligibly, were greatly delighted, regaled me with coffee and some sort of *kalte Schale*, told me all their secrets, hopes and desires, and within two days called me their friend and treated me still more hospitably to sweet, floury, cinnamon-cakes. Both were fairly well educated, that is, they knew Schiller by heart, played the piano, and sang German songs. There the likeness between them ended. The dispen-

[14] On the other hand, the enlightened government appointed as French master in the same Vyatka high school the celebrated Orientalist Vernikovsky, who was a colleague of Kovalevsky's and Mickiewicz's and was exiled in connection with the case of the Philarets.†

† The Philarets or 'lovers of virtue' formed a secret students' society at Vilna University in the first quarter of the nineteenth century. Their object was to promote learning, to help the poor, and to preach ideals of goodness and justice. Towjanski and Mickiewicz were members of it. (*Tr.*) In 1822-3 many of them were imprisoned, exiled or ordered to serve as private soldiers. (*A.S.*)

ser's wife was a tall, fair, lymphatic woman, very good-looking but sleepy and listless; she was extremely good-natured and, indeed, with her physique it would have been hard to be anything else. Being once convinced that her husband was her husband, she loved him quietly and steadily, looked after the kitchen and the linen, read novels in her spare moments, and in due time successfully bore the chemist a daughter with white eyebrows and eyelashes, who was scrofulous.

Her friend, a short, swarthy brunette, vigorously healthy, with big, black eyes and an air of independence, was a beauty of the sturdy peasant type; a great deal of energy was apparent in her words and movements, and when at times the dispenser, a dull, close-fisted fellow, made somewhat discourteous observations to his wife, and she listened to them with a smile on her lips and a tear on her eyelash, Paulina would flush crimson and give the irate husband such a look that he would instantly subside, pretend to be very busy, and go off to his laboratory to pound and mix all sorts of nasty things for the restoration of the health of the officials of Vyatka.

I liked the simple-hearted girl who knew how to stand up for herself, and I do not know how it happened, but it was to her I first talked of my love and translated some of Natalie's letters. Only one who has lived for long years with people who are complete strangers know how precious are these heart-to-heart talks. I rarely talk of my feelings, but there are moments, even now, when the longing to speak out becomes unbearable, and at that time I was four-and-twenty, and I had only just realised my love. I could bear separation, I could have borne silence too, but, meeting with another child on the threshold of womanhood, in whom everything was so unaffectedly simple, I could not restrain myself from blurting out my secret to her. And how grateful to me she was for this, and how much good she did me!

I was sometimes wearied by Vitberg's conversation, which was always serious, and, since I was fretted by my difficult relationship with Madame R——, I could not be at my ease with her. In the evening I often used to go off to Paulina, read foolish stories aloud to her, listen to her ringing laugh and to her singing, especially for my benefit, 'Das Mädchen aus der Fremde'—by which she and I understood another 'maiden from a strange land'; and the clouds were dissipated, there was an unfeigned gaiety, an un-

troubled serenity in my heart, and I would go home at peace.
Then the dispenser, after stirring his last mixture and smearing his
last plaster with ointment, would arrive to bore me with absurd
political inquiries—not, however, before he had drunk off his 'medicine' and eaten the herring salad prepared by the little white hands
der Frau Apothekerin.

Madame R—— suffered, while I with pitiful weakness waited
for time to bring some chance solution, and prolonged the half-
deception. A thousand times I wanted to go to Madame R——,
to throw myself at her feet, to tell her everything, to face her wrath,
her contempt . . . but it was not indignation that I feared—I should
have been glad of that—I feared her tears. One must have experienced much evil to be able to endure a woman's tears, to be able
to doubt while they trickle still warm over the flushed cheek. Besides,
her tears would have been genuine.

A good deal of time passed like this. It began to be rumoured
that my exile might soon come to an end. The day no longer seemed
so remote on which I should fling myself into a chaise and dash off
to Moscow; familiar faces hovered before my eyes and among them,
foremost of them, the cherished features; but scarcely had I abandoned myself to these dreams when the pale, sad form of Madame
R—— would appear at the other side of the chaise with tear-stained
eyes, full of pain and reproach, and my joy was dimmed: I felt sorry
for her, mortally sorry.

I could no longer remain in a false position, and plucking up
all my courage I resolved to break out of it. I wrote her a full confession. Warmly, frankly, I told her the whole truth. On the next
day she said she was ill and did not leave her room. All the sufferings
of a criminal, all the fear that he will be detected, I went through
on that day. She had another attack of her nervous stupor—I dared
not visit her.

I needed a greater penance. I shut myself up with Vitberg in my
study and told him my whole story. At first he was astonished, then
he listened to me not as a judge but as a friend, did not torment me
with questions, did not preach to me with stale morality, but devoted
himself to helping me find means to soften the blow—he alone could
do that. His affection was very warm for those of whom he was fond.
I had been afraid of his rigorous morals, but his affection for me
and for Madame R—— completely outweighed that. Yes, in his

hands I could leave the unhappy woman to whose disconsolate existence I had given the finishing blow; in him she found strong moral support and authority. She respected him like a father.

In the morning Matvey gave me a note. I had scarcely slept all night. With a trembling hand I broke the seal. She wrote gently, in a noble and deeply mournful spirit; the flowers of my eloquence had not concealed the asp beneath them; in her words of resignation could be heard the stifled moan of a wounded heart, the cry of pain, repressed by a supreme effort. She blessed me on my way to my new life, wished me happiness, called Natalie a sister, and held out a pleading hand to us for forgetfulness of the past and friendship for the future—as though she had been to blame!

Sobbing, I read her letter over and over again. *Qual cuor tradisti!*

Later on I met her. She gave me the hand of friendship, but we felt uncomfortable; each of us had left something unsaid: there was something that each of us tried to avoid alluding to.

A year ago I heard of her death.

When I left Vyatka I was tormented for a long time by the memory of Madame R——. When I regained my composure I set to work to write a story of which she was the heroine. I described a young nobleman of the period of Catherine who has abandoned the woman who loves him and married another. She pines away and dies. The news of her death is a heavy blow to him, he becomes sombre and melancholy, and eventually goes out of his mind. His wife, who is the ideal of gentleness and self-sacrifice, after trying everything, leads him in one of his quieter moments to the Devichy Convent and kneels down with him at the unhappy woman's grave, asking for her forgiveness and intercession. From the windows of the convent the words of a prayer reach them, soft feminine voices sing of forgiveness—and the young man recovers. The story was a failure. At the time when I wrote it Madame R—— had no thought of coming to Moscow, and the only man who guessed that there had been anything between us was the 'wandering German', K. I. Sonnenberg. After my mother's death in 1851 we heard no word of him. In 1860 a tourist, describing his acquaintance with Karl Ivanovich, now a man of eighty, showed me a letter from him. In a postscript the old man told him of the death of Madame R—— and said that *my brother* had had her buried in the Devichy Convent!

I need hardly say that neither of them knew of the story I wrote.

Chapter 22

In Moscow while I was Away

My peaceful life at Vladimir was soon troubled by news from Moscow which now reached me from all sides and distressed me deeply. To make this intelligible I must go back to 1834.

The day after I was arrested in 1834 was the name-day of my aunt, the princess, and so when Natalie had parted from me in the graveyard she had said: 'Until to-morrow'. She was expecting me, and several members of the family had arrived, when suddenly my cousin appeared and told them the full details of my arrest. She was shocked by this news, so utterly unexpected; she got up to go into another room, and after taking two steps fell unconscious on the floor. The princess saw it all and understood it all; she determined to oppose this dawning love by every means in her power.

What for?

I do not know: she had recently, that is since I had finished my studies, been very well disposed to me; but my arrest and rumours of our *free-thinking* attitude, of our betrayal of the Orthodox Church by entering the Saint-Simon 'sect' infuriated her; from that time forward she never spoke of me except as 'the political criminal' or 'that unfortunate son of my brother Ivan'. The Senator had to use all his authority to induce her to allow Natalie to come to the Krutitsky Barracks to say good-bye to me.

Fortunately I was in exile and the princess had plenty of time before her.

'And where is this Perm or Vyatka? He'll be sure to break his neck there, or have it broken for him; and he'll forget her there: that's the main thing.'

But as though to spite the princess, I had an excellent memory. Natalie's correspondence with me, long concealed from the old lady, was at last discovered, and she strictly forbade the maids and menservants to transmit letters to the young girl, or to take her letters to the post. In two years there began to be talk of my return. 'So I dare say some fine morning that unfortunate son of my brother's will open the door and walk in; it's no use wasting time thinking about it, and putting things off—we'll make a match for her and save her from the political criminal who has no religion or principles.'

Formerly the princess had used to sigh and say of the poor, forlorn girl that she had scarcely anything, that it would not do for her to pick and choose, and that she would like to see her settled *somehow* in her own lifetime. She had indeed, with the help of her hangers-on, *somehow* settled the fate of one distant cousin who had no dowry by marrying her off to an attorney of some sort. A nice, good-natured, well-educated girl, she married to satisfy her mother; two years later she died, but the attorney was still alive, and from gratitude was still looking after her Excellency's affairs. In this case, quite the contrary, the orphan was by no means a penniless bride; the princess was prepared to give her in marriage like a daughter of her own, to give her a dowry of a hundred thousand roubles in cash alone and to leave her something in her will besides. On such terms suitors are always to be found, not only in Moscow but anywhere you like, especially when there is the title of princess as well as a 'lady companion' and the nomadic old ladies.

The whispering, negotiations, rumours and the maid-servants brought Princess Marya Alexeyevna's intention to the ears of the unhappy victim of so much solicitude. She told the 'lady companion' that she would certainly not accept any proposal. Then began an incessant, outrageous and ruthless persecution without one trace of delicacy, a petty persecution that attacked her every minute and clutched her at every step, at every word.

'Imagine bad weather, fearful cold, wind, rain, an overcast sky without expression, a nasty little room which looks as though a corpse had just been carried out of it, and these *children,* without object or even enjoyment, make a din, shout, break and defile everything near them; and it would be bad enough if one had simply to look at them, but when one is forced to live among them . . .' So she writes in a letter from the country where the princess had gone in the summer; and she goes on: 'there are three old women sitting here with us, and they are all three describing how their late husbands were paralysed and how they looked after them; and it is chilly enough without that.'

Now to this environment was added systematic persecution, and it was carried on not by the princess alone but also by the wretched old women, who constantly tormented Natalie, exhorting her to marry and abusing me; as a rule she said nothing in her letters of the continual annoyances she had to endure, but sometimes bitterness, humiliation and boredom were too much for her. 'I don't know,' she writes, 'whether they can invent anything more to oppress me with. Will they possibly have wit enough for that? Do you know that I am actually forbidden to go into another room, or even to move to another seat in the same room? It is a long while since I played the piano; lights were brought and I went into the drawing-room, thinking they might be merciful, but no, they brought me back and made me knit; perhaps, at least I might sit at another table—I can't endure being beside them—might I do even that? No, I must sit just here beside the priest's wife, listen, look, and talk, while they do nothing but talk about Filaret or criticise you. For a moment I was angry and grew red, but suddenly my heart was weighed down by a feeling of bitter sadness, not because I had to be their slave, no . . . I felt mortally sorry for them.'

The matchmaking was officially beginning.

'A lady has been here who is fond of me, and whom for that reason I do not like. . . . She is doing her very utmost to get me settled, and she made me so angry that as she left I sang—

> *"I had rather be dressed in my winding-sheet*
> *Than the wedding veil without my sweet."* '

A few days later, 26th October, 1837, she writes: 'What I have been through to-day, my dear, you can't imagine. They dressed me up and took me off to Madame S——*, who has been extremely gracious to me ever since I was a child; Colonel Z——* goes there every Tuesday to play cards. Imagine my situation: on the one side the old ladies at the card-table, on the other various ugly figures, and he. The conversation, the company—everything was so alien to me, so strange and repugnant, so lifeless and vulgar, that I was more like a statue than a living creature. Everything that was going on seemed like an oppressive, suffocating nightmare. I kept asking to go home, like a child: they would not heed me. The attention of the host and of *the visitor* overwhelmed me; he got as far as writing

N

half my monogram in chalk. Oh heavens, I am not strong enough and I can look for support to no one among those who might be a help; I am all alone on the edge of a precipice, and a whole crowd of them are doing everything they can to push me over; sometimes I am weary, my strength fails me, and you are not near and in the distance I cannot see you; but the mere thought of you—and my soul is stirred and ready to do battle again in the armour of love.'

Meanwhile everyone liked the Colonel: the Senator was friendly to him, and my father gave it as his opinion that 'a better match could not be expected and should not be desired'. 'Even his Excellency D.P. (Golokhvastov) is pleased with him,' wrote Natalie. The princess said nothing directly to Natalie, but restricted her freedom even more severely and tried to hasten things up. Natalie tried to pretend in his presence to be a complete imbecile, hoping to frighten him off, but not at all; he went on coming more and more frequently.

'Yesterday,' she writes, 'Emilia was here and this is what she said: "If I heard that you were dead I should cross myself with joy and thank God." She is right in a great deal but not altogether; her soul living by grief alone[1] could fully grasp the suffering of my heart, but the bliss with which love fills it she can hardly understand.'

But the princess was not losing heart. 'Wishing to have a clear conscience, the princess summoned a priest who is acquainted with Z——— and asked him whether it would not be a sin to marry me by force. The priest said it would be actually a godly work to make provision for an orphan. I am sending for my own priest,' Natalie adds, 'and shall tell him the whole story.'

'*October 30th.*—My clothes are here, my attire for to-morrow, and the ikon, the rings; there is fuss and preparations, and not a word to me. The Nasakins and others have been invited. They are preparing a surprise for me and I am preparing a surprise for them.

'*Evening.*—Now a family council is going on. Lev Alexeyevich (the Senator) is here. You urge me to be strong—there is no need, my dear. I am equal to extricating myself from the awful, loathsome scenes into which they are dragging me on the chain. Your image is bright above me, there is no need to fear for me, and my very distress and sadness are so sacred and have taken so firm a hold on my soul that tearing them away would hurt even more, the wounds would re-open.'

---

[1] A reference to the break between Emilia Aksberg and N. M. Satin. (*A.S.*)

However, though they did their best to mask and cover up the
affair, the Colonel could not avoid seeing the determined aversion of
his proposed bride; he began to be less frequent in his visits, declared
himself ill, and even hinted at some addition to the dowry; this
greatly incensed the princess, but she got over even that humiliation
and was ready to give her estate near Moscow as well. This concession he had not apparently expected, for after it he disappeared
altogether.

Two months passed quietly. All at once the news came that I
had been transferred to Vladimir. Then the princess made her last
desperate effort to marry off her *protégée*. One of her acquaintances
had a son, an officer, who had just returned from the Caucasus; he
was young, cultivated, and a very decent fellow. The princess cast
away her pride and herself suggested to his sister that she should
'sound' her brother and see whether he cared for the match. He
yielded to his sister's suggestion. My young cousin did not care to
play the same disgusting and tedious part a second time, so, seeing
that the affair was taking a serious turn, she wrote to the young man
a letter, told him directly, openly, and simply that she loved another
man, trusted herself to his honour and begged him not to add to
her sufferings.

The officer with great delicacy drew back. The princess was
amazed and affronted and made up her mind to find out what had
happened. The officer's sister, to whom Natalie had spoken herself,
and who had given her word to her brother to pass nothing on to
the princess, told the whole story to the 'lady companion'; the latter
of course at once reported it to her mistress.

The princess almost choked with indignation. Not knowing what
to do, she ordered the young girl to go upstairs to her room and not
to let her set eyes on her; not content with that, she ordered her
door to be locked and put two maids on guard; then she wrote notes
to her two brothers and one of her nephews and asked them to
come and give her advice, saying that 'she was so distressed and
upset that she could not think what to do in the misfortune that
had befallen her'. My father refused, saying that he had plenty of
worries of his own, that there was no need to attach such importance
to what had happened, and that he was a poor judge in affairs of
the heart. The Senator and D. P. Golokhvastov appeared the next
evening in answer to her summons.

They talked for a long time without reaching any agreement and at last asked to see the prisoner. The young girl came in, but she was no longer the shy, silent orphan they had known. Unshakable firmness and irreversible determination were apparent in the calm, proud expression of her face; this was no child, but a woman who had come to defend her love—my love.

The sight of the 'accused' confounded the Areopagus. They felt uncomfortable; at last Dmitry Pavlovich, *l'orateur de la famille*, expatiated at length on the cause of their coming together, the distress of the princess, her heartfelt desire to settle her *protégée's* future, and the strange opposition on the part of the one for whose benefit it was all being done. The Senator with a nod and a movement of his forefinger expressed his assent to his nephew's words. The princess said nothing but sat with her head turned away, sniffing salts.

The 'accused' heard all they had to say and asked with straight-forward simplicity what they required of her.

'We have no thought of requiring anything from you,' observed the nephew. 'We are here at Aunt's desire to give you sincere advice. A match is being offered to you that is excellent in all respects.'

'I cannot accept it.'

'What is your reason for that?'

'You know it.'

The orator of the family coloured a little, took a pinch of snuff, and screwing up his eyes went on:

'There is a great deal here to which objection might be urged. I would call your attention to the precariousness of your hopes. It is so long since you have seen our unfortunate Alexander; he is so young and impetuous—are you certain of him?'

'Yes, and whatever his intentions may be, I cannot change mine.'

The nephew was *au bout de son Latin*; he got up saying: 'God grant that you may not regret it! I feel very anxious about your future.'

The Senator frowned; the luckless girl now appealed to him.

'You have always shown sympathy for me,' she said to him. 'I implore you, save me: do what you like, but take me out of this life. I have done no harm to anyone, I ask for nothing, I am not trying to do anything, I am only refusing to deceive a man and ruin myself by marrying him. What I have to endure on account of it you cannot imagine; it pains me to have to say this in the presence of the princess, but to put up with the slights, the insulting words, the hints of her friend is too much for me. I cannot, I ought not to allow it, for insulting me is insulting. . . .'

Her nerves gave way and the tears gushed from her eyes; the Senator leapt up and walked about the room in agitation.

Meanwhile the 'lady companion', boiling over with fury, could not restrain herself and said, addressing the princess:

'So that's our nice, modest girl: there's gratitude for you.'

'Of whom is she speaking?' shouted the Senator, 'Eh? How is it, sister, you allow that woman, devil knows who she is, to speak like that of your brother's daughter in your presence? And if it comes to that, why is this creature here at all? Did you invite her to the family council too? Is she a relation or what?'

'My dear,' answered the terrified princess, 'you know what she is to me and how she looks after me.'

'Yes, yes, that's all very nice, let her give you your medicine and what's necessary; that's not what I am talking about. I ask you, *ma soeur*, why is she here when family affairs are being discussed, and how dare she open her mouth? One might think, after this, that she runs the whole show, and then you complain—Hey, my carriage!'

The 'lady companion' flushed, and ran out of the room in tears.

'Why do you spoil her like this?' the Senator went on, carried away; 'she fancies she is sitting in a pot-house at Zvenigorod; how is it you aren't disgusted by it?'

'Leave off, my dear, please,' the poor princess groaned, 'my nerves are so upset—oh! You can go upstairs and stay there,' she added, addressing her niece.

'It's time to be done with all this Bastille business. It's all nonsense and leads to nothing,' observed the Senator and took his hat.

Before driving away he went upstairs; Natalie, overcome by all that had passed, was sitting in an armchair with her face hidden, weeping bitterly. The old man patted her on the shoulder and said:

'Calm yourself, calm yourself, it'll all be thrashed out. You must just try to stop my sister being angry with you; she is an invalid: she must be humoured; after all, she only wishes for your good, you know; but, there, you shan't be married against your will, I'll answer for that.'

'Better a nunnery, a boarding-school, to go to my brother[2] at Tambov, or to Petersburg, than endure this life any longer,' she answered.

[2] 'The Chemist'. (*A.S.*)

'Come, that'll do! try and soothe my sister, and as for that fool of a woman I'll teach her not to be rude.'

The Senator, as he crossed the great hall, met the 'lady companion': 'I'll ask you not to forget yourself,' he shouted at her, holding up a menacing finger; she went sobbing into the bedroom where the princess was already lying on the bed while four maids rubbed her hands and feet, moistened her temples with vinegar, and poured Hoffman's drops on lumps of sugar.

So ended the family council.

It is clear that the girl's situation was hardly likely to be improved by what had happened; the 'lady companion' was more on her guard, but, now cherishing a personal hatred for Natalie, and desirous of avenging her own injury and humiliation, she poisoned her existence by petty, indirect means. I need hardly say that the princess participated in this ignoble persecution of a defenceless girl.

This had to be ended. I made up my mind to come forward, and wrote a long, calm, frank letter to my father. I told him of my love and, foreseeing his reply, added that I did not want to hurry him, that I should give him time to see whether it was a passing feeling or not, and that all that I begged of him was that the Senator and he would put themselves in the poor girl's place and would remember that they had the same rights over her as the princess herself.

My father answered that he could not endure meddling in other people's affairs, that what the princess did in her own house was not his business; he advised me to abandon foolish ideas 'engendered by the idleness and *ennui* of exile', and added that I would do better to prepare myself for travel in foreign lands. We had often talked in past years of a tour abroad; he knew how passionately I wished for it, but he had found endless obstacles and had always ended by saying: 'You must first close my eyes, then you'll be free to go to the ends of the earth.' In exile I had lost all hope of going abroad soon. I knew how hard it would be to get his permission and, besides, it would have seemed a lack of delicacy to insist on a voluntary separation after the enforced one. I remembered the tears quivering on his old eyelids when I was setting off to Perm . . . and now here was my father taking the initiative and suggesting I should go!

I had been open, I had spared the old man in my letter, had asked so little—and he had answered with irony and artifice.

'He doesn't want to do anything for me,' I said to myself; 'like Guizot he advocates *la non-intervention*. Very well then, I'll act myself, and now amen to concessions.' I had not once before thought about the ordering of the future; I believed, I knew that it was mine, that it was ours, and I left the details to chance; the consciousness of love was enough for us, and our desires did not go beyond a momentary interview. My father's letter forced me to take the future into my own hands. It was nothing to expect—*cosa fatta capo ha!* My father was not very sentimental, while as for the princess—

> *'Let her weep,*
> *Her tears mean nought to her!'*[3]

Just at that time my brother[4] and Ketscher came to stay at Vladimir. Ketscher and I spent whole nights together, talking, recalling the past, laughing through our tears, and laughing till we cried. He was the first of our set whom I had seen since I left Moscow. From him I heard the chronicles of our circle, what changes had taken place and what questions were absorbing it, what fresh people had arrived, where those were who had left Moscow, and so on. When we had talked everything over I told him of my plans. After considering how I ought to act, Ketscher concluded with a proposal the absurdity of which I appreciated afterwards. Desirous of exhausting all peaceful means, he offered to go to my father, whom he scarcely knew, and to talk to him *seriously*. I agreed.

Ketscher, of course, was better fitted for anything good or for anything bad, than for diplomatic negotiations, particularly with my father. He was endowed in the highest degree with everything that was bound to ruin any chance of success. His very appearance was enough to depress and alarm any conservative. A tall figure, with hair strangely dishevelled and arranged on no fixed principle, with a harsh countenance reminiscent of a number of the members of the Convention of 1793, especially of Marat, with the same big mouth, the same hard, disdainful lines about the lips, and the same expression of mournful and exasperated gloom; to this must be added spectacles, a wide-brimmed hat, extreme irritability, a loud voice, lack of all habit of self-control, and the power of arching his eyebrows higher and higher as he grew more indignant. Ketscher was like Laravigny in George Sand's excellent novel, *Horace*, with an admix-

---

[3] M. Yu. Lermontov's poem, 'A Testament'. (*A.S.*)
[4] See p. 13, fnn. (*R.*)

ture of something of the Pathfinder and Robinson Crusoe, as well as an element purely Muscovite. His open, generous temperament had set him from childhood in direct conflict with the world surrounding him; he did not conceal this antagonism and was accustomed to it. A few years older than we were, he was continually scolding us and was dissatisfied with everything. He used to quarrel and bring accusations against us, and he covered it all with the simple good nature of a child. His words were rude, but his feelings were tender and we forgave him much.

Imagine him, this last of the Mohicans with the face of a Marat, the 'friend of the people', setting off to admonish my father! Many times afterwards I made Ketscher describe their interview; my imagination was unequal to picturing all the oddity of this diplomatic intervention. It happened so unexpectedly that for a moment my old father lost his bearings and began explaining all the weighty considerations which led him to oppose my marriage; then, recovering himself, he changed his tone and asked Ketscher on what grounds he had come to discuss a matter which was none of his business. The conversation became more embittered. The diplomatist, seeing that the situation was deteriorating, tried to frighten the old man about my health, but it was already too late for that, and the interview ended, as might have been expected, in a series of malignant sarcasms from my father and rude rejoinders from Ketscher.

He wrote to me: 'Expect nothing from the old man.' That was all I needed to know. But what was I to do? How was I to begin? While I was thinking over a dozen different plans a day and unable to decide among them, my brother prepared to go to Moscow.

That was on the first of March 1838.

Chapter 23[1]

The Third of March and the Ninth of May, 1838[*]

In the morning I wrote letters; when I had finished we sat down to dinner. I could not eat, and we said nothing; I felt unbearably oppressed—it was between four and five, and at seven the horses were to come round. At the same time next day he would be in Moscow while I—and every minute my pulse beat faster.

'I say,' I said at last to my brother, looking at my plate, 'will you take me with you to Moscow?'

He put down his fork and looked at me, uncertain whether he had heard me aright.

---

[1] A fragment of this chapter was published in *The Pole Star,* Vol. I, page 79, together with the following note:

Who is entitled to write his reminiscences?

Everyone.

Because no one is obliged to read them.

In order to write one's reminiscences it is not at all necessary to be a great man, nor a notorious criminal, nor a celebrated artist, nor a statesman—it is quite enough to be simply a human being, to have something to tell, and not merely to desire to tell it but at least have some little ability to do so.

Every life is interesting; if not the personality, then the environment, the country are interesting, the life itself is interesting. Man likes to enter into another existence, he likes to touch the subtlest fibres of another's heart, and to listen to its beating . . . he compares, he checks it by his own, he seeks for himself confirmation, sympathy, justification. . . .

But may not memoirs be tedious, may not the life described be colourless and commonplace?

Then we shall not read it—there is no worse punishment for a book than that.

Moreover, the right to indite one's memoirs is no relief for the chagrin of this. Benvenuto Cellini's *Diary* is not interesting because he was an excellent worker in gold but because it is in itself as interesting as any novel.

The fact is that the very word 'entitled' to this or that form of composition does not belong to our epoch, but dates from an era of intellectual immaturity, from an era of poet-laureates, doctors' caps, corporations of savants, certificated philosophers, diploma'ed metaphysicians and other Pharisees of the Christian world. Then the act of writ-

'Take me through the town gate as your servant; I don't need anything more: do you agree?'

'Yes if you like, only, you know, afterwards you'll. . . .'

It was too late: his 'if you like' was already in my blood, in my brain. The idea that had only flashed upon me a minute before had now taken deep root.

'What is there to discuss? Anything may happen—so you'll take me?'

'Of course—I'm quite ready—only. . . .'

I jumped up from the table.

'Are you going?' asked Matvey, wanting to say something.

'I am,' I answered in such a tone that he said no more. 'I'll be back the day after to-morrow. If anyone comes, tell them I have a headache and am asleep. In the evening light the candles, and now get me my linen and my bag.'

The bells were tinkling in the yard.

'Are you ready?'

'Yes, and so good luck to us.'

---

ing was regarded as something sacred, a man writing for the public used a high-flown, unnatural, choice language; he 'expounded' or 'sang'.

We simply talk; for us writing is the same sort of secular pursuit, the same sort of work or amusement as any other. In this connection it is difficult to dispute 'the right to work'. Whether the work will find recognition and approval is quite a different matter.

A year ago I published in Russian part of my memoirs under the title of *Prison and Exile*. I published it in London at the beginning of the war. I did not reckon upon readers nor upon any attention outside Russia. The success of that book exceeded all expectations: the *Revue des Deux Mondes*, the most chaste and conceited of journals, published half the book in a French translation; the clever and learned *Athenaeum* printed extracts in English; the whole book has appeared in German and is being published in English.

That is why I have decided to print extracts from other parts.

In another place I speak of the immense importance my memoirs have for me personally, and the object with which I began writing them. I confine myself now to the general remark that the publication of contemporary memoirs is particularly useful for us Russians. Thanks to the censorship we are not accustomed to anything being made public, and the slightest publicity frightens, checks, and surprises us. In England any man who appears on any public stage, whether as a huckster of letters or a guardian of the press, is liable to the same critical examination, to the same hisses and applause as the actor in the lowest theatre in Islington or Paddington. Neither the Queen nor her husband are excluded. It is a mighty curb!

Let our imperial *actors* of the secret and open police, who have been so well protected from publicity by the censorship and paternal punishments, know that sooner or later their deeds will come into the light of day.

The above note is by H. From 'Who is entitled' to the end it appears in D (II, 597), headed 'Foreword to the chapters of Part IV, published in *The Pole Star*'. (R.)

By dinner-time next day the bells ceased tinkling, and we were at Ketscher's door. I bade them call him out. A week before, when he had left me at Vladimir, there had been no idea of my coming, and hence he was so surprised on seeing me that at first he did not say a word and then went off into a peal of laughter: but soon he looked anxious and led me indoors. When we were in his room he carefully locked the door and asked me: 'What has happened?'

'Nothing.'

'Then what have you come here for?'

'I couldn't stay at Vladimir; I want to see Natalie—that's all, and you must arrange it, and this very minute, because I must be back there to-morrow.'

Ketscher looked into my face and raised his eyebrows.

'What folly! The devil knows what to call it, to come like this with no need and nothing prepared! Have you written? Have you fixed a time?'

'I have written nothing.'

'Upon my word, my boy, but what are we to do with you? It's beyond anything, it's raving madness!'

'That's just the point—that we must think what to do without losing a minute.'

'You're a fool,' said Ketscher with conviction, raising his eyebrows higher than ever. 'I should be glad, extremely glad, if it didn't come off: it would be a lesson to you.'

'And rather a long lesson if I am caught. Listen: as soon as it is dark we'll drive to the princess's house; you shall call someone out into the street, one of the servants, I'll tell you which—and then we'll see what to do. That's all right, eh?'

'Well, there's no help for it, let's go; but how I should like it not to be a failure! Why didn't you write yesterday?'—and Ketscher, pulling his broad-brimmed hat over his brows with an air of dignity, threw on a black cloak lined with red.

'Oh, you damned grumbler!' I said to him as we went out, and Ketscher, laughing heartily, repeated: 'But really it's enough to make a hen laugh, to come like this without sending a word; it's beyond anything.'

I could not stay at Ketscher's—he lived terribly far away, and his mother had visitors that day. He took me to an officer of hussars whom he knew to be an honourable man, and who had never been mixed up with political affairs, and so was not under police supervision. The officer, a man with long moustaches, was sitting at dinner when we went in; Ketscher told him what we had come about. In reply the officer poured me out a glass of red wine and thanked us for the confidence we put in him; then he took me into his bedroom, which was adorned with saddles and saddle-cloths, so that one might have supposed that he slept on horseback.

'Here is a room for you,' he said; 'no one will disturb you here.'

Then he called his orderly, a hussar like himself, and ordered him not to let anyone into that room on any pretext. I found myself once more under the guardianship of a soldier, with this difference, that at the Krutitsky Barracks the gendarme had been keeping me from all the world, while here the hussar was keeping all the world from me.

When it was quite dark Ketscher and I set off. My heart beat violently when I saw the familiar streets and houses again which I had not seen for nearly four years . . . Kuznetsky Most, Tverskoy Boulevard . . . and here was Ogarëv's house; they had clapped a huge heraldic crest on it and it looked strange. On the ground floor, where we spent such happy youthful days, a tailor was living. . . . Here was Povarskaya Street—I held my breath: in the corner window of the attic room there was a candle burning: that was her room, she was writing to me, she was thinking of me, the candle twinkled so gaily, it seemed twinkling *to me*.

While we were considering how best to call someone out into the street, one of the princess's young footmen ran towards us.

'Arkady,' I said, going up to him. He did not recognise me. 'What's the matter with you?' I said, 'Don't you know your own people?'

'Oh, is it you, sir?' he cried.

I put my finger on my lips and said: 'If you would like to do me a friendly service, deliver this little note at once, as quickly as you can, through Sasha or Kostinka, do you understand? We will wait for the answer round the corner in the alley, and don't breathe a word to anyone about having seen me in Moscow.'

'Don't be uneasy, we'll pull it off in a flash,' answered Arkady, and he trotted into the house.

We walked up and down the alley for about half an hour before a little, thin, old woman came hurrying out, looking about her; this was that same spirited servant girl who in 1812 had asked the French soldiers for '*manger*' for me; we had called her Kostinka ever since

I was a child. The old woman took my face in both hands and showered kisses upon it.

'So you've flown to see us,' she said. 'Ah, you headstrong boy, when will you calm down, you rogue, you!—and you've given our young lady such a fright that she almost fainted.'

'And have you a note for me?'

'Yes, yes, see how impatient he is,' and she gave me a scrap of paper.

A few words had been scribbled in pencil with a trembling hand: 'My God, can it be true—you, here! To-morrow between five and six in the morning I shall expect you. I can't believe it, I can't believe it! Surely it must be a dream!'

The hussar again put me into his orderly's keeping. At half-past five next morning I stood leaning against a lamp-post, waiting for Ketscher, who had gone in at the wicket-gate of the princess's house. I shall not attempt to describe what was passing in me while I waited at the lamp-post; such moments remain one's own secret because there are no words for them.

Ketscher beckoned to me. I went in at the little gate. A boy who had grown up since I left showed me in with a friendly smile, and here I was in the hall which at one time I used to enter with a yawn, and now I was ready to fall on my knees and kiss every plank in the floor. Arkady led me into the drawing-room and went out. I sank exhausted on the sofa, my heart throbbed so violently that it was painful; and besides I was frightened. I linger over my story for the sake of spending longer with these memories, though I see that my words give a poor idea of them.

She came in all in white, dazzlingly lovely; three years of separation and the struggles she had been through had given the finishing touches to her features and her expression.

'It is you,' she said in her soft, gentle voice.

We sat down on the sofa and remained silent.

The expression of joy in her eyes resembled one of suffering. I suppose that when the feeling of gladness reaches its highest pitch it is mingled with an expression of pain, for she said to me: 'How tormented you look!'

I held her hand, she leaned her head on the other, and we had nothing to say to each other . . . a few brief phrases, two or three reminiscences, words from our letters, some idle remarks about Arkady, about the hussar, about Kostinka, that was all.

Then Kostinka came in, saying that it was time for me to go, and I got up without protesting, and she did not try to keep me . . . our hearts were so full, all thoughts of more or less, of shorter or longer, all vanished before the fullness of the present. . . .

When we had passed the town gate, Ketscher asked: 'Well, have you settled anything?'

'Nothing.'

'But you talked to her?'

'Not a word about that.'

'Does she consent?'

'I didn't ask. Of course she consents.'

'Well, upon my soul, you behave like a child, or a lunatic,' observed Ketscher, raising his eyebrows and shrugging his shoulders with indignation.

'I'll write to her and then to you, and now, good-bye. Now get along, all three of you!'[2]

It was thawing, the spongy snow was black in places, the endless white plain lay on both sides, little villages flashed by with their smoke, and then the moon rose and shed a different light on everything; I was alone with the driver and kept looking out, yet all the while was there with her, and the road and the moon and the fields were somehow mingled with the princess's drawing-room. And, strange to say, I remembered every word uttered by Kostinka, by Arkady, even by the maid who had led me out to the gate, but what I had said to her and what she had said to me I could not remember!

Two months were spent in an incessant bustle. I had to borrow money, and to get her baptismal certificate; it appeared that the princess had taken it. One of my friends—crawling, bribing, treating policemen and clerks—succeeded by all sorts of false statements in getting another from the Consistory.

When everything was ready, we, that is Matvey and I, set off.

At dawn on the eighth of May we were at the last posting-station before Moscow. The drivers had gone to get horses. The air was heavy, there were drops of rain, and it seemed as though a storm was coming on; I remained in the *kibitka* and hurried up my driver. Someone spoke near me in a strange, high, whining, sing-song voice. I turned round and saw a pale, thin girl of about sixteen, begging.

[2] The horses in the *troika*. (R.)

She was in rags, with her hair hanging about her; I gave her some small silver coin; she laughed when she saw it, but instead of going away she clambered on to the driver's seat, turned towards me and began muttering half-coherent sentences, looking straight into my face; her eyes were clouded and pitiful, wisps of hair fell over her face. Her sickly face, her unintelligible mutterings, together with the light of early morning, aroused a sort of nervous timidity in me.

'She's crazy, you know, that is, she is simple,' observed the driver. 'And where are you poking yourself? I'll give you a lash with the whip and then you'll know! Upon my soul, I will, you saucy hussy!'

'Why are you scolding, what have I done to you—here your master's given me a silver bit, and what have I done to you?'

'Well, he's given it to you, and so be off to your devils in the forest.'

'Take me with you,' added the girl, looking piteously at me, 'do, really, take me. . . .'

'To put you in a show in Moscow as a freak, some sea monster,' observed the driver. 'Come, get down, we're just off.'

The girl made no attempt to move, but kept looking pitifully at me. I begged the driver not to hurt her, and he lifted her gently in his arms and set her on the ground. She burst out crying and I was ready to cry with her.

Why had this creature crossed my path just on that day, just as I was driving into Moscow? I thought of Kozlov's 'Mad Girl'; he had met her near Moscow, too.

We drove on: the air was full of electricity, unpleasantly heavy and warm. A dark blue storm-cloud with grey streamers reaching to the earth was slowly trailing over the fields, and all at once a zig-zag of lightning ran slanting through it, there was a clap of thunder and the rain came down in torrents. We were nearly seven miles from the Rogozhsky Gate and after reaching Moscow had an hour's drive to the Devichy field. We reached the Astrakovs',[3] where Ketscher was to wait for me, literally without a dry stitch on us.

Ketscher was not there. He was at the bedside of a dying woman, Ye. G. Levashev. This woman was one of those marvellous pheno-mena of Russian life which reconcile one to it, one of those whose

[3]Astrakov, Nikolay Ivanovich (1809-42), a teacher of mathematics, and Tatyana Alexeyevna (1814-92), his wife, an authoress and a link between H. and his friends in Russia. (*A.S.*)

whole existence is a heroic feat, unknown to any but a small circle of friends. How many tears she had wiped away, how much comfort she had brought to more than one broken heart, of how many young lives she had been the support, and how much she had suffered herself! 'She spent herself in love,' I was told by Chaadayev, one of her closest friends, who dedicated to her his celebrated letter about Russia.*

Ketscher could not leave her, and wrote that he would come about nine o'clock. I was alarmed by this news. A man absorbed by a great passion is a dreadful egoist; in Ketscher's absence I could see nothing but a delay. . . . When it struck nine, when the bells began ringing for evening service and then another quarter of an hour passed, I was overcome by feverish anxiety and cowardly despair. . . . Half-past nine—no, he would not come; the sick woman was probably worse, and what was I to do? I could not remain in Moscow: one incautious word from the maid or from Kostinka in the princess's house would give everything away. It was possible to go back, but I felt I had not the strength to go back.

At a quarter to ten Ketscher appeared, in a straw hat and with the crumpled face of a man who has not slept all night. I rushed up to him and as I embraced him I showered him with reproaches. Ketscher looked at me with a frown and asked: 'Why, isn't half an hour enough to get from the Astrakovs' to the Povarskaya? I might have been gossiping with you here for an hour, and I dare say it would have been very nice, but I could not bring myself to leave a dying woman sooner than I needed for the sake of that. She sends you her greetings,' he added; 'she blessed me with her dying hand, and wished us success and gave me a warm shawl in case of need.' The dying woman's greeting was particularly dear to me. The warm shawl was very useful in the night, and I had no time to thank her nor to press her hand . . . soon afterwards she died.

Ketscher and Astrakov set off. Ketscher was to drive out of the town with Natalie, and Astrakov was to come back and tell me whether everything had gone off successfully and what I was to do. I was left waiting with his beautiful, delightful wife; she had herself only lately been married and, being of an ardent, passionate nature, she took the warmest interest in our doings. She tried with feigned gaiety to assure me that everything would go off splendidly, though she was herself so fretted by anxiety that her face was continually changing its expression. We sat together in the window and conversation did not flow easily; we were like children shut up in an empty room as a punishment. Two hours passed in this way.

There is nothing in the world more shattering, more unendurable than inactivity and suspense at such moments. Friends make a great mistake in taking the whole burden off the shoulders of the principal *patient*. They ought to invent duties for him if there are none, to overwhelm him with physical exertions, to distract his mind with bustle and fuss.

At last Astrakov came in, and we rushed to meet him.

'Everything is going marvellously; I saw them gallop off,' he shouted to us from the yard. 'You go out at the Rogozhsky Gate at once; there by the little bridge you will see the horses not far from Perov's tavern. Good luck to you! And change your cab half-way, so that your second cabman may not know where you have come from.'

I flew like an arrow from the bow. . . . And here was the little bridge not far from Perov's; there was no one there, and on the other side of the bridge, too, there was no one. I drove as far as the Izmaylovsky Menagerie: there was no one. I dismissed the cabman and went forward on foot. I walked backwards and forwards, and eventually saw a carriage on another road. A handsome young coachman was standing by it. 'Hasn't a tall gentleman in a straw hat driven by here,' I asked him, 'and not alone, with a young lady?'

'I have seen no one,' the coachman answered reluctantly.

'With whom did you come here?'

'With gentlefolks.'

'What is their name?'

'What is that to you?'

'What a fellow you are, really! If it was nothing to do with me, I should not be asking you.'

The coachman gave me a searching look and smiled—apparently my appearance disposed him more favourably to me.

'If you have business with them then you ought to know their names yourself: who do you want?'

'You are a regular flint; well, I want a gentleman named Ketscher.'

The coachman smiled again, and pointing towards the graveyard said: 'Over there, do you see something black in the distance? That's himself, and the young lady is with him; she did not bring a hat, so Mr Ketscher gave her his, seeing it was a straw one.'

This time we again met in a graveyard!

With a faint cry she flung herself on my neck.

'And it's for ever!' she cried.

'For ever,' I repeated. Ketscher was touched and tears gleamed in his eyes; he took our hands and said in a trembling voice, 'Friends, be happy!' We embraced him. This was our *real* wedding!

For over an hour we waited in a private room at Perov's tavern, and still the carriage with Matvey did not come! Ketscher frowned. The possibility of trouble had never entered our heads, we were so happy there, the three of us, and as much at home as though we had always been together. There was a wood in front of the windows, and from the storey below came strains of music and a gypsy chorus; the weather was lovely after the storm.

I was not afraid, like Ketscher, of the police being put on our track by the princess; I knew that she had too much pride to involve a policeman in our family affairs. Besides, she never took any step without consulting the Senator, nor the Senator without consulting my father; my father would never consent to the police stopping me in Moscow or near Moscow, which would mean my being sent to Bobruysk or to Siberia for disobedience to the will of His Majesty. The only possible danger was from the secret police, but it had all been done so quickly that it was hard for them to know. Besides, if they had got an inkling of anything, it would never occur to anyone that a man who had secretly returned from exile and was eloping with his bride would be sitting calmly in Perov's tavern where there was a crush of people from morning to night.

At last Matvey appeared with the carriage.

'One more glass,' commanded Ketscher, 'and off you go!'

And then we were alone, that is, the two of us, flying along the Vladimir road.

At Bunkovo while the horses were being changed we went into the inn. The old hostess came to ask us whether we would like anything, and, looking at us good-naturedly, she said: 'How young and pretty your good lady is, and the two of you, God bless you, make a pretty pair.' We blushed up to our ears and did not dare to look at each other, but asked for tea to cover our confusion. After five o'clock the next day we reached Vladimir. There was no time to be lost; leaving Natalie with the family of an old married official, I rushed off to find whether everything was ready. But who was there to get things ready at Vladimir?

There are good-natured people everywhere. A Siberian regiment of

Uhlans was stationed at Vladimir at the time; I was only slightly acquainted with the officers but, meeting one of them rather often in the public library, I had taken to bowing to him; he was polite and very nice. A month later he admitted that he knew me and my 1834 story, and told me that he had himself been a student at Moscow University. When I was leaving Vladimir and looking about for someone in whose hands to leave various arrangements, I had thought of this officer, had driven to his place and told him frankly what I was up to. Genuinely touched by my confidence, he pressed my hand, promised to do everything, and kept his word.

He was waiting for me in full uniform, with white facings, his shako with no cover, with a cartridge-belt across his shoulder, and all sorts of cords and lace. He told me that the bishop had given the priest permission to marry us, but had ordered the baptismal certificate to be shown first. I gave the officer the baptismal certificate, while I went off to another young man who had also been a Moscow student. He was serving his two *provincial years* in accordance with the new regulation, in the governor's office, and was almost dying of boredom.

'Would you like to act as groomsman?'

'Whose?'

'Mine.'

'What, yours?'

'Yes, yes, mine.'

'Delighted. When?'

'Now.'

He thought that I was joking, but when I hastily told him how it was he skipped with joy. To be groomsman at a clandestine wedding, to bustle about, possibly to get into trouble, and all that in a little town absolutely without any diversions! He promised at once to get me a carriage and four and ran to his chest of drawers to see whether he had a clean white waistcoat.

As I drove away, I met my Uhlan with a priest sitting on his knee. Imagine an officer, spruced up in his variegated uniform, in a little drozhki with a stout priest, adorned with big, combed-out beard, and arrayed in a silk cassock, which kept catching in all the Uhlan's unnecessary accoutrements. This sight alone might have attracted attention not only in the street that led from the Golden Gate at Vladimir, but on the Paris boulevards, or in Regent Street itself. But the Uhlan had not thought of that, and indeed I only thought of it afterwards.

The priest had been going from house to house holding services, since it was St Nicholas's Day, and my cavalry officer had captured him by force somewhere and requisitioned him. We drove off to the bishop's.

To explain the situation I must describe how the bishop came to be involved in it at all. The day before I went away the priest who had agreed to marry us suddenly announced that he would not do it without the bishop's sanction, that he had heard something and was afraid. In spite of all my eloquence, as well as the Uhlan's, the priest was obstinate and stuck to his point. The Uhlan suggested trying the priest of his regiment. This man, a priest with a cropped head and shaven skin, wearing a long, full-skirted coat and trousers tucked into his high boots, and placidly smoking a soldier's pipe, though attracted by certain details in our proposal, yet refused to marry us, declaring, in a mixture of Polish and White Russian, that he was strictly and absolutely forbidden to marry 'civilians'.

'And we are still more strictly forbidden to be witnesses and groomsmen at marriages without permission,' the officer observed. 'And yet I'm going, you see.'

'It's a different matter if one stands before Jesus, as I do; it's a different matter.'

'God helps those who help themselves,' I said to the Uhlan. 'I'll go straight to the bishop. And by the way, why don't you ask permission?'

'That won't do. The Colonel would tell his wife and she'd gossip about it all over the place. Besides, he'd very likely refuse.'

Bishop Parfeny of Vladimir was an intelligent, austere, rough old man; managing and self-willed, he might equally well have been a governor or a general, and, indeed, I think he would have been more in his right place as a general than as a monk; but it had turned out otherwise, and he ran his diocese as he would have run a division in the Caucasus. I noticed in him, on the whole, far more of the qualities of an administrator than of one dead to the things of this life. He was, besides, rather severe than ill-natured; like all business-like men, he grasped questions quickly and clearly and was furious when people talked nonsense to him or did not understand him. It is far easier to come to an understanding with a man of this sort than with people who are mild, but weak and irresolute. In accordance with the custom at all provincial towns, on arriving at Vladimir I had gone once after mass to call on the bishop. He received me cordially, gave me his blessing, and regaled me with salmon; then he invited me to come one day and spend the evening talking with him, saying that his eyes were failing and he could not read in the evening. I went two or three times; he talked about literature, knew all the new Russian books and read the magazines, and so we got on splendidly together. Nevertheless, it was with some alarm that I knocked at his episcopal door.

It was a hot day. His Reverence the bishop received me in the garden. He was sitting under a big, shady lime tree, and had taken off his cowl and let his grey locks flow in freedom. A bald, well set up head-priest was standing before him, bareheaded, and right in the sun, reading some document aloud; his face was crimson and big drops of perspiration stood out on his forehead: he screwed up his eyes at the dazzling whiteness of the paper with the sunlight upon it, yet he did not dare to move nor did the bishop tell him to step out of the sun.

'Sit down,' said the bishop after blessing me, 'we are just finishing; these are our little Consistory affairs. Read on,' he added to the head-priest, and he, after mopping his face with a dark blue handkerchief and coughing aside, started reading again.

'What news have you to tell me?' Parfeny asked me, handing the pen to the head-priest, who seized this excellent opportunity to kiss his hand.

I told him of the priest's refusal.

'Have you the necessary papers?'

I showed him the governor's permission.

'Is that all?'

'Yes.'

Parfeny smiled: 'And on the lady's side?'

'There is her baptismal certificate; it will be brought on the day of the wedding.'

'When is the wedding?'

'In two days.'

'You've found a house, then?'

'Not yet.'

'Now see here,' Parfeny said to me, putting his finger on his lip and hooking his mouth towards his cheek, one of his favourite tricks; 'you're an intelligent and well-read man, but you won't catch an old sparrow by putting salt on its tail. There is something shady about it, so, since you have come to me, you had much better tell your business according to your conscience, as if you were at confession. Then I'll tell you straight what can be done and what can't, and in any case my advice will do you no harm.'

My business seemed to me so clear and so just that I told him the whole story, without, of course, going into unnecessary details. The old man listened attentively and often looked into my face. It appeared he was an old acquaintance of the princess's, and therefore could to some extent judge for himself of the truth of my account.

'I understand, I understand,' he said when I had finished. 'Well, let me write a letter to the princess on my own account.'

'I assure you that no peaceful means will lead to anything: her humours and obduracy have gone too far. I have told your Reverence all about it, as you desired; now I must add that if you refuse to help me I shall be forced to do secretly, stealthily, by bribes, what I am now doing quietly, but straightforwardly and openly. I can assure you of one thing: neither prison nor a fresh term of exile shall stop me.'

'You see,' said Parfeny, getting up and stretching, 'what a head-strong fellow you are. Perm has not been enough for you; steep hills have not broken you in yet. Am I saying that I forbid it? Get married if you like, there is nothing unlawful about it; but it would be better to do it peacefully, with the consent of the family. Send me your priest, I'll prevail on him somehow; only remember one thing: without the proper papers on the bride's side don't even attempt it. So it's a case of "Neither prison nor exile"—upon my word, what are people coming to nowadays! Well, the Lord be with you! Good luck to you, only you'll get me into trouble with the princess.'

And so, in addition to the Uhlan officer, a part in our plot was also taken by his Reverence Parfeny, Bishop of Vladimir and Suzdal.

When as a preliminary measure I had asked the governor's permission, I had in no way represented my marriage as being secret; this was the surest method of avoiding talk about it, and nothing could be more natural than the arrival of my future bride in Vladimir, since I had been deprived of the right to leave it. It was also natural that under the circumstances we should wish our wedding to be as modest as possible.

When we arrived with the priest at the bishop's on the ninth of May, his servitor told us that he had gone to his out-of-town house that morning and would not be back until night. It was already between seven and eight in the evening, one cannot marry after ten, and the next day was Saturday. What was to be done? The priest was scared. We went in to see the head-monk, the bishop's chaplain; he was drinking tea with rum in it and was in the most benign frame of mind. I told him our business, and he poured me out a cup of tea and insisted on my adding rum to it; then he took out some huge silver spectacles, read the baptismal certificate, turned it over, looked at the other side where there was nothing written, folded it up, and giving it back to the priest said: 'In the most perfect possible order.'

The priest still hesitated. I told the chaplain that if I were not married that day it would upset me terribly.

'Why put it off?' he said. 'I will tell his Reverence; marry them, Father Ioann, marry them—in the name of the Father, the Son, and the Holy Ghost, Amen!'

There was nothing for the priest to say; he drove off to write out a certificate that we were not related within the prohibited degrees, while I galloped off for Natalie.

When we were driving alone together out of the Golden Gate, the sun, which had till then been hidden by clouds, shed a dazzling light upon us with its last, bright-red rays, and so triumphantly and joyously that we both said in one breath: 'That's to see us off!' I remember her smile at the words and the pressure of her hand.

The drivers' little church, two miles from the town, was empty; there were neither choristers nor lighted candelabra. Five or six troopers of the Uhlan regiment came in as they were passing, and went out again. The old clerk chanted in a soft, faint voice; Matvey looked at us with tears of joy, the young groomsmen stood behind us with the heavy crowns with which all the Vladimir drivers had been married one after another. The deacon with a shaky hand passed us the silver bowl of union . . . it grew dark in the church, with only a few candles glowing here and there; all this was, or seemed to us, extremely fine, from its very simplicity. The bishop drove by, and seeing the church doors open stopped and sent to inquire what was happening. The priest, turning a little pale, went out to him himself, and returned a minute later with a cheerful face, saying to us: 'His Reverence sends you his episcopal blessing and bade me tell you he is praying for you.'

By the time we were driving home the news of our clandestine marriage was all over the town; ladies were waiting on the balconies and the windows were open. I let down the carriage windows and was a little vexed that the darkness prevented me from showing my 'young woman'.

At home we drank two bottles of wine with Matvey and the groomsmen; the latter stayed twenty minutes with us, and then we were left alone, and again, as at Perov's, this seemed so simple and natural that we were not in the least surprised at it, though for months afterwards we could not get over the wonder of it.

We had three rooms. We sat at a little table in the drawing-room, and forgetting the fatigue of the last few days we talked away part of the night. . . .

To have a crowd of outsiders at wedding festivities has always seemed to me something coarse, unseemly, almost cynical; why this premature lifting of the veil from love, this initiation of indifferent casual spectators into the privacy of the family? How all these hack-neyed greetings, commonplace vulgarities, stupid allusions, must wound the poor girl who is thrust into the public eye in the part of the bride . . . not one delicate feeling is spared: the luxury of the bridal chamber, the charm of the night attire, are displayed not only for the visitors to admire but for every idle vagrant. And after this the first days of the new life that is beginning, in which every minute is precious, which ought to be spent far away in solitude, are, as though in mockery, passed in endless dinners and exhausting balls, among a crowd.

Next morning we found in the *salon* two rose-bushes and an im-mense bouquet. Nice, kind Yuliya Fëdorovna (the governor's wife), who had taken a warm interest in our romance, had sent them. I embraced and kissed her footman and then we went off to see her. Since the bride's trousseau consisted of two dresses, the one in which she had travelled and the other in which she had been married, she put on the wedding dress.

From Yuliya Fëdorovna's we drove to the bishop's; the old man himself led us into the garden, with his own hands cut a nosegay of flowers, told Natalie how I had tried to frighten him with the prospect of my own ruin, and in conclusion advised her to study housekeeping. 'Do you know how to salt cucumbers?' he asked Natalie.

'I do,' she answered, laughing.

'Oh, that's hard to believe. And you know, it is essential!'

In the evening I wrote a letter to my father. I begged him not to be angry at the accomplished fact, and, 'since God had united us', to forgive me and add his blessing. My father as a rule wrote me a few lines once a week; he did not write one day earlier or later in reply, and even began his letter as usual: 'I received your letter of the 10th of May at half-past five the day before yesterday, and from it learned, not without distress, that God had united you with Natasha. I do not cross the will of God in anything, but submit blindly to the trials which He lays upon me. But since the money is mine and you have not thought it necessary to comply with my wishes, I must inform you that I shall not add one kopeck to your present allowance of one thousand silver roubles a year.'

How whole-heartedly we laughed at this distinction between the spiritual and temporal power.

And yet how we needed something more! The money I had borrowed was all spent. We had nothing, absolutely nothing, no clothes, no linen, no crockery. We sat like prisoners in a little flat because we had nothing to go out in. Matvey with a view to economy made a desperate effort to transform himself into a cook, but except beef-steaks and chops he could cook nothing, and so for the most part confined himself to provisions that needed little cooking: ham, salt fish, milk, eggs, cheese, and extremely hard cakes flavoured with mint and not in their first youth. Dinner was an endless source of amusement to us; sometimes we had milk first by way of soup, and sometimes last by way of dessert. Over this Spartan fare we used to smile as we recalled the long procession at the celebration of dinner at the princess's and at my father's, where half a dozen flunkeys ran about the room with bowls and dishes, cloaking under the magnificent *mise en scène* the really very uninventive fare.

So we struggled along in poverty for a year. 'The Chemist' sent us ten thousand paper roubles; more than six thousand of this had to go to pay our debts, but what remained was a great help. At last even my father was tired of trying to take us by hunger, like a fortress, and without adding to my allowance he began sending us presents of money, though I never dropped a hint about money after his famous *distinguo!*

I began looking for other quarters. A big, neglected manor-house with a garden was to let on the other side of the river Lybed. It belonged to the widow of a prince who had ruined himself at cards, and it was being let particularly cheaply because it was far away and inconvenient, and chiefly because the princess bargained to keep part of it, in no way separated from the rest, for her son, a spoilt fellow of thirty, and for his servants. No one would agree to this partial possession;[4] I at once accepted it, for I was fascinated by the loftiness of the rooms, the size of the windows, and the big, shady garden. But this very loftiness and spaciousness made a very amusing contrast with our complete lack of movable belongings and articles of the first necessity. The princess's housekeeper, a good-natured old woman, who was greatly attracted by Matvey, provided us, at her own risk, first with a table-cloth, then with cups, then with sheets, then with knives and forks.

What bright and untroubled days we spent in the little three-roomed flat at the Golden Gate and in the princess's huge house! . . . There was a big, scarcely furnished *salon*, in which we were sometimes over-taken by such childishness that we raced about it, jumped over the chairs, lit candles in all the candelabra fastened to the wall, and after illuminating the room *a giorno*, recited poetry. Matvey and our maid, a young Greek girl, took part in everything and played the fool as much as we did. Order 'did not triumph'[5] in our household.

And for all this childishness our life was full of a profound earnestness. Cast away in the quiet, peaceful little town, we were completely devoted to each other. From time to time came news of one of our friends, a few words of warm sympathy, and then again we were alone, absolutely alone. But in this solitude our hearts were not closed by our happiness; on the contrary, they were more open to every interest than ever before; we led a full and many-sided life, we thought and read, gave ourselves up to every pursuit and again concentrated on our love; we compared our thoughts and dreams, and saw with amazement how endless was our sympathy, how in all the subtlest, evanescent intricacies and ramifications of feeling and thought, tastes and antipathies, all was kinship and harmony. The only difference was that Natalie brought into our union a gentle, mild, gracious element, the characteristics of a young girl with all the poetry of a loving woman, while I brought lively activity, my *semper in motu*, infinite love and, moreover, a medley of earnest ideas, laughter, 'dangerous' thoughts and unfeasible projects.

'. . . . My desires had reached a standstill, I was satisfied, I lived in the present, I expected nothing from the morrow, I trusted care-

---

[4] There is a metaphor here from the Russian strip-system of farming. (R.)

[5] He is referring ironically to what was said by Sebastian, Minister for Foreign Affairs under Louis-Philippe, in the Chamber of Deputies in 1831, when France was against any military intervention in Poland: *'L'ordre règne à Varsovie.'* (R.)

lessly that it would take nothing from me. Personal life could give nothing more, this was the limit; any change could but diminish it, in some way or another.[6]

'In the spring Ogarëv came from his exile for a few days. He was then at the very height of his powers; he too was soon to pass through painful experiences; at moments he seemed to feel that misfortune was at hand, but he could still turn aside and take the lifted hand of destiny for a dream. I myself thought then that these storm-clouds would be dissipated; carelessness is characteristic of everyone young and not devoid of strength; it expresses a confidence in life and in oneself. The feeling of complete mastery over one's fate lulls us asleep . . . while dark powers and black-hearted people draw us without a word to the edge of the precipice.

'And well it is that man either does not suspect, or can shut his eyes and forget. Where there is apprehension there can never be complete happiness; complete happiness is serene as the sea in the calm of summer. Apprehension gives its morbid, feverish intoxication which pleases like the thrill of suspense at cards, but this is far from the feeling of harmonious, everlasting peace. And so, whether it be a dream or not, I prize most highly that trust in life, before life itself has called it in question and woken one up. . . . Chinese die of a crude intoxication with opium. . . .'[7]

So I ended this chapter in 1853 and so I end it now.

[6] The following lines are omitted here, which were published in *The Pole Star*, Vol. I, p. 79: But fate knows no moderation. 'Misfortunes,' says Hamlet [*sc.* Claudius] 'come not singly but in a throng,' and happiness exactly likewise.

[7] The following lines are omitted here, which were printed in *The Pole Star*, Vol. I, p. 81: Our trio exhibited a marvellous harmony. Nowhere in it were there confines or limits, or those imperceptible contradictions which in reality point to a boundary line and say, 'No further'. We were entirely united and entirely free.

Here ends the lyrical part of our life. Ahead there are labour, successes, encounters, activity, a wide circle of acquaintances, a long path to travel, other places, revolutions, history. . . . Ahead there are children, cares, struggle . . . further ahead still all will perish . . . on the one hand a grave, on the other loneliness and life in a foreign country!

Chapter 24

The Thirteenth of June, 1839[1]

ONE long, winter evening towards the end of 1838 we were sitting alone, as always, reading and not reading, talking and being silent, and in silence continuing the talk. There was a hard frost outside, and in the room it was not at all warm. Natasha did not feel well and was lying on the sofa, covered with a cloak, and I was sitting on the floor near her. My reading did not get on: she was absent-minded, thinking of something else, absorbed in something, and her face kept changing.

'Alexander,' she said, 'I have a secret: come nearer and I will tell you in your ear. Or no: guess it yourself.'

I did guess, but insisted on her telling me. I longed to hear this news from her: she told me; we looked at each other in excitement and with tears in our eyes.

How rich is the human heart in the capacity for happiness, for joy, if only people know how to give themselves up to it without being distracted by trifles. The present is usually disturbed by external worries, empty cares, irritable obstinacy, all the rubbish which is brought upon us in the midday of life by the vanity of vanities, and the stupid ordering of our everyday life. We waste our best minutes; we let them slip through our fingers as though we had heaven knows how many of them. We are generally thinking of to-morrow, of next year, when we ought to be clutching with both hands the brimming cup which life itself, unbidden, with her customary lavishness, holds out to us, and to drink and drink of it until the cup passes into other hands. Nature does not care to spend a long time offering us her treat.

[1] The date of the birth of the Herzens' first child, Alexander. (*A.S.*)

One would have thought that nothing could have been added to our happiness, and yet the news of the coming child opened new tracts of the heart, new raptures, hopes and alarms of which we had before known nothing.

When rather frightened and alarmed, love grows more tender, is more anxious in its solicitude: from the selfishness of two it becomes not a mere selfishness of three but the self-denial of two for a third; family life begins with children. A new element is entering into life, a mysterious person is knocking at the door, a guest who as yet is not, and who is indispensable, who is passionately awaited. Who is he? No one knows but, whoever he is, he is a fortunate stranger: with what love he is met on the threshold of life!

And then there is the agonising anxiety: will he be born alive or not? There are so many unhappy possibilities. The doctor smiles at the questions: 'He understands nothing, or he doesn't want to say,' one thinks; everything is still concealed from outsiders; there is no one to ask—besides one is ashamed to.

And then the child gives signs of life. I know no loftier and more religious emotion than that which fills the heart at feeling the first movements of the future being, struggling to get out and stretching its unready muscles, that first laying on of hands with which the father gives assent and blessing to the existence of the newcomer and yields him a share of his life.

'My wife,' a French *bourgeois* said to me once, 'my wife'—he looked round and, seeing that there were neither ladies nor children present, added half-audibly—'is pregnant.'

Indeed, the muddle of all our moral conceptions is such that pregnancy is looked upon as something improper. Though absolute respect is demanded for the mother, whoever she may be, a veil is drawn over the mystery of birth, not from a feeling of respect or inward modesty, but from a regard for propriety. All this is the depravity of idealism, the corruption of monasticism, the accursed immolation of the flesh; it is all that unhappy dualism in which like the Magdeburg hemispheres[2] we are dragged in different directions. Jeanne Deroin,[3] in spite of her socialism, hints in her *Almanach des Femmes* that in

---

[2] An experiment suggested by Otto von Guericke (d. 1686), the inventor of the air-pump. The hemispheres fit together air-tight; the air between them is exhausted, and great force is required to separate them. (*R.*)

[3] Jeanne Deroin was a disciple of Saint-Simon who published an *Almanach des Femmes* in 1851. (*Tr.*)

time children will be born differently. How differently?—As the
angels are born.—Well, that's clear enough.

Honour and glory to our teacher, the old realist Goethe. He had
the courage to set the woman with child beside the chaste maidens of
romanticism, and did not fear to mould in his mighty verse the
changing forms of the future mother, comparing them with the
supple limbs of the future woman.

Truly the woman who bears, together with the memory of past
transports, the whole cross of love, all its burden, offering up beauty,
time and suffering, feeding from her own breast, is one of the most
exquisite and touching figures.

In the *Roman Elegies*, in *The Spinner*, in Gretchen and her des-
pairing prayer, Goethe has expressed all the solemnity with which
nature surrounds the ripening fruit and all the thorns with which
society crowns this vessel of future life.

Poor mothers, who hide, like a disgrace, the traces of love, how
brutally and mercilessly the world persecutes them, and persecutes
them at the very time when the woman needs peace and kindness,
savagely poisoning for her those irreplaceable moments of fulfilment
in which life droops fainting under the excess of happiness. . . .

Little by little, with horror, the secret is discovered: the luckless
mother tries at first to persuade herself that it is fancy, but soon doubt
is impossible; with despair and tears she follows every movement of
her babe: she would like to check the secret working of life, to turn
it back; she hopes for some misfortune as clemency, as an absolution
—but ineluctable nature goes its way; she is young and healthy!

To make a mother wish for the death of her child, and sometimes,
what is more, to make of her its executioner and then to have her
punished by our executioner, or to cover her with disgrace if her
woman's heart is too strong for her—what a sensible, moral arrangement!

And who has weighed, who has considered what passed in her
heart while the mother traversed the terrible path from love to fear,
from fear to despair, to crime, to madness, for infanticide is a physio-
logical absurdity? She too has had, of course, moments of forgetfulness, in which she has passionately loved her coming little one, and
the more because his existence was a secret between the two of them;
there have been times when she has dreamed of his little feet, of his
milky smile, has kissed him in his sleep, has found in him a likeness
to one who has been so dear to her. . . .

'But do they feel it? Of course there are unfortunate victims . . . but . . . the others, the general run?'

It would be hard, one fancies, to sink lower than those bats that flit about at night in the fog and slush of the London streets, those victims of ignorance, poverty, and hunger, with whom society guards its respectable women from the superfluous passionateness of their admirers . . . in them, of course, it would be hardest of all to assume a trace of maternal feeling, would it not?

Allow me to tell you of a little incident that happened to me. Three years ago I met a beautiful young girl. She belonged to the honourable citizenship of debauchery, that is, she did not democratically *faire le trottoir*, but lived in *bourgeois* style, kept by a merchant. It was at a public ball; the friend who was with me knew her and invited her to drink a bottle of wine with us in the gallery; as may be supposed, she accepted the invitation. She was a merry, carefree creature, and probably, like Laura in Pushkin's *Don Juan*, was never worried by the fact that far away in Paris it was cold while she heard the watchman in Madrid cry 'The sun is shining.' . . . After swallowing the last glass she rushed once more into the ponderous whirl of the English dances and I lost sight of her.

This winter, one wet evening, I made my way across the street to stand under the Arcade in Pall Mall to escape the streaming rain; a poorly dressed woman was standing under the lamp-post in the archway, probably looking for prey and shivering with cold. Her features struck me as familiar; she glanced at me, turned away and tried to shrink out of sight, but I had time to recognise her.

'What has happened to you?' I asked her with sympathy.

Her sunken cheeks were suffused with bright crimson, whether from shame or consumption I do not know, but it did not seem to be rouge; in two years and a half she had grown ten years older.

'I was ill for a long time and very unlucky,' with an air of intense affliction she drew my attention with a glance to her worn clothes.

'But where is your friend?'

'He was killed in the Crimea.'

'Why, but he was a merchant, wasn't he?'

She was confused, and instead of answering she said: 'I am very ill even now, and besides I have no work at all. Why, have I changed so much?' she asked, looking at me suddenly in embarrassment.

'Very much: in those days you were like a little girl, and now I shouldn't mind betting that you have children of your own.'

She flushed crimson, and with something like terror she asked: 'How did you find that out?'

'Well, you see, I do know. Now tell me, what really has been happening to you?'

'Nothing, only you are right: I have got a little boy . . . if only you knew,' and at those words her face brightened, 'what a splendid, handsome little fellow he is; even the neighbours all admire him. But that man married a rich girl and went away to the Continent. The baby was born afterwards. He is to blame for my situation. At first I had money and used to buy him everything in the biggest shops, but then things got worse and worse, and I have taken everything to "uncle". I have been advised to put baby out in the country, it certainly would be better for him, but I can't. I look at him, I just look at him and say to myself, "No, we had better die together". I tried to find a place, but they won't take me with the baby. I went back to mother's, she's all right, she's got a kind heart, she forgave me, she is fond of the boy and makes a lot of him; but for five months now she's lost the use of her legs—what with the doctor to pay so many times and the chemist and then, as you know yourself, coal and bread and everything so dear this year, there's nothing for it but to die of hunger. So I—' she paused, 'of course, it would be better to chuck myself in the Thames than . . . but there's baby and I'm sorry for him; who should I leave him to? and you know he's such a darling!'

I gave her something and took out a shilling as well and said:

'And spend that on something for your baby.'

She took the coin gladly, held it in her hand, and suddenly gave it back to me, adding with a mournful smile:

'If you are so kind, buy him something yourself in a shop here, a toy or something—no one has ever given him a present, poor baby, since he was born.'

I looked with emotion at this 'lost' woman and friendlily pressed her hand.

People who are so zealous for the rehabilitation of all those ladies with camellias and pearls would do better to leave velvet furniture and rococo boudoirs alone and look a bit more closely at this unhappy, starved, shivering harlotry, the fatal harlotry which forces its victim down the road to ruin and gives no chance of recovery or repentance. Scavengers more often find precious stones in the gutter than when they pick up the spangles from tawdry finery.

This reminded me of that clever translator of *Faust*, poor Gérard de Nerval, who shot himself last year. He had not been home for five or six days. It was discovered at last that he was spending his time in the lowest dens near the town gates, as Paul Niquet used to do, that there he had made friends with thieves, with low creatures of all sorts, was treating them to drink, playing cards with them, and sometimes sleeping under their protection. His old friends tried to persuade him to come away, and to put him to shame. Nerval, defending himself good-naturedly, once said to them:

'Let me tell you, my friends, you are fearfully prejudiced. I assure you that the society of these people is decidedly no worse than that of any others I have been among.' He had been suspected of madness; after that, I imagine, the suspicion passed into certainty!

The fatal day was approaching and everything became more and more frightening. I looked at the doctor and the mysterious face of the midwife with slavish reverence. Neither Natasha nor I nor our young maid knew anything about this sort of thing; luckily, at my father's request, an elderly lady, Praskovya Andreyevna, a sensible, practical and capable woman, came from Moscow to stay with us. Seeing our helplessness she autocratically took the reins of management into her own hands and I obeyed her like a negro.

One night I felt a hand touch me: I opened my eyes, and Praskovya Andreyevna was standing before me in a nightcap and dressing-gown with a candle in her hand; she told me to send for the doctor and the midwife. I was petrified, just as though the news were something I had not in the least expected. If I could have drunk some opium, turned over on the other side and slept through the danger . . . but there was no help for it: I dressed with trembling hands and hurried to wake Matvey.

A dozen times I ran out from the bedroom into the front hall to listen for a carriage coming in the distance. Everything was still but for the faint, faint rustle of the breeze of morning in the warm June air of the garden; the birds were beginning to sing, the crimson dawn threw a light flush over the leaves, and again I hurried back to the bedroom, pestered kind Praskovya Andreyevna with stupid questions, squeezed Natasha's hands convulsively, did not know what to do, trembled and was in a fever . . . but at last the drozhki rattled on the bridge across the Lybed—thank God, it was in time!

M

At eleven o'clock in the morning I started as though from a violent electric shock when the loud cry of a new-born baby reached my ear. 'A boy,' Praskovya Andreyevna called to me as she went towards the cradle; I would have taken the baby from the pillow, but I could not, my hands trembled so violently. The thought of danger (which often begins only at this stage) that had constricted my chest vanished at once, a turbulent joy took possession of my heart as though in it all the bells were pealing for a festival of festivals! Natasha smiled at me, smiled at the baby, wept and laughed, and only her broken, spasmodic breathing, her weary eyes, and deathly pallor reminded me of the struggle, the agony that she had just been through.

Then I left the room, for I could bear no more. I went into my study and flung myself on the sofa, quite at the end of my strength, and lay for half an hour without any definite thought, without any definite emotion, in a sort of agony of bliss.

That face of triumph and exhaustion, that joy hovering, together with the hint of death, upon the mother's young forehead, I recognised again in Van Dyck's Madonna in the Corsini Gallery at Rome. The baby has just been born, they are holding it up to the mother; exhausted, with not a drop of blood in her face, faint and weary, she smiles, while her tired eyes rest on the baby with a look of infinite love.

It must be admitted that the Virgin Mother is quite out of keeping with the celibate religion of Christianity. With her, life, love, gentleness break involuntarily into the everlasting funeral, the dread day of judgment, and the other horrors of Church theodicy.

That is why Protestantism has cast out *only* the Mother of God from its barn-like chapels, from its factories of God's word. She really does interfere with Christian propriety; she cannot be separated from her earthly nature, she warms the cold church, and in spite of everything remains a woman, a mother. She avenges the unnatural conception with the natural birth, and snatches a blessing on her womb from the lips of monastic worshippers who curse everything bodily.

Michelangelo and Raphael realised all this with their brush.

In 'The Day of Judgment' in the Sistine Chapel, that massacre of St Bartholomew in the other world, we see the Son of God going to preside over the executions; He has already lifted His hand . . . He will give the signal, and tortures, agonies will follow, the last trump will sound, the universal *auto-da-fé* will begin crackling; but—the woman, this Mother, trembling and sorrowing for all, has pressed up to Him in horror, and is imploring Him on behalf of the sinners; looking at her He will perhaps relent and forget His cruel 'Woman, what hast thou to do with me?' and will not give the signal.

The Sistine Madonna is Mignon after the child's birth; she is frightened at her unprecedented fate, lost . . .

'Was hat man dir, du armes Kind, gethan?'

Her inner peace is shattered, she has been assured that her son is the Son of God, that she is the Mother of God; she looks with a sort of nervous rapture; with mesmeric clairvoyance she seems to be saying: 'Take Him, He is not mine.' But at the same time she presses Him to herself as though, if she could, she would run with Him to somewhere far away and would simply fondle and feed at her breast not the Saviour of the world but her own son. And all this is because she is a human mother and is no sister of Isis, Rhea and the other gods of the female sex.

That is why it has been so easy for her to conquer the cold Aphrodite, that Ninon L'Enclos of Olympus, whose children no one troubles about. Mary with her babe in her arms, with her eyes meekly looking down upon Him, surrounded by the halo of womanliness and the holiness of the estate of motherhood, is nearer to our hearts than her golden-haired rival.

To my thinking Pius IX and his Conclave were very consistent in proclaiming the unnatural or, in their language, *immaculate* conception of the Virgin. Mary, born naturally like you and me, would naturally stand up for mankind and sympathise with us: in her the living reconciliation of flesh and spirit would steal into religion. If she too was not humanly born, there is nothing in common between her and us; she will not be sorry for us, and the flesh is once more damned—and the Church more needful than ever for salvation.

It is a pity that the Pope is a thousand years too late. That, it seems, is Pius IX's fate. *Troppo tardi, Santo Padre, siete sempre e sempre—troppo tardi!*

Appendix

Letters to N. A. Zakharin[1]

WHEN I wrote this part of my Memoirs I did not have our old letters. I got them in 1856. After reading them over I had to correct two or three passages, not more. My memory here had not betrayed me. I should have liked to add a few of Natalie's letters, and at the same time I am restrained by a kind of fear, and cannot decide whether I ought to lay bare our life even further, and whether those lines so dear to me might not meet with a cold smile.

Among Natalie's papers I found my own notes to her, written some before prison and some from the Krutitsky Barracks. Some of them I append to this part. Perhaps they will not seem superfluous to those who are fond of tracing the rise of men's destinies, perhaps they will read them with that nervous interest with which we look through the microscope at the development of the living organism.

I[2]

August 15th, 1832.

Most dear Natalya Alexandrovna,—To-day is your birthday; I should very much have liked to congratulate you on it in person, but there really is no possibility. I am sorry I have not been to see you for so long, but circumstances have quite prevented me from disposing of my time as I should have liked. I hope that you will forgive me, and I wish you the full development of all your talents and all the store of happiness which fate bestows on the pure in heart.—
Your devoted A. H.

[1] These letters quoted are by no means always identical with the originals that have been preserved; nor is their dating always correct. (R.)

[2] These little notes were kept by Natalie, and on many of them she wrote a few words in pencil. I could not preserve any of the letters she wrote to me in prison. I was obliged to destroy them all at once.

II

July 5th or 6th, 1833.

You are wrong, Natalya Alexandrovna. You are quite wrong in thinking that I should confine myself to one letter—here is another for you. It is extremely pleasant to write to persons with whom one is in sympathy; there are so few of them, so few that one wouldn't use a quire of paper on them in a year.

I am a graduate, that is true, but it wasn't me they gave the gold medal to. I have a silver medal—*one of three!*

A. H.

P.S.—To-day there was the prize-giving, but I didn't go for I don't care to be second.

III

(At the beginning of 1834.)

Natalie! we are expecting you impatiently. M—— hopes that in spite of Y—— I——'s[3] threats yesterday Emilia Mikhaylovna[4] will be sure to come too, and so, till we meet,—Wholly yours,

A. H.

IV

KRUTITSKY BARRACKS,
December 10th, 1834.

I have just written a letter to the colonel,[5] in which I have asked for a permit for you; there is no answer yet. It will be harder for you to arrange it, but I rely on Mother. You were in luck in regard to me; you were the last of my friends whom I saw before my arrest [we parted confidently hoping to see each other soon, at nine o'clock; but at two I was already in the police-station], and you will be the first to see me again. Knowing you, I know that that will give you pleasure; let me assure you that it will me too. To me you are a sister.

There is not much for me to say about myself. I have settled down and grown used to being a prisoner. The most dreadful thing for me is the separation from Ogarëv, for he is essential to me. I have not seen him once—that is, not properly—though on one occasion I was

---

[3] H.'s elder brother (see p. 13, fn.) (R.)
[4] Aksberg (see p. 314 and fn.) (R.)
[5] I. S. Semënov (see p. 185). (A.S.)

sitting alone in a little lobby (at the committee), my examination was over; from my window the lighted front hall could be seen; a drozhki was brought round, I rushed instinctively to the window, opened the little pane and saw an adjutant get in, and Ogarëv with him. The drozhki drove off and he had no chance to see me. Can we be fated to perish by a mute, inglorious death, of which no one will hear? Why then has nature given us spirits craving for activity, for glory? Can that be a mockery? But no, faith, strong and living, glows here in my heart: there is a providence! I am reading with delight *The Lives of the Saints*; there you have examples of self-sacrifice, there you have men!

I have just received the answer, it is not cheering—they refuse the permit.

Good-bye, remember and love your brother.

[no signature]

V

December 31st, 1834.

I will never take upon myself the responsibility which you lay upon me, never! You have a great deal that is *your own*, why then do you surrender yourself to my will like this? I want you to make *of yourself whatever you can make of yourself*; for my part I undertake to assist that development, to remove obstacles.

As for your situation, it is not so bad for your development as you imagine. You have a great advantage over many; as soon as you began to understand yourself, you found yourself alone, alone in the whole world. Others have known a father's love and a mother's tenderness—you have not had them. No one has cared to interest himself in you, you have been left to yourself. What can be better for development? Thank your fates that no one was interested in you; they would have instilled something alien to you, they would have warped your childish soul—now it is too late.

[no signature]

VI

KRUTITSKY BARRACKS,
February 8, 1835.

I am told you have an idea of going into a nunnery; don't expect me to smile at the idea: I understand it, but it needs to be very, very carefully weighed. Can it be that the thought of love has never stirred your bosom? A nunnery means despair; there are no nunneries now for prayer. Can you doubt that you will one day meet a man who will love you, whom you will love? I shall be glad to press his hand and yours. He will be fortunate. If that *he* does not appear—then go into a nunnery; that is a million times better than a vulgar marriage.

I understand *le ton d'exaltation* of your letters—*you are in love!* If you write to me that you are in love in earnest I'll say nothing—a brother's authority stops at that. But I must have you say those words. Do you know what ordinary men are? They may of course make some people happy—but can they make you happy, Natasha? You think too little of yourself! Better into a nunnery than into the common herd. Remember one thing, that I say this because I am your brother, *because I am proud of you and for you.*

I have received another letter from Ogarëv; here is an extract from it:

'*L'autre jour donc je repassais dans ma mémoire toute ma vie. Un bonheur qui ne m'a jamais trahi, c'est ton amitié. De toutes mes passions une seule, qui est restée intacte, c'est mon amitié pour toi, car mon amitié est une passion.*'

In conclusion, one word more. What is so strange about it if he does love you? What would he be if he did not love you, seeing a shade of attention on your side? But I beseech you don't tell him of your love—not for a long time.

Farewell.—Your brother, ALEXANDER.

VII

[February 1835.] KRUTITSKY BARRACKS

What marvels happen in the world, Natalie! Before I got your last letter I had answered all your questions. I have heard that you were ill and sad. Take care of yourself, drink resolutely the—not so much bitter as—loathsome cup which your *benefactors* fill for you.

And after that on another sheet of paper follows:

[March 1835.]

Natasha, my dear, my sister, for God's sake don't lose heart, despise these abominable egoists, you make too much allowance for them, despise them all—they are wretches! It was an awful moment for me when I read your letter to Emilie. My God, what a situation I am in! What can I do for you? I swear that no brother loves his sister more than I do you, but what can I do?

I received your letter and am pleased with you. Forget him, if that is how it is; it was an experiment, and if it had really been love it would not have been expressed like that.

[no signature]

VIII

KRUTITSKY BARRACKS,
April 2nd [1835]

My heart is torn to shreds, I have not been so crushed, so shattered, all the while I have been in prison as now. It is not exile that is the cause of it. What do I care whether it is Perm or Moscow? Moscow is no better than Perm. Let me tell you all about it.

On the 31st of March we were summoned to hear our sentence. It was a glorious, magnificent day. Twenty fellows were gathered together, who were to be immediately scattered, some to cells in fortresses, others to distant towns; and all of them had spent nine months in captivity. They all sat, a noisy, merry company, in the big hall. When I went in, Sokolovsky, with a beard and a moustache, threw himself on my neck, and Satin was there too. Ogarëv was brought in a good while after me, and all rushed to greet him; we embraced with tears and a smile. Everything came to life in my heart, I lived, I was a young man, I pressed everyone's hand; in a word, it was one of the happiest moments of my life. I had not a gloomy thought. At last the sentence[6] was read out.

All was well, but yesterday—damnation take it!—has shattered me in every nerve. Obolensky is being confined in the same place with me. When the sentence had been read us, I asked leave of Tsynsky for us to see each other and was given permission. On returning I went to see him, and meanwhile they had forgotten to tell the colonel about the permission. Next day that blackguard of an officer S—— reported the matter to the colonel, and in that way I implicated three of the very best officers, who had done me God knows how many kindnesses; they were all reprimanded and all punished, and now have to be on duty for three weeks (and it is Easter!) without being relieved. Vasilev the gendarme has been flogged, and all through

[6] I omit it.

me. I bit my fingers, wept, raged, and the first thought that came into my head was revenge. I told things about the officer which might ruin him (he has gone off somewhere with a prisoner), and then remembered that he is a poor man and the father of seven children; but ought one to spare a man who peaches? Did he spare others?

[no signature]

IX

April 10th, 1835. Nine o'clock
A few hours before departure I am still writing, and writing to you—my last word as I go away shall be for you. Painful is the feeling of separation, and involuntary separation, but such is the fate to which I have committed myself; it draws me on and I submit. When shall we see each other? Where? All that is dark, but bright is the thought of your affection, the exile will never forget his charming sister.

Perhaps . . . but I cannot finish, for they have come for me—and so farewell for a long time, but, on my word, not for ever, I cannot think that.

All this is written in the presence of the gendarmes.

[no signature]

Traces of tears can be seen on this note and the word *perhaps* has been twice underlined by her. Natalie carried this note about with her for several months.

NOTES TO VOLUME ONE[1]

Selected from the Complete Works of A. I. Herzen (Moscow Academy of Sciences, 1956). These notes are indicated by asterisks in the text.

Dedication to N. P. Ogarëv

Page xliv . . . *written in a fine hand* . . . from Herzen's first cousin, Natalya Alexandrovna Zakharin, whom he married.

Page xliv . . . *some four months!* . . . From 2nd January (when Herzen arrived at Vladimir to 9th May (when he married N. A. Zakharin), 1838.

Page xliv . . . *misfortunes, mistakes* . . . Herzen is speaking of his experiences after the defeat of the revolution of 1848, and also of the misfortunes which befell his family: the loss of his mother and son in a shipwreck in 1851, and the death of his wife on 2nd May, 1852.

Page xlvi . . . *our childish Grütli* . . . According to tradition representatives of the Uri, Schwyz and Unterwalden cantons took an oath in 1307, in Grütli Meadow in Uri canton, to fight for the liberation of their country. The alliance of the three cantons laid the foundation of the actual independence of the Swiss State. Herzen is comparing this legendary oath with the oath taken by himself and N. P. Ogarëv on the Sparrow Hills at Moscow: see chapter 4. (Rütli or Grütli is a meadow on the west side of Lake Lucerne. It is possible that the oath of 1307 was a renewal of an oath taken in 1291. *R.*)

PART I

Chapter 2

Page 22 . . . *I was thirteen* . . . Herzen was not more than eight at this time.

[1] See Preface p. viii, last paragraph.

Chapter 3

Page 45 . . . See Byron's *Don Juan*, canto IV, stanza 44. ('Her father's blood before her father's face Boil'd up, and proved her truly of his race.' *R*.)

Page 49 . . . *the terrible news of the fourteenth of July* . . . The execution of the Decembrists took place on 13th July, 1826.

Page 49 . . . *the death penalty* de jure *did not exist* . . . By an *ukaz* of Yelizaveta Petrovna of 30th September, 1754, the death penalty (in case of the award of it) was commuted to another punishment (penal servitude, branding, etc.). Catherine II confirmed, by an *ukaz* of 6th April, 1775, the legality of the *ukaz* of 1754; but the *ukaz* of Yelizaveta Petrovna was interpreted as not being applicable to state (extraordinary) crimes (hence the executions of Mirovich and Pugachëv). The question of capital punishment in Russia was put before the State Council in 1823, in connection with the forming of a scheme for a universal code. Some members of the Council interpreted the *ukaz* of 1754 as having abolished capital punishment for all crimes, including state crimes; but the majority of the members, relying upon the fact that in the text of the *ukaz* of 1754 only common crimes were spoken of, and finding support in the practice of Catherine II, pronounced that capital punishment in cases of state crimes was juridically valid. Nicholas I availed himself of this later in awarding the sentences for the Decembrist affair.

Page 49 . . . *into his Code* . . . By the Code of Laws published in 1832 the death penalty was prescribed for political crimes, military crimes (in time of military operations) and crimes against quarantine regulations.

Page 50 . . . *The whole of the Royal Family* . . . Nicholas I was not present at this service.

Chapter 6

Page 93 . . . *'committee examinations'* . . . From 1809 until 1834 civil servants, who had received no higher education and who wished to attain the rank of collegiate assessor, might be examined at Russian universities by special committees, which consisted of several professors and lecturers. The entrants were examined in the basic branches of learning which were studied in the physico-mathematical, literary and moral-political (i.e. juridical) faculties. Entrants who were successful in the 'committee examinations' received a certificate to that effect . . . Evening courses were organised to prepare entrants for examinations of this kind.

Page 96 . . . *together with the law about passports* . . . Herzen is obviously referring to Nicholas I's *ukaz* about passports, promulgated in 1844, which led to further restrictions on the issue of passports to persons travelling abroad. Thus on the basis of the *ukaz* of 15th March the issue of passports for foreign countries was in the hands of the Ministry of Internal Affairs, and they were issued only to persons who had attained the age of twenty-five years; if it was desired to travel abroad for medical attention, not only police permission but also medical testimony of illness, and so on were required.

Page 96 . . . *religious intolerance* . . . Herzen is thinking of Nicholas I's measures directed against various confessions in order that official orthodoxy might triumph: the incorporation of the Uniats in the official Church (1839); the struggle against the Old Believers; the violence done to the Christianity of the Volga, Ural, Caucasian and Siberian peoples.

Page 97 . . . *seminarists and Germans* . . . As a rule it was the children of foreigners working in Russia, chiefly as physicians, apothecaries or teachers of foreign languages, who were most eager to enter the medical faculty, for which a knowledge of Latin was necessary. A shortage of doctors (principally in the army) evoked a series of governmental measures to increase the supply of medical students at the universities, and at the special instructional institutions, from the number of seminarists who knew Latin. Universities admitted pupils from the seminaries every year, who were enrolled in regular detachments as state-supported students in the medical faculties.

Page 100 . . . *Cuvier* . . . *Candolle* . . . Baron G. Cuvier: *Discours sur les révolutions de la surface du globe*; Aug.-Pyr. de Candolle: *Organographie végétale*.

Page 111 . . . *eight days* . . . In a written deposition given to the Commission of Inquiry in 1834 Herzen testified that he had been under arrest for seventy-two hours in 1831 in connection with the Malov case.

Page 114 . . . *observations on the magnetic needle* . . . According to *Moskovskiye Vedomosti*, No. 90 of 9th November, 1829, Humboldt did speak on this occasion of the observations on magnetism that he had made during his travels in the Urals.

Page 114 . . . *ten years later Liszt* . . . Liszt visited Russia in 1842, and also in 1843 and 1847.

Page 125 . . . *Vadim* . . . *hated the autocracy* . . . His father, Vasily Vasilevich Passek, had advanced ideas for his time. When he was arrested in 1794 there were discovered in his possession copies in manuscript of A. N. Radishchev's *Journey from Petersburg to Moscow* (an attack on Russian autocracy and serfdom, 1790) and some liberal, antimonarchical verses of his own, written under the influence of Radishchev.

Page 134 . . . *on the lists of the secret police* . . . Ogarëv and Satin had been under secret police surveillance since the summer of 1833, in connection with the Sungurov affair. In December, 1833, the police observed Ogarëv and Sokolovsky singing the Marseillaise at the entrance to the Maly Theatre. Obolensky had been under surveillance by the police since 1832.

Chapter 7

Page 142 . . . *the manuscript of* Khever . . . It was not his dramatic poem *Khever* that Sokolovsky published at this time, but a novel, *One and Two*, or *The Love of a Poet*.

Page 148 . . . *You write* . . . *1833* . . . In this extract Herzen has considerably toned down the juvenile, enthusiastic, romantic, elevated style of the original.

Page 150 . . . *the Code Napoléon* . . . The Saint-Simonists were tried in 1832, under Article 291 of the Criminal Code, brought into effect in 1811, for an offence against public morals. Herzen is thinking of the philistinism and hypocrisy of this bourgeois Criminal Code, and also of the Civil Code of 1804, which was re-named in 1807 the 'Code Napoléon'.

Page 150 . . . *the religion of Orléans* . . . Herzen's irony. The period of the July (Orléans) Monarchy was marked by the extreme moral dissoluteness of the governing financial aristocracy. Moreover the July authorities accused the Saint-Simonists, who were preaching a 'new religion' and the equality of the sexes, of immorality and of advocating the 'community of women'.

PART II

Chapter 8

Page 166 . . . *six years later* . . . This should read 'eight years later', since Herzen was arrested in 1834 and Orlov died in 1842.

Chapter 10

Page 175 . . . *a stout man* . . . It has been possible to establish the identity of this official. He was Dmitry Ignatevich Studenikin, who had been a student at Moscow University from 1820 to 1823.

Chapter 12

Page 201 . . . *he became a mystic* . . . In 1841 Ibayev published a small book, *The Anatomist's Knife,* or *A Glance at the Inner Man,* which was very adversely reviewed in *Otechestvenniye Zapiski* because of its mystical tone. Herzen was working for this periodical at that time, and must have known of the review, which evidently gave him grounds for calling Ibayev a mystic.

Chapter 14

Page 234 . . . *to introduce at elections* . . . Herzen is speaking of the plans for electoral reform which were mooted in France between the years 1840 and 1848. In particular it was demanded that the right to vote should be granted to persons who possessed an academic degree.

Chapter 16

Page 275 . . . *the oppressive feeling of remorse* . . . Herzen is hinting at his *liaison* at Vyatka with Praskovya Petrovna Medvedyev (see pp. 323ff.).

Chapter 18

Page 290 . . . *a master at the high school* . . . This was D. V. Nebaba (see p. 293).
Page 290 . . . *the* Provincial News *on its feet* . . . Certain writings by Herzen were printed in the *Vyatka Provincial News*, but by the time these began to appear, in January 1838, he had already been transferred to Vladimir.
Page 291 . . . *were introduced in 1837* . . . A 'Provincial News' began to be published in forty-two provinces in 1838.
Page 291 . . . *in Sadovaya Street* . . . The house was in the Spiridonovka (now Alexey Tolstoy Street). It was pulled down in 1893.